Contemporary Drama
Performing Identity
Revised Edition

Edited by James Utz

Ithaca College

San Diego, CA

First published in the United States of America in 2010 by Cognella, a division of University Readers, Inc.

14 13 12 11 10   1 2 3 4 5

Printed in the United States of America

ISBN: 978-1-935551-17-1

www.cognella.com 800.200.3908

Contents

Introduction   1

Sizwe Bansi Is Dead   3
By Athol Fugard (1932–), John Kani (1943–), and
Winston Ntshona (1941–)

Jelly's Last Jam   39
By George C. Wolfe (1954–)

Our Country's Good   121
By Timberlake Wertenbaker (1951–)

Six Characters in Search of an Author   193
By Luigi Pirandello (1867–1936)

Oleanna   247
By David Mamet (1947–)

Six Degrees of Separation   285
By John Guare (1938–)

Topdog/Underdog   341
By Suzan-Lori Parks (1963–)

Fire in the Basement   405
By Pavel Kohout (1928–)

Introduction

By James Utz

In selecting plays for this anthology, I considered that this book was intended for use in an introductory theatre class, and that this placed specific demands upon the text. I think of an introductory theatre class as a specific entity: it is not a theatre history course, nor is it a course in dramatic literature. At most colleges and universities, such courses are available alongside introductory theatre courses, and I would advise any students interested in pursuing theatre beyond the introductory level to take these classes. "Introduction to Theatre" courses are frequently delivered as general-education courses, fulfilling an "arts" or "humanities" requirement and intended for those students *not* majoring in theatre. They are often survey courses, covering such subjects as stage spaces, professions and practices, genres and styles of plays, and contemporary trends in the craft. An anthology of plays for such a class, then, has certain expectations and limitations placed upon it. It should provide a selection of plays common enough to be part of a casual spectator's vocabulary of experience, but not narrowly focused in terms of period, nationality, style, or theme.

Timeliness of material and the avoidance of redundancy were two of my major concerns in considering material for inclusion here. It has been my experience that most college undergraduates have encountered the works of Shakespeare, for example, in high school if not earlier. If they have somehow managed to avoid Shakespeare, they have most likely been exposed to Henrik Ibsen, Arthur Miller, Tennessee Williams, one of the ancient Greek tragedians, or even Molière. More important than the concern with exposure is my desire to combat the widely held perception (especially among non-theatre majors) that theatre is an archaic or obsolete discipline. This is not an unfounded preconception, especially when one considers the preponderance of electronically-delivered dramatic entertainment—film, television, and streaming Internet video—and its seeming advantage in terms of currency and profitability. I have found students receptive to modern and post-modern works (in both the temporal and artistic senses of these terms), as these plays frequently have a greater claim to immediate pertinence and a greater ability to challenge received beliefs about the theatre. While the earliest plays included here, *Six Characters in Search of an Author*, is too old to be considered "contemporary," I considered it worthy of inclusion simply because of its author's massive influence on subsequent drama.

One thread that connects all of the plays assembled here is the idea of performance. At first glance, this statement seems so obvious as to be ridiculous: *of course* a play, since it is meant to be performed, is bound up in the idea of performance. But I refer to performance in the everyday sense, meaning that we frequently find ourselves playing roles in the presence of other people. Here, I do not mean that we intentionally deceive, or fantasize, or fake our way through life, although deception is certainly one example of the sort of "acting" we employ or encounter in everyday situations. More commonly, however, we find ourselves "performing" familial roles, social roles, and professional roles. As the Father in *Six Degrees of Separation* observes, we are frequently different people in different social contexts, without even intending to be. Further, our everyday choices in terms of habits, language, clothing, and other behaviors that define us as individuals contribute to the perception that even "self" is something that is to an extent performed.

The scripts in this collection explore the idea of everyday performance in various ways. Kohout's *Fire in the Basement* and Mamet's *Oleanna* discuss the enactment of professional roles and their connection to political power. Wertenbaker's *Our Country's Good* features the use of role-playing as a means of self-discovery and personal redefinition, while Fugard, Kani, and Ntshona's *Sizwe Bansi is Dead* treats these purposes as absolute necessities in an oppressive political environment. Wolfe and Birkenhead's *Jelly's Last Jam* overtly concerns itself with the performance of race. Parks' *Topdog/Underdog* is a classic story of sibling rivalry, played out through emulation. Finally, Guare's *Six Degrees of Separation* and Pirandello's *Six Characters in Search of an Author* investigate the effects of performance on both "actors" and "spectators," with the latter play eventually blurring the line between art and reality.

Ultimately, the most important criterion for a script's inclusion in this collection was artistic excellence. Aside from the classroom discussions that these plays might engender, I personally feel, and am confident you will agree, that these plays display an abundance of the qualities we demand from dramatic entertainment: inventive, surprising plots, distinctive characters, sharp dialogue, relevant and compelling themes, and playful experimentation. Realistically, no anthology is likely to be regarded as perfect, and I do not expect every class requiring this anthology to accommodate every script included here, or to avoid supplementing this anthology with additional scripts. However, I believe that teachers and students will find that this collection enlightens and entertains. More importantly, I suspect that it will inspire curiosity about the craft of theatre, and affirm, if affirmation is needed, the connection and pertinence of theatre to everyday life.

James Utz, Ph.D.
Ithaca College
December 2009

Sizwe Bansi Is Dead
(1972)

By Athol Fugard (1932–), John Kani (1943–), and
Winston Ntshona (1941–)

Like *Fire in the Basement*, *Sizwe Bansi is Dead* is a play that depicts life in an oppressive society: in this case, South Africa under *apartheid*, a system of legalized segregation that characterized life in that country from 1948 to 1994. Under apartheid, South Africans were classified by race (white, black, Indian, or "colored," meaning mixed-race). Residential areas were segregated, as were public institutions such as schools and hospitals. Interracial marriage was prohibited, and interaction between racial groups was made difficult by a series of regulations that governed most aspects of daily life. Even cultural events, such as plays, were not immune to the effects of apartheid.

In this context, it is remarkable that Athol Fugard, a white man, and John Kani and Winston Ntshona, two black men, should collaborate on a play. All three were members of the Serpent Players, an interracial company that Fugard formed in the 1960s—the name comes from the company's first venue, an former snake pit at a zoo. The company performed minimal, low-tech plays and relied on the sort of presentational acting style called for in *Sizwe Bansi is Dead*.

The play opens with an extended monologue by Styles, the owner of a photography studio. Styles (originally played by Kani, who along with Ntshona won a Tony Award for Best Actor in a Play for his performance in *Sizwe Bansi*) tells us the story of how he decided to go into business for himself, a decision that grew out of years of humiliation that he endured while working at a Ford plant. Styles recounts the fateful day when Henry Ford, Jr. visited the plant, a visit which prompted the local bosses to put on a show for the American executive, including costumes (clean new uniforms for the workers), properties (shiny new tools), and music ("You must sing," Styles tells his co-workers. "The joyous songs of the days of old before we had fools like this one next to me to worry about"). During the monologue, Styles enacts the behavior of his bosses, marveling at the fact that for one day they were forced to grovel and smile as he always did.

In the present, and in his new role, Styles encounters a customer, a man claiming to be Robert Zwelinzima (but who we learn is actually Sizwe Bansi). "Robert" wants to take a picture to send home to his wife, who lives in the territory of Ciskei. Ciskei was a *bantustan* or "self-governing" territory for blacks. Under apartheid, blacks in South Africa were legally residents of these territories—indeed, forced relocation was utilized to this end. On account of their residency in these "independent" homelands, blacks were deprived of full citizenship in South Africa, unable to vote and prohibited from working without a proper permit. The right to seek work in a city enabled a black person to live there—otherwise he would be relegated to the impoverished, remote Bantustan, where a dangerous mining job might be his best hope. Black families were not permitted to live together in cities reserved for whites; frequently, black workers in the city would send money back home to provide for their families.

The flash of Styles's camera triggers a flashback in which we learn that Sizwe, having lost his right to work and having his "pass book" (a form of identification all blacks were required to carry) stamped for relocation to the homeland, is at his wit's end when an unusual opportunity presents itself. His friend, Buntu, finds a dead body in the street, that of a man killed by "tsotsis" (robbers or thugs). Taking the dead man's pass book, Buntu discovers that the man (Robert Zwelinzima) has permission to seek work in town. Buntu then hatches the plan on which the action of the play turns: he will replace Robert's passbook photo with Sizwe's. "We burn this book," Buntu says, referring to Sizwe's original passbook, "and Sizwe disappears off the face of the earth." Sizwe will assume Robert's identity, in the process garnering his opportunity to work, and Robert's corpse will simply remain unidentifiable.

The play's dramatic conflict, then, relies upon Sizwe's sense of identity and personal integrity. Should he keep his name, the one which he has bestowed upon his children, and thus resign himself to the poverty to which he has been sentenced, or should he embrace his new identity and the hope that it bestows upon him? Styles, earlier in the play, had established that this would not be an easy choice: "we own nothing except ourselves," he tells us. "This world and its laws, allows us nothing, except ourselves. There is nothing we can leave behind when we die, except the memory of ourselves." Sizwe himself wonders how to live as "another man's ghost." Buntu argues that, given the daily humiliation he must endure as a black man living under apartheid, Sizwe has never been anything but a ghost. "When the white man sees you walk down the street and calls out, 'Hey, John! Come here' … to you, *Sizwe Bansi* … isn't that a ghost? Or when his little child calls you 'Boy' … you a man, circumcised with a wife and four children … isn't that a ghost? Stop fooling yourself. All I'm saying is be a real ghost, if that is what they want, what they've turned us into. Spook them into hell, man!"

Buntu's argument also relies upon economic considerations—a man in Sizwe's position, with a family to support, cannot afford intangible luxuries such as integrity and pride. "If I didn't have anyone to worry about or look after except myself," he says, "maybe then I'd be prepared to pay some sort of price for a little pride." Ultimately, pride is reserved for those with power, those not forced to play a subservient role in life. "Shit on our pride," Buntu continues, "if we only bluff ourselves that we are men." Sizwe, we must remember, aspires to the sort of blue-collar job that Styles used to work at the Ford plant. That this hope should be so desperate that Sizwe should sacrifice his identity to attain it speaks volumes. Whatever optimism the play provides us at the end is premised on Sizwe's hope that he can collect a weekly wage-packet in exchange for the sort of work that made Styles feel like a "monkey," always "wearing a mask of smiles." Ultimately, then, *Sizwe Bansi is Dead* is relentless in criticizing its society, one in which even the most outlandish quests for personal freedom and renewal deliver minimal benefits.

CHARACTERS

STYLES
SIZWE BANSI
BUNTU

This play was given its first performance on 8 October 1972 at The Space, Cape Town, and was directed by Athol Fugard with the following cast:

Styles and Buntu	John Kani
Sizwe Bansi	Winston Ntshona

SIZWE BANSI IS DEAD

Styles's Photographic Studio in the African township of New Brighton, Port Elizabeth. Positioned prominently, the name-board:

> *Styles Photographic Studio. Reference Books; Passports; Weddings; Engagements; Birthday Parties and Parties.*
>
> *Prop.—Styles.*

Underneath this a display of photographs of various sizes. Centre stage, a table and chair. This is obviously used for photographs because a camera on a tripod stands ready a short distance away.

There is also another table, or desk, with odds and ends of photographic equipment and an assortment of 'props' for photographs.

The setting for this and subsequent scenes should be as simple as possible so that the action can be continuous.

Styles walks on with a newspaper. A dapper, alert young man wearing a white dustcoat and bowtie. He sits down at the table and starts to read the paper.

STYLES. [*reading the headlines*] 'Storm buffets Natal. Damage in many areas … trees snapped like … what? … matchsticks. …'
[*He laughs.*]
They're having it, boy! And I'm watching it … in the paper.
[*Turning the page, another headline.*]
'China: A question-mark on South West Africa.' What's China want there? *Yo!* They better be careful. China gets in there … ! [*Laugh.*] I'll tell you what happens …
[*Stops abruptly. Looks around as if someone might be eavesdropping on his intimacy with the audience.*]
No comment.
[*Back to his paper.*]
What's this? … *Ag!* American politics. Nixon and all his votes. Means buggerall to us.
[*Another page, another headline.*]
'Car plant expansion. 1.5 million rand plan.' *Ja.* I'll tell you what *that* means … more machines, bigger buildings … never any expansion to the pay-packet. Makes me fed-up. I know what I'm talking about. I worked at Ford one time. We used to read in the newspaper … big headlines! … 'So and so from America or London made a big speech: "… going to see to it that the conditions of their non-white workers in Southern Africa were substantially improved."' The talk ended in the bloody newspaper. Never in the pay-packet.
Another time we read: Mr Henry Ford Junior Number two or whatever the hell he is … is visiting the Ford Factories in South Africa!
[*Shakes his head ruefully at the memory.*]
Big news for us, man! When a big man like that visited the plant there was usually a few cents more in the pay-packet at the end of the week.
Ja, a Thursday morning. I walked into the plant … 'Hey! What's this?' … Everything was quiet! Those big bloody machines that used to make so much noise made my

head go around ... ? Silent! Went to the notice-board and read: Mr Ford's visit today!

The one in charge of us ... [*laugh*] hey! I remember him. General Foreman Mr 'Baas' Bradley. Good man that one, If you knew how to handle him ... he called us all together:

[*Styles mimics Mr 'Baas' Bradley. A heavy Afrikaans accent.*]

'Listen, boys, don't go to work on the line. There is going to be a General Gleaning first.'

I used to like General Gleaning. Nothing specific, you know, little bit here, little bit there. But that day! Yessus ... In came the big machines with hot water and brushes—sort of electric mop—and God alone knows what else. We started on the floors. The oil and dirt under the machines was thick, man. All the time the bosses were walking around watching us:

[*Slapping his hands together as he urges on the 'boys'.*]

'Come on, boys! It's got to be spotless! Big day for the plant!' Even the *big* boss, the one we only used to see lunch-times, walking to the canteen with a big cigar in his mouth and his hands in his pocket ... that day? Sleeves rolled up, running around us:

'Come on! Spotless, my boys! Over there, John. ...' I thought: What the hell is happening? It was beginning to feel like hard work, man. I'm telling you we cleaned that place—spot-checked after fifteen minutes! ... like you would have thought it had just been built.

First stage of General Cleaning finished. We started on the second. Mr 'Baas' Bradley came in with paint and brushes. I watched.

W – h – i – t – e   l – i – n – e

[*Mr 'Baas' Bradley paints a long white line on the floor*]

What's this? Been here five years and I never seen a white line before. Then:

[*Mr 'Baas' Bradley at work with the paint-brush.*]

CAREFUL THIS SIDE. TOW MOTOR IN MOTION.

[*Styles laughs.*]

It was nice, man. Safety-precautions after six years. Then
another gallon of paint.

Y – e – l – l – o – w   l – i – n – e –

NO SMOKING IN THIS AREA. DANGER!

Then another gallon:

G – r – e – e – n   l – i – n – e –

I noticed that that line cut off the roughcasting section, where we worked with the rough engine blocks as we got them from Iscor. Dangerous world that. Big machines! One mistake there and you're in trouble. I watched them and thought: What's going to happen here? When the green line was finished, down they went on the floor—Mr 'Baas' Bradley, the lot! — with a big green board, a little brush, and a tin of white paint. EYE PROTECTION AREA. Then my big moment:

'Styles!'

'Yes, sir!'

[*Mr 'Baas' Bradley's heavy Afrikaans accent*] 'What do you say in your language for this? Eye Protection Area.'

It was easy, man!

'*Gqokra Izi Khuselo Zamehlo Kule Ndawo.*'

Nobody wrote it!

'Don't bloody fool me, Styles!'

'No, sir!'

Then spell it … slowly.'

[*Styles has a big laugh.*]

Hey! That was my moment, man. Kneeling there on the floor … foreman, general foreman, plant supervisor, plant manager … and Styles? Standing!

[*Folds his arms as he acts out his part to the imaginary figures crouched on the floor.*]

'*G – q – o – k – r – a*' … and on I went, with Mr. 'Baas' Bradley painting and saying as he wiped away the sweat:

'You're not fooling me, hey!'

After that the green board went up. We all stood and admired it. Plant was looking nice, man! Colourful!

Into the third phase of General Cleaning. 'Styles!'

'Yes, sir!'

'Tell all the boys they must now go to the bathroom and wash themselves clean.'

We needed it! Into the bathroom, under the showers … hot water, soap … on a Thursday! Before ten? *Yo!* What's happening in the plant? The other chaps asked me: What's going on, Styles? I told them: 'Big-shot cunt from America coming to visit you.' When we finished washing they gave us towels … [*laugh*].

Three hundred of us, man! We were so clean we felt shy! Stand there like little ladles in front of the mirror. From there to the General Store.

Handed in my dirty overall.

'Throw it on the floor.'

'Yes, sir!'

New overall comes, wrapped in plastic. Brand new, man! I normally take a thirty-eight but this one was a forty-two. Then next door to the tool room … brand new tool bag, set of spanners, shifting spanner, torque wrench—all of them brand new—and because I worked in the dangerous hot test section I was also given a new asbestos apron and fire-proof gloves to replace the ones I had lost about a year ago. I'm telling you I walked back heavy to my spot. Armstrong on the moon! Inside the plant it was general meeting again. General Foreman Mr 'Baas' Bradley called me.

'Styles!'

'Yes, sir.'

'Come translate.'

'Yes, sir!'

[*Styles pulls out a chair. Mr 'Baas' Bradley speaks on one side, Styles translates on the other.*]

'Tell the boys in your language, that this is a very big day in their lives.'

'Gentlemen, this old fool says this is a hell of a big day in our lives.'

The men laughed.

'They are very happy to hear that, sir'

'Tell the boys that Mr Henry Ford the Second, the owner of this place, is going to visit us. Tell them Mr Ford is the big Baas. He owns the plant and everything in it.'

'Gentlemen, old Bradley says this Ford is a big bastard. He owns everything in this building, which means you as well.'

A voice came out of the crowd:

'Is he a bigger fool than Bradley?'

'They're asking, sir, is he bigger than you?'

'Certainly … [*blustering*] … certainly. He is a very big baas. He's a … [*groping for words*] … he's a Makulu Baas.'

I loved that one!

'Mr "Baas" Bradley says most certainly Mr Ford is bigger than him. In fact Mr Ford is the grandmother baas of them all … that's what he said to me.'

'Styles, tell the boys that when Mr Henry Ford comes into the plant I want them all to look happy. We will slow down the speed of the line so that they can sing and smile while they are working.'

'Gentlemen, he says that when the door opens and his grandmother walks in you must see to it that you are wearing a mask of smiles. Hide your true feelings, brothers. You must sing. The joyous songs of the days of old before we had fools like this one next to me to worry about.' [*To Bradley.*] 'Yes, sir!'

'Say to them, Styles, that they must try to impress Mr Henry Ford that they are better than those monkeys in his own country, those niggers in Harlem who know nothing but strike, strike.'

Yo! I liked that one too.

'Gentlemen, he says we must remember, when Mr Ford walks in, that we are South African monkeys, not American monkeys. South African monkeys are much better trained …'

Before I could even finish, a voice was shouting out of the crowd:
'He's talking shit!' I had to be careful!
[*Servile and full of smiles as he turns back to Bradley.*]
'No, sir! The men say they are much too happy to behave like those American monkeys.'
Right! Line was switched on nice and slow—and we started working.
[*At work on the Assembly Line; singing.*]
'*Tshotsholoza … Tshotsholoza … kulezondawo …*'
We had all the time in the world, man! … torque wrench out … tighten the cylinder-head nut … wait for the next one. … [*Singing*] '*Vyabaleka … vyabaleka … kulezondawo …*' I kept my eye on the front office, I could see them—Mr 'Baas' Bradley, the line supervisor—through the big glass window, brushing their hair, straightening the tie. There was some General Cleaning going on there too.
[*He laughs.*]
We were watching them. Nobody was watching us. Even the old Security Guard. The one who every time he saw a black man walk past with his hands in his pockets he saw another spark-plug walk out of the plant. Today? To hell and gone there on the other side polishing his black shoes. Then, through the window, I saw three long black Galaxies zoom up. I passed the word down the line: He's come! Let me tell you what happened. The big doors opened; next thing the General Superintendent, Line Supervisor, General Foreman, Manager, Senior Manager, Managing Director … the bloody lot were there … like a pack of puppies!
[*Mimics a lot of fawning men retreating before an important person.*]
I looked and laughed! 'Yessus, Styles, they're all playing your part today!' They ran, man! In came a tall man, six foot six, hefty, full of respect and dignity … I marvelled at him! Let me show you what he did.
[*Three enormous strides*] One … two … three … [*Cursory look around as he turns and takes the same three strides hack.*]
One … two … three … OUT! Into the Galaxie and gone! That's all. Didn't talk to me, Mr 'Baas' Bradley, Line Supervisor or anybody. He didn't even look at the plant! And what did I see when those three Galaxies disappeared?
The white staff at the main switchboard,
'Double speed on the line! Make up for production lost!'

It ended up with us working harder that bloody day than ever before. Just because that big … [*shakes his head.*]

Six years there. Six years a bloody fool.

[*Back to his newspaper. A few more headlines with appropriate comment, then …*]

[*Reading*] The Mass Murderer! Doom!'

[*Smile of recognition.*]

'For fleas … Doom. Flies … Doom. Bedbugs … Doom. For cockroaches and other household pests. The household insecticide … Doom.' Useful stuff. Remember, Styles? *Ja.* [*To the audience.*] After all that time at Ford I sat down one day. I said to myself:

'Styles, you're a bloody monkey, boy!'

'What do you mean?'

'You're a monkey, man.'

'Go to hell!'

'Come on, Styles, you're a monkey, man, and you know it. Run up and down the whole bloody day! Your life doesn't belong to you. You've sold it. For what, Styles? Gold wrist-watch in twenty-five years time when they sign you off because you're too old for anything any more?'

I was right. I took a good look at my life. What did I see? A bloody circus monkey! Selling most of his time on this earth to another man. Out of every twenty-four hours I could only properly call mine the six when I was sleeping. What the hell is the use of that?

Think about it, friend. Wake up in the morning, half-past six, out of the pyjamas and into the bath-tub, put on your shirt with one hand, socks with the other, realize you got your shoes on the wrong bloody feet, and all the time the seconds are passing and if you don't hurry up you'll miss the bus … 'Get the lunch, dear. I'm late. My lunch, please, darling! … then the children come in … 'Daddy, can I have this? Daddy, I want money for that.' 'Go to your mother. I haven't got time. Look after the children, please, sweetheart!!'… grab your lunch … 'Bye Bye!!' and then run like I-don't-know-what for the bus stop. You call that living? I went back to myself for another chat:

'Suppose you're right. What then?'

'Try something else.'

'Like what?'

Silly question to ask. I knew what I was going to say. Photographer! It was my hobby in those days. I used to pick up a few cents on the side taking cards at parties, weddings, big occasions. But when it came to telling my wife and parents that I wanted to turn professional ... !!

My father was the worst,

'You call that work ? Click-click with a camera. Are you mad?' I tried to explain. 'Daddy, if I could stand on my own two feet and not be somebody else's tool, I'd have some respect for myself. I'd be a man.'

'What do you mean? Aren't you one already? You're circumcised, you've got a wife ...'

Talk about the generation gap!

Anyway I thought: To hell with them. I'm trying it.

It was the Christmas shutdown, so I had lots of time to look around for a studio. My friend Dhlamini at the Funeral Parlour told me about a vacant room next door. He encouraged me. I remember his words. 'Grab your chance. Styles. Grab it before somebody in my line puts you in a box and closes the lid.' I applied for permission to use the room as a studio. After some time the first letter back: 'Your application has been received and is being considered.' A month later: 'The matter is receiving the serious consideration of the Board.' Another month: 'Your application is now on the director's table.' I nearly gave up, friends. But one day, a knock at the door—the postman—I had to sign for a registered letter, 'We are pleased to inform you ...'

[*Styles has a good laugh.*]

I ran all the way to the Administration Offices, grabbed the key, ran all the way back to Red Location, unlocked the door, and walked in!

What I found sobered me up a little bit. Window panes were all broken; big hole in the roof, cobwebs in the corners. I didn't let that put me off though. Said to myself: 'This is your chance. Styles. Grab it.' Some kids helped me clean it out. The dust! *Yo!* When the broom walked in the Sahara Desert walked out! But at the end of that day it was reasonably clean, I stood here in the middle of the floor, straight! You know what that means? To stand straight in a place of your own? To be your own ... General Foreman, Mr 'Baas', Line Supervisor—the lot! I was tall, six foot six and doing my own inspection of the plant.

So I'm standing there—here—feeling big and what do I see on the walls? Cockroaches, *Ja*, cockroaches ... in *my* place I don't mean those little things that ran all over the place when you pull out the kitchen drawer. I'm talking about the big bastards, the paratroopers as we call them. I didn't like them. I'm not afraid of them but I just don't like them! All over. On the floors, the walls. I heard the one on the wall say: 'What's going on? Who opened the door?' The one on the floor answered: 'Relax. He won't last. This place is condemned.' That's when I thought: Doom. Out of here and into the Chinaman's shop, 'Good day, sir, I've got a problem. Cockroaches.'

The Chinaman didn't even think, man, he just said: 'Doom!' I said: 'Certainly.' He said: 'Doom, seventy-five cents a tin.' Paid him for two and went back. *Yo!* You should have seen me! Two-tin Charlie!

[*His two tins at the ready, forefingers on the press-buttons, Styles gives us a graphic re-enactment of what happened. There is a brief respite to 'reload'—shake the tins—and tie a handkerchief around his nose after which he returns to the fight. Styles eventually backs through the imaginary door, still firing, and closes it. Spins the tins and puts them into their holsters.*]

I went home to sleep, *I* went to sleep. Not them [*the cockroaches*]. What do you think happened here? General meeting under the floorboards. All the bloody survivors. The old professor addressed them: 'Brothers, we face a problem of serious pollution … contamination! The menace appears to be called Doom, I have recommended a general inoculation of the whole community. Everybody inline, please. [*Inoculation proceeds.*] Next … next … next …' While poor old Styles is smiling in his sleep! Next morning I walked in … [*He stops abruptly.*] … What's this? Cockroach walking on the floor? Another one on the ceiling? Not a damn! Doom did it yesterday. Doom does it today. [*Whips out the two tins and goes in fighting. This time, however, it is not long before they peter out.*] Pssssssss … pssssss … pssss … pss [*a last desperate shake, but he barely manages to get out a squirt*].

Pss.

No bloody good! The old bastard on the floor just waved his feelers in the air as if he was enjoying air-conditioning. I went next door to Dhlamini and told him about my problem. He laughed. 'Doom? You're wasting your time Styles. You want to solve your problem, get a cat. What do you think a cat lives on in the township? Milk? If there's any the baby gets it. Meat? When the family sees it only once a week? Mice? The little boys got rid of them years ago. Insects, man, township cats are insect-eaters. Here …'

He gave me a little cat. I'm … I'm not too fond of cats normally. This one was called Blackie … I wasn't too fond of that name either. But … Kitsy! Kitsy! Kitsy … little Blackie followed me back to the studio.

The next morning when I walked in what do you think I saw? Wings. I smiled. Because one thing I do know is that no cockroach can take his wings off. He's dead!

[*Proud gesture taking in the whole of his studio.*] So here it is!

[*To his name-board.*]

'Styles Photographic Studio. Reference Books; Passports; Weddings; Engagements; Birthday Parties and Parties. Proprietor: Styles.'

When you look at this, what do you see? Just another photographic studio? Where people come because they've lost their Reference Book and need a photo for the new one? That I sit them down, set up the camera … 'No expression, please.'… click-click … 'Come back tomorrow, please'… and then kick them out and wait for the next? No, friend. It's more than just that. This is a strong-room of dreams. The dreamers? My people. The simple people, who you never find mentioned in the history books, who never get statues erected to them, or monuments commemorating their great deeds. People who would be forgotten, and their dreams with them, if it wasn't for Styles. That's what I do, friends, Put down, in my way, on paper the dreams and hopes of my people so that even their children's children will remember a man … 'This was our Grandfather' … and say his name. Walk into the houses of New Brighton and on the walls you'll find hanging the story of the people the writers of the big books forget about

[*To his display-board.*]

This one [*a photograph*] walked in here one morning. I was just passing the time. Midweek, Business is always slow then. Anyway, a knock at the door. Yes! I must explain something, I get two types of knock here. When I hear … [*knocks solemnly on the table*] … I don't even look up, man, 'Funeral parlour is next door,' But when I hear … [*energetic rap on the table … he laughs*] … that's *my* sound, and I shout 'Come in!'

In walked a chap, full of smiles, little parcel under his arm, I can still see him, man!

[*Styles acts both roles.*]

'Mr Styles?'

I said: 'Come in!'

'Mr Styles, I've come to take a snap, Mr Styles.'

I said: 'Sit down! Sit down, my friend!'

'No, Mr Styles. I want to take the snap standing. [*Barely containing his suppressed excitement and happiness*] Mr Styles, take the card, please!'

I said: 'Certainly, friend,'

Something you mustn't do is interfere with a man's dream. If he wants to do it standing, let him stand. If he wants to sit, let him sit. Do exactly what they want! Sometimes they come in here, all smart in a suit, then off comes the jacket and shoes and socks … [*adopts a boxer's stance*] … 'Take it, Mr Styles. Take it!' And I take it. No questions! Start asking stupid questions and you destroy that dream. Anyway, this chap I'm telling you about … [*laughing warmly as he remembers*] … I've seen a lot of smiles in my business, friends, but that one gets first prize, I set up my camera, and just as I was ready to go … 'Wait, wait, Mr Styles! I want you to take the card with this.' Out of his parcel came a long piece of white paper … looked like some sort of document … he held it in front of him. *[Styles demonstrates.]* For once I didn't have to say, 'Smile!' Just: 'Hold it!' … and, click, … finished. I asked him what the document was.

'You see, Mr Styles, I'm forty-eight years old. I work twenty-two years for the municipality and the foreman kept on saying to me if I want promotion to Boss-boy I must try to better my education. I didn't write well, Mr Styles. So I took a course with the Damelin Correspondence College. Seven years, Mr Styles! And at last I made it. Here it is. Standard Six Certificate, School Leaving, Third Class! I made it, Mr Styles. I made it. But I'm not finished. I'm going to take up for the Junior Certificate, then Matric … and you watch, Mr Styles. One day I walk out of my house, graduate, self-made! Bye-bye, Mr Styles,' … and he walked out of here happy man, self-made.

[*Back to his display-board; another photograph.*]

My best. Family Card. You know the Family Card? Good for business. Lot of people and they all want copies. One Saturday morning. Suddenly a hell of a noise outside in the street. I thought: What's going on now? Next thing that door burst open and in they came! First the little ones, then the five- and six-year-olds … I didn't know what was going on, man! Stupid children, coming to mess up my place. I was still trying to chse them out when the bigger boys and girls came through the door. Then it clicked. Family Card!

[*Changing his manner abruptly.*]

"Come in! Come in!'

[*Ushering a crowd of people into his studio.*]

… now the young men and women were coming in, then the mothers and fathers, uncles and aunties … the eldest son, a mature man, and finally …

[*Shaking his head with admiration at the memory.*]

the Old Man, the Grandfather! [*The 'old man' walks slowly and with dignity into the studio and sits down in the chair.*]

I looked at him. His grey hair was a sign of wisdom, His face, weather-beaten and lined with experience. Looking at it was like paging the volume of his history, written by himself. He was a living symbol of Life, of all it means and does to a man. I adored him. He sat there—half smiling, half serious—as if he had already seen the end of his road. The eldest son said to me: 'Mr Styles, this is my father, my mother, my brothers and sisters, their wives and husbands, our children. Twenty-seven of us, Mr Styles, We have come to take a card. My father …' he pointed to the old man, '… my father always wanted it.' I said: 'Certainly. Leave the rest to me.' I went to work.

[*Another graphic re-enactment of the scene as he describes it.*]

The old lady here, the eldest son there. Then the other one, with the other one. On this side I did something with the daughters, aunties, and one bachelor brother. Then in front of it all the eight-to-twelves, standing, in front of them the four-to-sevens, kneeling, and finally right on the floor everything that was left, sitting. Jesus, it was hard work, but finally I had them all sorted out and I went behind the camera.

[*Behind his camera.*]

Just starting to focus …

[*Imaginary child in front of the lens; Styles chases the child back to the family group.*]

'… Sit down! Sit down!'

Back to the camera, start to focus again … Not One Of Them Was Smiling! I tried the old trick, 'Say cheese, please.' At first they just looked at me, 'Come on! Cheese!' The children were the first to pick it up,

[*Child's voice*] 'Cheese. Cheese. Cheese.' Then the ones a little bit bigger—'Cheese'—then the next lot—'Cheese'—the uncles and aunties—'Cheese'—and finally the old man himself— 'Cheese'! I thought the roof was going off, man! People outside in the street came and looked through the window. They joined in: 'Cheese.' When I looked again the mourners from the funeral parlour were there wiping away their tears and saying 'Cheese.' Pressed my little button and there it was—New Brighton's smile, twenty-seven variations. Don't you believe those bloody fools who make out we don't know how to smile!

Anyway, you should have seen me then. Moved the bachelor this side, sister-in-laws that side. Put the eldest son behind the old man. Reorganized the children … [*Back behind his camera.*] 'Once again, please! Cheese!' Back to work … old man and old woman together, daughters behind them, sons on the side. Those that were kneeling now standing, those that were standing, now kneeling … Ten times, friends! Each one different!

[*An exhausted Styles collapses in a chair.*]

When they walked out finally I almost said Never Again! A week later the eldest son came back for the cards. I had them ready. The moment he walked through that door I could see he was in trouble. He said to me: 'Mr Styles, we almost didn't make it. My father died two days after the card. He will never see it.' 'Come on,' I said. 'You're a man. One day or the other everyone of us must go home. Here …' I grabbed the cards. 'Here. Look at your father and thank God for the time he was given on this earth.' We went through them together. He looked at them in silence. After the third one, the tear went slowly down his cheek.

But at the same time … I was watching him carefully … something started to happen as he saw his father there with himself, his brothers and sisters, and all the little grandchildren. He began to smile. 'That's it, brother,' I said. 'Smile! Smile at your father. Smile at the world.'

When he left, I thought of him going back to his little house somewhere in New Brighton, filled that day with the little mothers in black because a man had died. I saw my cards passing from hand to hand. I saw hands wipe away tears, and then the first timid little smiles.

You must understand one thing. We own nothing except ourselves. This world and its laws, allows us nothing, except ourselves. There is nothing we can leave behind when we die, except the memory of ourselves. I know what I'm talking about, friends—I had a father, and he died.

[*To the display-board.*]

Here he is. My father. That's him. Fought in the war. Second World War. Fought at Tobruk. In Egypt. He fought in France so that this country and all the others could stay Free, When he came back they stripped him at the docks—his gun, his uniform, the dignity they'd allowed him for a few mad years because the world needed men to fight and be ready to sacrifice themselves for something called Freedom, in return they let him keep his scoff-tin and gave him a bicycle. Size twenty-eight I remember, because it was too big for me. When he died, in a rotten old suitcase amongst some of his old rags, I found that photograph. That's all. That's all I have from him,

[*The display-board again.*]

Or this old lady, Mrs Matothlana. Used to stay in Sangocha Street, You remember! Her husband was arrested …

[*Knock at the door.*]

Tell you about it later. Come in!

[A man *walks nervously into the studio. Dressed in an ill-fitting new double-breasted suit. He is carrying a plastic bag with a hat in it. His manner is hesitant and shy. Styles takes one look at him and breaks into an enormous smile.*]

[*An aside to the audience.*] A Dream! [*To the man.*] Come in, my friend.

MAN. Mr Styles?

STYLES. That's me. Come in! You have come to take a card?

MAN. Snap.

STYLES. Yes, a card. Have you got a deposit?

MAN. Yes.

STYLES. Good. Let me just take your name down. You see, you pay deposit now, and when you come for the card, you pay the rest.

MAN. Yes.

STYLES. [*to his desk and a black book for names and addresses*]. What is your name? [*The man hesitates, as if not sure of himself.*]

Your name, please?

[*Pause.*]

Come on, my friend. You must surely have a name.

MAN. [*pulling himself together, but still very nervous*]. Robert
Zwelinzima.

STYLES. [*writing*]. 'Robert Zwelinzima.' Address? MAN [*swallowing*]. Fifty, Mapija Street.

STYLES. [*writes, then pauses*]. 'Fifty, Mapija?'

MAN. Yes.

STYLES. You staying with Buntu? MAN. Buntu.

STYLES. Very good somebody that one. Came here for his Wedding Card. Always helping people. If that man was white they'd call him a liberal.

[*Now finished writing. Back to his customer.*] All right. How many cards do you want?

MAN. One card.

STYLES [*disappointed*]. Only one?

MAN. One.

STYLES. How do you want to take the card?

[*The man is not sure of what the question means.*] You can take the card standing …

[*Styles strikes a stylish pose next to the table.*] sitting …

[*Another pose … this time in the chair.*] anyhow. How do you want it?

MAN. Anyhow.

STYLES. Right. Sit down.

[*Robert hesitates.*] Sit down!

[*Styles fetches a vase with plastic flowers, dusts them off, and places them on the table.
Robert holds up his plastic bag.*]

What you got there?

[*Out comes the hat.*]

Aha! Stetson. Put it on my friend.

[*Robert handles it shyly.*]

You can put it on, Robert.

[*Robert pulls it on. Styles does up one of his jacket buttons.*]

What a beautiful suit, my friend! Where did you buy it?

MAN. Sales House.

STYLES [*quoting a sales slogan*]. 'Where the Black world buys the best. Six months to
pay. Pay as you wear.'

[*Nudges Robert.*]

… and they never repossess!

[*They share a laugh.*]

What are you going to do with this card?

[*Chatting away as he goes to his camera and sets it up for the photo. Robert watches the preparations apprehensively.*]

MAN. Send it to my wife.

STYLES. Your wife!

MAN. Nowetu.

STYLES. Where's your wife?

MAN. King William's Town.

STYLES [*exaggerated admiration*]. At last! The kind of man I like. Not one of those foolish young boys who come here to find work and then forget their families back home. A man, with responsibility!

Where do you work?

MAN. Feltex.

STYLES. I hear they pay good there.

MAN. Not bad.

[*He is now very tense, staring fixedly at the camera. Styles straightens up behind it.*]

STYLES. Come on, Robert! You want your wife to get a card with her husband looking like he's got all the worries in the world on his back? What will she think? 'My poor husband is in trouble!' You must smile!

[*Robert shamefacedly relaxes a little and starts to smile.*] That's it!

[*He relaxes still more. Beginning to enjoy himself Uncertainly produces a very fancy pipe from one of his pockets. Styles now really warming to the assignment.*]

Look, have you ever walked down the passage to the office with the big glass door and the board outside: 'Manager—Bestuurder'. Imagine it, man, you, Robert Zwelinzima, behind a desk in an office like that! It can happen, Robert. Quick promotion to Chief Messenger. I'll show you what we do, [*Styles produces a Philips' class-room map of the world, which he hangs behind the table as a backdrop to the photo.*]

Look at it, Robert, America, England, Africa, Russia, Asia! [*Carried away still further by his excitement, Styles finds a cigarette, lights it, and gives it to Robert to hold. The latter is now ready for the 'card' ... pipe in one hand and cigarette in the other. Styles stands behind his camera and admires his handiwork.*]

Mr Robert Zwelinzima, Chief Messenger at Feltex, sitting in his office with the world behind him. Smile, Robert. Smile!

[*Studying his subject through the viewfinder of the camera.*]

Lower your hand, Robert ... towards the ashtray ... more ... now make a four with your legs ...

[*He demonstrates behind the camera. Robert crosses his legs.*]

Hold it, Robert … Keep on smiling … that's it … [*presses the release button—the shutter clicks.*]

Beautiful! All right, Robert.

[*Robert and his smile remain frozen.*]

Robert. You can relax now. It's finished! MAN. Finished?

STYLES. Yes. You just want the one card? MAN. Yes.

STYLES. What happens if you lose it? Hey? I've heard stories about those postmen, Robert. *Yo!* Sit on the side of the road and open the letters they should be delivering! 'Dear wife …' —one rand this side, letter thrown away. 'Dear wife …'—another rand this side, letter thrown away. You want that to happen to you? Come on! What about a movie, man?

MAN. Movie?

STYLES. Don't you know the movie?

MAN. No.

STYLES. Simple! You just walk you see …

[*Styles demonstrates; at a certain point freezes in mid-stride.*]

… and I take the card! Then you can write to your wife:

'Dear wife, I am coming home at Christmas …' Put the card in your letter and post it. Your wife opens the letter and what does she see? Her Robert, walking home to her! She shows it to the children. 'Look, children, your daddy is coming!' The children jump and clap their hands: 'Daddy is coming! Daddy is coming!'

MAN [*excited by the picture Styles has conjured up*]. All right!

STYLES. You want a movie?

MAN. I want a movie.

STYLES. That's my man! Look at this, Robert.

[*Styles reverses the map hanging behind the table to reveal a gaudy painting of a futuristic city.*]

City of the Future! Look at it. Mr Robert Zwelinzima, man about town, future head of Feltex, walking through the City of the Future!

MAN [*examining the backdrop with admiration. He recognizes a landmark*]. OK.

STYLES. OK Bazaars … [*the other buildings*] … Mutual Building Society, Barclays Bank … the lot!

What you looking for, Robert?

MAN. Feltex.

STYLES. Yes … well, you see, I couldn't fit everything on, Robert. But if I had had enough space Feltex would have been here.

[*To his table for props.*]

Walking-stick … newspaper …

MAN [*diffidently*]. I don't read.

STYLES. That is not important, my friend. You think all those monkeys carrying newspapers can read? They look at the pictures.

[*After 'dressing' Robert with the props he moves back to his camera.*] This is going to be beautiful, Robert. My best card. I must send one to the magazines.

All right, Robert, now move back. Remember what I showed you. Just walk towards me and right in front of the City of the Future. I'll take the picture. Ready? Now come, Robert ... [*Pipe in mouth, walking-stick in hand, newspaper under the other arm, Robert takes a jaunty step and then freezes, as Styles had shown him earlier.*]

Come, Robert. . . .

[*Another step.*]

Just one more, Robert. . . .

[*Another step.*]

Stop! Hold it, Robert. Hold it!

[*The camera flash goes off; simultaneously a blackout except for one light on Robert, frozen in the pose that will appear in the picture. We are in fact looking at the photograph. It 'comes to life' and dictates the letter that will accompany it to Nowetu in King William's Town.*]

MAN. Nowetu ...

[*Correcting himself*]

Dear Nowetu,

I've got wonderful news for you in this letter. My troubles are over, I think. You won't believe it, but I must tell you. Sizwe Bansi, in a manner of speaking, is dead! I'll tell you what I can.

As you know, when I left the Railway Compound I went to stay with a friend of mine called Zola. A very good friend that, Nowetu. In fact he was even trying to help me find some job. But that's not easy, Nowetu, because Port Elizabeth is a big place, a very big place with lots of factories but also lots of people looking for a job like me. There are so many men, Nowetu, who have left their places because they are dry and have come here to find work!

After a week with Zola, I was in big trouble. The headman came around, and after a lot of happenings which I will tell you when I see you, they put a stamp in my passbook which said I must leave Port Elizabeth at once in three days time. I was very much unhappy, Nowetu. I couldn't stay with Zola because if the headman found me there again my troubles would be even bigger. So Zola took me to a friend of his called Buntu, and asked him if I could stay with him until I decided what to do ...

[*Buntu's house in New Brighton. Table and two chairs. Robert, in a direct continuation of the preceding scene, is already there, as Buntu, jacket slung over his shoulder, walks in. Holds out his hand to Robert.*]

BUNTU. Hi, Buntu.

[*They shake hands.*]

MAN. Sizwe Bansi.

BUNTU. Sit down.

[*They sit.*]

Zola told me you were coming. Didn't have time to explain anything. Just asked if you could spend a few nights here. You can perch yourself on that sofa in the corner. I'm alone at the moment My wife is a domestic … sleep-in at Kabega Park … only comes home weekends. Hot today, hey?

[*In the course of this scene Buntu will busy himself first by having a wash—basin and jug of water on the table—and then by changing from his working clothes preparatory to going out. Sizwe Bansi stays in his chair.*]

What's your problem, friend?

MAN. I've got no permit to stay in Port Elizabeth.

BUNTU. Where do you have a permit to stay?

MAN. King William's Town.

BUNTU. How did they find out?

MAN [*tells his story with the hesitation and uncertainty of the illiterate. When words fail him he tries to use his hands.*]

I was staying with Zola, as you know. I was very happy there. But one night … I was sleeping on the floor … I heard some noises and when I looked up I saw torches shining in through the window … then there was a loud knocking on the door. When I got up Zola was there in the dark … he was trying to whisper something, I think he was saying I must hide. So I crawled under the table. The headman came in and looked around and found me hiding under the table … and dragged me out.

BUNTU. Raid?

MAN. Yes, it was a raid, I was just wearing my pants. My shirt was lying on the other side. I just managed to grab it as they were pushing me out … I finished dressing in the van. They drove straight to the administration office … and then from there they drove to the Labour Bureau. I was made to stand in the passage there, with everybody looking at me and shaking their heads like they knew I was in big trouble. Later I was taken into an office and made to stand next to the door … The white man behind the desk had my book and he also looked at me and shook his head. Just then one other white man came in with a card …

BUNTU. A card?

MAN. He was carrying a card.

JUNTU. Pink card?

MAN. Yes, the card was pink.

BUNTU. Record card. Your whole bloody life is written down on that. Go on.

MAN. Then the first white man started writing something on the card … and just then somebody came in carrying a …

[*demonstrates what he means by banging a clenched fist on the table.*] BUNTU. A stamp?

MAN. Yes, a stamp. [*Repeats the action.*] He was carrying a stamp.

BUNTU. And then?

MAN. He put it on my passbook. BUNTU. Let me see your book?

[*Sizwe produces his passbook from the back-pocket of his trousers. Buntu examines it.*]
Shit! You know what this is? [*The stamp.*]

MAN. I can't read.

BUNTU. Listen … [*reads*], 'You are required to report to the Bantu Affairs Commissioner, King William's Town, within three days of the above-mentioned date for the …' You should have been home yesterday! … 'for the purpose of repatriation to home district.' Influx Control.

You're in trouble, Sizwe.

MAN. I don't want to leave Port Elizabeth.

BUNTU, Maybe. But if that book says go, you go.

MAN. Can't I maybe burn this book and get a new one?

BANTU. Burn that book? Stop kidding yourself, Sizwe! Anyway suppose you do. You must immediately go apply for a new one. Right? And until that new one comes, be careful the police don't stop you and ask for your book. Into the Courtroom, brother. Charge: Failing to produce Reference Book on Demand. Five rand or five days. Finally the new book comes. Down to the Labour Bureau for a stamp … it's got to be endorsed with permission to be in this area. White man at the Labour Bureau takes the book, looks at it—doesn't look at you!—goes to the big machine and feeds in your number …

[*Buntu goes through the motions of punching out a number on a computer.*]
… card jumps out, he reads: 'Sizwe Bansi. Endorsed to King William's Town …' Takes your book, fetches that same stamp, and in it goes again. So you burn that book, or throw it away, and get another one. Same thing happens.

[*Buntu feeds the computer; the card jumps out.*]
'Sizwe Bansi, Endorsed to King William's Town …' Stamp goes in the third time … But this time it's also into a van and off to the Native Commissioner's Office; card around your neck with your number on it; escort on both sides and back to King William's Town. They make you pay for the train fare too!

MAN. I think I will try to look for some jobs in the garden.

BUNTU. You? Job as a garden-boy? Don't you read the newspapers ?

MAN. I can't read.

BUNTU. I'll tell you what the little white ladies say: 'Domestic vacancies, I want a garden-boy with good manners and a wide knowledge of seasons and flowers. Book in order.' Yours in order? Anyway what the hell do you know about seasons and flowers? [*After a moment's thought.*] Do you know any white man who's prepared to give you a job?

MAN. No, I don't know any white man.

BUNTU. Pity. We might have been able to work something then. You talk to the white man, you see, and ask him to write a letter saying he's got a job for you. You take that letter from the white man and go back to King William's Town, where you show it to the Native Commissioner there. The Native Commissioner in King William's Town reads that letter from the white man in Port Elizabeth who is ready to give you the job. He then writes a letter back to the Native Commissioner in Port Elizabeth. So you come back here with the two letters. Then the Native Commissioner in Port Elizabeth reads the letter from the Native Commissioner in King William's Town together with the first letter from the white man who is prepared to give you a job, and he says when he reads the letters: Ah yes, this man Sizwe Bansi can get a job. So the Native Commissioner in Port Elizabeth then writes a letter which you take with the letters from the Native Commissioner in King William's Town and the white man in Port Elizabeth, to the Senior Officer at the Labour Bureau, who reads all the letters. Then he will put the right stamp in your book and give you another letter from himself which together with the letters from the white man and the two Native Affairs Commissioners, you take to the Administration Office here in New Brighton and make an application for Residence Permit, so that you don't fall victim of raids again. Simple.

MAN. Maybe I can start a little business selling potatoes and …

BUNTU. Where do you get the potatoes and …?

MAN. I'll buy them.

BUNTU. With what?

MAN. Borrow some money …

BUNTU. Who is going to lend money to a somebody endorsed to hell and gone out in the bush? And how you going to buy your potatoes at the market without a Hawker's Licence? Same story, Sizwe. You won't get that because of the bloody stamp in your book.

There's no way out, Sizwe. You're not the first one who has tried to find it. Take my advice and catch that train back to King William's Town. If you need work so bad go knock on the door of the Mines Recruiting Office. Dig gold for the white man. That's the only time they don't worry about Influx Control.

MAN. I don't want to work on the mines. There is no money there. And it's dangerous, under the ground. Many black men get killed when the rocks fall. You can die there.

BUNTU [*stopped by the last remark into taking possibly his first real look at Sizwe*].

You don't want to die.

MAN. I don't want to die.

BUNTU [*stops whatever he is doing to sit down and talk to Sizwe with an intimacy that was not there before.*]

You married, Sizwe?

MAN. Yes.

BUNTU. How many children?

MAN. I've got four children.

BUNTU. Boys? Girls?

MAN. I've got three boys and one girl.

BUNTU. Schooling?

MAN. Two are schooling. The other two stay at home with their mother.

BUNTU. Your wife is not working.

MAN. The place where we stay is fifteen miles from town. There is only one shop there. Baas van Wyk. He has already got a woman working for him. King William's Town is a dry place Mr Buntu … very small and too many people. That is why I don't want to go back.

BUNTU. *Ag,* friend … I don't know! I'm also married. One child.

MAN. Only one?

BUNTU. *Ja,* my wife attends this Birth Control Clinic rubbish. The child is staying with my mother.

[*Shaking his head.*] *Hai,* Sizwe! If I had to tell you the trouble I had before I could get the right stamps in my book, even though I was born in this area! The trouble I had before I could get a decent job … born in this area! The trouble I had to get this two-roomed house … born in this area!

MAN. Why is there so much trouble, Mr Buntu?

BUNTU. Two weeks back I went to a funeral with a friend of mine. Out in the country. An old relative of his passed away. Usual thing … sermons in the house, sermons in the church, sermons at the graveside. I thought they were never going to stop talking!

At the graveside service there was one fellow, a lay preacher … short man, neat little moustache, wearing one of those old-fashioned double-breasted black suits … *Haai!* He was wonderful. While he talked he had a gesture with his hands … like this … that reminded me of our youth, when we learnt to fight with kieries. His text was 'Going Home'. He handled it well, Sizwe. Started by saying that the first man to sign the Death Contract with God, was Adam, when he signed in Eden. Since that day, wherever Man is, or whatever he does, he is never without his faithful companion, Death. So with Outajacob … the dead man's name … he has at last accepted the terms of his contract with God.

But in his life, friends, he walked the roads of this land. He helped print those footpaths which lead through the bush and over the veld … footpaths which his children are now walking. He worked on farms from this district down to the coast and north as far as Pretoria. I knew him. He was a friend. Many people knew Outa jacob. For a long time he worked for Baas van der Walt. But when the old man died his young son Hendrik said: 'I don't like you. Go!' Outa jacob picked up his load and put it on his shoulders. His wife followed. He went to the next farm … through the fence, up to the house … : 'Work, please, Baas.' Baas Potgieter took him. He stayed a long time there too, until one day there was trouble between the Madam and his wife. Jacob and his wife were walking again. The load on his back was heavier, he wasn't so young any more, and there were children behind them now as well. On to the next farm. No work. The next one. No work. Then the next one. A little time there. But the drought was bad and the farmer said: 'Sorry, Jacob. The cattle are dying. I'm moving to the city.' Jacob picked up his load yet again. So it went, friends. On and on … until he arrived there. [*The grave at his feet.*] Now at last it's over. No matter how hard-arsed the boer on this farm wants to be, he cannot move Outa Jacob. He has reached Home.

[*Pause.*]

That's it, brother. The only time we'll find peace is when they dig a hole for us and press our face into the earth.

[*Putting on his coat.*]

Ag, to hell with it. If we go on like this much longer we'll do the digging for them.

[*Changing his tone.*]

You know Sky's place, Sizwe?

MAN. No.

BUNTU. come. Let me give you a treat. I'll do you there.

[*Exit Buntu.*

Blackout except for a light on Sizwe. He continues his letter to Mowetu.]

MAN. Sky's place? [*Shakes his head and laughs.*] Hey, Nowetu! When I mention that name again, I get a headache … the same headache I had when I woke up in Buntu's place the next morning. You won't believe what it was like. You cannot! It would be like you walking down Pickering Street in King William's Town and going into

Koekemoer's Cafe to buy bread, and what do you see sitting there at the smart table and chairs? Your husband, Sizwe Bansi, being served ice- cream and cool drinks by old Mrs Koekemoer herself. Such would be your surprise if you had seen me at Sky's place. Only they weren't serving cool drinks and ice-cream. No! First-class booze, Nowetu. And it wasn't old Mrs Koekemoer serving me, but a certain lovely and beautiful lady called Miss Nkonyemi. And it wasn't just your husband Sizwe sitting there with all the most important people of New Brighton, but *Mister* Bansi.
[*He starts to laugh.*] Mister Bansi!
[*As the laugh gets bigger, Sizwe rises to his feet.*]
[*The street outside Sky's Shebeen in New Brighton. Our man is amiably drunk. He addresses the audience.*]

MAN. Do you know who I am, friend? Take my hand, friend. Take my hand, I am Mister Bansi, friend. Do you know where I come from? I come from Sky's place, friend. A most wonderful place. I met everybody there, good people. I've been drinking, my friends—brandy, wine, beer … Don't you want to go in there, good people? Let's all go to Sky's place. [*Shouting.*] Mr Buntu! Mr Buntu!
[*Buntu enters shouting goodbye to friends at the Shebeen. He joins Sizwe. Buntu, though not drunk, is also amiably talkative under the influence of a good few drinks.*]

BUNTU [*discovering the audience*]. Hey, where did you get all these wonderful people?

MAN. I just found them here. Mr Buntu,

BUNTU. Wonderful!

MAN. I'm inviting them to Sky's place, Mr Buntu.

BUNTU. You tell them about Sky's?

MAN. I told them about Sky's place, Mr Buntu.

BUNTU [*to the audience*]. We been having a time there, man! MAN. They know it. I told them everything.

BUNTU [*laughing*]. Sizwe! We had our fun there.

MAN. Hey … hey …

BUNTU. Remember that Member of the Advisory Board?

MAN. Hey … Hey … Mr Buntu! You know I respect you, friend. You must call me nice.

BUNTU. What do you mean?

MAN [*clumsy dignity*]. I'm not just Sizwe no more. He might have walked in, but Mr Bansi walked out!

BUNTU [*playing along*]. I am terribly sorry, Mr Bansi. I apologize for my familiarity. Please don't be offended. [*Handing over one of the two oranges he is carrying.*] Allow me … with the compliments of Miss Nkonyeni.

MAN [*taking the orange with a broad hut sheepish grin*]. Miss
   Nkonyeni!

BUNTU. Sweet dreams, Mr Bansi.

MAN [*tears the orange with his thumbs and starts eating it messily*].
   Lovely lady, Mr Buntu.

BUNTU [*leaves Sizwe with a laugh. To the audience*]. Back there in the Shebeen a Member
   of the Advisory Board hears that he comes from King William's Town. He goes up
   to Sizwe, 'Tell me, Mr Bansi, what do you think of Ciskeian Independence?'

MAN [*interrupting*]. *Ja*, I remember that one. Bloody Mister Member of the Advisory
   Board. Talking about Ciskeian Independence!

   [*To the audience.*]

   I must tell you, friend … when a car passes or the wind blows up the dust, Ciskeian
   Independence makes you cough. I'm telling you, friend … put a man in a pon-
   dok and call that Independence? My good friend, let me tell you … Ciskeian
   Independence is shit!

BUNTU. Or that other chap! Old Jolobe. The fat tycoon man! [*to the audience*] Comes to
   me … [*pompous voice*] … 'Your friend, Mr Bansi, is he on an official visit to town?'
   'No,' I said, 'Mr Bansi is on an official walkout!' [*Buntu thinks this is a big joke.*]

MAN [*stubbornly*]. I'm here to stay.

BUNTU [*looking at his watch*]. Hey, Sizwe …

MAN [*reproachfully*]. Mr Buntu!

BUNTU [*correcting himself*]. Mr Bansi, it is getting late. I've got to work tomorrow. Care
   to lead the way, Mr Bansi? MAN. You think I can't? You think Mr Bansi is lost?

BUNTU. I didn't say that.

MAN. You are thinking it, friend. I'll show you. This is Chinga Street.

BUNTU. Very good! But which way do we … ?

MAN [*setting off*]. This way.

BUNTU [*pulling him back*]. Mistake. You're heading for Site and Service and a lot of
   trouble with the Tsotsis.

MAN [*the opposite direction*]. That way.

BUNTU. Lead on. I'm right behind you.

MAN. *Ja*, you are right, Mr Buntu. There is Newell High School. Now …

BUNTU. Think carefully!

MAN. … when we were going to Sky's we had Newell in front.
   So when we leave Sky's we put Newell behind. BUNTU. Very good!

   [*An appropriate change in direction. They continue walking, and eventually arrive at
   a square, with roads leading off in many directions. Sizwe is lost. He wanders around,
   uncertain of the direction to take.*]

MAN. *Haai*, Mr Buntu … ! BUNTU. Mbizweni Square.

MAN. *Yo!* Cross-roads to hell, wait … [*Closer look at landmark.*]… that building … Rio Cinema! So we must …

BUNTU. Rio Cinema? With a white cross on top, bell outside, and the big show on Sundays?

MAN [*sheepishly*]. You're right, friend. I've got it, Mr Buntu.

That way.

[*He starts off. Buntu watches him.*]

BUNTU. Goodbye. King William's Town a hundred and fifty miles. Don't forget to write.

MAN [*hurried about-turn*]. *Haai… haai …*

BUNTU. Okay, Sizwe, I'll take over from here. But just hang on for a second I want to have a piss. Don't move!

[*Buntu disappears into the dark.*]

MAN. *Haai*, Sizwe! You are a country fool! Leading Mr Buntu and Mr Bansi astray. You think you know this place New Brighton? You know nothing!

[*Buntu comes running back.*]

BUNTU [*urgently*]. Let's get out of here.

MAN. Wait, Mr Buntu, I'm telling that fool Sizwe …

BUNTU. Come on! There's trouble there … [*pointing in the direction from which he has come*] … let's move.

MAN. Wait, Mr Buntu, wait. Let me first tell that Sizwe …

BUNTU. There's a dead man lying there!

MAN. Dead man?

BUNTU. I thought I was just pissing on a pile of rubbish, but when I looked carefully I saw it was a man. Dead. Covered in blood. Tsotsis must have got him. Let's get the hell out of here before anybody sees us.

MAN. Buntu … Buntu …

BUNTU. Listen to me, Sizwe! The Tsotsis might still be around.

MAN. Buntu …

BUNTU. Do you want to join him? MAN. I don't want to join him, BUNTU. Then come.

MAX. Wait, Buntu.

BUNTU. Jesus! If Zola had told me how much trouble you were going to be!

MAN. Buntu, … we must report that man to the police station. BUNTU. Police Station! Are you mad? You drunk, passbook not in order … 'We've come to report a dead man, Sergeant.'

'Grab them!' Case closed. We killed him.

MAN. Mr Buntu, … we can't leave him …

BUNTU. Please, Sizwe!

MAN. Wait. Let's carry him home.

BUNTU. Jst like that! Walk through New Brighton streets, at this hour, carrying a dead man. Anyway we don't know where he stays. Come.

MAN. Wait, Buntu, ... listen ...

BUNTU. Sizwe!

MAN. Buntu, we can know where he stays. That passbook of his will talk. It talks, friend, like mine. His passbook will tell you. BUNTU [*after a moment's desperate hesitation*]. You really want to land me in the shit, hey.

[*Disappears into the dark again.*]

MAN. It will tell you in good English where he stays. My passbook talks good English too ... big words that Sizwe can't read and doesn't understand. Sizwe wants to stay here in New Brighton and find a job; passbook says, 'No! Report back.'

Sizwe wants to feed his wife and children; passbook says,

'No, Endorsed out.'

Sizwe wants to ...

[*Buntu reappears, a passbook in his hand. Looks around furtively and moves to the light under a lamp-post.*]

They never told us it would be like that when they introduced it. They said: Book of Life! Your friend! You'll never get lost! They told us lies.

[*He joins Buntu who is examining the book.*]

BUNTU. *Haai!* Look at him [*the photograph in the book, reading*].

'Robert Zwelinzima. Tribe: Xhosa. Native identification Number ...'

MAN. Where does he stay, Buntu?

BUNTU [*paging through the book*]. Worked at Dorman Long seven years ... Kilomet Engineering ... eighteen months ... Anderson Hardware two years ... now unemployed. Hey, look, Sizwe! He's one up on you. He's got a work-seeker's permit.

MAN. Where does he stay, Buntu?

BUNTU. Lodger's Permit at 42 Mdala Street. From there to Sangocha Street ... now at ...

[*Pause. Closes the book abruptly.*]

To hell with it I'm not going *there*.

MAN. Where, Buntu?

BUNTU [*emphatically*]. I Am Not Going There!

MAN. Buntu ...

BUNTU. You know where he is staying now? Single Men's Quarters! If you think I'm going there this time of the night you got another guess coming.

[*Sizwe doesn't understand.*]

Look, Sizwe … I stay in a house, there's a street name and a number. Easy to find. Ask anybody … Mapija Street? That way. You know what Single Men's Quarters is? Big bloody concentration camp with rows of things that look like train carriages. Six doors to each! Twelve people behind each door! You want me to go there now? Knock on the first one: 'Does Robert Zwelinzima live here?' 'No!' Next one: 'Does Robert …?' 'Buggeroff, we're trying to sleep!' Next one: 'Does Robert Zwelinzima … ?' They'll fuck us up, man! I'm putting this book back and we're going home.

MAN. Buntu!

BUNTU [*half-way back to the alleyway*]. What?

MAN. Would you do that to me, friend? If the Tsotsis had stabbed Sizwe, and left him lying there, would you walk away from him as well?

[*The accusation stops Buntu.*]

Would you leave me lying there, wet with your piss? I wish I was dead. I wish I was dead because I don't care a damn about anything any more.

[*Turning away from Buntu to the audience.*]

What's happening in this world, good people? Who cares for who in this world? Who wants who?

Who wants me, friend? What's wrong with me? I'm a man. I've got eyes to see, I've got ears to listen when people talk. I've got a head to think good things. What's wrong with me?

[*Starts to tear off his clothes.*]

Look at me! I'm a man. I've got legs. I can run with a wheelbarrow full of cement! I'm strong! I'm a man. Look! I've got a wife. I've got four children. How many has he made, lady? [*The man sitting next to her.*] is he a man? What has he got that I haven't … ?

[*A thoughtful Buntu rejoins them, the dead man's reference book still in his hand.*]

BUNTU. Let me see your book?

[*Sizwe doesn't respond.*] Give me your book!

MAN. Are you a policeman now, Buntu?

BUNTU. Give me your bloody book, Sizwe!

MAN [*handing it over*]. Take It, Buntu. Take this book and read it carefully, friend, and tell me what it says about me. Buntu, does that book tell you I'm a man?

[*Buntu studies the two hooks. Sizwe turns back to the audience.*]

That bloody book … ! People, do you know? No! Wherever you go … it's that bloody book. You go to school, it goes too. Go to work, it goes too. Go to church and pray and sing lovely hymns, it sits there with you. Go to hospital to die, it lies there too!

[*Buntu has collected Sizwe's discarded clothing.*]

BUNTU. Come!

[*Buntu's house, as earlier. Table and two chairs. Buntu pushes Sizwe down into a chair. Sizwe still muttering, starts to struggle back into his clothes. Buntu opens the two reference books and places them side by side on the table. He produces a pot of glue, then very carefully tears out the photograph in each book. A dab of glue on the back of each and then Sizwe's goes back into Robert's book, and Robert's into Sizwe's. Sizwe watches this operation, at first uninterestedly, but when he realizes what Buntu is up to, with growing alarm. When he is finished, Buntu pushes the two books in front of Sizwe.*]

MAN [*shaking his head emphatically*]. Yo! *Haai, haai.* No, Buntu.

BUNTU. It's a chance.

MAN. *Haai, haai, haai …*

BUNTU. It's your only chance!

MAN. No, Buntu! What's it mean? That me, Sizwe Bansi …

BUNTU. Is dead.

MAN. I'm not dead, friend.

BUNTU. We burn this book … [*Sizwe's original*] … and Sizwe Bansi disappears off the face of the earth.

MAN. What about the man we left lying in the alleyway?

BUNTU. Tomorrow the Flying Squad passes there and finds him. Check in his pockets … no passbook. Mount Road Mortuary. After three days nobody has identified him. Pauper's Burial. Case closed.

MAN. And then?

BUNTU. Tomorrow I contact my friend Norman at Feltex. He's a boss-boy there. I tell him about another friend, Robert Zwelinzima, book in order, who's looking for a job. You roll up later, hand over the book to the white man. Who does Robert Zwelinzima look like? You! Who gets the pay on Friday? You, man!

MAN. What about all that shit at the Labour Bureau, Buntu?

BUNTU. You don't have to there. This chap had a work-seeker's permit, Sizwe. All you do is hand over the book to the white man. *He* checks at the Labour Bureau. They check with their big machine. 'Robert Zwelinzima has the right to be employed and stay in this town.'

MAN. I don't want to lose my name, Buntu.

BUNTU. You mean you don't want to lose your bloody passbook! You love it, hey?

MAN. Buntu. I cannot lose my name.

BUNTU [*leaving the table*]. All right, I was only trying to help. As Robert Zwelinzima you could have stayed and worked in this town, As Sizwe Bansi …? Start walking, friend. King William's Town. Hundred and fifty miles. And don't waste any time! You've got to be there by yesterday. Hope you enjoy it.

MAN. Buntu …

BUNTU. Lots of scenery in a hundred and fifty miles,

MAN. Buntu! …

BUNTU. Maybe a better idea is just to wait until they pick you up. Save yourself all that walking. Into the train with the escort! Smart stuff, hey. Hope It's not too crowded though. Hell of a lot of people being kicked out, I hear.

MAN. Buntu! …

BUNTU. But once you're back! Sit down on the side of the road next to your pondok with your family … the whole Bansi clan on leave … for life! Hey, that sounds okay. Watching all the cars passing, and as you say, friend, cough your bloody lungs out with Ciskeian independence.

MAN [*now really desperate*]. Buntu!!!

BUNTU. What you waiting for? Go!

MAN. Buntu.

BUNTU. What?

MAN. What about my wife, Nowetu?

BUNTU. What about her?

MAN [*maudlin tears*]. Her loving husband, Siwze Bansi, is dead!

BUNTU. So what! She's going to marry a better man.

MAN [*bridling*]. Who?

BUNTU. You … Robert Zwelinzima.

MAN [*thoroughly confused*]. How can I marry my wife, Buntu?

BUNTU. Get her down here and I'll introduce you.

MAN. Don't make jokes, Buntu. Robert … Sizwe … I'm all mixed up. Who am I?

BUNTU. A fool who is not taking his chance.

MAN. And my children! Their father is Sizwe Bansi. They're registered at school under Bansi …

BUNTU. Are you really worried about your children, friend, or are you just worried about yourself and your bloody name? Wake up, man! Use that book and with your pay on Friday you'll have a real chance to do something for them.

MAN. I'm afraid. How do I get used to Robert? How do I live as another man's ghost?

BUNTU. Wasn't Sizwe Bansi a ghost?

MAN. No!

BUXTU. No? When the white man looked at you at the Labour Bureau what did he see? A man with dignity or a bloody passbook with an N.I. number? Isn't that a ghost? When the white man sees you walk down the street and calls out 'Hey, John! Come here' … to you, *Sizwe Bansi* … isn't that a ghost? Or when his little child calls you 'Boy' … you a man, circumcised with a wife and four children … isn't that a ghost?

Stop fooling yourself. All I'm saying is be a real ghost, if that is what they want, what they've turned us into. Spook them into hell, man!

[*Sizwe is silenced. Buntu realizes his words are beginning to reach the other man. He paces quietly, looking for his next move. He finds it.*]

Suppose you try my plan. Friday. Roughcasting section at Feltex. Paytime. Line of men—non-skilled labourers. White man with the big box full of pay-packets.

'John Kani!' 'Yes, sir!' Pay-packet is handed over. 'Thank you, sir.'

Another one. [*Buntu reads the name on an imaginary pay-packet.*] 'Winston Ntshona!' 'Yes, sir!' Pay-packet over. 'Thank you, sir!' Another one. 'Fats Bhokolane!' *'Hier is ek, my baas!'* Pay-packet over. *"Dankie, my baas!"* Another one. 'Robert Zwelinzima!' [*No response from Sizwe.*] 'Robert Zwelinzima!'

MAN. Yes, sir.

BUNTU [*handing him the imaginary pay-packet*]. Open it. Go on. [*Takes back the packet, tears it open, empties its contents on the table, and counts it.*]

Five … ten … eleven … twelve … and ninety-nine cents. In *your* pocket!

[*Buntu again paces quietly, leaving Sizwe to think. Eventually …*] Saturday. Man in overalls, twelve rand ninety-nine cents

in the back pocket, walking down Main Street looking for Sales House. Finds it and walks in. Salesman comes forward to meet him,

'I've come to buy a suit.' Salesman is very friendly, 'Certainly. Won't you take a seat. I'll get the forms. I'm sure you want to open an account, sir. Six months to pay. But first I'll need all your particulars.'

[*Buntu has turned the table, with Sizwe on the other side, into the imaginary scene at Sales House.*]

BUNTU [*pencil poised, ready to fill in a form*]. Your name, please, sir?

MAN [*playing along uncertainly*]. Robert Zwelinzima.

BUNTU [*writing*]. Robert Zwelinzima.' Address?

MAN. Fifty, Mapija Street.

BUNTU. Where do you work?

MAN. Feltex.

BUNTU. And how much do you get paid?

MAN. Twelve … twelve rand ninety-nine cents.

BUNTU. N.I. Number, please?

[*Sizwe hesitates.*]

Your Native Identity number please?

[*Sizwe is still uncertain. Buntu abandons the act and picks up Robert Zwelinzima's passbook. He reads out the number.*]

N – I – 3 – 8 – 1 – 1 – 8 – 6 – 3.

Burn that into your head, friend. You hear me? It's more important than your name. N.I. number … three …

MAN. Three.

BUNTU. Eight.

MAN. Eight.

BUNTU. One.

MAN. One.

BUNTU. One.

MAN. One.

BUNTU. Eight.

MAN. Eight.

BUNTU. Six. MAN. Six.

BUNTU. Three.

MAN. Three.

BUNTU. Again. Three.

MAN. Three.

BUNTU. Eight,

MAN . Eight.

BUNTU. One.

MAN. One.

BUNTU. One.

MAN. One.

BUNTU. Eight.

MAN. Eight.

BUNTU. Six.

MAN. Six.

BUNTU. Three.

MAN. Three.

BUNTU [*picking up his pencil and returning to the role of the salesman*]. N.I. number, please.

MAN [*pausing frequently, using his hands to remember*]. Three … eight … one … one … eight … six … three …

BUNTU [*abandoning the act*]. Good boy.

[*He paces, Sizwe sits and waits.*]

Sunday. Man in a Sales House suit, hat on top, going to church. Hymn book and bible under the arm. Sits down in the front pew. Priest in the pulpit.

[*Buntu jumps on to a chair in his new role. Sizwe kneels.*] The Time has come!

MAN. Amen!

BUNTU. Pray, brothers and sisters … Pray … Now!

MAN. Amen.

BUNTU. The Lord wants to save you. Hand yourself over to him, while there is still time, while Jesus is still prepared to listen to you.

MAN [*carried away by what he is feeling*]. Amen, Jesus!

BUNTU. Be careful, my brothers and sisters …

MAN. Hallelujah!

BUNTU. Be careful lest when the big day comes and the pages of the big book are turned, it is found that your name is missing. Repent before it is too late.

MAN. Hallelujah! Amen.

BUNTU. Will all those who have not yet handed in their names for membership of our burial society please remain behind.

[*Buntu leaves the pulpit and walks around with a register.*]

Name, please, sir? Number? Thank you.

Good afternoon, sister. Your name, please.

Address? Number? God bless you. [*He has reached Sizwe.*]

Your name, please, brother?

MAN. Robert Zwelinzlma.

BUNTU. Address?

MAN. Fifty, Mapija Street.

BUNTU. N.I. number.

MAN [*again tremendous effort to remember*]. Three … eight … one … one … eight … six … three …

[*They both relax.*]

BUNTU [*after pacing for a few seconds*]. Same man leaving the church … walking down the street.

[*Buntu acts out the role while Sizwe watches. He greets other members of the congregation.*]

'God bless you. Brother Bansi. May you always stay within the Lord's mercy.'

'Greetings, Brother Bansi. We welcome you into the flock of Jesus with happy spirits.'

'God bless you, Brother Bansi. Stay with the Lord, the Devil is strong.'

Suddenly …

[*Buntu has moved to behind Sizwe. He grabs him roughly by the shoulder.*]

Police!

[*Sizwe stands up frightened. Buntu watches him carefully.*]

No, man! Clean your face.

[*Sizwe adopts an impassive expression. Buntu continues as the policeman.*]

What's your name?

MAN. Robert Zwelinzima.

BUNTU. Where do you work? MAN. Feltex.

BUNTU. Book!

[*Sizwe hands over the book and waits while the policeman opens it, looks at the photograph, then Sizwe, and finally checks through its stamps and endorsements. While all this is going on Sizwe stands quietly, looking down at his feet, whistling under his breath. The book is finally handed back.*]

Okay. [*Sizwe takes his book and sits down.*]

MAN [*after a pause*]. I'll try it, Buntu.

BUNTU. Of course you must, if you want to stay alive.

MAN. Yes, but Sizwe Bansi is dead.

BUNTU. What about Robert Zwelinzima then? That poor bastard I pissed on out there in the dark. So *he's* alive again. Bloody miracle, man.

Look, if someone was to offer me the things I wanted most in my life, the things that would make me, my wife, and my child happy, in exchange for the name Buntu … you think I wouldn't swop?

MAN. Are you sure, Buntu?

BUNTU [*examining the question seriously*]. If there was just me … I mean, if I was alone, if I didn't have anyone to worry about or look after except myself … maybe then I'd be prepared to pay some sort of price for a little pride. But if I had a wife and four children wasting away their one and only life in the dust and poverty of Ciskeian Independence … if I had four children waiting for me, their father, to do something about their lives … *ag*, no, Sizwe …

MAN. Robert, Buntu.

BUNTU [*angry*]. All right! Robert, John, Athol, Winston … Shit on names, man! To hell with them if in exchange you can get a piece of bread for your stomach and a blanket in winter. Understand me, brother, I'm not saying that pride isn't a way for us. What I'm saying is shit on our pride if we only bluff ourselves that we are men. Take your name back, Sizwe Bansi, if it's so important to you. But next time you hear a white man say 'John' to you, don't say *'Ja, Baas?'* And next time the bloody white man says to you, a man, 'Boy, come here,' don't run to him and lick his arse like we all do. Face him and tell him: 'White man. I'm a Man!' *Ag kak!* We're bluffing ourselves.

It's like my father's hat. Special hat, man! Carefully wrapped in plastic on top of the wardrobe in his room, God help the child who so much as touches it! Sunday it goes on his head, and a man, full of dignity, a man I respect, walks down the street. White man stops him: 'Come here, kaffir!' What does he do?

[*Buntu whips the imaginary hat off his head and crumples it in his hands as he adopts a fawning, servile pose in front of the white man.*]

'What is it, Baas?'

If that is what you call pride, then shit on it! Take mine and give me food for my children,

[*Pause.*]

Look, brother, Robert Zwelinzima, that poor bastard out there in the alleyway, if there *are* ghosts, he is smiling tonight. He is here, with us, and he's saying: 'Good luck, Sizwe! I hope it works,' He's a brother, man.

MAN. For how long, Buntu?

BUNTU. How long? For as long as you can stay out of trouble, Trouble will mean police station, then fingerprints off to Pretoria to check on previous convictions … and when they do that … Siswe Bansi will live again and you will have had it.

MAN. Buntu, you know what you are saying? A black man stay out of trouble? Impossible, Buntu. Our skin is trouble.

BUNTU [*wearily*]. You said you wanted to try.

MAN. And I will.

BUNTU [*picks up his coat*]. I'm tired, … Robert. Good luck. See you tomorrow.

[*Exit Buntu, Sizwe picks up the passbook, looks at it for a long time, then puts it in his back pocket. He finds his walking-sticky newspaper, and pipe and moves downstage into a solitary light. He finishes the letter to his wife.*]

MAN. So. Nowetu, for the time being my troubles are over. Christmas I come home. In the meantime Buntu is working a plan to get me a Lodger's Permit. If I get it, you and the children can come here and spend some days with me in Port Elizabeth. Spend the money I am sending you carefully. If all goes well I will send some more each week. I do not forget you, my dear wife.

Your loving Husband, Sizwe Bansi

[*As he finishes the letter, Sizwe returns to the pose of the photo. Styles Photographic Studio. Styles is behind the camera.*]

STYLES. Hold it, Robert. Hold it just like that. Just one more. Now smile, Robert … Smile … Smile …

[*Camera flash and blackout.*]

Jelly's Last Jam
(1992)

By George C. Wolfe (1954–)

INTRODUCTION

Having staged *Angels in America, Bring in 'Da Noise, Bring in 'Da Funk,* and *Topdog/Underdog,* George C. Wolfe is perhaps more widely known as a director than as a playwright. He also served as the artistic director and producer of the New York Shakespeare Festival from 1993 to 2004. However, as a playwright, Wolfe is both humorous and intelligent, combining social commentary with acerbic wit. In his most famous script, *The Colored Museum* (1986), Wolfe dismantles prevalent Black stereotypes in a series of mostly comical vignettes. *Jelly's Last Jam* treats the subject of race more personally and more historically, giving the performance of ethnicity moral and even metaphysical dimensions.

This musical forces its main character, the jazz musician Jelly Roll Morton, to "tell [his] tale and save [his] soul." Given this, it is not surprising that the action of the play takes place at the end of Jelly's life, and in a setting "somewhere between heaven and hell." What is slightly more surprising is that even Jelly's afterlife is racially determined. The process of judgment by which Jelly will be "saved" or (presumably) damned takes place in the "Jungle Inn," a jazz nightclub in the middle of a "black void," and is presided over by a character known as the Chimney Man, the ultimate arbiter of blackness: "Just think of me as the coffee in your family's cream."

Since this play shows us events not as if they were happening right now but as they are recalled from past experience, one of the major conflicts in this play takes place between Jelly and the Chimney Man, as the two characters debate how Jelly's story should be told. "This is my life," Jelly says, "n' I'm gonna tell it my way." However, the Chimney Man acts as an editor of sorts, ferreting out embellishments, exaggerations, and falsehoods. "For every tale you lace with a lie," he says, "I'm gonna be there."

The Chimney Man's insistence on emphasizing pain seems unnecessary, even though he sensibly points out that "ya gotta have grit to go with the gravy." Jelly's tale is already full of pain; the pain of exclusion and difference is an intrinsic part of Jelly's character, and his existential crisis leads to many of his unfortunate choices. Jelly (born Ferdinand Joseph Le Menthe Morton) comes from a New Orleans family of Creoles, and his life under the "watchful gaze" of his mixed-race ancestors is one of repression, as they seek to emphasize their difference from blacks: "NOT A GRIT OR COLLARD GREEN, COME WHAT MAY." Jelly's self-image is bound up in performance, in more ways than one: he expresses himself through the piano, but the classical music he is forced to play speaks for someone other than himself. "WHAT IF I COULD VARY THAT," he sings, "CHANGE A RHYTHM, ADD A FLAT / UNTIL IT FEELS MORE LIKE ME?"

This search for what seems like intuitive, intrinsic self-expression leads him away from his family, but into a world in which he is again out of place. At thirteen, Jelly finds inspiration in the blues clubs, "where good Creoles didn't go," but is immediately recognized and taunted as an outsider. Buddy Bolden asks him, "Say Frenchy, yo' Mama know you hangin' out with us darktown folk?" Likewise, Buddy upbraids Jelly for his training and taste, telling him that "The Miserere" from *Il Trovatore* "ain't no music; the notes is written out, tellin' ya what's gon' come next. That's like wakin' up in the mornin' n' knowin' you gonna be alive at the end of the day. That might be the way you Creoles live, but it is not the way we do things uptown!" Buddy, like Jelly, equates music with life and self: life is an improvisation, so music must be one as well. Having found a kindred spirit, Jelly embraces the "uptown" crowd, but pays a terrible price. He is disowned by his family: "You are not fit to be Creole," he is told.

Perhaps it is this exclusion, and the ensuing isolation, that led him to "believe that the message was him," that is, give himself sole credit for inventing jazz instead of crediting the community from which he learned it, but this does not excuse the cruelty with which he treats his friend and accomplice, Jack the Bear. When Jelly gives Jack a red doorman's jacket and tells him, "the only thing a nigga can do for me is scrub my steps n' shine my shoes," we see not only Jelly's disdain for dark-skinned blacks, but his inability to reciprocate friendship, a problem that dogs him throughout his life. Jack's presence in Jelly's story synthesizes these two issues.

However, it is the racial implications of the act, and of Jelly's self-aggrandizement, that concern the Chimney Man, who asserts the final control over the story, and it is these crimes for which Jelly must atone. The play begins with a roll call of famous jazz musicians ("Basie, Bolden, n' Bechet"), a list which excludes Jelly, and ultimately the "Last Rites" of the play concern themselves with Jelly's place in this history. In the end Jelly is faced with a choice: continue performing the persona he has created for himself, the solitary genius who utilizes his black heritage when it suits him, or drop the façade and embrace the larger community, joining it as an authentic—if humbled—soul.

ACT ONE

PROLOGUE

Lights reveal a large door, carved with Yoruba motifs, floating in the middle of a black void. The stillness is cut by the faint sound of piano riffs, dissonant yet melodic. The door to the void slowly opens and light from within casts the Silhouette of a Man in a top hat and cutaway. Percussive underscore.

The Man slowly enters the void, riding on "a shaft of darkness." It is the Chimney Man—ageless, elegant, otherworldly.

CHIMNEY MAN:
N' it came to pass that a people were born.
Then torn from the land that was their home.
The story of their pain was set forth in music,
Destined to conquer, take the world by storm.
N' so messengers were called to spread its glory; Go forth Armstrong,
Go forth Ellington,
Go forth Basic, Bolden, n' Bechet.
N' it came to pass that a messenger was called
Who came to believe that the message was him.
Yes, he of diamond tooth n' flashy threads;
Yes, he who drinks from the vine of syncopation
But denies the black soil from which this rhythm was born.
… Denies the black soil from which this rhythm was born!

On the Chimney Man's signal, there is a blast of music and the black void begins to magically transform into …

SCENE I
THE JAM

The Jungle Inn, a run-down club, "somewhere's 'tween heaven n' hell." Its denizens, hereafter known as the Crowd—a colorful array of lowdown types—are "dancin' hard n' gettin' down," as the music continues to wail.

On the Chimney Man's signal, three "creatures" appear. They are the Hunnies, chorus girls—ethereal and low. As they begin to "entertain," the Chimney Man "dissolves" into the black void which still encases the club.

HUNNIE ONE: Welcome to the Jungle Inn.
HUNNIE TWO: A lowdown club somewhere's between …
HUNNIES: Heaven n' hell.
HUNNIE THREE: Where we jammin'! CROWD: *Yeah!*
HUNNIE THREE: With Jelly!
CROWD: *Yeah!*
HUNNIES/CROWD: Tonight!

SONG: JELLY'S JAM

HUNNIE ONE:
    TELL YO' MAMA
    AIN'T COMIN' HOME TONIGHT
HUNNIES TWO & THREE:
    WE'RE GONNA JUMP DOWN
    N' JAM WITH JELLY
HUNNIE TWO:
    THE BAND IS BLOWIN'
    THE GIN IS FLO WIN'
HUNNIES ONE & THREE:
    WE GONNA SLUM IT
    N' SLAM WITH JELLY
HUNNIE THREE:
    GIT IT SHAKIN'
    WE GONNA WAIL TONIGHT
HUNNIES ONE & TWO:
    JUMP IN THE BUCKET
    N' JAM WITH JELLY

HUNNIES:
  OOH PAPA
  TIME TO PULL THE STOPPA'
  RAISIN' HELL AT JELLY'S JAM
HUNNIE ONE:
    HO'S N' HIGH-TONES
    HUSTLIN' HONKY TONKS
JELLY'S LAST JAM
HUNNIES/CROWD:
  GITTIN' LOWDOWN
  TO JAM WITH JELLY
HUNNIE TWO:
  A LOTTA LOWLIFES
  A LOTTA NO-LIFES
HUNNIES/CROWD:
  GONNA JOIN UP
  N' JAM WITH JELLY
HUNNIE THREE:
  TURN THE HEAT ON
  WE GONNA COOK TONIGHT
HUNNIES/CROWD:
  SO GIT THE JUICE OUT
  N' JAM WITH JELLY
HUNNIES:
  OOH SISTA'
  HOT ENOUGH TO BLISTA'
CROWD:
  RAISIN' HELL AT JELLY'S JAM

  IT'S THE BEST DAMN JAM SINCE WAY BACK
    WHEN
  IT'S THE ONE LAST CHANCE TO HOWL AGAIN
  IT'S THE "LET'S GIT DRUNK, WHO GIVES A
    DAMN?"
  LOOK OUT IT'S JELLY'S JAM

  STOMP N' SHOUT
  TURN IT OUT

PUT YOUR FOOT DOWN DADDY
HERE I AM
RAISIN' HELL AT JELLY'S JAM

The Crowd's dancing is raucous and low. The music is blaring and hot. The Hunnies corral the energy of the music and the Crowd as they begin to "conjure up" the spirit of Jelly Roll Morton.

HUNNIES:
C'MON JELLY WE WANT YOUR SOUL
HUNNIES/CROWD:
GONNA JAM JELLY ROLL
WE GITTIN' READY FOR THE ROLL
WE GITTIN' READY FOR THE ROLL
WE GITTIN' READY FOR THE ROLL

AAAAAAHHHH!

The Hunnies and the Crowd continue conjuring up the spirit of Jelly Roll Morton. The dance builds until a slumped figure magically ascends to the stage from below.

HUNNIES/CROWD:
JAZZ ME JELLY ROLL
JAZZ ME JELLY ROLL
JAZZ ME JELLY ROLL
OOOOOOH
JAZZ ME JAZZ ME
JAZZ ME JAZZ ME
JAZZ ME JELLY ROLL
OOOOOOH

The slumped figure enters the club. It's Jelly Roll Morton. As the music and dance continue, Jelly begins to grow in stature until, at the number's end, he is strutting, arrogant and proud.

HUNNIES/CROWD (*Beckoning Jelly*):
COME ON IN!

WHERE YA BEEN?
LET'S GIT DRUNK
WHO GIVES A DAMN?
IT'S PAPA JELLY'S JAM
SWEET PAPA JELLY'S JAM
SMOOTH PAPA JELLY'S JAM
HOT PAPA JELLY
IT'S JELLY'S
JAM!
JAM!
JAM!
Yeah!

> *The number ends. The Hunnies and the Crowd are busy celebrating Jelly. The Chimney Man appears. On his signal, the action freezes.*

CHIMNEY MAN: Well, well, well …
WILL YOU LOOK WHO JUST NOW UP N' DIED
COULD IT BE
MISTER JELLY ROLL?

WELCOME JELLY TO THE OTHER SIDE
TIME TO TELL YOUR TALE
N' SAVE YOUR SOUL

IT'S THE NOW OR NEVER,
EVERMORE
END OF THE LINE

N' from this moment on,

YOUR ASS IS MINE

> *On Chimney Man's signal, the action continues with the Hunnies and the Crowd cheering and hanging on Jelly. Music underscore.*

CROWD MEMBER ONE: Jelly, my man, you remember that club just outside of Chicago. (*To the audience*) Y'all remember, that little club.

CROWD MEMBER TWO: The first time I saw "The Roll" was back in .... er, urn, nineteen aught four.

CROWD MEMBER THREE (*A woman; overlapping*): Ooh child I could dance all night to the Chicago Stomp!

CROWD MEMBER FOUR: Remember all them diamonds you had …

CROWD MEMBER FIVE: All them suits you had …

CROWD MEMBER SIX (*A woman*): All them women you had …

CROWD MEMBER SEVEN (*A woman*): You ought to know 'cause he had you twice.

CROWD MEMBER EIGHT: Remember Jelly?

JELLY: Shit yeah, I remember. I remember you … n' you. (*To Crowd Member Six*) I don't remember you, but I wish I did. (*To the Crowd*) Maybe a little later she'll remind me.

The Crowd laughs.

JELLY: I remember it all.

SONG: IN MY DAY

JELLY:

I'M TELLIN' YA
IN MY DAY
THIS MAN WAS MADE OF MONEY
YOU KNOW IT, YEAH IN MY DAY
THESE HANDS WERE DRIPPIN' HONEY
I'D FLASH 'EM THAT *SAVOIR FAIRE*
N' TOSS 'EM A SMILE

CROWD MEMBER FOUR: Diamond-studded smile!

JELLY:

WHAT YOU FOLKS CALLED "STYLE"
I USETA CALL THE "HIGH-TONE"
THE "WHOZZAT?"
THE "HOW YOU LEARN TO USE-ZAT!"

IN MY DAY
THIS MAN CAME UP WITH A SOUND
N' INCIDENTALLY IN MY DAY
IT GOT TO GETTIN' AROUND

CROWD (*A trio*):
   FROM HIGH-FALUTIN'
   TO A HOLE IN THE GROUND

JELLY:
   'CAUSE I WAS—
   OOH YEAH, GOOD AS THAT!
   MISTER MOZART WOULDA
   TIPPED HIS HAT
   BELIEVE ME WHEN I SAY
   I WAS SOMETHIN' IN MY DAY
   REALLY SOMETHIN' IN MY DAY

HUNNIES:
   THEY CALLED HIM CREOLE BOY
   SWEET PAPA JELLY JOY
   OOH HOW THAT HARD-LOVIN' DADDY
   COULD PLAY
   HOT LICKIN' PIANA MAN
   COULD ROLL LIKE NO ONE CAN
   N' SQUEEZE YOUR LITTLE
   TEASE YOUR LITTLE TROUBLES AWAY
   OH HOW HIS HANDS WOULD EASE
   DOWN THE PIANA KEYS
   IT'S LIKE HE WAS STRUTTIN' THE MUSIC
   WHENEVER HE'D PLAY

   Jelly, "struttin' as if strokin'," dances about, flaunting his prowess and his charm. As Jelly begins to sing again, the Jungle Inn reality begins to fade. Lights reveal Gran Mimi, dressed for mourning and floating in the void, holding a rose and rosary. Jelly is oblivious to her presence.

JELLY:
   THEN ONE NIGHT
   IT GETS TO FEELIN' TOO STILL
   THEN ONE NIGHT
   YOU FEEL A SHARP LITTLE CHILL
   N' THERE'S THIS—

HUNNIE THREE:
   DARKNESS

HUNNIE TWO:
   IN THE AIR
HUNNIE ONE:
   COMIN' CLOSER
   TILL IT'S EVERYWHERE
JELLY:
   COMIN'. TO STEAL MY STORY
   BURY MY NAME, DENY MY GLORY
   COMIN' TO BLOW OUT MY LIGHT
   TONIGHT!
   TONIGHT!

   Chimney Man emerges from the void.

CHIMNEY MAN:
   TONIGHT!

   Music underscore. As Chimney Man speaks, Jelly begins to gasp for air—reliving the sensation of his death.

CHIMNEY MAN: N' in one breath, a man becomes a memory. All he was, what he dreamed, those he loved, lost forever. *Fini.* No more.

   On Chimney Man's signal, Jelly recovers. Lights up on the Jungle Inn and the Crowd celebrating Jelly. And floating in the void, Gran Mimi.

CHIMNEY MAN: But if any man's tale deserves to be told, it's The Roll's.

   The Crowd commiserates.

JELLY: I couldn't have said it better myself. I don't believe I've had the pleasure.
CHIMNEY MAN: Why I'm him what they call, De Chimney Man. I stand at the corner of Cadaver Avenue and Last Gasp Lane n' sweep folks along the way. Jes' think of me as de doe'man. Or *le concierge* to your soul.
JELLY: I like that.
CHIMNEY MAN: I figured you would.
JELLY: *Le concierge* to my soul. So Chim … (*Confidentially*) … does this mean that I'm already … ?

CHIMNEY MAN: Terminally inclined? Afraid so. Which is why there's not a moment to lose. There are so many tales—

JELLY: Left untold.

CHIMNEY MAN: So many truths—

JELLY: Locked inside of lies.

CHIMNEY MAN: But tonight is your night Jelly.

JELLY: My night!

CHIMNEY MAN: To relive n' recreate that which was.

CHIMNEY MAN: N' in a flash, that which you remember, becomes real. N' the Crowd, this club, this audience, this night, the veiled lady who stands so stunningly reposed, are here to serve only you. Ah yes, tonight we gonna jam Jelly!	CROWD (*Whispered*): JAZZ ME JELLY ROLL JAZZ ME JELLY ROLL JAZZ ME JELLY ROLL (*Etc.*)

JELLY: You mean Jam wit' Jelly. CHIMNEY MAN: But of course.

    Music up.

CROWD:
    JAM!

JELLY:
    MOVE OVER, HERE I AM!

CROWD:
    JAM!

CHIMNEY MAN:
    GIT READY! TIME TO JAM!

CROWD:
JAM! JELLY/CHIMNEY MAN:
    THE STORY OF THE ROLL

CHIMNEY MAN:
    HIS HEART

JELLY:
    HIS SONG

CHIMNEY MAN:

HIS SOUL

JELLY/CHIMNEY MAN/HUNNIES/CROWD:
    IT'S JELLY'S …
    JAM!
    JAM!
    JAM!

> As the music blares, the Crowd and the Jungle Inn disappear into the void. Jelly and
> Chimney Man look on as the Hunnies take center stage.

SCENE 2
IN THE BEGINNING

HUNNIE THREE: Introducing …
HUNNIE ONE: The blueprint for perfection …
HUNNIE TWO: Ferdinand Le Menthe Morton!

> Jelly is joined by Young Jelly, early teens. He is as rakishly charming as his older
> self.

YOUNG JELLY: Also known as … Young Jelly.
JELLY: Same classic profile.
YOUNG JELLY: Same regal brow.
JELLY (*Indicating Young Jelly*): It's hard to believe someone who looks this good ….
YOUNG JELLY (*Indicating Jelly*): Could get even better, but …
JELLY/YOUNG JELLY: What can we say.
JELLY: 'Course now "The Roll" wasn't always so in control. For you see I …
YOUNG JELLY: Me …
JELLY: We … are the progeny of one of the oldest—
YOUNG JELLY:—and most genteel Creole families in New Orleans.

> Lights reveal a turn-of-the-century New Orleans parlor, replete with five "ancestors"
> holding frames to simulate portraits of Creole Ancestors. Two young Creole girls,
> Amede and Viola, stand perfectly posed holding white fans.

JELLY: Classically trained by the finest musicians of the day, while those of darker hues lived in shacks n' crooned the blues, I would sit in the parlor, under the watchful gaze of my Creole ancestors …

YOUNG JELLY: And I would play the piano …

JELLY: As my two beautiful sisters, Amede and Viola, would sing … and dance …

As Young Jelly "plays," Amede and Viola dance and the Ancestors sing.

SONG: THE CREOLE WAY

AMEDE/VIOLA:
 LA LA LA LA
 LA LA LA LA
ANCESTORS:
 OUR SKIN IS FAIR
 OUR BLOOD EUROPEAN
 OUR WAVY HAIR
 SOMEWHERE IN BETWEE-EN
 NOT A GRIT OR COLLARD GREEN
 COME WHAT MAY
AMEDE/VIOLA:
 LA LA LA LA LA LA
ANCESTOR ONE:
 DON'T YOU AGREE?
ANCESTOR TWO:
 OF COURSE
ANCESTORS THREE & FIVE:
 MAIS OUI
AMEDE/VIOLA:
 LA LA LA LA
ANCESTORS:
 THAT'S THE CREOLE WAY

ANCESTOR FOUR: AMEDE/VIOLA:
 WHILE OTHERS WILL   LA LA LA LA
 DEBAUCH THEMSELVES
  NIGHTLY

ANCESTOR TWO:

 WE DANCE QUADRILLES   LA LA LA LA
 AND MINGLE POLITELY

ANCESTORS/AMEDE/VIOLA:

 TO A TUNE THAT'S
 BRILLIANTLY LIGHT
 AND GAY!

YOUNG JELLY: ANCESTORS/AMEDE/VIOLA:

 ALL I DO IS PLAY AND   LA LA
  PLAY   LA LA
 PLAY WHAT I PLAYED   LA LA LA LA
  YESTERDAY   LA LA LA
 SAME OLD LA LA LA   LA LA LA LA
 IN THE SAME OLD KEY   LA LA LA LA
 WHAT IF I COULD VARY
  THAT
 CHANGE A RHYTHM,
  ADD A FLAT
 UNTIL IT FEELS MORE
  LIKE ME?

The Ancestors abruptly stop singing.

ANCESTORS/AMEDE/VIOLA: Like you! (*Cornering Young Jelly*)

ANCESTOR ONE:

 You're given notes
 And so you will play them

ANCESTORS THREE & FOUR:

 You're given rules
 And you will obey them

ANCESTORS:

 GOOD BOYS LEARN TO FOLLOW
 FOOLS DECIDE TO STRAY
 WHICH SHALL IT BE?
 WHICH SHALL IT BE?
 ANSWER US BOY!

YOUNG JELLY (*Defeated*):

 THE CREOLE WAY

ANCESTORS/AMEDE/VIOLA:
  THE CREOLE WAY

>   *Lights out on the Ancestors, Amede and Viola. As Jelly crosses to console Young Jelly, the Parlor fades away.*

SONG: THE WHOLE WORLD'S WAITIN' TO SING YOUR SONG

JELLY (*Scatting*):
  WAH-WAH-WAH-WAH
  WAH-WAH-WAH-WAH-WAH-WAH
  THAT AINT YOU
  NOT THE "YOU" YOU GONNA BE
  THE MAN YOU WANNA BE IS ME
  YEAH YEAH YEAH
YOUNG JELLY:
  YEAH, YEAH … NO
JELLY:
  READY OR NOT, BOY
  GONNA BE HOT, BOY
  THE WHOLE WORLD'S WAITIN'
  TO SING YOUR SONG!
  I TELL YA

  YOU WANT A NEW
  A "NEVER-BEFORE" SOUND
  I'LL TAKE YOU TO
  A "SOON-TO-BE-YOUR" SOUND
  THE WHOLE WORLD'S WAITIN'
  TO SING YOUR SONG
YOUNG JELLY: But they just said …
JELLY:
  FORGET WHAT THEY TOLD YOU
  C'MON AHEAD
  AIN'T NUTHIN' TO HOLD YOU
  THE WHOLE WORLD'S WAITIN' TO SING YOUR SONG

YOU'LL BE
MISTER "KEEP-'EM-COMIN'"
KING OF THE GOOD-TIME RAG
FAST LICKS
FANCY SYNCOPATION
JELLY/YOUNG JELLY:
N' ALL KINDS OF REASON TO BRAG!

JELLY:	YOUNG JELLY:
YOU ARE THE ONE	… THE ONE
THE SUN'S GONNA	… GONNA
THE ONE THE WORLD	RISE ON
IS KEEPIN' ITS EYES ON	
THE WHOLE WORLD'S WAITIN'	
TO SING …	

Jelly illustrates a riff of syncopation—i.e., tap or scat—as lights reveal stylized frag-
ments of the French Quarter and the People of the Street. Their patchwork attire,
colorful wares and percussive street cries envelop the stage.

BEIGNET MAN: Fresh hot beignets!
JELLY: There's a whole other world beyond these parlor walls.
RAG MAN: Get your rags, man!
JELLY: A symphony of sound to be orchestrated …
GATOR MAN: Snake oil!
TIN-A-FEEX MAN: Fix yuh tin!
JELLY: Syncopated …
GUMBO LADY: Gumbo filé ya-ya!
JELLY: N' they're all waiting on you.
YARD GIRLS (*The Hunnies*):
WAH-OOH WAH-OOH WAH-OOH
JELLY: Yard girls everywhere.
YARD GIRLS:
DO DADDY DO
DO DADDY DO
DO DADDY DO DA
JELLY'S LAST JAM
JELLY: Spasm band …

 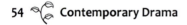

A Spasm Band—black boys in tattered clothes—plays washboards, pots and pans.

JELLY: Here comes the beignet man!

BEIGNET MAN:

FRESH HOT BEIGNETS!
FRESH HOT BEIGNETS!
BEIG-NETS!

JELLY: The lady with the gumbo pan …

GUMBO LADY:

GIT IT WHILE IT'S HOTTA
HOTTA-HOTTA
GIT IT WHILE IT'S HOTTA

JELLY: The Brick-Dust lady …

BRICK-DUST LADY:

ZOZO LA BRIQUE

JELLY: Tin-a-Feex and Gator Man …

TIN-A-FEEX MAN:

TIN TIN TIN-A-FEEX
FIX YUH TIN

GATOR MAN:

I GOT YUH SNAKE OIL

JELLY: Root man, Ragman, Green Sass Man …

RAGMAN:

GIT YOUR RAGS-AH READY
FO' DE OLE RAGMAN

GREEN SASS MAN:

CANTAL-OPE-AH
FROM DE GREEN SASS MAN

ROOT MAN:

ROOTS! ROOTS!
ROOTS FOR LOVIN'
ROOTS FOR LIVIN'
ROOT MAN

The People of the Street abruptly freeze.

JELLY: The whole world's waitin' … *make your song …*

Young Jelly stands motionless, overwhelmed by his task. He then begins to conduct, adding rhythm on top of rhythm.

YARD GIRLS:
DO DADDY DO
DO DADDY DO
DO DADDY DO DA
OH-WAH-OOH
WAH-OH WAH-OH

SPASM BAND: (*Rhythms—four bars*)

BEIGNET MAN:
COME BUY-O BEIGNET MAN

GUMBO LADY:
LADY WITH THE GUMBO PAN …
GET IT WHILE IT'S HOTTA, HOTTA, HOTTA

BRICK-DUST LADY:
ZOZO LA BRIQUE

TIN-A-FEEX MAN:
TIN TIN TIN-A-FEEX
FIX YUH TIN

GATOR MAN:
I GOT YUH SNAKE OIL

GREEN SASS MAN:
CANTAL-OPE-AH

RAGMAN:
GET YUH RAGS AH READY
FOR DE RAGMAN . …

ROOT MAN:
ROOTS! ROOTS!
ROOTS FOR LOVIN'
ROOTS FOR LIVIN' (*Etc.*)

Jelly steps in. He dances/scats a percussive rhythm. Young Jelly repeats it. Jelly creates another rhythm. Young Jelly repeats it. The call and response grows and grows until Jelly and Young Jelly are dancing/scatting as if one.

PEOPLE OF THE STREET:
YOU! YOU! YOU! YOU!

 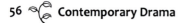

YOU! YOU! YOU! YOU!

YOU'RE THE ONE
THE SUN'S GONNA RISE ON
THE ONE WE'RE KEEPIN' OUR EYES ON
JUST WAITIN' TO SING YOUR SONG
YEAH! YEAH! YEAH!

SLIDE THAT SOUND
ROLL THAT RHYTHM
SYNCOPATE THE STREET-BEAT WITH 'EM
THE WHOLE WORLD, THE WHOLE WORLD
IS WAITING TO SING YOUR …

> *Final tap break.*

PEOPLE OF THE STREET:
    … YOUR SONG.

> *The street fades away as Jelly and Young Jelly applaud/toast one another. The Chimney Man and the Hunnies appear. Lights out on Young Jelly.*

CHIMNEY MAN: Bravo Jelly, bravo. But how did your ancestors feel about you cavorting with *un gens du commun.* They couldn't have been too pleased.

> *The Hunnies hold up a picture frame as Chimney Man "becomes" a Creole Ancestor.*

CHIMNEY MAN:
    FERDINAND!
JELLY (*Amused*): You? One of my ancestors?
CHIMNEY MAN (*Aside*): Some folks like a bit of cream in their coffee. Just think of me as the coffee in your family's cream. (*As Ancestor; recitative*)

HOW MANY TIMES DO WE HAVE TO TELL YOU
WE ARE WHO WE ARE
N' WE ARE NOT WHO WE ARE NOT!
BEATING ON POTS NEVER HAS BEEN

AND NEVER WILL BE MUSIC
MUSIC IS THE FRENCH OPERA HOUSE

Music underscore.

CHIMNEY MAN: Ah yes, the French Opera House, that bastion of culture n' grace, where the lilting melodies of Massenet warmed the hearts of all Creoles. But not the soul of Creole boy. Jelly, you forgot to tell them that when you was just a lad, yo' daddy run off n' yo' mama up n' died.

JELLY: Wait a minute. Wait a—

CHIMNEY MAN (*Overlapping*): N' when you got a case of them lonely boy blues, Massenet is simply not enough.

On the Chimney Man's signal, lights reveal Miss Mamie.

JELLY: … this is my life n' I'm gonna tell it my way.

MAMIE: (*Overlapping*): Oooh child, I'd know that behind of yours a mile away.

JELLY: Mamie!

They embrace.

MAMIE: Little Sweet Butt!

JELLY (*Nuzzling Mamie's cleavage*): Big Mamie.

MAMIE: Git yo' head outta there, boy!

JELLY (*To audience*): Everybody, I'd like y'all to meet the melodic, the magnificent, the mellifluous Miss Mamie—known 'round N'awlins as the Blues Queen of Rampart Street n' Perdito.

MAMIE (*Asking the audience*): Y'all ever hear of me? (*Pause for audience response …*) I said, d'yall ever hear of me? (*Once the audience responds ….*) Folks'll lie as soon as lookin' at you. (*Laughs*) Darlin', don't feel bad. My story lasted 'bout as long as my song. (*To Jelly*) Not like some folks who done gone off n' got famous. Aww but in my day, from the tip of my titties to the bottom of my shoes …

I DRANK, DRUNK, FEEL, FUNK, FELT ME SOME BLUES

N' these ain't no pretend titties, so you know my shit wuz strong. N' there wuzn't but one man who could do the blues the way the blues ought to be done!

JELLY (*Modestly*): Well now, Mamie, I've never considered the blues my forte, however …

 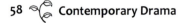

MAMIE: Sweet Butt, ain't nobody tawkin' 'bout you. Now when it comes to strokin', you the one. But when it comes to smokin' you know there was none other than—
JELLY/MAMIE: Buddy Bolden!

Lights reveal Buddy Bolden playing his cornet.

MAMIE: The man hit notes only colored folks n' heaven could hear.
JELLY: I remember the first time I went sneakin' off n' met King Buddy.

Lights reveal Young Jelly cautiously walking down a series of alleyways and streets depicted by doorframes.

JELLY: I musta been 'bout thirteen at the time. It was just past near dark, n' I was out walkin' where good Creoles didn't go, when I heard this

SOULFULLY, WOEFULLY, LOWDOWN SOUND ...

Buddy plays a riff.

HUNNIE TWO:
FOLLOW THAT UPTOWN-RAGTIME-TAG-ALONG

Young Jelly walks down an alley full of Crib Girls— uptown prostitutes.

HUNNIE THREE:
FOLLOW THAT UPTOWN-RAGTIME-TAG-ALONG

Young Jelly walks down a street where a couple is grinding, and gets caught in the middle of Two Men fighting. Buddy Bolden plays.

HUNNIE ONE:
FOLLOW THAT UPTOWN-RAGTIME-TAG-ALONG
HUNNIES:
BARRELHOUSE BLUES.

Young Jelly comes to a doorway. As he walks through it, lights reveal ...

SCENE 3
GOIN' UPTOWN

Buddy Bolden takes command of the club stage. He is joined by a Piano Player and Miss Mamie. The Jungle Inn Crowd becomes Buddy's Uptown Crowd as they gather in a circle on chairs around Buddy and Miss Mamie.

SONG: MICHIGAN WATER

MISS MAMIE:
 MICHIGAN WATER
 TASTE LIKE SHERRY WINE
 MEAN SHERRY WINE
 MICHIGAN WATER
 TASTE LIKE SHERRY WINE
 MISSISSIPPI WATER
 TASTE LIKE TURPENTINE

BUDDY:
 RAMPART STREET GAL
 SHE GOT A BLACK CAT BONE

MISS MAMIE:
 A BLACK CAT BONE

BUDDY:
 OH RAMPART STREET GAL
 SHE GOT A BLACK CAT BONE

MISS MAMIE:
 A BLACK CAT BONE

BUDDY:
 THE HO' DID HER HOODOO
 N' NOW I CAN'T LEAVE HER ALONE

 Music underscore.

BUDDY: *(To audience):* How many y'all ever loved yo'selves a brownskin gal?

 The Crowd responds.

BUDDY: Oooowee, wuzn't it sweet.

The Crowd responds.

BUDDY: Ya git to understand why God made the earth like he did. All rich n' dark. Jes' makes ya wanna plow all night long.

I loved me a brownskin gal. N' thought she loved me till one day she got up, put on her Sumday-go-to-meetin'-dress, n' some waves in her head, n' went downtown. Said she wanted to git herself a high-tone man.

I said, "Now babee, did ya git hit in the head doin' Miss Ann's laundry or what? They don't want you downtown, 'cauz jes' like yo' ass, yo' face is brown. What you be wantin' after some Creole priss, wit' his nose all up in the air. He may know the right way to hold a fork. But a good fork ain't nuthin' compared to a good …

Buddy makes his cornet "growl." The Crowd responds.

BUDDY: All them Creoles is good for is …

Buddy sees Young Jelly standing around, "feeling" the music.

BUDDY: Well now, what have's we here? Say Frenchy, yo' Mama know you hangin' out with us darktown folk?

The Crowd taunts Young Jelly.

YOUNG JELLY: My name's not Frenchy! It's Ferdinand Le Menthe Morton!
BUDDY: Sure as shit sounds like Frenchy to me. Ya look like ya got music in ya. Whatcha play?
YOUNG JELLY: Everything.
BUDDY: Do tell?
YOUNG JELLY: Piano, guitar, mandolin …
BUDDY: We fresh outta mandolins, how 'bout "throwin' a roll"?
YOUNG JELLY: Huh?
BUDDY: The piano!

The Piano Player steps aside and lets Young Jelly take his place.

BUDDY: Ya know "Lonesome Bed Blues"?

Young Jelly shakes his head "no."

BUDDY: "Conti Street Blues"?

Young Jelly shakes his head "no."

BUDDY: "Creole-Boy-Don't-Know-Shit Blues?"
YOUNG JELLY: I know "The Miserere" from *Il Trovatore.*
BUDDY: That ain't no music; the notes is written out, tellin' ya what's gon' come next. That's like wakin' up in the mornin' n' knowin' you gonna be alive at the end of the day. That may be the way you Creoles live, but it is not the way we do things uptown!

The Crowd commiserates.

BUDDY: Frenchy, meet Too-Tight Nora n' Three-Finger Jake.

Nora and Jake, two rough types, join Buddy.

BUDDY: Jake, show 'em that walk you do called "Shootin' the Agaite."

Jake "walks." Buddy, Young Jelly and the Uptown Crowd cheer him on.

BUDDY: Nora baby, strut that strut that gits the sun so hot, it's got to go home for the night n' cool off.

Nora "struts." Buddy, Young Jelly and the Crowd go wild.

MISS MAMIE:
NOW WHEN YOU PLAYIN'
WHAT THEY WALKIN'
THAT'S MUSIC!
(*Spoken*; *to Young Jelly*) Go on Sweet Butt, n' play that piana!

Buddy and Young Jelly play; the Crowd dances.

MISS MAMIE:
I'M GONNA WEAR OSTRICH PLUMES N' SATIN
A HORSEHAIR WIG THREE FEET HIGH
SO ALL YOU GUMBO-EATIN' BITCHES

CAN KISS MY ASS GOODBYE
MISSISSIPPI WATER AIN'T NO FRIEND OF MINE
MICHIGAN WATER TASTE LIKE SHERRY WINE
WE SAY
MISSISSIPPI WATER TASTE LIKE TURPENTINE

The number ends.

MAMIE: Ferdinand took to sneakin' off n' hangin' with Buddy n' that uptown, lowdown
    Crowd.
JELLY: Tradin' swaggers n' swills n' thrillin' the Crowd …
YOUNG JELLY: … with my high-brow know-how!
JELLY: N' it was 'round about now that I invented jazz.

On the Chimney Man's signal, Jelly and the Crowd freeze.

CHIMNEY MAN:
    And it came to pass that a messenger was called
    Who came to believe that the message was him …

*On a second signal, Chimney Man "unfreezes" Jelly and the Crowd and the action
continues. As Young Jelly plays the piano, the Uptown Crowd, Buddy, Mamie, Jelly,
and the Hunnies as Storyville Whores celebrate and embrace Young Jelly and his
music.*

SONG: SHORT PIANO ROLL

UPTOWN CROWD:
    SWEET AS JELLY ON A ROLL
    SWEET JELLY ON A ROLL
    GO ON JELLY N' PLAY THAT ROLL
    THAT'S WHY THEY CALL HIM MISTER
    THAT'S WHY THEY CALL HIM MISTER
    THAT'S WHY THEY CALL HIM MISTER
    JELLY ROLL
    ROLL …
    ROLL …
    ROLL …

During the above, the uptown world begins to fade into the void. Jelly and Young Jelly find themselves enveloped in the shadow of a Veiled Woman standing in front of a New Orleans door.

CHIMNEY MAN: *Je me presente … Madame Mimi Pachet …*

The Veiled Woman lifts her veil. It's Gran Mimi, matronly, elegant, severe.

GRAN MIMI: *Vint citi*! I said come here.

Young Jelly runs to her.

CHIMNEY MAN: Wrought iron draped in lace n' brocade.
GRAN MIMI: How many times do I have to tell you, we are who we are and we are not who we are not.
YOUNG JELLY: But I was only—
GRAN MIMI: Silence!
CHIMNEY MAN: What Jelly left out of his revisionist reverie, is *la vérité* … (*Aside*) … that's French for "the boy be tellin' lies." For you see, after his mama was no more, he n' his sisters were raised by Gran Mimi. *N'est pas*, Jelly?
JELLY (*Nonchalant*): This never happened.
CHIMNEY MAN: N' once she found out 'bout you jammin' wit' them niggas n' messin' wit' them whores—
GRAN MIMI: You are not fit to be Creole. You are no grandchild of mine.
YOUNG JELLY: If you'd only let me—
GRAN MIMI: I said silence!
JELLY (*With growing intensity*): This never happened.
CHIMNEY MAN (*Overlapping*): Shall I tell 'em what came next or shall you—
JELLY (*Emphatic*): I said this never happened!
CHIMNEY MAN: I'd be delighted! Ole Mimi got so beside herself, she jes' hauled off n' … *Gran Mimi slaps Young Jelly. Music underscore.*
CHIMNEY MAN: In case y'all didn't git that, she just hauled off n'—

Gran Mimi slaps again. This time Jelly responds as if he's been hit. Young Jelly falls and cowers on the ground.

SONG: THE BANISHMENT

GRAN MIMI:

GET AWAY, BOY
WANT YOU AWAY FROM MY DOOR
GET AWAY, BOY
WANT YOU AWAY FROM MY DOOR

I KNOW YOU BEEN STAYING OUT
EVERY NIGHT
KNOW YOU BEEN SNEAKING HOME
'FORE IT'S LIGHT

COME BACK HERE SMELLING OF ALL
THAT'S LOW
OF THINGS I DON'T WANT TO KNOW
OOOOOHHHHHHH

IF YOU SPIT IN THE WATER
THERE'S NO GOING BACK TO THE WELL

You shame the name of *la famille* …

SPIT IN THE WATER
OH, THERE'S NO GOING BACK TO THE WELL

You shame the memory of your mother …

YOU LAY DOWN WITH DIRT
YOU GONNA CARRY THAT SMELL

(*Scats*)

OOOH
WOH
OH
WOH-WOH-WOH-WOH
OOOOH
OH-WOH-WOH-QH-WOH

TU N'EST PAS CREOLE
YOU ARE NOT CREOLE!
YOU BEEN LAYING WITH DIRT
YOU ARE NOT CREOLE!
THAT'S WHY I'M TELLING YOU
YOU HAVE NO FAMILY—NOW GO!

YOUNG JELLY:
PLEASE!

GRAN MIMI:
GO!

YOUNG JELLY:
PLEASE!

GRAN MIMI:
VA!
VA!
VA!

Jelly crosses in to console his younger self.

JELLY:
LONELY BOY, HE
HURTIN' SO BAD INSIDE
LOST WHATEVER KIND OF
LOVIN' HE'S KNOWN
LONELY BOY,
HURTIN' SO BAD INSIDE
FROM NOW ON
GONNA FEEL SO ALONE
ALONE
ALONE

GRAN MIMI:
GET AWAY FROM MY DOOR

Gran Mimi and her door fade. Young Jelly fades into the void. The number ends. The Chimney Man crosses to Jelly.

JELLY: You shouldn't have done that.

CHIMNEY MAN: I know, I know. It's your life, and you want to tell it your way. But in telling the story of Jelly, the story of jazz, ya gotta have grit to go with the gravy—ya gotta have pain, to go with the song.

JELLY: Listen Shine, why don't you just go stand over in the dark somewhere, n' leave the light on me.

CHIMNEY MAN: N' because you said so I'm supposed to go? Because your Creole ass commanded, I'm supposed to obey? I hate to disappoint you Jelly, but I'm up n' in yo' shit'n' I'm gonna stay there till I break you.

JELLY: Aww he'p me he'p me Shine 'cause I do's be scared.

CHIMNEY MAN: You have no idea—

JELLY: No, you're the one who has no idea. All my life I been fightin' to git what should have been given n' I'll be damned if I'm gonna let you or anybody else tell me a damn thing about my life or the way I lived it. I know what I deserve n' I'm gonna—

CHIMNEY MAN: What you deserve? What you deserve is for me to sweep your arrogant ass straight to hell.

JELLY: Well, why don't you "Kiss my arrogant Creole ass."

Music underscore.

CHIMNEY MAN: I take that back. Hell's too good for you. Ever hear of East St. Louis? Piss me off again n' you gonna be giggin' in ole West Hell. Even the devil doesn't go there after dark.

JELLY: Out my way, Shine, I'm gittin' mine tonight.

CHIMNEY MAN: To relive your past with none of the pain is a lie. N' for every tale you lace with a lie, I'm gonna be there.

JELLY: N' so will I, Shine. Go on n' try, Shine.

CHIMNEY MAN: I'm gonna drag you through it.

JELLY: Alright Shine, let's do it!

Just as Jelly turns, Chimney Man "vanishes" and Jelly finds standing before him Jack the Bear—dark-skinned, and with an easy-going Southern charm. Music underscore continues.

SCENE 4
THE JOURNEY TO CHICAGO

JELLY (*Overjoyed*): Jack!
JACK: Jelly … my partner!
JELLY: My man!
JACK: My "I cover your back."
JELLY: N' you cover mine.
JELLY/JACK: Brothers to the end!

They laugh and embrace.

JELLY: Everybody, meet my ace-boon-coon. Jack the Bear!
JACK: How y'all doin?
JELLY: Jack n' I first met ridin' the rails to anywhere's other than where we was from. Jack, tell 'em where ya got ya name.
JACK (*Embarrassed*): Jelly man, they don't wanna hear 'bout how—
JELLY: He stole it. Ha! Took it from this Mississippi gangster n' claimed it as his own.
JACK: Hell, his ass wuz dead. Lotta good it was gonna do him. 'Sides, I like the way it fit me. "Jack … the Bear."
JELLY: Tell 'em what your real name is.
JACK: Awww man …
JELLY: His mama named him Clovis. Ha! (*Laughs*) Clovis n' Ferd. Two of the sorriest lookin' fools you'd ever wanna see. Me with my high wata' pants n' oversized suit.
JACK: My hat too big n' these hand-me-down shoes. Good thing we never walked 'cross no mirror. Otherwise I'd ah gone runnin' back to 'Bama n' you to New Orleans.
JELLY: Jack my man, ya don't understand. The world's gonna be our home. Lotsa money's gon' be our home. Too many women …

Music out.

JELLY: … that'll be my home. But I'll let you come visit.

Hunnies bring on "hick" jackets and hats for Jack and Jelly. A cattle car appears. During the whole "Somethin' More" sequence, the cattle car transforms into various locales; i.e., a Pool Hall, a Dance Hall, etc.

SONG: SOMETHIN' MORE

JACK:
> GOT NO LUNCH

JELLY:
> WE GOT NO DINNER

JACK:
> POCKETS THIN

JELLY:
> N' GITTIN' THINNER

JACK:
> GOT NO BED
> 'CEPT THE FLOOR

JELLY:
> NO, THAT AIN'T IT
> THERE'S SOMETHIN' MORE
>
> HENRY FORD,
> HE'S GITTIN' RICHER
> WHY NOT US?
> YA GET THE "PITCHER?"

JACK:
> WELL, WHAT THE HELL
> WE WAITIN' FOR

JELLY/JACK:
> SO LET US GIT US SOMETHIN' MORE!

JELLY:
> LOTSA SUITS——THE HANDMADE KIND
> WEAR SIX A DAY IF I'VE A MIND

JACK:
> SHOES THAT FIT—LIVIN' FAT
> N' A BIG WIDE COMFORTABLE BED

JELLY:
> BRAND NEW TOWNS
> NEW WAY OF TALKIN'

JACK:
> RIDE THE RAILS
> INSTEAD OF WALKIN'

JELLY/JACK:
FORGET THE OLD US
OUT-IN-THE-COLD US
FORGET WHAT WE AIN'T HAD BEFORE
TIME TO HUSTLE US
SOMETHIN' MORE!
SOMETHIN' MORE!
SOMETHIN' …

Jelly and Jack find themselves inside a Pool Hall. The lights are dim and the Men dangerous. The Hunnies appear as Low Girls. A Bouncer hands Jelly a pool cue, bets are placed and the game begins.

The Pool Game

An oily Pool Player takes his first shot.

HUNNIES (*Chanting seductively*):
Nine ball—*unnh!*
In the pocket!

The Player takes another shot.

HUNNIES:
Ten ball—*unnh!*
In the pocket!

The Player takes another shot.

HUNNIES:
You—*unnh!*
Missed the pocket! Next!

Jelly takes his first shot.

JELLY: I'm gonna hit that one. N' that one's gonna hit that one. N' they both gonna go in. I hope.
HUNNIES:

Seven, five—*unnh! Unnh!* In the pocket!

Jelly takes his next shot.

HUNNIES:
Four, three—*unnh! unnh!*
In the pocket!

As Jelly prepares to take his next shot …

HUNNIES:
Eight ball
Take it home now …
Take it home now …
Take it home now …

They all watch the ball slowly roll in.

HUNNIES:
Unnh!

As Jelly goes to retrieve his winnings, lights out on the Hunnies. The Pool Player covers the money with his foot. Jelly feigns surrender. He and Jack turn to go. The Pool Player and his Men begin to laugh. Their laughter is cut short when Jelly turns back and hits the Player with his cue. On the hit, lights out on pool scene and up on Chimney and the Hunnies. Percussive underscore.

CHIMNEY MAN:
SINCE GRANDMA KICKED HIM OUT THE DO'
HUNNIES:
HE WANTS SOMETHIN' MO'
HE WANTS SOMETHIN' MO'
CHIMNEY MAN:
DON'T PLAY HIS MUSIC LIKE HE DID BEFO'
HUNNIES:
HE WANTS SOMETHIN' MO' HE WANTS SOMETHIN' MO'
CHIMNEY MAN:
GOT AN EMPTY SPACE

INSIDE OF HIM
N' HE'S OUT TO FILL IT
TO THE BRIM
WITH A HANDOUT

HUNNIE THREE:
A HUSTLE

HUNNIE ONE:
A FIVE-DOLLAR HO'

HUNNIE TWO:
FROM A CINCINNATI CATHOUSE

HUNNIE THREE:
TO A DIVE IN MONROE

CHIMNEY MAN:
CREOLE BOY WANTS

CHIMNEY MAN/HUNNIES/CROWD:
MO' MO' MO' MO'
MO' MO' MO' MO'

A Bordello

Lights reveal Jack caught up in a card game and Jelly surrounded by Women.

HUNNIES:
IN A SPORTIN' HOUSE DOWN NATCHEZ WAY
JACK N' JELLY STOP TO PLAY

JELLY:
JACK PULLS OFF A POKER PLOY

CROWD (*At card table; amazed*):
OOOOH!

JACK:
WHILE JELLY'S INSIDE SPREADIN' JOY

WOMEN (*Orgasmically*):
AAAAAH!

Jelly and Jack dance/strut to the next locale.

A Chain Gang

HUNNIES:
    IN MOBILE
    WE DO MEAN 'BAMA
    ALMOST SWUNG A CHAIN-GANG HAMMA
CHAIN-GANG MEN:
    UNNH!
    UNNH!
JACK:
    JUDGE SAID FO' YEARS"
JELLY:
    WE SAID "NO YEARS—-
    SO LONG 'BAMA—"
JACK:
    "GOTTA SCRAM-A!"

    Jelly and Jack "escape."

HUNNIES/CROWD:
    OOH YEAH! OOH YEAH!
    BA-DA-BA-DA-BA-DA-BA-DA-BA-DA
HUNNIES:
    LEFT KENTUCKY
    FEELIN' LUCKY
    TURNIN' NASHVILLE
    INTO CASH-VILLE
    SITTIN' PRETTY IN
    YAZOO CITY
    PUT SOME JUICE IN
    TUSCALOOS—

    Jelly and Jack reappear in dapper attire.

JELLY/JACK:
    EVERY DAY
    ALONG THE WAY
JELLY:
    GITTIN' SMARTER
JACK:

GITTIN' QUICKER

JELLY:

SMOOTHER

JACK:

BETTER

JELLY/JACK:

SHARPER
SLICKER

GOOD TIMES KNOCKIN'
AT OUR DOOR—

As Jelly and Jack traverse the countryside, men strut past them announcing the shifting locales—"Entering Memphis"; "70 Miles to Biloxi"; "Cincinnati Population 451,160"; "Brownsville, Southernmost Town in USA".

HUNNIES:

SOMETHIN' MORE
SOMETHIN' MORE
SOMETHIN' MORE
 SOMETHIN' MORE
SOMETHIN' MORE
SOMETHIN' MORE
SOMETHIN' MORE
SOMETHIN' MORE

The Hunnies envelop Jelly and sing seductively.

HUNNIES:

CHICAGO—THAT'S WHERE THE MONEY'S FLYIN'
CHICAGO—THAT'S WHERE THE MUSIC'S SWINGIN'
CHICAGO
CHICAGO
CHICAGO
YEAH!

JELLY (*To Jack*): Jack pack yo' bags n' a new attitude. We headin' for Chi-ca-go!

JACK: Jelly my man, I'm all for somethin' more, as long as it ain't too much. Now, a cousin of mine, he went to this Chicago place, n' was never heard from again.

 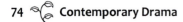

JELLY: That's 'cause it's hard to write home when ya got a woman in your left hand n' a wad of money in your right. Jes' look at us. We too pretty to touch, n' too smart to lose. Chicago is our kinda town. I hear they got buildings as high as the Tower of Babel; trains that fly like Ezekiel's wheel; n' women … like Bath-sheba …

JACK: Good God!

JELLY: Who love to be touched … in all the wrong places.

Music underscore out.

JACK: Jelly?

JELLY: Yeah Jack?

JACK: What say we go git us—

Music up.

JELLY:
SOMETHIN' MORE—

JACK:
WE TALKIN' WOMEN

JELLY:
SOMETHIN' MORE—

JACK:
STARK NAKED WOMEN

JELLY:
SOMETHIN' MORE—

JACK:
YES LORD, BATHSHEBA

JELLY:
SOMETHIN' …

JACK:
WAITIN' …

JELLY:
SOMETHIN' …

JACK:
WANTIN' …

JELLY/JACK:
MORE

The Dance Hall

> *Jelly and Jack turn to find themselves in a run-down Dance Hall. A mediocre Piano Flayer is pounding out a tune as Couples half-heartedly dance.*

JACK: This dive ain't Chicago! Where's Bathsheba?

JELLY: Before we hit big time, I gotta make sure I've still got the touch.

JACK: But this ain't no pool hall, it's a dance hall.

JELLY: These hands can do more than jes' curl their way 'round a cue. (*Loud-talking*) Jack my man, I thought you told me this was a hot juke joint. Sheeet! Nuthin' but cheap liquor, beat chicks n' bad music.

> *The Piano Player stops playing, couples stop dancing. Jelly continues to loud-talk, oblivious to the shift in attitude.*

JELLY (*Laughing*): We tawkin' three strikes n' yo' ass is out.

WAITRESS (*Threatening; to Jack*): Whut he say?

JACK: Ha-ha-ha. He was just mumblin' 'bout what a warm establishment y'all got here. So y'all jes' go on back to playin' n' dancin'. Go on.

> *No sooner has the Piano Player resumed playing …*

JELLY: You call that playin'? That fool couldn't hit a piana wit' a BRICK.

> *The Piano Player slams down the piano lid and is about to go charging after Jelly when a large man—Sam—sitting at a table, signals him to stop.*

SAM: Fo' a yella runt, you sho' be tawkin' a ton-ah-shit.

JELLY: Yeah well, I calls 'em as I see's 'em n' slays 'em as I go. Folks call me Sweet Papa Jelly Roll, finest piana man ever lived.

SAM (*Rising from table and crossing to Jelly*): Folks call me Foot-in-yo'-Ass Sam. If you don't live up to yo' name title, I guess I'm gon' have to live up to mine.

> *Jelly crosses to the piano.*

JACK: Ah, Jelly … you do know how to play?

SONG: THAT'S HOW YOU JAZZ

JELLY: (*Begins to play*):
I'LL SHOW YA HOW TO PLAY
LIKE FOLKS DOWN N'AWLINS WAY
SHOW YOU THE STYLISH FINGERS THEY HAS

Jelly plays a dazzling piano riff. The Crowd is instantly impressed.

OOOH WHAT A NOISE THEY MAKE
STOMP TILL THE WINDOWS SHAKE

START MIXIN'
C'MON N' GITCHA LICKS IN
OOH-OOH-OOH
THAT'S HOW YA JAZZ

In order to get goin', what I like to call "Sweet Papa Jelly's Jazz," ya got to start off with a lowdown foundation … (*He plays a phrase on the piano*)
MEN (*Imitating tubas*):
BOM BOM
BOM BOM
BOM BOM
BOM BOM
BOM BOM
BOM BOM
BOM-BUH-DOM-DOM
JELLY: Then ya add some sweet-ass syncopation …

The Men, as tubas, continue their licks as the women add in …

WOMEN (*As banjos*):
PLUNK-A-PLUNK
A-PLUNK-A-PLUNK-A-PLUNK
PLUNK-A-PLUNK
A-PLUNK-A-PLUNK-A-PLUNK
PLUNK-A-PLUNK
A-PLUNK-A-PLUNK-A-PLUNK
BIDDELEY-DIDDELEY-DUM

BIDDELEY-DIDDELEY-DUM

JELLY: Next, I need some bluesy "Variations."

He plays a blues lick. Vocal tuba and banjo licks continue as the "horns" add in.

MEN/WOMEN (*As horns*):
    WAH-AAH
    WAH-AAH
    WAH-AAH
    WAH-AAH

The three figures—tubas, banjos and horns—continue under Jelly's text.

JELLY: N' you can leave the melody to me.

Jelly begins to sing, with the Dance Hall Crowd as his vocal orchestra.

JELLY:
    TAKE BUDDY BOLDEN'S BLUES
    SOME CREOLE CURLICUES
    ADD SOME STREET-RAG RAZZMATAZZ
CROWD (*Banjos only*):
    BIDDELEY-DIDDELEY-DA
    BIDDELEY-DIDDELEY-DA
JELLY:
    THAT TUNE STRUT-STRUTS ALONG
    JUST LIKE IT OWNS THE SONG
    THEN YA HIT IT WITH A—
CROWD:
    DO-WEE-DEE-LAH-DO
    WHOOP-DE-DAH-DAH
JELLY:
    THAT'S HOW YOU JAZZ
    N' NOW THE TUNE IS GOIN'
WOMEN:
    OOOH DADDY SING TO ME
JELLY:
    GIMME SOME "UNNH"

 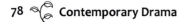

OR IT—

CROWD:

DON'T MEAN A THING TO ME

JELLY:

WATER DON'T COME WETTA
PIANA MEN DON'T COME BETTA

CROWD:

UNH UNH UNH
C'MON LET'S JAZZ!

The Crowd clears the floor and looks on in amazement as Jelly uses tap or scat to illustrate jazz.

CROWD:

THAT'S HOW YOU JAZZ!

Jelly tap/scat break.

CROWD:

THAT'S JAZZ!

Jelly tap/scat break.

CROWD:

THAT'S HOW YOU JAZZ!

Jelly tap break/scat.

CROWD:

THAT'S JAZZ!

Jelly encourages the Dance Hall Crowd to join in. And they do—cautiously at first, until the music and rhythms free them. An exuberant dance of syncopation and scat ensues. Five members of the Crowd form a vocal quintet at the piano.

QUINTET/ CROWD/:

JAZZ!
JAZZ!

JAZZ!
OOOOH!
JAZZ!
JAZZ!
JAZZ!

QUINTET:
OOOOH!
JAZZ!
JAZZ!
JAZZ!

Tap/scat break—Jelly with the Crowd.

QUINTET:
OOOOH!

Tap/scat break—Jelly with the Crowd.

QUINTET:
OOOOOH!
WAH WAH-WAH
WAH-WAH
WAH-WAH

QUINTET/CROWD:
N' NOW THE TUNE IS GOIN'
THE WAH-WAH IS SHOWIN'
WATER DON'T COME WETTA
PIANA MEN DON'T COME BETTA
OOH OOH OOH
THAT'S HOW YA JAZZ

N' NOW THE TUNE IS GOIN'
THE WAH-WAH'S SHOWIN'

OOOOOH …
OOOOOH …
OOOOOH …
OOOOH-OOOOH

N' NOW THE TUNE IS GOIN'
OOH DADDY SING TO ME
GIMME SOME "UNNH"
OR IT DON'T MEAN A THING TO ME
WATER DON'T COME WETTA
PIANA MEN DON'T COME BETTA
OOH OOH OOH
THAT'S HOW YOU JAZZ
OOH OOH OOH
THAT'S HOW YOU JAZZ
OOH OOH OOH
THAT'S HOW …
YOU …
JAZZ …
JAZZ …
JAZZ …
That's how you jazz!

Reprise.

CROWD:
OH-OH-OH
THAT'S HOW YOU JAZZ!
OH-OH-OH
THAT'S HOW YOU JAZZ!
OH-OH-OH
THAT'S HOW . …
YOU. …

The exuberant energy transforms into an invocatory jazz-prayer.

CROWD:
JAZZ
JAZZ

Lights out on Jelly and the Dance Hall. As Jack does the following scat/speech, the Crowd maintains the above invocation.

JACK: A brownskin gal in ah Sunday dress
   WAS INSIDE OF JELLY'S SONG.
   Sittin' down to a meal by yo' mama after bein' gone too long from home
   WAS INSIDE OF JELLY'S SONG.
   Standin' on some open road, not knowin' where you goin', but knowin' it's gotta be
   better than the pain you leavin' behind
   WAS INSIDE OF JELLY'S SONG.
   A "Feel good, head high, strut low" kinda song!
   A "HIGH LIFE OR NO LIFE, YA STILL GOTTA LIVE
       YO' LIFE" KINDA SONG.
   N' everywhere we went, folks claimed us as their own.
   N' Jelly's music was like Moses, partin' the water n' pavin' the way for … Chi-ca-
   go!

SCENE 5
CHICAGO!

   Drumroll.

VOICE-OVER: The Rooftop Garden, Chicago's sepia supper club, proudly presents Jelly
   Roll Morton n' his Red Hot Peppers!

SONG: THE CHICAGO STOMP (Instrumental)

   *Flashing lights. Blaring music. Jelly and the Red Hot Peppers, his orchestra, are
   revealed, jamming away. A Chicago Crowd dances exuberantly.*

   Lights out on Jelly and the Crowd, and up on the Chimney Man.

CHIMNEY MAN:
   RECORD DEAL WITH RCA
   TURN OUT SIX HIT TUNES A DAY
   DON'T LET NOBODY GET IN YOUR WAY
   DOIN' THE CHICAGO STOMP

   *Lights reveal Jelly, a Shoeshine Boy at his feet and the Chicago Crowd clamoring all
   around him. Off to one side, Jack.*

JELLY: Them boys in the recordin' session didn't know what hit 'em when I let 'em know I was the instigator, the procreator n' the high-tone imaginator of J-A-Double-Z.

Once I laid down how I'd come up with tonal variations, the shifts in syncopation, yet letting the melodic structure fly, they was too through. Know what I told 'em! "Play it the way I wrote it, or get out!"

As the Chicago Crowd laughs and applauds, lights out on Jelly and the Crowd and up on the Chimney Man.

CHIMNEY MAN:
PUT SOME NEW SUITS ON YOUR BACK
BUY A BIG NEW CADILLAC
TELL THE WORLD YOUR ASS AIN'T BLACK
DO THE CHICAGO STOMP

Lights reveal Jelly talking to a Reporter/Photographer and standing in front of his "Cadillac"—the Hunnies as the car's headlights and grille. Jack is in the background "buffing up the car."

JELLY: N'awlins born n' bred. But ya see what most folks don't understand is that my ancestors came directly from the shores of France. No coon stock in this Creole.

Jelly laughs and poses. As the camera goes "flash," lights out on Jelly, the Reporter, etc., and up on Chimney Man.

CHIMNEY MAN:
SLICK AS SOAP AND HARD AS STEEL
FIND NEW WAYS TO WHEEL AND DEAL
CAN'T GET HURT IF YOU DON'T FEEL
DO THE CHICAGO STOMP

Lights reveal Jelly sipping champagne as Jack, acting as Jelly's valet, cleans off his suit.

JELLY: Jack, I had to let them gangster boys know straight out that the way they nickel n' dime all the shine musicians in town was not gonna work with "The Roll." I told 'em fifteen hundred a night. N' guess what I got?

JELLY/JACK: Fifteen hundred a night!

The Chicago Crowd envelops Jelly. The dancing builds to a big finish. Jelly and his music have conquered Chicago.

CROWD (*Chanting*): Go Jelly go! Go Jelly go! (*Etc.*)

On the Chimney Man's signal, lights out on the Chicago Crowd as lights reveal Anita, young, beautiful, standing by a piano. Jelly is irresistibly drawn to her.

CHIMNEY MAN: Music flyin' n' money flowin'—life couldn't be better for "The Roll." Ah, but a one-night gig in a nearby town turns Jelly into jam. She's calling to you Jelly—waiting to replay the day you two first met.

SCENE 6
JELLY N' ANITA

Lights up on Anita's Club—small and intimate, with a piano, beaded curtains, etc. Anita abruptly turns to face Jelly, who now has Jack at his side.

ANITA: Piano man, you're late.
JELLY: Generally when folks first meet, they say "Hello."
ANITA: Greeting took place forty-five minutes ago. If you'd wanted to partake, ya should have been here.
JELLY: Jack?
JACK: In Chicago, things don't start till we arrive.
ANITA: Word's come my way you're all the rage there. But sugah, this ain't Chicago. It's Cal City, Illinois. N' here we do things on time. If you think you can live with that, we'll begin. Otherwise you can leave n' I'll look elsewhere.
JELLY: You're openin' a new club?

She nods. He sits at the piano.

JELLY: Well, if you're lookin' for the best, there is no elsewhere.
ANITA: You know "Play the Music for Me?"
JELLY: I probably wrote it. (*Laughing and very pleased with himself*) Jack, did you hear what I say? "I probably wrote it." Jelly, Jelly, Jelly!

Jack indicates to Jelly that Anita is waiting for him to play. Jelly begins to play.

 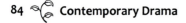

SONG: PLAY THE MUSIC FOR ME

ANITA:

OOH SAY IT
YEAH PLAY IT
PLAY ME A MIDNIGHT KEY
PLAY A SMOKY ROOM
PLAY A HE AND A SHE
OH—WOOWOOWEE
OOH SUGAH
PLAY THE MUSIC FOR ME

OH SING IT
YEAH SWING IT
SWEET POSSIBILITY
PLAY A SOFT CARESS
PLAY A "MAYBE, LET'S SEE"
NO GUARANTEE
OOH SUGAH
PLAY THE MUSIC FOR ME

MUSIC IN THE STRUTTIN'
OF A FINE LOOKIN' MAN
MUSIC IN THE STROKIN'
OF A SWEET-TALKIN' HAN'
MUSIC IN THE LYIN'
MUSIC IN THE LAUGHIN'
IN LOVIN' YOUR WOMAN LIKE NOBODY CAN
IT'S IN THE MUSIC
WHERE THE LOVIN' SHOULD BE
THE MUSIC'S IN THE LIVIN'
PLAY THE MUSIC FOR ME

Jelly plays a piano solo playfully and seductively. Anita starts to scat.

ANITA:

SHA-BA-DE-BA-BE-BA …

JELLY: Not yet.

He plays a bit more. She starts to scat.

ANITA:
SHA-BA-DE-BA …

JELLY: Not yet! (*He plays some more*) Jump in there anytime, Baby!

ANITA:
WHEN YOU'RE TALKIN'
YOU'RE TALKIN' THE MUSIC
WHEN YOU'RE WALKIN'
YOU'RE WALKIN' THE MUSIC
SUGAH, THAT'S THE WAY IT'S
GOTTA BE
THE MUSIC'S IN THE LIVIN'
PLAY ME THE MUSIC
THE MUSIC'S IN THE LIVIN'
PLAY THE MUSIC FOR ME

Jelly and Anita applaud one another, as does Jack.

ANITA: So piano man, you got a name?

JELLY (*Turning on the charm*): You want to know my name? Jack, tell her who I am.

JACK: This is *the* Jelly Roll Morton. Lover of women, inventor of jazz and owner of twenty-seven suits.

JELLY: N' you are … ?

ANITA: Not interested. (*Anita turns to go*)

JELLY: Ha! As many looks as you been throwin'.

ANITA: Just 'cause I throw a look, n' you catch it, don't mean it had your name on it. (*To Jack*) But you, Sugah, you ain't tell Sweet Anita your name.

Anita pours it on thick, flirting with Jack, enjoying how much it's annoying Jelly.

JACK (*Rising to the occasion*): Folks call me Jack the Bear. ANITA: Is that B-E-A-R or B-A-R-E?

JACK: Both.

He and Anita laugh.

JELLY (*Pulling Anita aside*): Wait—whoa. Anita come on now. Jack's like a brother to me, but … there's no comparison. (*Confidentially*) For one thing he's so …

ANITA: So what Jelly? So black? Sugah, if I'd wanted a white man, I'd get me the real thing, n' not some pale imitation thereof. 'Cause like the sayin' goes, "The blacker the berry, the sweeter the juice."

JELLY: You know Anita, when I first saw you, I said to myself, "Jelly, before you stands a real lady." I now see I was wrong. (*He turns to go*) Jack?

Jack reluctantly follows after him.

ANITA (*Calling after Jelly*): Oh is that what you lookin' for? "A lady!" Someone who smiles n' pours tea n' agrees with her man, no matter what. He says it's sunny, n' even though it's pourin', she stands there smiling, pretending to not be wet. If that's what you're lookin' for, sugah I can tell you now, ain't nobody home.

JELLY: If you think "The Roll" is gonna stand here while you—

ANITA (*Overlapping*): Now, if you lookin' for a woman … (*Seductively*) Full-hipped n' sweet-lipped, who says what she feels n' feels it to the bone, then maybe, just maybe somebody might be home.

Provided the man inquiring loved the way he played instead of the way he talked. If that's the case, I'd advise you to knock soon, 'cause Sweet Anita has no intention of waitin' around till you do.

Just as Anita is about to exit through the beaded-curtain …

JELLY: Knock, knock.

Jelly and Anita embrace. Music underscore. As they kiss, they strip down to their undergarments. Lights out on Anita's club and up on the Hunnies pushing a large curtained brass bed. Jelly and Anita fall into it.

SONG: LOVIN' IS A LOWDOWN BLUES

HUNNIES:
THEY SAY THAT LOVIN' IS A LOWDOWN BLUES
YOU AIN'T GOT NUTHIN' BUT YOUR LIFE TO LOSE
WHEN YOU CAN'T STOP YOURSELF FROM LOVIN'
LOVIN' IS A LOWDOWN BLUES

The Hunnies open the curtains to reveal Jelly and Anita having a post-coital conversation.

JELLY: Sweeeet-Anita. Sweet-Sweet-Anita. Never met a woman quite like you. (*Beat*) Well ... ain't you gonna say you never met a man quite like me?

Anita says nothing.

JELLY: Anita, come on now, it's common knowledge, can't nobody roll like "The Roll."

ANITA: Sugah, haven't you heard ... men who talk about how good they are, generally aren't.

Jelly starts to seduce her.

ANITA: Generally they aren't ... but occasionally ... they are.

The Hunnies close the curtains on Jelly and Anita.

HUNNIE TWO:
　　SHE THINKS HE'S
　　UNNH SO ...
HUNNIE ONE:
　　YEAH SO ...
HUNNIE THREE:
　　YOU KNOW ...
HUNNIES:
　　LIGHT MY FUSE
HUNNIE TWO:
　　HE THINKS SHE'S
　　YEAH SO ...
HUNNIE ONE:
　　UNNH SO ...
HUNNIE THREE:
　　JUST WHAT
HUNNIES:
　　HE CAN USE
　　UH-HUH

 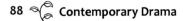

LOVIN' IS A FUCK-YOU BLUES

The Hunnies open the curtains.

JELLY: Anita, I don't have time to be owning no club. "The Roll" has big plans. We talkin' European tours. Maybe even a pit stop in that hick burg New York. Everywhere I go, they gonna love themselves some "Roll."

ANITA: Talkin' big is one thing. Thinkin' big is what counts.

JELLY: Oh so now I don't know how to think.

ANITA: If you would just listen to what I'm—

JELLY *(Overlapping)*: No, you're the one who needs to listen, 'cause see "The Roll" has gotten quite far in this world. "The Roll" has been able to—

ANITA *(Cutting him off)*: Aww Jelly to hell with "The Roll." This bed ain't big enough for you n' all your titles. There's only room for Jelly n' Anita.

JELLY: You know woman you talk a whole lotta trash.

ANITA: Yeah well man, so do you.

JELLY *(Grabbing her)*: I ought to …

ANITA: You ought to what … ?

The Hunnies close the curtains.

HUNNIE THREE:
   THEY'RE SO EXCITABLE
HUNNIES:
   UH-HUH
HUNNIE THREE:
   THEY'RE SO DELIGHTABLE
HUNNIES:
   UH-HUH
   IT LOOKS LIKE NUTHIN' BUT GOOD TIMES
   NUTHIN' BUT GOOD NEWS
   LOVIN' IS A SWEET-ASS BLUES

The Hunnies open the curtains.

JELLY: "*Va! Va!*" She told me to go, Anita. Said I was dirt. "You are not Creole." I sat on those steps, waiting for her to forgive me, let me in. She never did. "*Va. Va.*"

Anita kisses him long and hard.

ANITA: Don't none of that matter now, 'cause I'm your home.

After a beat …

JELLY: Anita? ANITA: Hmm?
JELLY: What you think of the name, "Jelly N' Anita's Midnight Inn?"
HUNNIE ONE:
    OOOOH
    WOH-WOH-WOH-WOH
    OOOOH
    WOH-WOH-WOH-WOH
ANITA (*During the above*): Oooh Jelly, the place I've found, you are going to love.
JELLY: Wait a minute. You've already picked out the club.
ANITA: I see a baby grand piano, crystal chandeliers. My man deserves nuthin' but the best.

As the Hunnies sing, Jelly and Anita "make love."

HUNNIE TWO:
    BUT WHEN IT DIES …
    THE WAY IT DOES …
    AIN'T NO SURPRISE …
HUNNIES:
    LOVIN' IS A SLY-DOG BLUES

Jelly and Anita's lovemaking transforms into a fight.

ANITA (*Swinging at Jelly*): You no-count-two-bit-two-timin'-son-of-a-bitch!
JELLY (*Overlapping*): Anita … Anita, wait—whoa … Anita calm down n' listen. 'Cause see I've written hundreds of songs, each special in their own way.
ANITA: What's that got to do with us?
JELLY: Every once in a while, a song comes along n' it's from this whole other place way deep down inside. That's the kinda song you are.
ANITA: Oh I see. N' so regardless of how many other songs or bitches pass through "The Roll's" hands, that's alright. 'Cause I'm still your "one special song."
JELLY: Exactly. (*He moves in to kiss her*)

 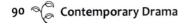

ANITA: Jelly you're good. You're real good. But like my mama used to say, "Jes' 'cause a man smiles while servin' shit don't mean it don't smell."

JELLY: You and yo' mama missed the point. (*Begins to get dressed*)

ANITA: Oh no sugah, your point was real clear. Just so long as you understand that that door swings both ways.

JELLY: What's that supposed to mean?

ANITA: You've been expanding your musical repertoire, well so have I.

JELLY: Shame on you, Anita. Sayin' you was with some man, just to get back at me.

ANITA: What makes you think it was a lie?

JELLY: Anita, a man knows things 'bout his woman that she don't know about herself. Like it or not woman, I got your game.

ANITA: Like it or not man, I got yours.

JELLY: Nobody's got "The Roll's" game. No sir, not "The Roll." But as far as bitches go, you come pretty close. Gotta go.

He stands to go, oblivious to the impact this last statement has had on her.

HUNNIES:
THEY SAY THAT LOVIN' IS A LOWDOWN BLUES
YOU AIN'T GOT NUTHIN' BUT YOUR LIFE TO LOSE
WHEN YOU CAN'T STOP YOURSELF FROM LOVIN'

ANITA: Jelly?

JELLY: Hmm?

ANITA: You gonna be seein' Jack?

JELLY: Yeah, we hangin' …

ANITA: Well, will you give him my best.

Anita kisses Jelly long and hard. On the last line of the song, Anita and Jelly stare at each.

HUNNIES:
LOVIN' IS A SLY-DOG
SWEET-ASS,
FUCK-YOU
LOWDOWN DIRTY BLUES

Lights isolate Jelly, dearly affected by the scene. Chimney Man enters holding a large gift box and crosses to Jelly.

CHIMNEY MAN: Remember how you felt Jelly? I mean the very idea that Anita would choose someone like Jack over someone like you. The very idea!

Remember how you waited till the opening of your club? (*He presents Jelly with the box*) Remember?

> *Jelly takes box and exits.*

SCENE 7
JELLY AND ANITA'S MIDNIGHT INN

> *Jelly and Anita's Midnight Inn, a stylish nightclub. Jack, in dapper attire, is surveying the place when Anita enters, also in elegant attire.*

JACK: (*Ad lib singing from "Somethin' More"*)

ANITA (*Upon seeing Jack*): Well I do declare, let me take a gander at Mr. Jack the Bear.

JACK: Pretty, huh? Oh n' check out the shoes … (*Confidentially*) Straight from the bovine's butt to my feet, with no hand-me-down stops along the way.

> *Jelly appears at entrance of the club holding the box given to him by the Chimney Man. He silently watches the following exchange.*

JACK: Aww but now, ain't you one to put the peacock to shame.

ANITA: Lookin' so good, I gots to be illegal. One touch a get ya five to ten.

JACK: Then I guess I'm gonna be servin' life.

> *Jack and Anita laugh and hug. Jelly enters the club.*

JACK (*Seeing Jelly*): Jelly my man, you git a load of that crowd? (*He laughs*)

ANITA: You're late. (*She starts to leave*)

JACK (*Catching her and bringing them all together*): Come on, Sweet Anita, lay off. Jes' for tonight, everybody loves everybody.

JELLY: I couldn't agree more.

> *He presents Jack with the box.*

JACK: Awww Jelly man, no!

JELLY: Go on, open it!

Jack takes from the box a bright red doorman's coat.

JACK: I don't understand …

JELLY: Well ya see back in N'awlins, Countess Willie Piazza used to have this colored midget that worked as her doorman. N' this white fella one time told me, he said "Jelly, I can't explain it, but havin' a li'l nigga in a red coat opening that door, makes me feel like I belong."

Jack starts a slow laugh which grows. Jelly returns the laughter.

JACK: Jelly, man you crazy man.

ANITA: Jelly, please.

JACK: She thinks you're serious. Jelly n' me always pullin' shit like this on each other. My ace-boon-coon.

JELLY: I'll be the ace n' you be the coon.

Jelly and Jack laugh.

ANITA: Jelly just stop it!

JELLY (*Overlapping; ignoring Anita*): After all, we want folks to feel like they belong? Well we got the li'l nigga—n' a sweet one to boot. "Blacker the berry …", so forth n' so on. N' we got the red coat. So what seems to be the problem?

JACK: Jelly man, why you doin' this?

JELLY: We share everything. What's yours is mine n' mine, yours. N' seein' as I'm the one who's got everything—the name, the money, the talent, the women … or should I say woman——you ain't got shit! So be a good nigga n' put on the coat.

The tension is broken as Jack throws the coat on the ground and then exits. Jelly crosses to the piano and begins to pick out a tune.

ANITA: Well now, I bet "The Roll" is feelin' real good. I bet he's flyin' high. Who was it Jelly? Was it some ho'? Or maybe it was yo' Grandma kickin' your ass out.

JELLY: You watch your mouth!

ANITA: Who hurt you so hard n' cut you so deep that the second you feel any kinda pain, you don't think, you don't feel, you just lash out.

Makin' you think there was somethin' goin' on between Jack n' me was wrong. But it was nuthin' compared to what you just did, to Jack, to me, to us. (*Pulling Jelly away from the piano*) Are you listening to me?

JELLY: You better go see 'bout your boy. He looked kinda upset.

ANITA: Don't do this. Don't treat me like I don't matter.

She stops, waits for Jelly to say something. He doesn't. She then turns to go.

JELLY: Anita wait …

Anita stops. He picks up the red coat.

JELLY: Jack forgot his coat.

Music cue. She exits. Lights isolate Jelly.

SONG: DR. JAZZ

JELLY (*With an edge*):
 LISTEN PEOPLE HERE COMES DOCTOR JAZZ
 HE'S GOT GLORY ALL AROUND HIM, YES HE HAS
 WHEN THE WORLD GOES WRONG
 N' YOU GOT THE BLUES
 HE'S THE MAN WHAT MAKES YOU GET OUT
 BOTH YOUR DANCIN' SHOES

On Jelly's signal, lights reveal the Crowd as a Chorus of Coons, in white lips and red doormen's jackets and caps.

CHORUS OF COONS (*Spoken*):
 Front n' center the inventor of jazz!
 Got the magic—
JELLY: Yes he has!
CHORUS OF COONS (*Sung*):
 AIN'T NO MEDICINE KNOWN TO MAN
JELLY/CHORUS OF COONS:
 CAN MAKE YOU FEEL GOOD LIKE THE DOCTOR CAN
CHORUS OF COONS: Only name that you need to know—
JELLY:
 WORLD'S GREATEST ONE-MAN SHOW
CHORUS OF COONS:

EVEN THE DEVIL, WHOEVER HE WAS
COULDN'T PLAY JAZZ THE WAY JELLY DOES
HELLO CENTRAL, GIVE ME GIVE ME DOCTOR JAZZ

JELLY:

HELLO CENTRAL, GIVE ME DOCTOR JAZZ
GOT GLORY ALL AROUND HIM, YES HE HAS
C'MON ON YOUR FEET N' SWING WITH THE ROLL
FEEL HIS RHYTHM RIPPIN' THROUGH YA
RIGHT DOWN TO YOUR SOUL
SO SPREAD THE WORD WHEREVER YOU MAY GO
YOU'VE SEEN THE LIGHT TONIGHT N' NOW YOU KNOW
BLAZE HIS NAME ACROSS THE SKY
FLAMING LETTERS TEN FEET HIGH
"J.R. MORTON, MISTER DOCTOR JAZZ"

As Jelly dances, his rage releases itself as a manic "showstopper"—driving himself and the Chorus of Coons in a dance break that is as exuberant as it is emotionally raw.

JELLY:

HELLO WORLD
You can call me Jelly
WHO DO YOU LOVE?

CHORUS OF COONS: Jelly!

JELLY: Louder!

CHORUS OF COONS:

EVERYBODY LOVES THEIR DOCTOR JAZZ!

Lights reveal Chimney Man.

CHORUS OF COONS:

DOCTOR JAZZ

On Chimney Man's signal, Jelly sees a face in the void—Anita.

CHORUS OF COONS:

DOCTOR JAZZ

On Chimney Man's signal, Jelly sees a second face in the void—Jack.

CHORUS OF COONS:
DOCTOR—

On Chimney Man's signal, Jelly sees—Gran Mimi, ordering him to go.

CHORUS OF COONS:
IT'S DOCTOR JAZZ!

Blackout.

ACT TWO

SCENE I
THE CHIMNEY MAN TAKES CHARGE

Lights reveal Jelly and the Chimney Man posed as they were at the end of Act One.

CHIMNEY MAN (*Laughs*): You know Jelly, you're having quite the night. "No coon stock in this Creole." "Be a good nigga n' put on the coat." N' my all-time favorite: "I invented jazz."

JELLY: Before there was Jelly, there was a bunch of shines moanin' the blues n' a ton of hacks bangin' on keys.
(*Mimes piano playing*)
Tonka-tonka-tonka-tonka-tonk!
Ooooh baby-baby—I's got the blues.
    I'm the one who took the shit n' made it soar—maintain the melody, throw in a break, add a riff, shift the syncopation, shift the syncopation. Jelly's jazz, Jelly's jazz.
    Ask any of them fools who came before me n' they haven't got a clue. Ask any of the ones who came after n' they'll tell you it all started with me.

CHIMNEY MAN: It all started with you, huh? Nothing but savages beatin' with sticks. N' then lo n' behold, there came forth "The Roll."

JELLY: Listen Shine, let me tell you one damn thing—

CHIMNEY MAN (*Overlapping*): No let me tell you!

On Chimney's signal, Jelly freezes.

CHIMNEY MAN: We're goin' on a journey Jelly, you n' me. To the deepest, darkest part of the night. It's a sweet little song we're gonna sing. N' once the music starts there's no turning back. First stop, New York City! Spotlight!

On Chimney Man's signal, lights out on Jelly. Music underscore.

CHIMNEY MAN: Now it's true that in Chicago they loved themselves some Roll. But when he left there and went to New York, it was Filet of Soul, a la "The Roll."

SCENE 2
THE NEW YORK SUITE

A glorious fanfare. Blazing lights. New York City. Lights reveal the Hunnies and Chimney Man done over stylish and slickin'.

SONG: GOOD OLE NEW YORK

HUNNIES:
> GOOD OLE NEW YORK
> OUR KIND OF TOWN

CHIMNEY MAN:
> BIG TIME BUCKS AND BROADWAY PALACES

HUNNIES:
> HOCK YOUR SOUL AND HIT THE HEIGHTS

CHIMNEY MAN:
> FRONT PAGE PICTURES IN THE PAPERS AND—

HUNNIES:
> PRESTO! THERE'S YOUR NAME IN LIGHTS

An overly zealous Jelly appears with Variety newspaper in hand.

JELLY:
> NEW YORK LOOK OUT!
> I own you starting now
> I'LL MAKE YOU SHOUT
> Stand back 'cause I know how!

CHIMNEY MAN/HUNNIES:

STEP RIGHT UP YOUR DREAM IS WAITING
IT'S TIME TO POP THE CORK
WELCOME TO GOOD OLE NEW YORK

As Jelly "rides" the A train.

CHIMNEY MAN/HUNNIES:
UPTOWN
HUNNIE ONE:
YOU WANNA GO WHERE
THEY KNOW HOW TO SYNCOPATE
CHIMNEY MAN/HUNNIES:
UPTOWN
HUNNIE TWO:
HOME OF THE "YEAH"
DO WE HAVE TO ELUCIDATE?
HUNNIE THREE:
THE PLACE WHERE THE PACE
IS STRICTLY JAZZ

Lights reveal the interior of a Harlem Club and the Harlem Folk, elegantly attired.

CHIMNEY MAN/HUNNIES/HARLEM FOLK:
HARLEM!

The Harlem Folk break into exuberant dancing.

CHIMNEY MAN/HUNNIES/HARLEM FOLK:
DO-WAH DO-WAH DO-WAH DO-WAY
WAH WAH-WAH WAH-WAY

SONG: TOO LATE, DADDY

JELLY:
I'LL SHOW YOU HOW TO PLAY
LIKE FOLKS DOWN N'AWLINS WAY
SHOW YOU THE STYLISH MUSIC THEY HAS

OOH WHAT A NOISE THEY MAKE
STOMP TILL THE WINDOWS SHAKE
FOLKS MIXIN'
C'MON N' GIT YOUR LICKS IN
OOH-OOH

> *Tap/scat break.*

JELLY:
OOH-OOH

> *Tap/scat break.*

JELLY:
THAT'S HOW …
YOU …

> *Jelly's rhythm is replaced by a swinging rhythm which all the Harlem Folk begin to dance to.*

HARLEM FOLK:
… JAZZ!

YOU'RE TOO LATE DADDY
WE'RE SWINGIN' A WHOLE NEW SONG
IT'S GOT US JUMPIN'
N' SWINGIN' THE WHOLE NIGHT LONG

WOMEN:
IT'S A REET SWEET BEAT
THAT'S COIN' 'ROUND

MEN:
THE JIM-JAM JIVE
THE SLAM-JAM SOUND

HARLEM FOLK:
YOU'RE TOO LATE DADDY
WE'RE SWINGIN' TO A WHOLE NEW SOUND

JELLY: Maybe you didn't hear me. The name is Jelly Roll Morton … the inventor of jazz.

HARLEM FOLK:
WHO NEEDS JELLY WHEN WE GOT LOUIS?

CROWD MEMBER TWO: (*Solo scat a la Louis Armstrong*)

JELLY: Louis Armstrong! That coon. That baboon.

HARLEM FOLK:
WHO NEEDS JELLY WHEN WE GOT THE DUKE?

CROWD MEMBER SIX: (*Solo scat a la Duke Ellington*)

JELLY: Duke Ellington ain't good enough to—

HARLEM FOLK:
BUT WE GOT BASIE!

CROWD MEMBER NINE: (*Solo scat a la Count Basie*)

HARLEM FOLK:
WE'RE SWINGIN' … TO A WHOLE NEW SOUND!

The Harlem Folk break into a raucous dance, driving Jelly off to the side.

HARLEM FOLK:
IT'S TOO LATE DADDY
WE'RE SWINGIN' SWINGIN' SWINGIN'
TO A WHOLE NEW SONG

JELLY: I'll be back, n' when I do you'll be throwin' me a parade!

CROWD MEMBER THREE: Honey, you better go downtown where they don't know what real music is!

The Hunnies and Chimney Man reappear. They sing as Jelly struts "Downtown."

CHIMNEY MAN/HUNNIES:
DOWNTOWN

HUNNIE ONE:
YOU BETTER GO WHERE THE DEALS AND THE DOLLARS ARE

CHIMNEY MAN/HUNNIES:
DOWNTOWN

HUNNIE TWO:
MEET WITH THE CATS WITH THE
HATS AND THE FAT CIGARS

HUNNIE THREE:
WHERE THE NAME OF THE GAME
IS "WHO'S ON TOP"

Lights reveal four Tin Pan Alley office doors.

HUNNIES:
TIN PAN ALLEY!

Jelly sings and plays the piano as if auditioning.

JELLY:
I'M THE MAN YOU ALL BEEN WAITIN' FOR
I'M THE BEST THERE IS, THERE AIN'T NO MORE
WHEN IT COMES TO JAZZ, "THE ROLL" IS IT
WAIT … LOOK! THIS TUNE'S A HIT!

(*Demonstrating piano licks*)

COUPLE OF FRILLS
COUPLE OF FILLS
GIVE 'EM A GLISS
NOW LISTEN TO THIS
WOW!
POW!

From behind one of the doors pop the Melrose Brothers—Frank and Al—fast-talking, fast-dancing, ex-vaudevillians turned music publishers, holding a contract and pen.

MELROSE BROTHERS: yeah-yeah-yeah-yeah-yeah-yeah-yeah-yeah …

SONG: THAT'S THE WAY WE DO THINGS IN NEW YAWK

FRANK:
JELLY BABY
SO YOU'RE SAYIN' YOU WANNA GO FAR?
AL: Then sign on the dotted line …
FRANK:
AIN'T NO MAYBE, BABY
WE'RE GONNA MAKE YOU A STAR!
AL: So sign on the dotted line …
FRANK:

DEPEND ON FRANK N' AL …

AL: The leading publishers …

FRANK:

THE MELROSE BROTHERS, PAL

AL: Of colored music.

JELLY:

ALRIGHT FELLAS
WHAT MONEY WE TALKIN'?

FRANK:

THE MINOR POINTS WE WON'T DISCUSS

AL:

WE DO FOR YOU, YOU DO FOR US

JELLY:

WON'T TALK MONEY? C'MON DO I LOOK LIKE A FOOL?

MELROSE BROTHERS:

YA KNOW WE'RE GONNA DO RIGHT BY YOU!

JELLY:

I DONE BETTER
PITCHIN' PENNIES AND HUSTLIN' POOL!

MELROSE BROTHERS:

C'MON, WE'RE GONNA DO RIGHT BY YOU!
THEY'RE BOUND TO SCREW YOU DOWN THE PIKE
WHY NOT BE SCREWED BY FOLKS YOU LIKE?

AL:

YOU JUST GIVE US A TUNE WE CAN DANCE TO

FRANK:

YOU GET TO SEE YOUR NAME IN LIGHTS

AL:

WE GET TO KEEP THE COPYRIGHTS

MELROSE BROTHERS:

SIGN!

JELLY:

NO!

MELROSE BROTHERS:

SIGN!

JELLY:

NO!

MELROSE BROTHERS:

OR TAKE A WALK
'CAUSE THAT'S THE WAY WE DO THINGS

JELLY:
WELL THAT'S NOT THE WAY THAT "THE ROLL" DOES THINGS

MELROSE BROTHERS:
THAT'S THE WAY WE DO THINGS IN NEW YORK

The Melrose Brothers exit through two separate doors.

HUNNIES: You think they're bad, Jelly, you ain't seen nuthin' yet.

Two Gangsters enter, Nick and Gus. Lights out on the Chimney Man and the Hunnies.

NICK:
GO ON PLAY
PLAY A TUNE, MR. PIANO MAN
THE NAME'S NICK

GUS:
N' GUS

NICK:
YOU PLAY, YOU PLAY FOR US

GUS:
WE TELL YOU
WHAT N' WHO
YOU'LL BE PLAYING FOR
WE'RE SO TO SPEAK YOUR "PATRONS OF DE ARTS"

NICK:
LIKE WE SAID
PLAY A TUNE, MR. PIANO MAN

GUS:
PLAY ANY CLUB OR HALL

NICK:
GUESS WHAT, WE OWN 'EM ALL

GANGSTERS:
YOU WANNA MAKE IT BIG HERE
SIDDOWN, WE'LL TALK

They offer Jelly a chair. He doesn't move.

GANGSTERS:
SIDDOWN, WE'LL TALK

Jelly doesn't move.

GUS: Jelly, listen, let us give you a piece of advice or you'll be outta here yesterday. You step on someone's feet, n' nigga you don't eat.

JELLY (*Exploding*): Now you listen n' listen good! I'm not some wooly-headed coon dancin' n' catchin' coins on a corner. When you're prepared to deal with me as a Creole, we'll talk.

NICK: What's he tawkin' 'bout?

GUS: Creole, shmeole! There's kikes, niggers n' wops. I leave anybody out? NICK: Nope.

GANGSTERS: That's the way we do things in New York.

JELLY: I don't need any of them. After all …
I'M THE ONE YOU SPORTS CAN'T WAIT TO SEE

Lights reveal the Gangsters, the Harlem Folk and the Hunnies, who become the doors of the city.

PEOPLE OF NEW YORK:
DOOR SLAM! DOOR SLAM!

JELLY:
IF YOU TALKIN' JAZZ YOU TALKIN' ME

PEOPLE OF NEW YORK:
DOOR SLAM! DOOR SLAM!

JELLY:
GONNA TURN THIS CITY—

PEOPLE OF NEW YORK:
SLAM! SLAM! SLAM!

The Chimney Man struts on a la Cab Calloway.

CHIMNEY MAN:
EVERYWHERE HE TURNS

HUNNIES:

EVERYWHERE HE TURNS

CHIMNEY MAN:
EVERYTHING HE TRIES

HUNNIES:
EVERYTHING HE TRIES

HUNNIES/PEOPLE OF NEW YORK:
DOOR SLAM! DOOR SLAM!
DOOR SLAM! DOOR SLAM!

CHIMNEY MAN:
FROM THE RITZIEST CLUBS
TO THE RAUNCHIEST DIVES

HUNNIES/PEOPLE OF NEW YORK:
DOOR SLAM! DOOR SLAM!
DOOR SLAM! DOOR SLAM!
DOOR SLAM!
ALONE … ALONE …

CHIMNEY MAN:
ALONE

The People of New York fade away. In isolated light, Jelly. As the Chimney Man talks, Jelly dances/scats his mounting frustration. The Hunnies maintain a chant.

HUNNIES:
HOW YA DOIN' MR. PIANO MAN … HOW YA DOIN' MR. PIANO MAN
…

CHIMNEY MAN: "Who needs Jelly when we got Louis?" "Come on, we're gonna do right by you." "Too late Daddy, we're swingin' to a whole new sound." "Door slam! Door slam!" "You step on someone's feet, n' nigga you don't eat." "Siddown, we'll talk." "Siddown, we'll talk." "Siddown, we'll talk."

Music out. Lights reveal a New York Railroad Flat— a piano covered with crumpled sheet music; a radio on top of the piano; etc.

DANCE: JELLY IN ISOLATION

Jelly, alone, overwhelmed by the silence, begins to dance, trying to find his rhythm. Anxiety builds until be explodes and is left standing powerless. All of a sudden, be hears a rhythm. It's Young Jelly. The two engage in a dance of innocence, celebration and triumph. Jelly has regained his confidence. He crosses to his piano and is about to begin writing when the Chimney Man appears and clicks on the radio.

ANNOUNCER (*Voice-over of Chimney Man*): Alright Mrs. Mary Joe Jones of Jones, Indiana, for the all-important bonus round, who invented jazz?

Jelly sits up and begins to listen intently.

ANNOUNCER (*Voice-over*): Was it "A," Paul Whiteman, "B," W. C. Handy or "C," Jelly Roll Morton? You now have five seconds.

JELLY: You got that right! Jelly Roll Morton!

CONTESTANT (*Voice-over*): Oh—ah—ooo—let me see, now. "A," Paul Whiteman.

Buzzer sound.

ANNOUNCER (*Voice-over*): Aw, sorry Mary Joe …

JELLY (*Overlapping*): Sorry, Mary Joe!

ANNOUNCER (*Voice-over*): … it's "B," W. C. Handy. Next week on *Ripley's Believe It or Not*, the bonus jackpot will be worth …

JELLY: No! No!

Jelly switches off the radio and sits at the piano, totally defeated.

CHIMNEY MAN:
THE PAIN IS REAL
RELAX N' DON'T FIGHT IT
TAKE WHAT YOU FEEL
Now go ahead, write it.

Jelly begins to play as if writing a song. Isolated light reveals Anita, now many years older than when last seen.

SONG: THE LAST CHANCE BLUES

ANITA:
ONE DAY THE WORLD IS SITTIN'
IN YOUR SWEET YOUNG HAND
THEN ALL AT ONCE YOU TURN AROUND

N' THERE YOU STAND
A FACE YOU BARELY RECOGNIZE
THE LITTLE LINES AROUND THE EYES
TALKIN' 'BOUT THE LAST CHANCE BLUES

JELLY:

LEGS ARE GETTIN' SLOWER
N' I GOT NOWHERE TO GO
MONEY GETTIN' LOWER
N' PEOPLE SAYIN' NO
BROKEN DREAMS N' WASTED BETS
NOW AND THEN A FEW REGRETS
TALK ABOUT YOUR LAST CHANCE BLUES

ANITA:

AIN'T IT FUN …

JELLY:

AIN'T IT GREAT … DRESSED TO THE NINES

ANITA:

N' TEN YEARS OUT OF DATE

JELLY:

NEW YORK TIMES SAYS
I'M YESTERDAY'S NEWS
I GOT THE LAST CHANCE BLUES

ANITA:

WHAT IF I WHISPERED LOW
"SWEET MAN, I NEED YOU SO"
JUST ONCE KEPT MY FINGER OFF THE FUSE?
BUT NO, I HAD TO FIGHT
PROVE I WAS RIGHT
WELL THAT'S THE THING ABOUT
THE LAST CHANCE BLUES

JELLY:

WHAT IF I NEVER LIED
WHAT IF JUST ONCE I TRIED TO SAY HOW I REALLY FEEL
'STEAD OF PUSHIN' HER AWAY
IF I'D KNOWN
HOW MUCH I HAD TO LOSE
I WOULDN'T BE SINGIN'
THE LAST CHANCE BLUES

JELLY/ANITA: (*Scat verse*)

JELLY:
  IF I

ANITA:
  IF I SAW HIM

JELLY:	ANITA:
SAW HER THERE	STANDING THERE

JELLY:
  LOOKIN' HARDER THAN

JELLY:	ANITA:
HELL	MEAN AS HELL
I DON'T CARE	I WOULDN'T CARE
I'D,	I WOULD TELL HIM "HEY
MAKE HER LISTEN	YOU GOTTA LISTEN TO ME"
HEY BABY	SHOUT SO HE COULD HEAR
I LOVE YOU	SWEET MAN I LOVE YOU

JELLY/ANITA:
  DON'T MAKE ME SING THE
  LAST CHANCE BLUES
  NOW THAT I KNOW WHAT I COULD LOSE …

JELLY:
  I DON'T WANNA SING THE …

JELLY/ANITA:
  LAST CHANCE BLUES

  The lights crossfade to reveal …

SCENE 3
THE LAST CHANCE

  A small-time restaurant—a few tables; a piano. Anita sits, reflective, as Jelly slowly enters the place. Music underscore.

JELLY: Anita?

ANITA(*Incredulous*): Jelly?

She laughs, rushes to him. They embrace one another, like old friends.

ANITA: Just look at you.

JELLY: No, look at you!

They both feel themselves going to "that place" and decide to pull back.

JELLY/ANITA: So …

ANITA: … been a long time.

JELLY: Yep. See ya got yo'self a new place.

ANITA: Nuthin' like "Jelly N' Anita's Midnight Inn," but it feeds me n' a few other folks.

JELLY: Nice piano.

ANITA: N' from time to time I sing me a tune.

Jelly applauds.

ANITA: I don't know why you're applauding. You never encouraged me before.

JELLY: I said a lot of things back then. But so did you. Lord knows I tried to git along with you.

ANITA: You! Sugah, I know I'm goin' to heaven after all the hell you put me through.

They laugh.

JELLY: I always loved the way you said "Sugah." Even when you was evil, it still sounded sweet.

They smile at one an other. Chimney Man enters to observe the scene. After a beat …

JELLY: Anita?

ANITA: Hmm?

JELLY: Is that red beans n' rice I smell?

ANITA (*Laughs*): Umhm. N' on Fridays, it's Gumbo a la Anita.

JELLY: Enough to make a person wanna hang his hat n' stick around for a few.

ANITA: Not to mention a sign out front sayin' "Mr. Jelly Roll Morton Appearin' Here Tonight!"

JELLY (*Playful*): Seein' as I am the inventor of jazz ... so forth n' so on, what kinda pay we tawkin'?

ANITA: All the Gumbo a la Anita you can take.

JELLY: Well now, good gumbo outside of N'awlins is mighty hard to find. But it can be done. N' in my life I've seen a whole lotta signs sayin' "Jelly Roll Morton Appearing Tonight."

But the thing that could make a person really consider hangin' for a few, is the "a la Anita." Ah, could you tell me how's that served?

ANITA: Hot. N' over a bed of rice.

JELLY: He'p me Jesus! Already dreamin' 'bout seconds n' I ain't finished firsts.

ANITA: As "The Roll" used to say, "Nuthin' to it, but to do it."

Music fades out.

JELLY: Ya know, Anita—you're the closest I've ever come to feelin' like I belong.

Just as they are about to hug, Jack enters.

JACK: Look out! I done died n' gone to hell!

Anita and Jelly turn to find Jack standing before them.

JACK: Got's to be hell, 'cause where else but would I run into "The Roll!"

Jack rushes and hugs Jelly, who is instantly on edge.

JACK: Jelly! My man! I don't believe It! Anita did you know 'bout this?

ANITA: I'm as surprised as you.

JACK: Damn it's good to see you. Why jes' the other night me n' Sweet Anita was tawkin' 'bout all the "way backs" that are long gone. I remember thinkin', "Damn what mess Jelly's gone n' got us into now. Things can't git no worse!" I now realize, things was never better. Wish I'd known it at the time. Woulda enjoyed 'em even more!

He looks to Anita who motions him to "get lost."

JACK: Well … let me let you two talk, while I take care of a few things. You are stickin' around? Anita?

ANITA: We're workin' on it.

JACK: Well work away. (*As he exits, sings*)
Ha-ha!
GOT NO LUNCH
AIN'T GOT NO DINNER
POCKETS THIN

ANITA (*Laughing*): Some things never change.

JELLY (*With an edge*): N' they never will.

ANITA: Now about you performing, I can't afford neon. But I figure we rig up a few lights, make a big sign n'—

JELLY (*Exploding*): Goddammit Anita, shut up!

ANITA: Did I miss something?

JELLY: N' don't try n' act like you don't know what's goin' on. What the hell is he doing here?

ANITA: Don't do this Jelly. Don't come back talking the same kinda trash that killed what we had.

JELLY (*Overlapping*): Things happen. From the past. Things you've said n' done that over time, you regret. N' then "Bam," some shit goes n' hits you in the face n' you realize, Jelly, Jelly, Jelly, you were right all along.

ANITA: Oh, so, let me get this right? I've lived my entire life, probably even arranged the Depression, so that after we broke up, I moved to California, bumped into Jack, he needed work. N' for years we've been plugging away, barely gettin' by, just in case someday you might happen to walk through that door n' I could say, "Ooh Jelly, I don't love you. I never did. I love Jack. Sweet Jack! Hot Jack! Black Jack!"

JELLY: Once a ho', always a ho'.

Anita slaps Jelly.

ANITA: After all this time, is that all I am to you?

Jelly is silent.

ANITA: For once in your life Jelly, admit your pain n' quit treatin' people like they was dirt. Especially the ones you love n' the ones who love you. (*After a beat*) Dear God, you don't know how.

Jelly turns away, helpless.

ANITA: Listen Jelly, times are hard n' in honor of what once was, the offer still stands about you working here. It's decent pay, meals included.

JELLY (*Deeply wounded but determined to not show it*): Thank you very kindly Anita, but that won't be necessary. I'm out here on big business. A new club in Los Angeles, on Central Avenue, wants me to headline. Details of the deal are still being worked out. N' the motion picture people have expressed interest in my life story.

ANITA: I'm glad to hear it.

JELLY: So you see "Sweet Anita," I don't need your charity … n' I don't need you.

ANITA: Oh, Sugah …

Anita crosses to him and attempts to embrace him; he freezes up.

ANITA (*Sensing his resistance*): All my best. (*She exits*)

CHIMNEY MAN: Very good, Jelly. Brilliant. Just when you're about to get things right, you go n' say some stupid shit like you just did. Why, Jelly?

JELLY: I don't know.

CHIMNEY MAN: Why, Jelly?

JELLY: I don't know why. You tell me. Tell me goddamnit!

Jelly breaks down. Jack quickly appears.

JACK: Where's Anita?

JELLY (*Pulling himself together*): She's ah … off doin' …

JACK: Jelly, man what's wrong?

JELLY: Nuthin'.

JACK: Funny huh, us back together after all these years. You n' me n' Sweet Anita. So what can I get you? Me n' Sweet Anita got ourselves a cook, n' Jel-leee, the man can throw down a mean batch of red beans!

Jelly takes a beat and then looks Jack dead in the eye.

JELLY: Jack, when are you gonna learn the only thing a nigga can do for me is scrub my steps n' shine my shoes.

CHIMNEY MAN: Why, Jelly?

The club fades away.

JACK: Was I a nigga when we was on the road together?

CHIMNEY MAN: Why?

JACK: Was I a nigga when no matter what you said or did I was by your side, sayin' "Go Jelly Man. I'm wit'cha all the way." (*He grabs Jelly*) Call me a nigga again, n' I'm gonna kick your ass.

He exits into the void.

JELLY: Jack please ... please ...

SCENE 4
CENTRAL AVENUE

The rhythms of jitterbug and early bebop fill the air as Jelly finds himself thrown into the garish neon world of Central Avenue. Lights reveal three Zoot Suiters and the Hunnies with nurse's hats and sunglasses—messengers of death.

CROWD:
DO-DO DO-DO
CENTRAL A-VE-NEW
DO-DO DO-DO
CENTRAL A-VE-NEW
DO-DO DO-DO
CENTRAL A-VE-NEW AH-AHHH

Chimney Man, the essence of Forties' hipster, appears. Percussive underscore.

CHIMNEY MAN: Ooooh ease me, grease me Sweet Papa Jelly.

JELLY: This place—

CHIMNEY MAN: Whatsamattah Jelly? Don't like the new sounds goin' 'round on Central Avenue? It's where you wound up after you left Anita.

JELLY: I know what happens here.

CHIMNEY MAN: I realize L.A. is not exactly the best place to die. Hell, they've barely figured out how to treat the living, but we all gotta jam with Sweet Daddy Death.

HUNNIES:
TELL YO' MAMA
AIN'T COMIN' HOME TONIGHT

CHIMNEY MAN: It all starts with an argument—
CROWD (*Men*):
   STAB—STAB

> *Jelly is being taunted by three Zoot Suiters with knives and the Hunnies wearing nurse's caps.*

CHIMNEY MAN: N' ends with you wastin' away in the Colored Wing of Los Angeles County General.
HUNNIES:
   COME ON IN
   WHERE YOU BEEN
JELLY (*Cowering; scared*): Don't you touch me. Don't touch …
HUNNIES:
   COME ON IN
   WHERE YOU

> *Just when Jelly is about to he stabbed, Chimney Man halts the action.*

CHIMNEY MAN: Better yet, let's skip all that n' get to my favorite part, you givin' up the ghost.
JELLY: I can't die. Not now. I've got to tell Jack. … N' Anita … n' …
CHIMNEY MAN:
   NOOOOWWW!!!

> *On the Chimney Man's signal, Jelly releases a silent howl.*

SCENE 5
THE LAST RITES

> *Percussive explosion. Lights reveal the Procession of the Dead, an otherworldly New Orleans/African parade of death coming to claim Jelly's soul.*
> *The Chimney Man, who is carrying a large broom, "sweeps" and the Procession swirls around Jelly. He cowers in fear. When Jelly looks up, the Procession is gone and standing over him is Gran Mimi—tossing rose petals onto Jelly, as if he's in his grave.*

GRAN MIMI:

BOY PRETTY BOY
NEVER GAVE YOU MY LOVE
BOY PRETTY BOY
NEVER GAVE YOU ANY LOVE
WHEN YOU GET NO LOVIN'
YOU GOT NO LOVIN' TO GIVE

The people and voices of Jelly's life fill the stage.

JACK: Was I a nigga when we wuz on the road together?

ANITA: So after all this time that's all I am to you?

CROWD (*A trio*):

FROM HIGH-FALUTIN' TO A HOLE IN THE GROUND

MISS MAMIE: Ooh darlin', my story lasted about as long as my song!

BUDDY: That's like wakin' up in the morning knowin' you gonna be alive at the end of the day. SAM: For a yella runt—

AL: Sign the contract!

HUNNIES: You think they're bad—

HUNNIES ONE & TWO: Ooooooh	ENSEMBLE (*Chants*):
Daddy!	JAM!
CROWD MEMBER THREE: Dance	JAM!
all night to that Chicago Stomp …	JAM!

The vocal cacophony continues to build as the Ensemble burls at Jelly the insults and slurs he's uttered all night.

NORA: No coon stock in this
Creole.

SAM: Be a good nigga n' put on
the coat.

CROWD MEMBER SEVEN: The only
thing "shine" on me is the
diamond in my tooth.

CROWD MEMBER FIVE: I invented
jazz.

JACK: The only thing a nigga can
do for me is scrub my steps and
shine my shoes.

BRICK-DUST LADY/HUNNIE TWO:
Was I a nigga—
Was I a nigga—

ENSEMBLE (*Chants*):
JAM!
JAM!

JAM!
JAM!
JAM!
JAM!

JAM!
JAM!
JAM!
JAM!
JAM!
JAM

As the voices overlap and build to a peak. Jelly lets out a cry.

JELLY:
OHHH NO MORE
I SEE … I SEE

The Crowd fades into the void and Jelly is left alone.

SONG: CREOLE BOY/FINALE

JELLY:
CREOLE BOY GOES OUT ONE DAY
THINKIN' AIN'T HE SOMETHIN'
BRAG LIKE NUTHIN' YOU SEEN
BIG-TIME TALKIN' MACHINE
YEAH WELL LIVIN' IS MEAN
ALL THOSE FANCY SUITS YOU OWN
CREOLE BOY YOU STILL ALONE

CREOLE BOY SAYS "STEP ASIDE!
I GOT SOMETHIN' SPECIAL"
HIGH-TONE TALK ABOUT FAIR

HIGH-CLASS NOSE IN THE AIR
HEY, DON'T NOBODY CARE
CREOLE AIRS OR OTHERWISE
YOU STILL A NIGGER IN THEIR EYES

HE LIKES TO HANG WITH WHATCHA
MIGHT CALL LOW
UP WHERE THE BLUES IS BLOWIN'
MEAN N' SLOW
DOWN N' DARK AIN'T IN HIS JAM
"NO COON STOCK, HEY!
JE SUIS CREOLE
THAT'S WHAT I AM"
THE KING OF SWEET-ASS
SYNCOPATION
AIN'T NO BLACK NOTES IN MY SONG

(*Music fill*)

JELLY:
I WAS WRONG
CREOLE BOY ONCE WAY BACK WHEN
HAD THE WHOLE WORLD SINGIN'
HAD THIS SOUND IN HIM, HEY!
A PAIN TOO HEAVY TO SAY
A PAIN HE STARTED TO PLAY
INSIDE EVERY NOTE OF HIS
IS WHAT HE CAME FROM … WHO HE IS
INSIDE EVERY NOTE OF HIS
IS WHAT HE CAME FROM … WHO HE IS

As Jelly continues to sing, lights reveal Miss Mamie and Buddy.

MISS MAMIE/BUDDY:
WE ARE THE RHYTHMS THAT COLOR YOUR SONG
JELLY:
YOU ARE MY SONG.

Lights reveal Jack, Anita and Gran Mimi.

GRAN MIMI:
THE PAIN THAT MAKES THE MELODY STRONG

JELLY:
YOU ARE MY SONG …

JACK/ANITA/MISS MAMIE/BUDDY/GRAN MIMI:
WE ARE THE FEELING

ENSEMBLE:
WE ARE THE FEELING IN YOUR SONG

The People from His Past envelop him. As they sing, the Yoruba door and the "shaft of darkness" leading to it, from the top of the show, appear. Jelly begins his ascent to the door, leaving the People from His Past behind.

ENSEMBLE:
ALL THE LYIN'
THE NEEDIN'
THE USIN'

JELLY:
THEY ARE MY SONG

ENSEMBLE:
ALL THE CRYIN' THE BLEEDIN' THE BRUISIN'

JELLY:
MY GLORIOUS SONG

Jelly exits through the door.

ENSEMBLE:
ALL THE LOVIN'
THE LEAVIN'
THE LOSIN'
WHO WE ARE
AND WHAT WE USED TO BE
IT'S IN THE MUSIC
PLAY THE MUSIC FOR ME …

There is an instrumental explosion as lights reveal Jelly followed by a New Orleans Funeral Band, complete with "second liners," banners, images from his past—a celebration which builds until Jelly is bathed in glorious light.

ENSEMBLE:
   IT'S IN THE MUSIC

   The Chimney Man appears.

CHIMNEY MAN:
   Go forth Armstrong!
   Go forth Ellington!
   Go forth Basie, Balden, n' Bechet!
   Go forth Morton!
ENSEMBLE:
   PLAY THE MUSIC FOR ME!

   The Funeral Band and "second liners" fade into the void. Jelly is left alone, the faint sound of piano riffs in the background.
   Jelly dances and mimes playing the piano until there is …

   Blackness

Our Country's Good (1988)

By Timberlake Wertenbaker (1951–)

INTRODUCTION

Based on Thomas Keneally's novel *The Playmaker*, *Our Country's Good* depicts the first production of an English-language play on Australian soil—the 1789 staging of George Farquhar's restoration comedy *The Recruiting Officer*. What is interesting about this production is that it was undertaken not by theater professionals, but by the only English inhabitants of Australia at the time: soldiers and convicts. In 1789, Australia was an English penal colony, not a destination of choice for performers; conditions in the colony were harsh, and theater was an unnecessary (and, in the minds of some officials—an unwanted) luxury.

On the other hand—as Timberlake Wertenbaker points out—the English expatriates (for both convicts and soldiers felt exiled from their homeland) already enjoyed a theater of sorts—the barbaric spectacle of public executions. As Harry Brewer says, "The convicts laugh at hangings." Captain Arthur Phillip, the Governor, replies, "I would prefer them to see real plays." This is not an idle, casual remark. Phillip genuinely believes that theater will not only have a civilizing effect on the convicts but also a bonding effect on the entire society: "The convicts will speak a refined, literate language and express sentiments of a delicacy they are not used to. It will remind them that there is more to life than crime and punishment. And we—this colony of a few hundred—will watch it together and for a few hours no longer be the despised prisoners and the hated soldiers." Lieutenant Ralph Clark, a junior officer anxious to be noticed, takes on the task of rehearsing Farquhar's play, and eagerly confirms Phillip's hopes: "By saying those well-balanced lines of Mr. Farquhar, they seemed to acquire a dignity—they seemed to lose some of their corruption."

Our Country's Good, however, is more than a saccharine tale about the redemptive qualities of theater; doubt and resistance plague the production, and the merits of theater (and, particularly, of theater in the context of hardship) are given a substantive debate. Captain Tench warns Phillip, "A bunch of convicts making fools of themselves, mouthing words no doubt written by some London ass, will hardly change our society." Major Robbie Ross, Ralph's superior and his primary antagonist, frets over the content of the play. "This pluming play has muddled the muffy Lieutenant's mind," he charges. "It makes fun of officers, it shows an officer lying and cheating." Arscott and Kable—two actors released from their work assignments so that they could rehearse—escape from the camp while in the process stealing from the food supply. This incident seems to confirm Ross's concerns about the unraveling of discipline. Even Ralph has reservations about the task for which he has volunteered; originally considering staging *Lady Jane Grey*, he wonders aloud, "How could a whore play Lady Jane?" The inability of convicts to identify with their characters is also a concern for Ralph's paramour, Mary Brenham: "How can I play Sylvia? She's brave and strong. She couldn't have done what I've done."

Other convicts have their own personal stakes in the performance: personal redefinition, creative empowerment, or psychological escape. Ketch Freeman, ostracized from the other convicts because he has escaped execution by volunteering to be a hangman, is desperate for approval. "Some players came into our village once," he pleads to Ralph. "They were loved like the angels, Lieutenant, like the angels. ... I want to be an actor." Dabby Bryant—initially tickled at the idea of taking on a new persona ("Wait till I tell my husband I've become a lady," she quips)—soon becomes disgusted with the lack of realism in *The Recruiting Officer*: "I could write scenes, Lieutenant, women with real lives ... I want to play myself." Arscott, however, chastened by his unsuccessful escape and subsequent punishment, wants the opposite:

"I don't want to play myself. When I say Kite's lines I forget everything else. I forget the judge said I'm going to have to spend the rest of my natural life in this place getting beaten and working like a slave. I can forget that out there it's trees and burnt grass, spiders that kill you in four hours and snakes. I don't have to think about what happened to Kable, I don't have to remember the things I've done, when I speak Kite's lines I don't hate anymore. I'm Kite. I'm in Shrewsbury. Can we get on with the scene ... and stop talking?"

Ultimately, Farquhar's characters and dialogue give the characters the ability to reclaim their dignity and even resist authority. In the midst of being humiliated and dehumanized by Ross during a rehearsal, Sideway turns to Mary and uses the play's dialogue as a veiled critique: "What pleasures I may receive abroad are indeed uncertain;

but this I am sure of, I shall meet with less cruelty among the most barbarous nations than I have found at home."

In the end, Wertenbaker's play does not concern itself with results and outcomes. The dialogue and action do not tell us whether the performance of *The Recruiting Officer* was "successful" or not. We do not learn whether Governor Phillip's experiment produced the results he anticipated; we do not learn whether Ralph earns the promotion that he seeks or the punishment that Ross threatens; we do not learn what becomes of the convicts' newfound voices and ambitions. In refusing to answer these questions, the play leaves us with a consideration of the *process* of characterization and performance—and its effects on the individual, regardless of the final result.

CHARACTERS

Captain Arthur Phillip
Major Robbie Ross
Captain David Collins
Captain Watkin Tench
Captain Jemmy Campbell
Reverend Johnson
Lieutenant George Johnston
Lieutenant Will Dawes
Second Lieutenant Ralph Clark
Second Lieutenant William Faddy
Midshipman Harry Brewer
The Aborigine
John Arscott
Black Caesar
Ketch Freeman
Robert Sideway
John Wisehammer
Mary Brenham
Dabby Bryant
Liz Morden
Duckling Smith
Meg Long

Note: The play takes place in Sydney, Australia in 1788–9.

ACT ONE

SCENE ONE. THE VOYAGE OUT

The hold of a convict ship bound for Australia, 1787. The convicts huddle together in the semi-darkness. On deck, the convict **Robert Sideway** *is being flogged.* **Second Lieutenant Ralph Clark** *counts the lashes in a barely audible, slow and monotonous voice.*

Ralph Clark Forty-four, forty-five, forty-six, forty-seven, forty-eight, forty-nine, fifty.

> *Sideway is untied and dumped with the rest of the convicts. He collapses. No one moves. A short silence.*

John Wisehammer At night? The sea cracks against the ship. Fear whispers, screams, falls silent, hushed. Spewed from our country, forgotten, bound to the dark edge of the earth, at night what is there to do but seek English cunt, warm, moist, soft, oh the comfort, the comfort of the lick, the thrust into the nooks, the crannies of the crooks of England. Alone, frightened, nameless in this stinking hole of hell, take me, take me inside you, whoever you are. Take me, my comfort and we'll remember England together.

John Arscott Hunger. Funny. Doesn't start in the stomach, but in the mind. A picture flits in and out of a corner. Something you've eaten long ago. Roast beef with salt and grated horseradish.

Mary Brenham I don't know why I did it. Love, I suppose.

SCENE TWO. A LONE ABORIGINAL AUSTRALIAN DESCRIBES THE ARRIVAL OF THE FIRST CONVICT FLEET IN BOTANY BAY ON JANUARY 20, 1788

The Aborigine A giant canoe drifts on to the sea, clouds billowing from upright oars. This is a dream which has lost its way. Best to leave it alone.

SCENE THREE. PUNISHMENT

Sydney Cove. **Governor Captain Arthur Phillip, Judge Captain David Collins, Captain Watkin Tench, Midshipman Harry Brewer.** *The men are shooting birds.*

Phillip Was it necessary to cross fifteen thousand miles of ocean to erect another Tyburn?

Tench I should think it would make the convicts feel at home.

Collins This land is under English law. The court found them guilty and sentenced them accordingly. There: a bald-eyed corella.

Phillip But hanging?

Collins Only the three who were found guilty of stealing from the colony's stores. And that, over there on the Eucalyptus, is a flock of *Cacatua galerita*—the sulphur-crested cockatoo. You have been made Governor-in-Chief of a paradise of birds, Arthur.

Phillip And I hope not a human hell, Davey. Don't shoot yet, Watkin, let's observe them. Could we not be more humane?

Tench Justice and humaneness have never gone hand in hand. The law is not a sentimental comedy.

Phillip I am not suggesting they go without punishment. It is the spectacle of hanging I object to. The convicts will feel nothing has changed and will go back to their ways.

Tench The convicts never left their old ways, Governor, nor do they intend to.

Phillip Three months is not long enough to decide that. You're speaking too loud, Watkin.

Collins I commend your endeavour to oppose the baneful influence of vice with the harmonizing acts of civilization, Governor, but I suspect your edifice will collapse without the mortar of fear.

Philip Have these men lost all fear of being flogged?

Collins John Arscott has already been sentenced to 150 lashes for assault.

Tench The shoulder-blades are exposed at about 100 lashes and I would say that somewhere between 250 and 500 lashes you are probably condemning a man to death anyway.

Collins With the disadvantage that the death is slow, unobserved and cannot serve as a sharp example.

Phillip Harry?

Harry The convicts laugh at hangings, Sir. They watch them all the time.

Tench It's their favourite form of entertainment, I should say.

Phillip Perhaps because they've never been offered anything else.

Tench Perhaps we should build an opera house for the convicts.

Phillip We learned to love such things because they were offered to us when we were children or young men. Surely no one is born naturally cultured? I'll have the gun now.

Collins We don't even have any books here, apart from the odd play and a few Bibles. And most of the convicts can't read, so let us return to the matter in hand, which is the punishment of the convicts, not their education.

Phillip Who are the condemned men, Harry?

Harry Thomas Barrett, aged seventeen. Transported seven years for stealing one ewe sheep.

Phillip Seventeen!

Tench It does seem to prove that the criminal tendency is innate.

Phillip It proves nothing.

Harry James Freeman, age twenty-five, Irish, transported fourteen years for assault on a sailor at Shadwell Dock.

Collins I'm surprised he wasn't hanged in England.

Harry Handy Baker, marine and the thieves' ringleader.

Collins He pleaded that it was wrong to put the convicts and the marines on the same rations and that he could not work on so little food. He almost swayed us.

Tench I do think that was an unfortunate decision. My men are in a ferment of discontent.

Collins Our Governor-in-Chief would say it is justice, Tench, and so it is. It is also justice to hang these men.

Tench The sooner the better, I believe. There is much excitement in the colony about the hangings. It's their theatre, Governor, you cannot change that.

Phillip I would prefer them to see real plays: fine language, sentiment.

Tench No doubt Garrick would relish the prospect of eight months at sea for the pleasure of entertaining a group of criminals and the odd savage.

Phillip I never liked Garrick, I always preferred Macklin.

Collins I'm a Kemble man myself. We will need a hangman.

Phillip Harry, you will have to organize the hanging and eventually find someone who agrees to fill that hideous office.

Phillip shoots.

Collins Shot.

Tench Shot.

Harry Shot, Sir.

Collins It is my belief the hangings should take place tomorrow. The quick execution of justice for the good of the colony, Governor.

Phillip The good of the colony? Oh, look! We've frightened a kankaroo.

They look.

All Ah!

Harry There is also Dorothy Handland, eighty-two, who stole a biscuit from Robert Sideway.

Phillip Surely we don't have to hang an eighty-two-year-old woman?

Collins That will be unnecessary. She hanged herself this morning.

SCENE FOUR. THE LONELINESS OF MEN

Ralph Clark's tent. It is late at night. Ralph stands, composing and speaking his diary.

Ralph Dreamt, my beloved Alicia, that I was walking with you and that you was in your riding-habit—oh my dear woman when shall I be able to hear from you—

All the officers dined with the Governor—I never heard of any one single person having so great a power vested in him as Captain Phillip has by his commission as Governor-in-Chief of New South Wales—dined on a cold collation but the Mutton which had been killed yesterday morning was full of maggots—nothing will keep twenty-four hours in this dismal country I find—

Went out shooting after breakfast—I only shot one cockatoo—they are the most beautiful birds—

Major Ross ordered one of the Corporals to flog with a rope ELIZABETH Morden for being impertinent to Captain Campbell—the Corporal did not play with her but laid it home which I was very glad to see—she has long been fishing for it—

On Sunday as usual, kissed your dear beloved image a thousand times—was very much frightened by the lightning as it broke very near my tent—several of the convicts have run away.

He goes to his table and writes in his journal.

If I'm not made 1st Lieutenant soon …

Harry Brewer has come in.

Ralph Harry—

Harry I saw the light in your tent—

Ralph I was writing my journal.

Silence.

Is there any trouble?

Harry No. (*Pause.*) I just came.

Talk, you know. If I wrote a journal about my life it would fill volumes. Volumes. My travels with the Captain—His Excellency now, no less, Governor-in-Chief, power to raise armies, build cities—I still call him plain Captain Phillip. He likes it from me. The war in America and before that, Ralph, my life in London. That would fill a volume on its own. Not what you would call a good life.

Pause.

Sometimes I look at the convicts and I think, one of those could be you, Harry Brewer, if you hadn't joined the navy when you did. The officers may look down on me now, but what if they found out that I used to be an embezzler?

Ralph Harry, you should keep these things to yourself.

Harry You're right, Ralph.

Pause.

I think the Captain suspects, but he's a good man and he looks for different things in a man—

Ralph Like what?

Harry Hard to say. He likes to see something unusual. Ralph, I saw Handy Baker last night.

Ralph You hanged him a month ago, Harry.

Harry He had a rope—Ralph, he's come back.

Ralph It was a dream. Sometimes I think my dreams are real—But they're not.

Harry We used to hear you on the ship, Ralph, calling for your Betsey Alicia.

Ralph Don't speak her name on this iniquitous shore!

Harry Duckling's gone silent on me again. I know it's because of Handy Baker. I saw him as well as I see you. Duckling wants me, he said, even if you've hanged me. At least your poker's danced its last shindy, I said. At least it's young and straight, he said, she likes that. I went for him but he was gone. But he's going to come back, I know it. I didn't want to hang him, Ralph, I didn't.

Ralph He did steal that food from the stores.

Pause.

 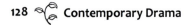

I voted with the rest of the court those men should be hanged, I didn't know His Excellency would be against it.

Harry Duckling says she never feels anything. How do I know she didn't feel something when she was with him? She thinks I hanged him to get rid of him, but I didn't, Ralph.

Pause.

Do you know I saved her life? She was sentenced to be hanged at Newgate for stealing two candlesticks but I got her name put on the transport lists. But when I remind her of that she says she wouldn't have cared. Eighteen years old, and she didn't care if she was turned off.

Pause.

These women are sold before they're ten. The Captain says we should treat them with kindness.

Ralph How can you treat such women with kindness? Why does he think that?

Harry Not all the officers find them disgusting, Ralph—haven't you ever been tempted?

Ralph Never! (*Pause.*) His Excellency never seems to notice me.

Pause.

He finds time for Davey Collins, Lieutenant Dawes.

Harry That's because Captain Collins is going to write about the customs of the Indians here—and Lieutenant Dawes is recording the stars.

Ralph I could write about the Indians.

Harry He did suggest to Captain Tench that we do something to educate the convicts, put on a play or something, but Captain Tench just laughed. He doesn't like Captain Tench.

Ralph A play? Who would act in a play?

Harry The convicts of course. He is thinking of talking to Lieutenant Johnston, but I think Lieutenant Johnston wants to study the plants.

Ralph I read *The Tragedy of Lady Jane Grey* on the ship. It is such a moving and uplifting play. But how could a whore play Lady Jane?

Harry Some of those women are good women, Ralph, I believe my Duckling is good. It's not her fault - if only she would look at me, once, react. Who wants to fuck a corpse!

Silence.

I'm sorry. I didn't mean to shock you, Ralph, I have shocked you, haven't I? I'll go.

Ralph Is His Excellency serious about putting on a play?

Harry When the Captain decides something, Ralph.

Ralph If I went to him—no. It would be better if you did, Harry, you could tell His Excellency how much I like the theatre.

Harry I didn't know that Ralph, I'll tell him.

Ralph Duckling could be in it, if you wanted.

Harry I wouldn't want her to be looked at by all the men.

Ralph If His Excellency doesn't like *Lady Jane* we could find something else.

Pause.

A comedy perhaps …

Harry I'll speak to him, Ralph. I like you.

Pause.

It's good to talk …

Pause.

You don't think I killed him then?

Ralph Who?

Harry Handy Baker.

Ralph No, Harry. You did not kill Handy Baker.

Harry Thank you, Ralph.

Ralph Harry, you won't forget to talk to His Excellency about the play?

SCENE FIVE. AN AUDITION

Ralph Clark, **Meg Long.** *Meg Long is very old and very smelly. She hovers over Ralph.*

Meg We heard you was looking for some women, Lieutenant. Here I am.

Ralph I've asked to see some women to play certain parts in a play.

Meg I can play, Lieutenant, I can play with any part you like. There ain't nothing puts Meg off. That's how I got my name: Shitty Meg.

Ralph The play has four particular parts for young women.

Meg You don't want a young woman for your peculiar, Lieutenant, they don't know nothing. Shut your eyes and I'll play you as tight as a virgin.

Ralph You don't understand, Long. Here's the play. It's called *The Recruiting Officer*.

Meg Oh, I can do that too.

Ralph What?

Meg Recruiting. Anybody you like. (*She whispers.*) You want women: you ask Meg. Who do you want?

Ralph I want to try some out.

Meg Good idea, Lieutenant, good idea. Ha! Ha! Ha!

Ralph Now if you don't mind—

Meg doesn't move.

Long!

Meg (*frightened but still holding her ground*) We thought you was a madge cull.

Ralph What?

Meg You know, a fluter, a mollie. (*impatiently*) A prissy cove, a girl! You having no she-lag on the ship. Nor here, neither. On the ship maybe you was seasick. But all these months here. And now we hear how you want a lot of women, all at once. Well, I'm glad to hear that, Lieutenant, I am. You let me know when you want Meg, old Shitty Meg.

She goes off quickly and Robert Sideway comes straight on.

Sideway Ah, Mr Clark.
He does a flourish.

I am calling you Mr Clark as one calls Mr Garrick Mr Garrick, we have not had the pleasure of meeting before.

Ralph I've seen you on the ship.

Sideway Different circumstances, Mr Clark, best forgotten. I was once a gentleman. My fortune has turned. The wheel … You are doing a play, I hear, ah, Drury Lane,

Mr Garrick, the lovely Peg Woffington. (*conspiratorially*) He was so cruel to her. She was so pale—

Ralph You say you were a gentleman, Sideway?

Sideway Top of my profession, Mr Clark, pickpocket, born and bred in Bermondsey. Do you know London, Sir, don't you miss it? In these my darkest hours, I remember my happy days in that great city. London Bridge at dawn—hand on cold iron for good luck. Down Cheapside with the market traders—never refuse a mince pie. Into St Paul's churchyard—I do love a good church—and begin work in Bond Street. There, I've spotted her, rich, plump, not of the best class, stands in front of the shop, plucking up courage, I pluck her. Time for coffee until five o'clock and the pinnacle, the glory of the day: Drury Lane. The coaches, the actors scuttling, the gentlemen watching, the ladies tittering, the perfumes, the clothes, the handkerchiefs.

> *He hands Ralph the handkerchief he has just stolen from him.*

Here, Mr Clark, you see the skill. Ah, Mr Clark, I beg you, I entreat you, to let me perform on your stage, to let me feel once again the thrill of a play about to begin. Ah, I see ladies approaching: our future Woffingtons, Siddons.

> **Dabby Bryant** *comes on, with a shrinking Mary Brenham in tow. Sideway bows.*

Ladies.

I shall await your word of command, Mr Clark, I shall be in the wings.

> *Sideway scuttles off.*

Dabby You asked to see Mary Brenham, Lieutenant. Here she is.

Ralph Yes—the Governor has asked me to put on a play. (*to Mary*) You know what a play is?

Dabby I've seen lots of plays, Lieutenant, so has Mary.

Ralph Have you, Brenham?

Mary (*inaudibly*) Yes.

Ralph Can you remember which plays you've seen?

Mary (*inaudibly*) No.

Dabby I can't remember what they were called, but I always knew when they were going to end badly. I knew right from the beginning. How does this one end. Lieutenant?

Ralph It ends happily. It's called *The Recruiting Officer*.

Dabby Mary wants to be in your play, Lieutenant, and so do I.

Ralph Do you think you have a talent for acting, Brenham?

Dabby Of course she does, and so do I. I want to play Mary's friend.

Ralph Do you know *The Recruiting Officer*, Bryant?

Dabby No, but in all those plays, there's always a friend. That's because a girl has to talk to someone and she talks to her friend. So I'll be Mary's friend.

Ralph Silvia—that's the part I want to try Brenham for—doesn't have a friend. She has a cousin. But they don't like each other.

Dabby Oh. Mary doesn't always like me.

Ralph The Reverend Johnson told me you can read and write, Brenham?

Dabby She went to school until she was ten. She used to read to us on the ship. We loved it. It put us to sleep.

Ralph Shall we try reading some of the play?

Ralph hands her the book. Mary reads silently, moving her lips.

I meant read it aloud. As you did on the ship. I'll help you, I'll read Justice Balance. That's your father.

Dabby Doesn't she have a sweetheart?

Ralph Yes, but this scene is with her father.

Dabby What's the name of her lover?

Ralph Captain Plume.

Dabby A Captain! Mary!

Ralph Start here, Brenham.

Mary begins to read.

Mary 'Whilst there is life there is hope, Sir.'

Dabby Oh, I like that, Lieutenant. This is a good play, I can tell.

Ralph Shht. She hasn't finished. Start again, Brenham, that's good.

Mary 'Whilst there is life there is hope, Sir; perhaps my brother may recover.'

Ralph That's excellent, Brenham, very fluent. You could read a little louder. Now I'll read.

'We have but little reason to expect it. Poor Owen! But the decree is just; I was pleased with the death of my father, because he left me an estate, and now I'm punished with the loss of an heir to inherit mine.'

Pause. He laughs a little.

This is a comedy. They don't really mean it. It's to make people laugh. 'The death of your brother makes you sole heiress to my estate, which you know is about twelve hundred pounds a year.'

Dabby Twelve hundred pounds! It must be a comedy.

Mary 'My desire of being punctual in my obedience requires that you would be plain in your commands, Sir.'

Dabby Well said, Mary, well said.

Ralph I think that's enough. You read very well, Brenham. Would you also be able to copy the play? We have only two copies.

Dabby Course she will. Where do I come in, Lieutenant? The cousin.

Ralph Can you read, Bryant?

Dabby Not those marks in the books, Lieutenant, but I can read other things. I read dreams very well, Lieutenant. Very well.

Ralph I don't think you're right for Melinda. I'm thinking of someone else. And if you can't read …

Dabby Mary will read me the lines, Lieutenant.

Ralph There's Rose …

Dabby Rose. I like the name. I'll be Rose. Who is she?

Ralph She's a country girl …

Dabby I grew up in Devon, Lieutenant. I'm perfect for Rose. What does she do?

Ralph She—well, it's complicated. She falls in love with Silvia.

Mary begins to giggle but tries to hold it back.

But it's because she thinks Silvia's a man. And she—they—she sleeps with her. Rose. With Silvia. Euh. Silvia too. With Rose. But nothing happens.

Dabby It doesn't? Nothing?

Dabby bursts out laughing.

Ralph Because Silvia is pretending to be a man, but of course she can't—

Dabby Play the flute? Ha! She's not the only one around here. I'll do Rose.

Ralph I would like to hear you.

Dabby I don't know my lines yet, Lieutenant. When I know my lines, you can hear me do them. Come on, Mary—

Ralph I didn't say you could—I'm not certain you're the right—Bryant, I'm not certain I want you in the play.

Dabby Yes you do. Lieutenant. Mary will read me the lines and I, Lieutenant, will read you your dreams.

There's a guffaw. It's **Liz Morden**.

Ralph Ah. Here's your cousin.

There is a silence. Mary shrinks away. Dabby and Liz stare at each other, each holding her ground, each ready to pounce.

Melinda. Silvia's cousin.

Dabby You can't have her in the play, Lieutenant.

Ralph Why not?

Dabby You don't have to be able to read the future to know that Liz Morden is going to be hanged.

Liz looks briefly at Dabby, as if to strike, then changes her mind.

Liz I understand you want me in your play, Lieutenant. Is that it?

She snatches the book from Ralph and strides off. I'll look at it and let you know.

SCENE SIX. THE AUTHORITIES DISCUSS THE MERITS OF THE THEATRE

Governor Arthur Phillip, **Major Robbie Ross,** *Judge David Collins, Captain Watkin Tench,* **Captain Jemmy Campbell Reverend Johnson,** *Lieutenant George Johnston,* **Lieutenant Will Dawes,** *Second Lieutenant Ralph Clark,* **Second Lieutenant William Faddy.**

It is late at night, the men have been drinking, tempers are high. They interrupt each other, overlap, make jokes under and over the conversation but all engage in it with the passion for discourse and thought of eighteenth-century men.

Ross A play! A f—

Revd Johnson Mmhm.

Ross A frippery frittering play!

Campbell Aheeh, aeh, here?

Ralph (*timidly*) To celebrate the King's birthday, on June the fourth.

Ross If a frigating ship doesn't appear soon, we'll all be struck with stricturing starvation—and you—a play!

Collins Not putting on the play won't bring us a supply ship, Robbie.

Ross And you say you want those contumelious convicts to act in this play. The convicts!

Campbell Eh, kev, weh, discipline's bad. Very bad.

Ralph The play has several parts for women. We have no other women here.

Collins Your wife excepted, Reverend.

Revd Johnson My wife abhors anything of that nature. After all, actresses are not famed for their morals.

Collins Neither are our women convicts.

Revd Johnson How can they be when some of our officers set them up as mistresses?

He looks pointedly at Lieutenant George Johnston.

Ross Filthy, thieving, lying whores and now we have to watch them flout their flitty wares on the stage!

Phillip No one will be forced to watch the play.

Dawes I believe there's a partial lunar eclipse that night. I shall have to watch that. The sky of this southern hemisphere is full of wonders. Have you looked at the constellations?

Short pause.

Ross Constellations. Plays! This is a convict colony, the prisoners are here to be punished and we're here to make sure they get punished. Constellations! Jemmy? Constellations!

He turns to Jemmy Campbell for support.

Campbell Tss, weh, marines, marines: war, phoo, discipline. Eh? Service—His Majesty.

Phillip We are indeed here to supervise the convicts who are already being punished by their long exile. Surely they can also be reformed?

Tench We are talking about criminals, often hardened criminals. They have a habit of vice and crime. Many criminals seem to have been born that way. It is in their nature.

Philip Rousseau would say that we have made them that way, Watkins: 'Man is born free, and everywhere he is in chains.'

Revd Johnson But Rousseau was a Frenchman.

Ross A Frenchman! What can you expect? We're going to listen to a foraging Frenchman now—

Collins He was Swiss actually.

Campbell Eeh, eyeh, good soldiers, the Swiss.

Phillip Surely you believe man can be redeemed, Reverend?

Revd Johnson By the grace of God and a belief in the true church, yes. But Christ never proposed putting on plays to his disciples. However, he didn't forbid it either. It must depend on the play.

Johnston He did propose treating sinners, especially women who have sinned, with compassion. Most of the convict women have committed small crimes, a tiny theft—

Collins We know about your compassion, not to say passion, for the women convicts, George.

Tench A crime is a crime. You commit a crime or you don't. If you commit a crime, you are a criminal. Surely that is logical? It's like the savages here. A savage is a savage because he behaves in a savage manner. To expect anything else is foolish. They can't even build a proper canoe.

Phillip They can be educated.

Collins Actually, they seem happy enough as they are. They do not want to build canoes or houses, nor do they suffer from greed and ambition.

Faddy (*looking at Ralph*) Unlike some.

Tench Which can't be said of our convicts. But really, I don't see what this has to do with a play. It is at most a passable diversion, an entertainment to wile away the hours of the idle.

Campbell Ttts, weh, heh, the convicts, bone idle.

Dawes We're wiling away precious hours now. Put the play on, don't put it on, it won't change the shape of the universe.

Ralph But it could change the nature of our little society.

Faddy Second Lieutenant Clark change society!

Phillip William!

Tench My dear Ralph, a bunch of convicts making fools of themselves, mouthing words written no doubt by some London ass, will hardly change our society.

Ralph George Farquhar was not an ass! And he was from Ireland.

Ross An Irishman! I have to sit there and listen to an Irishman!

Campbell Tss, tt. Irish. Wilde. Wilde.

Revd Johnson The play doesn't propagate Catholic doctrine, does it, Ralph?

Ralph He was also an officer.

Faddy Crawling for promotion.

Ralph Of the Grenadiers.

Ross Never liked the Grenadiers myself.

Campbell Ouah, pheuee, grenades, pho. Throw and run. Eh. Backs.

Ralph The play is called *The Recruiting Officer*.

Collins I saw it in London I believe. Yes. Very funny if I remember. Sergeant Kite. The devious ways he used to serve his captain …

Faddy Your part, Ralph.

Collins William, if you can't contribute anything useful to the discussion, keep quiet!

Silence.

Revd Johnson What is the plot, Ralph?

Ralph It's about this recruiting officer and his friend, and they are in love with these two young ladies from Shrewsbury and after some difficulties, they marry them.

Revd Johnson It sanctions Holy Matrimony then?

Ralph Yes, yes, it does.

Revd Johnson That wouldn't do the convicts any harm. I'm having such trouble getting them to marry instead of this sordid cohabitation they're so used to.

Ross Marriage, plays, why not a ball for the convicts!

Campbell Euuh. Boxing.

Phillip Some of these men will have finished their sentence in a few years. They will become members of society again, and help create a new society in this colony. Should we not encourage them now to think in a free and responsible manner?

Tench I don't see how a comedy about two lovers will do that, Arthur.

Phillip The theatre is an expression of civilization. We belong to a great country which has spawned great playwrights: Shakespeare, Marlowe, Jonson, and even in our own time, Sheridan. The convicts will be speaking a refined, literate language and expressing sentiments of a delicacy they are not used to. It will remind them that there is more to life than crime, punishment. And we, this colony of a few hundred, will be watching this together, for a few hours we will no longer be despised prisoners and hated gaolers. We will laugh, we may be moved, we may even think a little. Can you suggest something else that will provide such an evening, Watkin?

Dawes Mapping the stars gives me more enjoyment, personally.

Tench I'm not sure it's a good idea having the convicts laugh at officers, Arthur.

Campbell No. Pheeoh, insubordination, heh, ehh, no discipline.

Ross You want this vice-ridden vermin to enjoy themselves?

Collins They would only laugh at Sergeant Kite.

Ralph Captain Plume is a most attractive, noble fellow.

Revd Johnson He's not loose, is he Ralph? I hear many of these plays are about rakes and encourage loose morals in women. They do get married? Before, that is, before. And for the right reasons.

Ralph They marry for love and to secure wealth.

Revd Johnson That's all right.

Tench I would simply say that if you want to build a civilization there are more important things than a play. If you want to teach the convicts something, teach them to farm, to build houses, teach them a sense of respect for property, teach them thrift so they don't eat a week's rations in one night, but above all, teach them how to work, not how to sit around laughing at a comedy.

Phillip The Greeks believed that it was a citizen's duty to watch a play. It was a kind of work in that it required attention, judgement, patience, all social virtues.

Tench And the Greeks were conquered by the more practical Romans, Arthur.

Collins Indeed, the Romans built their bridges, but they also spent many centuries wishing they were Greeks. And they, after all, were conquered by barbarians, or by their own corrupt and small spirits.

Tench Are you saying Rome would not have fallen if the theatre has been better?

Ralph (*very loud*) Why not? (*Everyone looks at him and he continues, fast and nervously.*) In my own small way, in just a few hours, I have seen something change. I asked some of the convict women to read me some lines, these women who behave often no better than animals. And it seemed to me, as one or two—I'm not saying all of them, not at all—but one or two, saying those well-balanced lines of Mr Farquhar, they seemed to acquire a dignity, they seemed—they seemed to lose some of their corruption. There was one, Mary Brenham, she read so well, perhaps this play will keep her from selling herself to the first marine who offers her bread—

Faddy (*under his breath*) She'll sell herself to him, instead.

Ross So that's the way the wind blows—

Campbell Hooh. A tempest. Hooh.

Ralph (*over them*) I speak about her, but in a small way this could affect all the convicts and even ourselves, we could forget our worries about the supplies, the hangings and the floggings, and think of ourselves at the theatre, in London with our wives and children, that is, we could, euh—

Phillip Transcend—

Ralph Transcend the darker, euh—transcend the—

Johnston Brutal—

Ralph The brutality—remember our better nature and remember—

Collins England.

Ralph England.

A moment.

Ross Where did the wee Lieutenant learn to speak?

Faddy He must have had one of his dreams.

Tench (*over them*) You are making claims that cannot be substantiated, Ralph. It's two hours, possibly of amusement, possibly of boredom, and we will lose the labour of the convicts during the time they are learning to play. It's a waste, an unnecessary waste.

Revd Johnson I'm still concerned about the content.

Tench The content of a play is irrelevant.

Ross Even if it teaches insubordination, disobedience, revolution?

Collins Since we have agreed it can do no harm, since it might, possibly, do some good, since the only person violently opposed to it is Major Ross for reasons he has not made quite clear, I suggest we allow Ralph to rehearse his play. Does anyone disagree?

Ross I—I—

Collins We have taken your disagreement into account, Robbie.

Campbell Ah, eeh, I—I— (*He stops.*)

Collins Thank you, Captain Campbell. Dawes? Dawes, do come back to earth and honour us with your attention for a moment.

Dawes What? No? Why not? As long as I don't have to watch it.

Collins Johnston?

Johnston I'm for it.

Collins Faddy?

Faddy I'm against it.

Collins Could you tell us why?

Faddy I don't trust the director.

Collins Tench?

Tench Waste of time.

Collins The Reverend, our moral guide, has no objections.

Revd Johnson Of course I haven't read it.

Tench Davey, this is not an objective summing up, this is typical of your high-handed manner—

Collins (*angrily*) I don't think you're the one to accuse others of a high-handed manner, Watkin.

Phillip Gentlemen, please.

Collins Your Excellency, I believe, is for the play and I myself am convinced it will prove a most interesting experiment. So let us conclude with our good wishes to Ralph for a successful production.

Ross I will not accept this. You willy-wally wobbly words, Greeks, Romans, experiment, to get your own way. You don't take anything seriously, but I know this play—this play—order will become disorder. The theatre leads to threatening theory and you, Governor, you have His Majesty's commission to build castles, raise armies, administer a military colony, not fandangle about with a lewdy play! I am going to write to the Admiralty about this.

He goes.

Phillip You're out of turn, Robbie.

Campbell Aah - eeh - a. Confusion. (*He goes.*)

Dawes Why is Robbie so upset? So much fuss over a play.

Johnston Major Ross will never forgive you, Ralph.

Collins I have summed up the feelings of the assembled company, Arthur, but the last word must be yours.

Philip The last word will be the play, gentlemen.

SCENE SEVEN. HARRY AND DUCKLING GO ROWING

Harry Brewer, **Duckling Smith.** *Harry is rowing, Duckling is sulking.*

Harry It's almost beginning to look like a town. Look, Duckling, there's the Captain's house. I can see him in his garden.

Harry waves. Duckling doesn't turn around.

Sydney. He could have found a better name. Mobsbury. Lagtown. Duckling Cove, eh?

Harry laughs. Duckling remains morose.

The Captain said it had to be named after the Home Secretary. The courthouse looks impressive all in BRICK. There's Lieutenant Dawes' observatory. Why don't you look, Duckling?

Duckling glances, then turns back.

The trees look more friendly from here. Did you know the eucalyptus tree can't be found anywhere else in the world? Captain Collins told me that. Isn't that interesting? Lieutenant Clark says the three orange trees on his island are doing well. It's the turnips he's worried about, he thinks they're being stolen and he's too busy with his play to go and have a look. Would you like to see the orange trees, Duckling?

Duckling glowers.

I thought you'd enjoy rowing to Ralph's island. I thought it would remind you of rowing on the Thames. Look how blue the water is. Duckling. Say something. Duckling!

Duckling If I was rowing on the Thames, I'd be free.
Harry This isn't Newgate, Duckling.
Duckling I wish it was.
Harry Duckling!
Duckling At least the gaoler of Newgate left you alone and you could talk to people.
Harry I let you talk to the women.
Duckling (*with contempt*) Esther Abrahams, Mary Brenham!
Harry They're good women.
Duckling I don't have anything to say to those women, Harry. My friends are in the women's camp -
Harry It's not the women you're after in the women's camp, it's the marines who come looking for buttock, I know you, who do you have your eye on now, who, a soldier? Another marine, a corporal? Who, Duckling, who?

Pause.

You've found someone already, haven't you? Where do you go, on the beach? In my tent, like with Handy Baker, eh? Where, under the trees?

Duckling You know I hate trees, don't be so filthy.
Harry Filthy, you're filthy, you filthy whore.

Pause.

I'm sorry, Duckling, please. Why can't you?—can't you just be with me? Don't be angry. I'll do anything for you, you know that. What do you want, Duckling?

Duckling I don't want to be watched all the time. I wake up in the middle of the night and you're watching me. What do you think I'm going to do in my sleep, Harry? Watching, watching, watching. JUST STOP WATCHING ME.

Harry You want to leave me. All right, go and live in the women's camp, sell yourself to a convict for a biscuit. Leave if you want to. You're filthy, filthy, opening your legs to the first marine—

Duckling Why are you so angry with your Duckling, Harry? Don't you like it when I open my legs wide to you? Cross them over you—the way you like? What will you do when your little Duckling isn't there any more to touch you with her soft fingertips, Harry, where you like it? First the left nipple and then the right. Your Duckling doesn't want to leave you, Harry.

Harry Duckling …

Duckling I need freedom sometimes, Harry.

Harry You have to earn your freedom with good behaviour.

Duckling Why didn't you let them hang me and take my corpse with you, Harry? You could have kept that in chains. I wish I was dead. At least when you're dead, you're free.

Silence.

Harry You know Lieutenant Clark's play?

Duckling is silent.

Do you want to be in it?

Duckling laughs.

Dabby Bryant is in it too and Liz Morden. Do you want to be in it? You'd rehearse in the evenings with Lieutenant Clark.

Duckling And he can watch over me instead of you.

Harry I'm trying to make you happy, Duckling, if you don't want to—

Duckling I'll be in the play.

Pause.

How is Lieutenant Clark going to manage Liz Morden?

Harry The Captain wanted her to be in it.

Duckling On the ship we used to see who could make Lieutenant Clark blush first. It didn't take long, haha.

Harry Duckling, you won't try anything with Lieutenant Clark, will you?

Duckling With that Mollie? No.

Harry You're talking to me again. Will you kiss your Harry?

They kiss.

I'll come and watch the rehearsals.

SCENE EIGHT. THE WOMEN LEARN THEIR LINES

Dabby Bryant is sitting on the ground muttering to herself with concentration. She could be counting. Mary Brenham comes on.

Mary Are you remembering your lines, Dabby?

Dabby What lines? No. I was remembering Devon. I was on my way back to Bigbury Bay.

Mary You promised Lieutenant Clark you'd learn your lines.

Dabby I want to go back. I want to see a wall of stone. I want to hear the Atlantic breaking into the estuary. I can bring a boat into any harbour, in any weather. I can do it as well as the Governor.

Mary Dabby, what about your lines?

Dabby I'm not spending the rest of my life in this flat, brittle burnt-out country. Oh, give me some English rain.

Mary It rains here.

Dabby It's not the same. I could recognize English rain anywhere. And Devon rain, Mary, Devon rain is the softest in England. As soft as your breasts, as soft as Lieutenant Clark's dimpled cheeks.

Mary Dabby, don't!

Dabby You're wasting time, girl, he's ripe for the plucking. You can always tell with men, they begin to walk sideways. And if you don't—

Mary Don't start. I listened to you once before.

Dabby What would you have done without that lanky sailor drooling over you?

Mary I would have been less of a whore.

Dabby Listen, my darling, you're only a virgin once. You can't go to a man and say, I'm a virgin except for this one lover I had. After that, it doesn't matter how many men go through you.

Mary I'll never wash the sin away.

Dabby If God didn't want women to be whores he shouldn't have created men who pay for their bodies. While you were with your little sailor there were women in that stinking pit of a hold who had three men on them at once, men with the pox, men with the flux, men biting like dogs.

Mary But if you don't agree to it, then you're not a whore, you're a martyr.

Dabby You have to be a virgin to be a martyr, Mary, and you didn't come on that ship a virgin. 'A. H. I love thee to the heart', ha, tattooed way up there—

Dabby begins to lift Mary's skirt to reveal a tattoo high up on the inner thigh. Mary leaps away.

Mary That was different. That was love.

Dabby The second difficulty with being a martyr is that you have to be dead to qualify. Well, you didn't die, thanks to me, you had three pounds of beef a week instead of two, two extra ounces of cheese.

Mary Which you were happy to eat!

Dabby We women have to look after each other. Let's learn the lines.

Mary You sold me that first day so you and your husband could eat!

Dabby Do you want me to learn these lines or not?

Mary How can I play Silvia? She's brave and strong. She couldn't have done what I've done.

Dabby She didn't spend eight months and one week on a convict ship. Anyway, you can pretend you're her.

Mary No. I have to *be* her.

Dabby Why?

Mary Because that's acting.

Dabby No way I'm being Rose, she's an idiot.

Mary It's not such a big part, it doesn't matter so much.

Dabby You didn't tell me that before.

Mary I hadn't read it carefully. Come on, let's do the scene between Silvia and Rose. (*She reads.*) 'I have rested but indifferently, and I believe my bedfellow was as little pleased; poor Rose! Here she comes—

Dabby I could have done something for Rose. Ha! I should play Silvia.

Mary 'Good morrow, my dear, how d'ye this morning?' Now you say: 'Just as I was last night, neither better nor worse for you.'

Liz Morden comes on.

Liz You can't do the play without me. I'm in it! Where's the Lieutenant.

Dabby She's teaching me some lines.

Liz Why aren't you teaching me the lines?

Mary We're not doing your scenes.

Liz Well do them.

Dabby You can read. You can read your own lines.

Liz I don't want to learn them on my own.

Liz thrusts Dabby away and sits by Mary.

I'm waiting.

Dabby What are you waiting for, Liz Morden, a blind man to buy your wares?

Mary (*quickly*) We'll do the first scene between Melinda and Silvia, all right?

Liz Yea. The first scene.

Mary gives Liz the book.

Mary You start.

Liz looks at the book.

You start. 'Welcome to town, cousin Silvia'—

Liz 'Welcome to town, cousin Silvia'—

Mary Go on—'I envied you'—

Liz 'I envied you'—You read it first.

Mary Why?

Liz I want to hear how you do it.

Mary Why?

Liz Cause then I can do it different.

Mary 'I envied you your retreat in the country; for Shrewsbury, methinks, and all your heads of shires'—

Dabby Why don't you read it? You can't read!

Liz What?

She lunges at Dabby.

Mary I'll teach you the lines.

Dabby Are you her friend now, is that it? Mary the holy innocent and thieving bitch—

Liz and Dabby seize each other. **Ketch Freeman** *appears.*

Ketch (*with nervous affability*) Good morning, ladies. And why aren't you at work instead of at each other's throats?

Liz and Dabby turn on him.

Liz I wouldn't talk of throats if I was you, Mr Hangman Ketch Freeman.

Dabby Crap merchant.

Liz Crapping cull. Switcher.

Mary Roper.

Ketch I was only asking what you were doing, you know, friendly like.

Liz Stick to your ropes, my little galler, don't bother the actresses.

Ketch Actresses? You're doing a play?

Liz Better than dancing the Paddington frisk in your arms—noser!

Ketch I'll nose on you, Liz, if you're not careful.

Liz I'd take a leap in the dark sooner than turn off my own kind. Now take your whirligigs out of our sight, we have lines to learn.

Ketch slinks away as Liz and Dabby spit him off.

Dabby (*after him*) Don't hang too many people, Ketch, we need an audience!

Mary 'Welcome to town, cousin Silvia.' It says you salute.

Liz (*giving a military salute*) 'Welcome to town, cousin—Silvia.'

SCENE NINE. RALPH CLARK TRIES TO KISS HIS DEAR WIFE'S PICTURE

Ralph's tent. Candlelight. Ralph paces.

Ralph Dreamt my beloved Betsey that I was with you and that I thought I was going to be arrested.

He looks at his watch.

I hope to God that there is nothing the matter with you my tender Alicia or that of our dear boy—

He looks at his watch.

My darling tender wife I am reading Proverbs waiting till midnight, the Sabbath, that I might kiss your picture as usual.

He takes his Bible and kneels. Looks at his watch.

The Patrols caught three seamen and a boy in the women's camp.

He reads.

'Let thy fountain be blessed: and rejoice with the wife of thy youth.'
    Good God what a scene of whoredom is going on there in the women's camp.

He looks at his watch. Gets up. Paces.

Very hot this night.
    Captain Shea killed today one of the kankaroos—it is the most curious animal I ever saw.

He looks at his watch.

Almost midnight, my Betsey, the Lord's day—

He reads.

'And behold, there met him a woman with the attire of an harlot, and subtle of heart.
    So she caught him, and kissed him with an impudent face.'
    Felt ill with the toothache my dear wife my God what pain.

Reads.

'So she caught him, and kissed him with an impudent face ....'

'I have perfumed my bed with myrrh, aloes, cinnamon—' Sarah McCormick was flogged today for calling the doctor a c—midnight—

This being Sunday took your picture out of its prison and kissed it—God bless you my sweet woman.

> *He now proceeds to do so. That is, he goes down on his knees and brings the picture to himself. Ketch Freeman comes into the tent. Ralph jumps.*

Ketch Forgive me, Sir, please forgive me, I didn't want to disturb your prayers. I say fifty Hail Marys myself every night, and 200 on the days when—I'll wait outside. Sir.

Ralph What do you want?

Ketch I'll wait quietly, Sir, don't mind me.

Ralph Why aren't you in the camp at this hour?

Ketch I should be, God forgive me, I should be. But I'm not. I'm here. I have to have a word with you, Sir.

Ralph Get back to the camp immediately, I'll see you in the morning, Ketch.

Ketch Don't call me that, Sir, I beg you, don't call me by that name, that's what I came to see you about, Sir.

Ralph I was about to go to sleep.

Ketch I understand. Sir, and your soul in peace, I won't take up your time, Sir, I'll be brief.

Pause.

Ralph Well?

Ketch Don't you want to finish your prayers? I can be very quiet. I used to watch my mother, may her poor soul rest in peace, I used to watch her say her prayers, every night.

Ralph Get on with it!

Ketch When I say my prayers I have a terrible doubt. How can I be sure God is forgiving me? What if he will forgive me, but hasn't forgiven me yet? That's why I don't want to die, Sir. That's why I can't die. Not until I am sure. Are you sure?

Ralph I'm not a convict: I don't sin.

Ketch To be sure. Forgive me, Sir. But if we're in God's power, then surely he makes us sin. I was given a guardian angel when I was born, like all good Catholics, why didn't my guardian angel look after me better? But I think he must've stayed in Ireland. I think the devil tempted my mother to London and both our guardian angels stayed behind. Have you ever been to Ireland, Sir? It's a beautiful country. If I'd been an angel I wouldn't have left it either. And when we came within six fields of Westminster, the devils took over. But it's God's judgement I'm frightened of. And the women's. They're so hard. Why is that?

Ralph Why have you come here?

Ketch I'm coming to that, Sir.

Ralph Hurry up, then.

Ketch I'm speaking as fast as I can, Sir—

Ralph Ketch—

Ketch James, Sir, James, Daniel, Patrick, after my three uncles. Good men they were too, didn't go to London. If my mother hadn't brought us to London, may God give peace to her soul and breathe pity into the hearts of hard women—because the docks are in London and if I hadn't worked on the docks, on that day, May 23rd, 1785, do you remember it, Sir? Shadwell Dock. If only we hadn't left, then I wouldn't have been there, then nothing would have happened, I wouldn't have become a coal heaver on Shadwell Dock and been there on the 23rd of May when we refused to unload because they were paying us so badly, Sir. I wasn't even near the sailor who got killed. He shouldn't have done the unloading, that was wrong of the sailors, but I didn't kill him, maybe one blow, not to look stupid, you know, just to show I was with the lads, even if I wasn't, but I didn't kill him. And they caught five at random, Sir, and I was among the five, and they found the cudgel, but I just had that to look good, that's all, and when they said to me later you can hang or you can give the names, what was I to do, what would you have done, Sir?

Ralph I wouldn't have been in that situation. Freeman.

Ketch To be sure, forgive me, Sir. I only told on the ones I saw, I didn't tell anything that wasn't true. Death is a horrible thing, that poor sailor.

Ralph Freeman, I'm going to go to bed now—

Ketch I understand, Sir, I understand. And when it happened again, here! And I had hopes of making a good life here. It's because I'm so friendly, see, so I go along, and then I'm the one who gets caught. That theft, I didn't do it, I was just there, keeping a look out, just to help some friends, you know. But when they say to you, hang or be hanged, what do you do? Someone has to do it. I try to do it well. God had mercy on the whore, the thief, the lame, surely he'll forgive the hang—it's the women—they're without mercy - not like you and me, Sir, men. What I wanted to say. Sir, is that I heard them talking about the play.

Pause.

Some players came into our village once. they were loved like the angels, Lieutenant, like the angels. And the way the women watched them—the light of a spring dawn in their eyes.
    Lieutenant—
    I want to be an actor.

SCENE TEN. JOHN WISEHAMMER AND MARY BRENHAM EXCHANGE WORDS

Mary is copying The Recruiting Officer *in the afternoon light. John Wisehammer is carrying bricks and piling them to one side. He begins to hover over her.*

Mary 'I would rather counsel than command; I don't propose this with the authority of a parent, but as the advice of your friend'—
Wisehammer Friend. That's a good word. Short, but full of promise.
Mary 'That you would take the coach this moment and go into the country.'
Wisehammer Country can mean opposite things. It renews you with trees and grass, you go rest in the country, or it crushes you with power: you die for your country, your country doesn't want you, you're thrown out of your country.

Pause.

I like words.

Pause.

My father cleared the houses of the dead to sell the old clothes to the poorhouses by the Thames. He found a dictionary—Johnson's dictionary—it was as big as a bible. It went from A to L. I started with the A's. Abecedarian: someone who teaches the alphabet or rudiments of literature. Abject: a man without hope.
Mary What does indulgent mean?
Wisehammer How is it used?

Mary (*reads*) 'You have been so careful, so indulgent to me'—
Wisehammer It means ready to overlook faults.

Pause.

You have to be careful with words that begin with 'in'. It can turn everything upside down. Injustice. Most of that word is taken up with justice, but the 'in' twists it inside out and makes it the ugliest word in the English language.
Mary Guilty is an uglier word.
Wisehammer Innocent ought to be a beautiful word, but it isn't, it's full of sorrow. Anguish.

Mary goes back to her copying.

Mary I don't have much time. We start this in a few days.

Wisehammer looks over her shoulder.

I have the biggest part.
Wisehammer You have a beautiful hand.
Mary There is so much to copy. So many words.
Wisehammer I can write.
Mary Why don't you tell Lieutenant Clark? He's doing it.
Wisehammer No … no …I'm—
Mary Afraid?
Wisehammer Diffident.
Mary I'll tell him. Well, I won't. My friend Dabby will. She's—
Wisehammer Bold.

Pause.

Shy is not a bad word, it's soft. Mary But shame is a hard one.
Wisehammer Words with two L's are the worst. Lonely, loveless.
Mary Love is a good word.
Wisehammer That's because it only has one L. I like words with one L: Luck. Latitudinarian.

Mary laughs.

 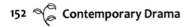

Laughter.

SCENE ELEVEN. THE FIRST REHEARSAL

Ralph Clark, Robert Sideway, John Wisehammer, Mary Brenham, Liz Morden, Dabby Bryant, Duckling Smith, Ketch Freeman.

Ralph Good afternoon, ladies and gentlemen—
Dabby We're ladies now. Wait till I tell my husband I've become a lady.
Mary Sshht.
Ralph It is with pleasure that I welcome you—
Sideway Our pleasure, Mr Clark, our pleasure.
Ralph We have many days of hard word ahead of us.
Liz Work! I'm not working. I thought we was acting.
Ralph Now, let me introduce the company—
Dabby We've all met before, Lieutenant, you could say we know each other, you could say we'd know each other in the dark.
Sideway It's a theatrical custom, the company is formally introduced to each other, Mrs Bryant.
Dabby Mrs Bryant? Who's Mrs Bryant?
Sideway It's the theatrical form of address. Madam. You may call me Mr Sideway.
Ralph If I may proceed—
Ketch Shhh! You're interrupting the director.
Dabby So we are, Mr Hangman.

The women all hiss and spit at Ketch.

Ralph The ladies first: Mary Brenham who is to play Silvia. Liz Morden who is to play Melinda. Duckling Smith who is to play Lucy, Melinda's maid.
Duckling I'm not playing Liz Morden's maid.
Ralph Why not?
Duckling I live with an officer. He wouldn't like it.
Dabby Just because she lives chained up in that old toss pot's garden.
Duckling Don't you dare talk of my Harry—
Ralph You're not playing Morden's maid, Smith, you're playing Melinda's. And Dabby Bryant, who is to play Rose, a country girl.

Dabby From Devon.
Duckling (*to Dabby*) Screw jaws!
Dabby (*to Duckling*) Salt bitch!
Ralph That's the ladies. Now, Captain Plume will be played by Henry Kable.

    He looks around.

Who seems to be late. That's odd. I saw him an hour ago and he said he was going to your hut to learn some lines, Wisehammer?

    Wisehammer is silent.

Sergeant Kite is to be played by John Arscott, who did send a message to say he would be kept at work an extra hour.
Dabby An hour! You won't see him in an hour!
Liz (*under her breath*) You're not the only one with new wrinkles in your arse, Dabby Bryant.
Ralph Mr Worthy will be played by Mr Sideway.

    Sideway takes a vast bow.

Sideway I'm here.
Ralph Justice Balance by James Freeman.
Duckling No way I'm doing a play with a hangman. The words would stick in my throat.

    More hisses and spitting. Ketch shrinks.

Ralph You don't have any scenes with him, Smith. Now if I could finish the introductions. Captain Brazen is to be played by John Wisehammer.
    The small parts are still to be cast. Now. We can't do the first scene until John Arscott appears.
Dabby There won't be a first scene.
Ralph Bryant, will you be quiet please! The second scene. Wisehammer, you could read Plume.

    Wisehammer comes forward eagerly.

No, I'll read Plume myself. So, Act One, Scene Two, Captain Plume and Mr Worthy.

Sideway That's me. I'm at your command.

Ralph The rest of you can watch and wait for your scenes. Perhaps we should begin by reading it.

Sideway No need, Mr Clark. I know it.

Ralph Ah, I'm afraid I shall have to read Captain Plume.

Sideway I know that part too. Would you like me to do both?

Ralph I think it's better if I do it. Shall we begin? Kite, that's John Arscott, has just left—

Dabby Running.

Ralph Bryant! I'll read the line before Worthy's entrance: 'None at present. 'Tis indeed the picture of Worthy, but the life's departed.' Sideway? Where's he gone?

Sideway has scuttled off. He shouts from the wings.

Sideway I'm preparing my entrance, Mr Clark, I won't be a minute. Could you read the line again, slowly?

Ralph 'Tis indeed the picture of Worthy, but the life's departed. What, arms-a-cross. Worthy!'

Sideway comes on, walking sideways, arms held up in a grandiose eighteenth-century theatrical pose. He suddenly stops.

Sideway Ah, yes, I forgot. Arms-a-cross. I shall have to start again.

He goes off again and shouts.

Could you read the line again louder please?

Ralph 'What, arms-a-cross, Worthy!'

Sideway rushes on.

Sideway My wiper! Someone's buzzed my wiper! There's a wipe drawer in this crew, Mr Clark.

Ralph What's the matter?

Sideway There's a pickpocket in the company.

Dabby Talk of the pot calling the kettle black.

Sideway stalks around the company threateningly.

Sideway My handkerchief. Who prigged my handkerchief?

Ralph I'm sure it will turn up, Sideway, let's go on.

Sideway I can't do my entrance without my handkerchief. (*furious*) I've been practising it all night. If I get my mittens on the rum diver I'll—

He lunges at Liz, who fights back viciously. They jump apart, each taking threatening poses and Ralph intervenes with speed.

Ralph Let's assume Worthy has already entered, Sideway. Now, I say: 'What arms-a-cross, Worthy! Methinks you should hold 'em open when a friend's so near. I must expel this melancholy spirit.'

Sideway has dropped to his knees and is sobbing in a pose of total sorrow.

What are you doing down there, Sideway?

Sideway I'm being melancholy. I saw Mr Garrick being melancholy once. That is what he did. *Hamlet* it was.

He stretches his arms to the ground and begins to repeat.

'Oh that this too, too solid flesh would melt. Oh that this too too solid flesh would melt. Oh that this too too—'

Ralph This is a comedy. It is perhaps a little lighter. Try simply to stand normally and look melancholy. I'll say the line again. (*Sideway is still sobbing.*) The audience won't hear Captain Plume's lines if your sobs are so loud, Sideway.

Sideway I'm still establishing my melancholy.

Ralph A comedy needs to move quite fast. In fact, I think we'll cut that line and the two verses that follow and go straight to Worthy greeting Plume.

Wisehammer I like the word melancholy.

Sideway A greeting. Yes. A greeting looks like this.

He extends his arms high and wide.

'Plume!' Now I'll change to say the next words. 'My dear Captain', that's affection isn't it? If I put my hands on my heart, like this. Now, 'Welcome'. I'm not quite sure how to do 'Welcome'.

Ralph I think if you just say the line.

Sideway Quite. Now.

He feels Ralph.

Ralph Sideway! What are you doing?

Sideway I'm checking that you're safe and sound returned. That's what the line says: 'Safe and sound returned.'

Ralph You don't need to touch him. You can see that!

Sideway Yes, yes. I'll check his different parts with my eyes. Now, I'll put it all together, 'Plume! My dear Captain, welcome. Safe and sound returned!'

He does this with appropriate gestures.

Ralph Sideway—it's a very good attempt. It's very theatrical. But you could try to be a little more—euh—natural.

Sideway Natural! On the stage! But Mr Clark!

Ralph People must —euh—believe you. Garrick after all is admired for his naturalness.

Sideway Of course. I thought I was being Garrick—but never mind. Natural. Quite. You're the director, Mr Clark.

Ralph Perhaps you could look at me while you're saying the lines.

Sideway But the audience won't see my face.

Ralph The lines are said to Captain Plume. Let's move on. Plume says: 'I 'scaped safe from Germany', shall we say—America? It will make it more contemporary—

Wisehammer You can't change the words of the playwright.

Ralph Mm, well, 'and sound, I hope, from London: you see I have—'

Black Caesar *rushes on.*

Ralph Caesar, we're rehearsing—would you—

Caesar I see that well, Monsieur Lieutenant. I see it is a piece of theatre, I have seen many pieces of theatre in my beautiful island of Madagascar so I have decided to play in your piece of theatre.

Ralph There's no part for you.

Caesar There is always a part for Caesar.

Sideway All the parts have been taken.

Caesar I will play his servant.

He stands next to Sideway.

Ralph Farquhar hasn't written a servant for Worthy.
Duckling He can have my part. I want to play something else.
Caesar There is always a black servant in a play, Monsieur Lieutenant. And Caesar is that servant. So, now I stand here just behind him and I will be his servant.
Ralph There are no lines for it, Caesar.
Caesar I speak in French. That makes him a more high up gentleman if he has a French servant, and that is good. Now he gets the lady with the black servant. Very chic.
Ralph I'll think about it. Actually, I would like to rehearse the ladies now. They have been waiting patiently and we don't have much time left. Freeman, would you go and see what's happened to Arscott. Sideway, we'll come back to this scene another time, but that was very good, very good. A little, a little euh, but very good.

Sideway bows out, followed by Caesar.

Now we will rehearse the first scene between Melinda and Silvia. Morden and Brenham, if you would come and stand here. Now the scene is set in Melinda's apartments. Silvia is already there. So, if you stand here, Morden. Brenham, you stand facing her.
Liz (*very, very fast*) 'Welcome to town cousin Silvia I envied you your retreat in the country for Shrewsbury methinks and all your heads of shires are the most irregular places for living—'
Ralph Euh, Morden—
Liz Wait, I haven't finished yet. 'Here we have smoke noise scandal affectation and pretension in short everything to give the spleen and nothing to divert it then the air is intolerable—'
Ralph Morden, you know the lines very well.
Liz Thank you, Lieutenant Clark.
Ralph But you might want to try and act them.

Pause.

Let's look at the scene.

Liz looks.

You're a rich lady. You're at home. Now a rich lady would stand in a certain way. Try to stand like a rich lady. Try to look at Silvia with a certain assurance.

Liz Assurance.

Wisehammer Confidence.

Ralph Like this. You've seen rich ladies, haven't you?

Liz I robbed a few.

Ralph How did they behave?

Liz They screamed.

Ralph I mean before you—euh—robbed them.

Liz I don't know. I was watching their purses.

Ralph Have you ever seen a lady in her own house?

Liz I used to climb into the big houses when I was a girl, and just stand there, looking. I didn't take anything. I just stood. Like this.

Ralph But if it was your own house, you would think it was normal to live like that.

Wisehammer It's not normal. It's not normal when others have nothing.

Ralph When acting, you have to imagine things. You have to imagine you're someone different. So, now, think of a rich lady and imagine you're her.

Liz begins to masticate.

What are you doing?

Liz If I was rich I'd eat myself sick.

Dabby Me too, potatoes.

The convicts speak quickly and over each other.

Sideway Roast beef and Yorkshire pudding.

Caesar Hearts of palm.

Wisehammer Four fried eggs, six fried eggs, eight fried eggs.

Liz Eels, oysters—

Ralph Could we get on with the scene, please? Brenham, it's your turn to speak.

Mary 'Oh, Madam, I have heard the town commended for its air.'

Liz 'But you don't consider Silvia how long I have lived in't!'

Ralph (*to Liz*) I believe you would look at her.

Liz She didn't look at me.

Ralph Didn't she? She will now.

Liz 'For I can assure you that to a lady the least nice in her constitution no air can be good above half a year change of air I take to be the most agreeable of any variety in life.'

Mary 'But prithee, my dear Melinda, don't put on such an air to me.'

Ralph Excellent, Brenham. You could be a little more sharp on the 'don't'.

Mary 'Don't.' (*Mary now tries a few gestures.*) 'Your education and mine were just the same, and I remember the time when we never troubled our heads about air, but when the sharp air from the Welsh mountains made our noses drop in a cold morning at the boarding-school.'

Ralph Good! Good! Morden?

Liz 'Our education cousin was the same but our temperaments had nothing alike.'

Ralph That's a little better, Morden, but you needn't be quite so angry with her. Now go on Brenham.

Liz I haven't finished my speech!

Ralph You're right, Morden, please excuse me.

Liz (*embarrassed*) No, no, there's no need for that, Lieutenant. I only meant—I don't have to.

Ralph Please do.

Liz 'You have the constitution of a horse.'

Ralph Much better, Morden. But you must always remember you're a lady. What can we do to help you? Lucy.

Dabby That's you, Duckling.

Ralph See that little piece of wood over there? Take it to Melinda. That will be your fan.

Ducking I'm not fetching nothing for Liz.

Ralph She's not Morden, she's Melinda, your mistress. You're her servant, Lucy. In fact, you should be in this scene. Now take her that fan.

Duckling (*gives the wood to Liz*) Here.

Liz Thank you, Lucy, I do much appreciate your effort.

Ralph No, you would nod your head.

Wisehammer Don't add any words to the play.

Ralph Now, Lucy, stand behind Morden.

Duckling What do I say?

Ralph Nothing.

Duckling How will they know I'm here? Why does she get all the lines? Why can't I have some of hers?

Ralph Brenham, it's your speech.

Mary 'So far as to be troubled with neither spleen, colic, nor vapours—

The convicts slink away and sink down, trying to make themselves invisible as Major Ross, followed by Captain Campbell, come on.

'I need no salt for my stomach, no—'

She sees the officers herself and folds in with the rest of the convicts.

Ralph Major Ross, Captain Campbell, I'm rehearsing.

Ross Rehearsing! Rehearsing!

Campbell Tssaach. Rehearsing.

Ross Lieutenant Clark is rehearsing. Lieutenant Clark asked us to give the prisoners two hours so he could rehearse, but what has he done with them? What?

Campbell Eeh. Other things, eh.

Ross Where are the prisoners Kable and Arscott, Lieutenant.

Campbell Eh?

Ralph They seem to be late.

Ross While you were rehearsing, Arscott and Kable slipped into the woods with three others, so five men have run away and it's all because of your damned play and your so-called thespists. And not only have your thespists run away, they've stolen food from the stores for their renegade escapade, that's what your play has done.

Ralph I don't see that the play—

Ross I said it from the beginning. The play will bring down calamity on this colony.

Ralph I don't see—

Ross The devil, Lieutenant, always comes through the mind, here, worms its way, idleness and words.

Ralph Major Ross, I can't agree—

Ross Listen to me, my lad, you're a Second Lieutenant and you don't agree or disagree with Major Ross.

Campbell No discipline, tcchhha.

Ross looks over the convicts.

Ross Caesar! He started going with them and came back.

Ralph That's all right, he's not in the play.

Caesar Yes I am, please Lieutenant, I am a servant.

Ross John Wisehammer!

Wisehammer I had nothing to do with it!

Ross You're Jewish, aren't you? You're guilty. Kable was last seen near Wisehammer's hut. Liz Morden! She was observed next to the colony's stores late last night in the company of Kable who was supposed to be repairing the door. (*to Liz*) Liz Morden, you will be tried for stealing from the stores. You know the punishment? Death by hanging. (*Pause.*) And now you may continue to rehearse, Lieutenant.

Ross goes. Campbell lingers, looking at the book.

Campbell Ouusstta. *The Recruiting Officer.* Good title. Arara. But a play, tss, a play.

He goes. Ralph and the convicts are left in the shambles of their rehearsal. A silence.

ACT TWO

SCENE ONE. VISITING HOURS

Liz, Wisehammer, Arscott, Caesar all in chains. Arscott is bent over, facing away.

Liz Luck? Don't know the word. Shifts its bob when I comes near. Born under a ha'penny planet I was. Dad's a nibbler, don't want to get crapped. Mum leaves. Five brothers, I'm the only titter. I takes in washing. Then. My own father. Lady's walking down the street, he takes her wiper. She screams, he's shoulder-clapped, it's not me, Sir, it's Lizzie, look, she took it. I'm stripped, beaten in the street, everyone watching. That night, I take my dad's cudgel and try to kill him. I prig all his clothes and go to my older brother. He don't want me. Liz he says, why trine for a make, when you can wap for a winne? I'm no dimber mort, I says. Don't ask you to be a swell mollisher, Sister, men want Miss Laycock, don't look at your mug. So I begin to sell my mother of saints. I thinks I'm in luck when I meet the swell cove. He's a bobcull: sports a different wiper every day of the week. He says to me, it's not enough to sell your mossie face, Lizzie, it don't bring no shiners no more. Shows me how to spice the swells. So Swell has me up the wall, flashes a pocket watch, I lifts it. But one time, I stir my stumps too slow, the swell squeaks beef, the snoozie hears. I'm nibbed. It's up the ladder to rest, I thinks when I goes up before the fortune teller, but no, the judge's a bobcull, I nap the King's pardon and it's seven years across the herring pond. Jesus Christ the hunger on the ship, sailors won't touch me: no rantum scantum, no food. But here, the Governor says, new life. You could nob it here, Lizzie, I thinks, bobcull Gov, this niffynaffy play, not too much work, good crew of rufflers, Kable, Arscott, but no, Ross don't like my mug, I'm nibbed again and now it's up the ladder to rest for good. Well. Lizzie Morden's life. And you, Wisehammer, how did you get here?

Wisehammer Betrayal. Barbarous falsehood. Intimidation. Injustice.

Liz Speak in English, Wisehammer.

Wisehammer I am innocent. I didn't do it and I'll keep saying I didn't.

Liz It doesn't matter what you say. If they say you're a thief, you're a thief.

Wisehammer I am not a thief. I'll go back to England to the snuff shop of Rickett and Loads and say, see, I'm back, I'm innocent.

Liz They won't listen.

Wisehammer You can't live if you think that way.

Pause.

I'm sorry. Seven years and I'll go back.

Liz What do you want to go back to England for? You're not English.

Wisehammer I was born in England. I'm English. What do I have to do to make people believe I'm English?

Liz You have to think English. I hate England. But I think English. And him, Arscott, he's not said anything since they brought him in but he's thinking English, I can tell.

Caesar I don't want to think English. If I think English I will die. I want to go back to Madagascar and think Malagasy. I want to die in Madagascar and join my ancestors.

Liz It doesn't matter where you die when you're dead.

Caesar If I die here, I will have no spirit. I want to go home. I will escape again.

Arscott There's no escape!

Caesar This time I lost my courage, but next time I ask my ancestors and they will help me escape!

Arscott (*shouts*) There's no escape!

Liz See. That's English. You know things.

Caesar My ancestors will know the way.

Arscott There's no escape I tell you.

Pause.

You go in circles out there, that's all you do. You go out there and you walk and walk and you don't reach China. You come back on your steps if the savages don't get you first. Even a compass doesn't work in this foreign upside-down desert. Here. You can read. Why didn't it work? What does it say?

He hands Wisehammer a carefully folded, wrinkled piece of paper.

Wisehammer It says north.
Arscott Why didn't it work then? It was supposed to take us north of China, why did I end up going in circles?
Wisehammer Because it's not a compass.
Arscott I gave me only shilling to a sailor for it. He said it was a compass.
Wisehammer It's a piece of paper with north written on it. He lied. He deceived you, he betrayed you, he betrayed you.

Sideway, Mary and Duckling come on.

Sideway Madam, gentleman, fellow players, we have come to visit, to commiserate, to offer our humble services.
Liz Get out!
Mary Liz, we've come to rehearse the play.
Wisehammer Rehearse the play?
Duckling The Lieutenant has gone to talk to the Governor. Harry said we could come see you.
Mary The Lieutenant has asked me to stand in his place so we don't lose time. We'll start with the first scene between Melinda and Brazen.
Wisehammer How can I play Captain Brazen in chains?
Mary This is the theatre. We will believe you.
Arscott Where does Kite come in?
Sideway (*bowing to Liz*) Madam I have brought you your fan. (*He hands her the 'fan', which she takes.*)

SCENE TWO. HIS EXCELLENCY EXHORTS RALPH

Phillip, Ralph.

Phillip I hear you want to stop the play, Lieutenant.

Ralph Half of my cast is in chains, Sir.

Phillip That is a difficulty, but it can be overcome. Is that your only reason. Lieutenant?

Ralph So many people seem against it. Sir.

Phillip Are you afraid?

Ralph No, Sir, but I do not wish to displease my superior officers.

Phillip If you break conventions, it is inevitable you make enemies, Lieutenant. This play irritates them.

Ralph Yes and I—

Phillip Socrates irritated the state of Athens and was put to death for it.

Ralph Sir—

Phillip Would you have a world without Socrates?

Ralph Sir, I—

Phillip In the Meno, one of Plato's great dialogues, have you read it, Lieutenant, Socrates demonstrates that a slave boy can learn the principles of geometry as well as a gentleman.

Ralph Ah—

Phillip In other words, he shows that human beings have an intelligence which has nothing to do with the circumstances into which they are born.

Ralph Sir—

Phillip Sit down, Lieutenant. It is a matter of reminding the slave of what he knows, of his own intelligence. And by intelligence you may read goodness, talent, the innate qualities of human beings.

Ralph I see—Sir.

Phillip When he treats the slave boy as a rational human being, the boy becomes one, he loses his fear, and he becomes a competent mathematician. A little more encouragement and he might become an extraordinary mathematician. Who knows? You must see your actors in that light.

Ralph I can see some of them, Sir, but there are others ... John Arscott—

Phillip He has been given 200 lashes for trying to escape. It will take time for him to see himself as a human being again.

Ralph Liz Morden—

Phillip Liz Morden—(He *pauses*.) I had a reason for asking you to cast her as Melinda. Morden is one of the most difficult women in the colony.

Ralph She is indeed, Sir.

Phillip Lower than a slave, full of loathing, foul mouthed, desperate.

Ralph Exactly, Sir. And violent.

Phillip Quite. To be made an example of.

Ralph By hanging?

Phillip No, Lieutenant, by redemption.

Ralph The Reverend says he's given up on her, Sir.

Phillip The Reverend's an ass, Lieutenant. I am speaking of redeeming her humanity.

Ralph I am afraid there may not be much there. Sir.

Phillip How do we know what humanity lies hidden under the rags and filth of a mangled life? I have seen soldiers given up for dead, limbs torn, heads cut open, come back to life. If we treat her as a corpse, of course she will die. Try a little kindness, Lieutenant.

Ralph But will she be hanged, Sir?

Phillip I don't want a woman to be hanged. You will have to help, Ralph.

Ralph Sir!

Phillip I had retired from His Majesty's Service, Ralph. I was farming. I don't know why they asked me to rule over this colony of wretched souls, but I will fulfil my responsibility. No one will stop me.

Ralph No, Sir, but I don't see—

Phillip What is a statesman's responsibility? To ensure the rule of law. But the citizens must be taught to obey the law of their own will. I want to rule over responsible human beings, not tyrannize over a group of animals. I want there to be a contract between us, not a whip on my side, terror and hatred on theirs. And you must help me, Ralph.

Ralph Yes, Sir. The play—

Phillip Won't change much, but it is the diagram in the sand that may remind—just remind the slave boy—Do you understand?

Ralph I think so.

Phillip We may fail. I may have a mutiny on my hands. They are trying to convince the Admiralty that I am mad.

Ralph Sir!

Phillip And they will threaten you. You don't want to be a Second Lieutenant all your life.

Ralph No, Sir!

Phillip I cannot go over the head of Major Ross in the matter of promotion.

Ralph I see.

Phillip But we have embarked, Ralph, we must stay afloat. There is a more serious threat and it may capsize us all. If a ship does not come within three months, the supplies will be exhausted. In a month, I will cut the rations again. (*Pause.*) Harry is not well. Can you do something? Good luck with the play, Lieutenant. Oh, and Ralph—

Ralph Sir—

Phillip Unexpected situations are often matched b-unexpected virtues in people, are they not?

Ralph I believe they are, Sir.

Phillip A play is a world in itself, a tiny colony we could almost say.

Pause.

And you are in charge of it. That is a great responsibility.

Ralph I will lay down my life if I have to, Sir.

Phillip I don't think it will come to that, Lieutenant. You need only do your best.

Ralph Yes, Sir, I will, Sir.

Phillip Excellent.

Ralph It's a wonderful play, Sir. I wasn't sure at first, as you know, but now—

Phillip Good, Good. I shall look forward to seeing it. I'm sure it will be a success.

Ralph Thank you, Sir. Thank you.

SCENE THREE. HARRY BREWER SEES THE DEAD

Harry Brewer's tent. Harry sits, drinking rum, speaking in the different voices of his tormenting ghosts and answering in his own.

Harry Duckling! Duckling! 'She's on the beach, Harry, waiting for her young Handy Baker.' Go away, Handy, go away! 'The dead never go away, Harry. You thought you'd be the only one to dance the buttock ball with your trull, but no one owns a whore's cunt, Harry, you rent.' I didn't hang you. 'You wanted me dead.' I didn't. 'You wanted me hanged.' All right, I wanted you hanged. Go away! (*Pause.*) 'Death is horrible, Mr Brewer, it's dark, there's nothing.' Thomas Barrett! You were hanged because you stole from, the stores. 'I was seventeen, Mr Brewer.' You lived a very wicked life. 'I didn't.' That's what you said that morning, 'I have led a very wicked life.' 'I had to say something, Mr Brewer, and make sense of dying. I'd heard the Reverend say we were all wicked, but it was horrible, my body hanging, my tongue sticking out.' You shouldn't have stolen that food! 'I wanted to live, go back to England, I'd only be twenty-four. I hadn't done it much, not like you.' Duckling! 'I wish I wasn't dead, Mr Brewer I had plans. I was going to have my farm, drink with friends and feel the strong legs of a girl around me—' You shouldn't have stolen.

'Didn't you ever steal?' No! Yes. But that was different. Duckling! 'Why should you be alive after what you've done?' Duckling! Duckling!

Duckling rushes on.

Duckling What's the matter, Harry?
Harry I'm seeing them.
Duckling Who?
Harry All of them. The dead. Help me.
Duckling I've heard your screams from the beach. You're having another bad dream.
Harry No. I see them.

Pause.

Let me come inside you.
Duckling Now?
Harry Please.
Duckling Will you forget your nightmares?
Harry Yes.
Duckling Come then.
Harry Duckling …

She lies down and lifts her skirts. He begins to go down over her and stops.

What were you doing on the beach? You were with him, he told me, you were with Handy Baker.

SCENE FOUR. THE ABORIGINE MUSES ON THE NATURE OF DREAMS

The Aborigine Some dreams lose their way and wander over the earth, lost. But this is a dream no one wants. It has stayed. How can we befriend this crowded, hungry and disturbed dream?

SCENE FIVE. THE SECOND REHEARSAL

Ralph Clark, Mary Benham and Robert Sideway are waiting. Major Ross and Captain Campbell bring the three prisoners Caesar, Wisehammer and Liz Morden. They are still in chains. Ross shoves them forward.

Ross Here is some of your caterwauling cast, Lieutenant.

Ross Unchain Wisehammer and the savage, Captain Campbell. (*Points to Liz.*) She stays in chains. She's being tried tomorrow, we don't want her sloping off.

Ralph I can't rehearse with one of my players in chains, Major.

Campbell Eeh. Difficult, Mmmm.

Ross We'll tell the Governor you didn't need her and take her back to prison.

Ralph No. We shall manage. Sideway, go over the scene you rehearsed in prison with Melinda, please.

Caesar I'm in that scene too. Lieutenant.

Ralph No, you're not.

Liz and Sideway Yes he is, Lieutenant.

Sideway He's my servant.

Ralph nods.

Ralph The rest of us will go from Silvia's entrance as Wilful. Where's Arscott?

Ross We haven't finished with Arscott yet. Lieutenant.

Campbell Punishment, eeh, for escape. Fainted. Fifty-three lashes left. Heeeh.

Ross (*pointing to Caesar*) Caesar's next. After Morden's trial.

Caesar cringes.

Ralph Brenham, are you ready? Wisehammer? I'll play Captain Plume.

Ross The wee Lieutenant wants to be in the play too. He wants to be promoted to convict. We'll have you in the chain gang soon, Mr Clark, haha. (A *pause. Ross and Campbell stand, watching. The Convicts are frozen.*)

Ralph Major, we will rehearse now.

Pause. No one moves.

We wish to rehearse.

Ross No one's stopping you, Lieutenant.

Silence.

Ralph Major, rehearsals need to take place in the utmost euh—privacy, secrecy you might say. The actors are not yet ready to be seen by the public.

Ross Not ready to be seen?

Ralph Major, there is a modesty attached to the process of creation which must be respected.

Ross Modesty? Modesty! Sideway, come here.

Ralph Major, Sideway—stay—

Ross Lieutenant. I would not try to countermand the orders of a superior officer.

Campbell Obedience. Ehh, first euh, rule.

Ross Sideway.

Sideway comes up to Ross.

Take your shirt off.

Sideway obeys Ross turns him and shows his scarred back to the company.

One hundred lashes on the *Sirius* for answering an officer. Remember, Sideway? Three hundred lashes for trying to strike the same officer.

I have seen the white of this animal's bones, his wretched blood and reeky convict urine have spilled on my boots and he's feeling modest? Are you feeling modest, Sideway?

He shoves Sideway aside.

Modesty.
  Bryant. Here.

Dabby comes forward.

On all fours.

Dabby goes down on all fours.

Now wag your tail and bark, and I'll throw you a biscuit. What? You've forgotten? Isn't that how you begged for your food on the ship? Wag your tail, Bryant, bark! We'll wait.

Brenham.

Mary comes forward.

Where's your tattoo, Brenham? Show us. I can't see it. Show us.

Mary tries to obey, lifting her skirt a little.

If you can't manage. I'll help you. (*Mary lifts her skirt a little higher.*) I can't see it.

But Sideway turns to Liz and starts acting, boldly, across the room, across everyone.

Sideway 'What pleasures I may receive abroad are indeed uncertain; but this I am sure of, I shall meet with less cruelty among the most barbarous nations than I have found at home.'

Liz 'Come, Sir, you and I have been jangling a great while; I fancy if we made up our accounts, we should the sooner come to an agreement.'

Sideway 'Sure, Madam, you won't dispute your being in my debt—my fears, sighs, vows, promises, assiduities, anxieties, jealousies, have run for a whole year, without any payment.'

Campbell Mmhem, good, that. Sighs, vows, promises, hehem, mmm. Anxieties.

Ross Captain Campbell, start Arscott's punishment. *Campbell goes.*

Liz 'A year! Oh Mr Worthy, what you owe to me is not to be paid under a seven years' servitude. How did you use me the year before—'

The shouts of Arscott are heard.

'How did you use me the year before—'

She loses her lines. Sideway tries to prompt her.

Sideway 'When taking advantage—'

Liz 'When taking the advantage of my innocence and necessity—'

But she stops and drops down, defeated. Silence, except for the beating and Arscott's cries.

SCENE SIX. THE SCIENCE OF HANGING

Harry, Ketch Freeman, Liz, sitting, staring straight ahead of her.

Ketch I don't want to do this.
Harry Get on with it, Freeman.
Ketch (*to Liz*) I have to measure you.

> *Pause.*

I'm sorry.

> *Liz doesn't move.*

You'll have to stand, Liz.

> *Liz doesn't move.*

Please.

> *Pause.*

I won't hurt you. I mean, now. And if I have the measurements right, I can make it quick. Very quick. Please.

> *Liz doesn't move.*

She doesn't want to get up, Mr Brewer. I could come back later.
Harry Hurry up.
Ketch I can't. I can't measure her unless she gets up. I have to measure her to judge the drop. If the rope's too short, it won't hang her and if the rope is too long, it could pull her head off. It's very difficult, Mr Brewer, I've always done my best.

> *Pause.*

But I've never hung a woman.

Harry (*in Tom Barrett's voice*) 'You've hung a boy.' (*to Ketch*) You've hung a boy.

Ketch That was a terrible mess, Mr Brewer, don't you remember. It took twenty minutes and even then he wasn't dead. Remember how he danced and everyone laughed. I don't want to repeat something like that, Mr Brewer, not now. Someone had to get hold of his legs to weigh him down and then—

Harry Measure her, Freeman!

Ketch Yes, Sir. Could you tell her to get up. She'll listen to you.

Harry (*shouts*) Get up you bitch.

Liz doesn't move.

Get up!

He seizes her and makes her stand.

Now measure her!

Ketch (*measuring the neck, etc., of Liz*) The Lieutenant is talking to the Governor again, Liz, maybe he'll change his mind. At least he might wait until we've done the play.

Pause.

I don't want to do this.

I know, you're thinking in my place you wouldn't. But somebody will do it, if I don't, and I'll be gentle. I won't hurt you.

Liz doesn't move, doesn't look at him.

It's wrong, Mr Brewer. It's wrong.

Harry (*in Tom Barrett's voice*) 'It's wrong. Death is horrible.' (*in his own voice to Ketch*) There's no food left in the colony and she steals it and gives it to Kable to run away.

Ketch That's true, Liz, you shouldn't have stolen that food. Especially when the Lieutenant trusted us. That was wrong, Liz. Actors can't behave like normal people, not even like normal criminals. Still, I'm sorry. I'll do my best.

Harry 'I had plans.' (*to Ketch*) Are you finished?

Ketch Yes, yes. I have all the measurements I need. No, one more. I need to lift her. You don't mind, do you, Liz?

He lifts her.

She's so light. I'll have to use a very long rope. The fig tree would be better, it's higher. When will they build me some gallows, Mr Brewer? Nobody will laugh at you, Liz, you won't be ashamed, I'll make sure of that.

Harry 'You could hang yourself.' Come on, Freeman. Let's go.

Ketch Goodbye, Liz. You were a very good Melinda. No one will be as good as you.

They begin to go.

Liz Mr Brewer.

Harry 'You wanted me dead.' I didn't. You shouldn't've stolen that food!

Ketch Speak to her, please, Mr Brewer.

Harry What?

Liz Tell Lieutenant Clark I didn't steal the food. Tell him—afterwards. I want him to know.

Harry Why didn't you say that before? Why are you lying now?

Liz Tell the Lieutenant.

Harry 'Another victim of yours, another body. I was so frightened, so alone.'

Ketch Mr Brewer.

Harry 'It's dark. There's nothing.' Get away, get away!

Liz Please tell the Lieutenant.

Harry 'First fear, then a pain at the back of the neck. Then nothing.' I can't see. It's dark. It's dark.

Harry screams and falls.

SCENE SEVEN. THE MEANING OF PLAYS

The Aborigine Ghosts in a multitude have spilled from the dream. Who are they? A swarm of ancestors comes through unmended cracks in the sky? But why? What do they need? If we can satisfy them, they will go back. How can we satisfy them?

Mary, Ralph, Dabby, Wisehammer, Arscott. Mary and Ralph are rehearsing. The others are watching.

Ralph 'For I swear, Madam, by the honour of my profession, that whatever dangers I went upon, it was with the hope of making myself more worthy of your esteem, and if I ever had thoughts of preserving my life, 'twas for the pleasure of dying at your feet.'

Mary 'Well, well, you shall die at my feet, or where you will; but you know, Sir, there is a certain will and testament to be made beforehand.'

I don't understand why Silvia has asked Plume to make a will.

Dabby It's a proof of his love, he wants to provide for her.

Mary A will is a proof of love?

Wisehammer No. She's using will in another sense. He must show his willingness to marry her. Dying is used in another sense, too.

Ralph He gives her his will to indicate that he intends to take care of her.

Dabby That's right, Lieutenant, marriage is nothing, but will you look after her?

Wisehammer Plume is too ambitious to marry Silvia.

Mary If I had been Silvia, I would have trusted Plume.

Dabby When dealing with men, always have a contract.

Mary Love is a contract.

Dabby Love is the barter of perishable goods. A man's word for a woman's body.

Wisehammer Dabby is right. If a man loves a woman, he should marry her.

Ralph Sometimes he can't.

Wisehammer Then she should look for someone who can.

Dabby A woman should look after her own interests, that's all.

Mary Her interest is to love.

Dabby A girl will love the first man who knows how to open her legs. She's called a whore and ends up here. I could write scenes, Lieutenant, women with real lives, not these Shrewsbury prudes.

Wisehammer I've written something. The prologue of this play won't make any sense to the convicts: 'In ancient times, when Helen's fatal charms' and so on. I've written another one. Will you look at it, Lieutenant?

Ralph does so and Wisehammer takes Mary aside.

You mustn't trust the wrong people, Mary. We could make a new life together, here. I would marry you, Mary, think about it, you would live with me, in a house. He'll have to put you in a hut at the bottom of his garden and call you his servant in public, that is, his whore. Don't do it, Mary.

Dabby Lieutenant, are we rehearsing or not? Arscott and I have been waiting for hours.

Ralph It seems interesting. I'll read it more carefully later.

Wisehammer You don't like it.

Ralph I do like it. Perhaps it needs a little more work. It's not Farquhar.

Wisehammer It would mean more to the convicts.

Ralph We'll talk about it another time.

Wisehammer Do you think it should be longer?

Ralph I'll think about it.

Wisehammer Shorter? Do you like the last two lines? Mary helped me with them.

Ralph Ah.

Wisehammer The first lines took us days, didn't they, Mary?

Ralph We'll rehearse Silvia's entrance as Jack Wilful. You're in the scene, Wisehammer. We'll come to your scenes in a minute, Bryant. Now, Brenham, remember what I showed you yesterday about walking like a gentleman? I've ordered breeches to be made for you, you can practise in them tomorrow.

Mary I'll tuck my skirt in. (*She does so and takes a masculine pose.*) 'Save ye, save ye, gentlemen.'

Wisehammer 'My dear, I'm yours.'

He kisses her.

Ralph (*angrily*) It doesn't say Silvia is kissed in the stage directions!

Wisehammer Plume kisses her later and there's the line about men kissing in the army. I thought Brazen would kiss her immediately.

Ralph It's completely wrong.

Wisehammer It's right for the character of Brazen.

Ralph No it isn't. I'm the director, Wisehammer.

Wisehammer Yes, but I have to play the part. They're equal in this scene. They're both captains and in the end fight for her. Who's playing Plume in our performance?

Ralph I will have to, as Kable hasn't come back. It's your line.

Wisehammer Will I be given a sword?

Ralph I doubt it. Let's move on to Kit's entrance, Arscott has been waiting too long.

Arscott 'Sir, if you please—'

Ralph Excellent, Arscott, but we should give you our last lines so you'll know when to come in. Wisehammer.

Wisehammer 'The fellow dare not fight.'

Ralph That's when you come in.

Arscott 'Sir, if you please—'

Dabby What about me? I haven't done anything either. You always rehearse the scenes with Silvia.

Ralph Let's rehearse the scene where Rose comes on with her brother Bullock. It's a better scene for you Arscott. Do you know it?

Arscott Yes.

Ralph Good. Wisehammer, you'll have to play the part of Bullock.

Wisehammer What? Play two parts?

Ralph Major Ross won't let any more prisoners off work. Some of you will have to play several parts.

Wisehammer It'll confuse the audience. They'll think Brazen is Bullock and Bullock Brazen.

Ralph Nonsense, if the audience is paying attention, they'll know that Bullock is a country boy and Brazen a captain.

Wisehammer What if they aren't paying attention?

Ralph People who can't pay attention should not go to the theatre.

Mary If you act well, they will have to pay attention.

Wisehammer It will ruin my entrance as Captain Brazen.

Ralph We have no choice and we must turn this necessity into an advantage. You will play two different characters and display the full range of your abilities.

Wisehammer Our audience won't be that discerning.

Ralph Their imagination will be challenged and trained. Let's start the scene. Bryant?

Dabby I think *The Recruiting Officer* is a silly play. I want to be in a play that has more interesting people in it.

Mary I like playing Silvia. She's bold, she breaks rules out of love for her Captain and she's not ashamed.

Dabby She hasn't been born poor, she hasn't had to survive, and her father's a Justice of the Peace. I want to play myself.

Arscott I don't want to play myself. When I say Kite's lines I forget everything else. I forgot the judge said I'm going to have to spend the rest of my natural life in this place getting beaten and working like a slave. I can forget that out there it's trees and burnt grass, spiders that kill you in four hours and snakes. I don't have to think about what happened to Kable, I don't have to remember the things I've done, when I speak Kite's lines I don't hate any more. I'm Kite. I'm in Shrewsbury. Can we get on with the scene, Lieutenant, and stop talking?

Dabby I want to see a play that shows life as we know it.

Wisehammer A play should make you understand something new. If it tells you what you already know, you leave it as ignorant as you went in.

Dabby Why can't we do a play about now?

Wisehammer It doesn't matter when a play is set. It's better if it's set in the past, it's clearer. It's easier to understand Plume and Brazen than some of the officers we know here.

Ralph Arscott, would you start the scene?

Arscott 'Captain, Sir, look yonder, a-coming this way, 'tis the prettiest, cleanest, little tit.'

Ralph Now Worthy—He's in this scene. Where's Sideway?

Mary He's so upset about Liz he won't rehearse.

Ralph I am going to talk to the Governor, but he has to rehearse. We must do the play, whatever happens. We've been rehearsing for five months! Let's go on. 'Here she comes, and what is that great country fellow with her?'

Arscott 'I can't tell, Sir.'

Wisehammer I'm not a great country fellow.

Ralph Act it, Wisehammer.

Dabby 'Buy chickens, young and tender, young and tender chickens?' This is a very stupid line and I'm not saying it.

Ralph It's written by the playwright and you have to say it. 'Here, you chickens!'

Dabby 'Who calls?'

Ralph Bryant, you're playing a pretty country wench who wants to entice the Captain. You have to say these lines with charm and euh—blushes.

Dabby I don't blush.

Ralph I can't do this scene without Sideway. Let's do another scene.

Pause.

Arscott, let's work on your big speeches. I haven't heard them yet. I still need Sideway. This is irresponsible, he wanted the part. Somebody go and get Sideway.

No one moves.

Arscott I'll do the first speech anyway, Sir. 'Yes, Sir, I understand my business, I will say it; you must know, Sir, I was born a gypsy, and bred among the crew till I was ten years old, there I learned canting and lying—'

Dabby That's about me!

Arscott 'I was bought from my mother Cleopatra by a certain nobleman, for three guineas, who liking my beauty made me his page—'

Dabby That's my story. Why do I have to play a silly milkmaid? Why can't I play Kite?

Mary You can't play a man, Dabby.

Dabby You're playing a man: Jack Wilful.

Mary Yes, but in the play, I know I'm a woman, whereas if you played Kite, you would have to think you were a man.

Dabby If Wisehammer can think he's a big country lad, I can think I'm a man. People will use their imagination and people with no imagination shouldn't go to the theatre.

Ralph Bryant, you're muddling everything.

Dabby No. I see things very clearly and I'm making you see clearly, Lieutenant. I want to play Kite.

Arscott You can't play Kite! I'm playing Kite! You can't steal my part!

Ralph You may have to play Melinda.

Dabby All she does is marry Sideway, that's not interesting.

Dabby stomps off. Ketch comes on.

Ketch I'm sorry I'm late, Lieutenant, but I know all my lines.

Ralph We'll rehearse the first scene between Justice Balance and Silvia. Brenham.

Arscott stomps off.

Mary 'Whilst there is life there is hope, Sir; perhaps my brother may recover.'

Ketch 'We have but little reason to expect it—'

Mary I can't. Not with him. Not with Liz—I can't. *She runs off.*

Ralph One has to transcend personal feelings in the theatre.

Wisehammer runs after Mary.

(*to Ketch*) We're not making much progress today, let's end this rehearsal.

He goes. Ketch is left alone, bewildered.

SCENE EIGHT. DUCKLING MAKES VOWS

Night. Harry, ill. Duckling.

Duckling If you live, I will never again punish you with my silence. If you live, I will never again turn away from you. If you live, I will never again imagine another man when you make love to me. If you live, I will never tell you I want to leave you. If you live, I will speak to you. If you live, I will be tender with you. If you live, I will look after you. If you live, I will stay with you. If you live, I will be wet and open to your touch. If you live, I will answer all your questions. If you live, I will look after you. If you live, I will love you.

Pause.

If you die, I will never forgive you.

She leans over him. Listens. Touches. Harry is dead.

I hate you.
  No. I love you.

She crouches into a foetal position, cries out. How could you do this?

SCENE NINE. A LOVE SCENE

The beach. Night. Mary, then Ralph.

Mary (*to herself*) 'Captain Plume, I despise your listing-money; if I do serve, 'tis purely for love—of that wench I mean. For you must know', etc. —
  'So you only want an opportunity for accomplishing your designs upon her?'
  'Well, Sir, I'm satisfied as to the point in debate; but now let me beg you to lay aside your recruiting airs, put on the man of honour, and tell me plainly what usage I must expect when I'm under your command.'

She tries that again, with a stronger and lower voice. Ralph comes on, sees her. She sees him, but continues.

'And something tells me, that if you do discharge me 'twill be the greatest punishment you can inflict; for were we this moment to go upon the greatest dangers in your profession, they would be less terrible to me than to stay behind you. And now your hand—this lists me—and now you are my Captain.'
Ralph (*as Plume*) 'Your friend.' (*Kisses her.*) ''Sdeath! There's something in this fellow that charms me.'

Mary 'One favour I must beg—this affair will make some noise—'
Ralph Silvia—

He kisses her again.

Mary 'I must therefore take care to be impressed by the Act of Parliament—'
Ralph 'What you please as to that. Will you lodge at my quarters in the meantime? You shall have part of my bed.' Silvia. Mary.
Mary Am I doing it well? It's difficult to play a man. It's not the walk, it's the way you hold your head. A man doesn't bow his head so much and never at an angle. I must face you without lowering my head, Let's try it again.
Ralph 'What you please as to that. —Will you lodge at my quarters in the meantime? You shall have part of my bed.' Mary!

She holds her head straight. Pause.

Will you?

Pause.

Mary Yes.

They kiss.

Ralph Don't lower your head. Silvia wouldn't.

She begins to undress, from the top.

I've never looked at the body of a woman before.
Mary Your wife?
Ralph It wasn't right to look at her. Let me see you.
Mary Yes.
Let me see you.
Ralph Yes.

He begins to undress himself.

SCENE TEN. THE QUESTION OF LIZ

Ralph, Ross, Phillip, Collins, Campbell.

Collins She refused to defend herself at the trial. She didn't say a word. This was taken as an admission of guilt and she was condemned to be hanged. The evidence against her, however, is flimsy.

Ross She was seen with Kable next to the food stores. That is a fingering fact.

Collins She was seen by a drunken sailor in the dark. He admitted he was drunk and that he saw her at a distance. He knew Kable was supposed to be repairing the door and she's known to be friends with Kable and Arscott. She won't speak, she won't say where she was. That is our difficulty.

Ross She won't speak because she's guilty.

Phillip Silence has many causes, Robbie.

Ralph She won't speak, Your Excellency, because of the convict code of honour. She doesn't want to beg for her life.

Ross Convict code of honour. This pluming play has muddled the muffy Lieutenant's mind.

Collins My only fear, Your Excellency, is that she may have refused to speak because she no longer believes in the process of justice. If that is so, the courts here will become travesties. I do not want that.

Phillip But if she won't speak, there is nothing more we can do. You cannot get at the truth through silence.

Ralph She spoke to Harry Brewer.

Phillip But Harry never regained consciousness before he died.

Ralph James Freeman was there and told me what she said.

Phillip Wasn't this used in the trial?

Collins Freeman's evidence wasn't very clear and as Liz Morden wouldn't confirm what he said, it was dismissed.

Ross You can't take the word of a crooked crawling hangman.

Phillip Why won't she speak?

Ross Because she's guilty.

Phillip Robbie, we may be about to hang the first woman in this colony. I do not want to hang the first innocent woman.

Ralph We must get at the truth.

Ross Truth! We have 800 thieves, perjurers, forgers, murderers, liars, escapers, rapists, whores, coiners in this scrub-ridden, dust-driven, thunder-bolted, savage-run, cretinous colony. My marines who are trained to fight are turned into ghouly gaolers, fed less than the prisoners—

Phillip The rations, Major, are the same for all, prisoners and soldiers.

Ross They have the right to more so that makes them have less. Not a ship shifting into sight, the prisoners running away, stealing, drinking and the wee ductile Lieutenant talks about the truth.

Phillip Truth is indeed a luxury, but its absence brings about the most abject poverty in a civilization. That is the paradox.

Ross This is a profligate prison for us all, it's a hellish hole we soldiers have been hauled to because they blame us for losing the war in America. This is a hateful, hary-scary, topsy-turvy outpost, this is not a civilization! I hate this possumy place.

Collins Perhaps we could return to the question of Liz Morden. (*Calls.*) Captain Campbell.

Campbell brings in Liz Morden.

Morden, if you don't speak, we will have to hang you: if you can defend yourself, His Excellency can overrule the court. We would not then risk a miscarriage of justice. But you must speak. Did you steal that food with the escaped prisoner Kable?

A silence.

Ralph She—

Collins It is the accused who must answer.

Phillip Liz Morden. You must speak the truth.

Collins We will listen to you.

Pause.

Ralph Morden. No one will despise you for telling the truth.

Phillip That is not so, Lieutenant. Tell the truth and accept the contempt. That is the history of great men. Liz, you may be despised, but you will have shown courage.

Ralph If that soldier has lied—

Ross There, there, he's accusing my soldiers of lying. It's that play, it makes fun of officers, it shows an officer lying and cheating. It shows a corrupt justice as well, Collins—

Campbell Good scene that, very funny, hah, scchhh.

Collins Et tu, Campbell?

Campbell What? Meant only. Hahah. 'If he be so good at gunning he shall have enough—he may be of use against the French, for he shoots flying,' hahaha. Good, and then there's this Constable ha—

Ross Campbell!

Phillip The play seems to be having miraculous effects already. Don't you want to be in it, Liz?

Ralph Morden, you must speak.

Collins For the good of the colony.

Phillip And of the play.

A long silence.

Liz I didn't steal the food.

Collins Were you there when Kable stole it?

Liz No. I was there before.

Ross And you knew he was going to steal it?

Liz Yes.

Ross Guilty. She didn't report it.

Collins Failure to inform is not a hangable offence.

Ross Conspiracy.

Collins We may need a retrial.

Phillip Why wouldn't you say any of this before?

Ross Because she didn't have time to invent a lie.

Collins Major, you are demeaning the process of law.

Phillip Why, Liz?

Liz Because it wouldn't have mattered.

Phillip Speaking the truth?

Liz Speaking.

Ross You are taking the word of a convict against the word of a soldier—

Collins A soldier who was drunk and uncertain of what he saw.

Ross A soldier is a soldier and has a right to respect. You will have revolt on your hands, Governor.

Phillip I'm sure I will, but let us see the play first. Liz, I hope you are good in your part.

Ralph She will be, Your Excellency, I promise that.

Liz Your Excellency, I will endeavour to speak Mr Farquhar's lines with the elegance and clarity their own worth commands.

SCENE ELEVEN. BACKSTAGE

Night. The Aborigine.

The Aborigine Look: oozing pustules on my skin, heat on my forehead. Perhaps we have been wrong all this time and this is not a dream at all.

The Actors come on. They begin to change and make up. The Aborigine drifts off.

Mary Are the savages coming to see the play as well?

Ketch They come around the camp because they're dying: smallpox.

Mary Oh.

Sideway I hope they won't upset the audience.

Mary Everyone is here. All the officers too.

Liz (*to Duckling*) Dabby could take your part.

Duckling No. I will do it. I will remember the lines.

Mary I've brought you an orange from Lieutenant Clark's island. They've thrown her out of Harry Brewer's tent.

Wisehammer Why? He wouldn't have wanted that.

Duckling Major Ross said a whore was a whore and I was to go into the women's camp. They've taken all of Harry's things.

She bursts into tears.

Mary I'll talk to the Lieutenant.

Liz Let's go over your lines. And if you forget them, touch my foot and I'll whisper them to you.

Sideway (*who has been practising on his own*) We haven't rehearsed the bow. Garrick used to take his this way: you look up to the circle, to the sides, down, make sure everyone thinks you're looking at them. Get in a line.

They do so.

Arscott I'll be in the middle. I'm the tallest.

Mary No, Arscott. (*Mary places herself in the middle.*)

Sideway Dabby, you should be next to Mary.

Dabby I won't take a bow.

Sideway It's not the biggest part, Dabby, but you'll be noticed.

Dabby I don't want to be noticed.

Sideway Let's get this right. If we don't all do the same thing, it will look a mess.

They try. Dabby is suddenly transfixed.

Dabby Hurray, hurray, hurray.

Sideway No, they will be shouting bravo, but we're not in a line yet.

Dabby I wasn't looking at the bow, I saw the whole play, and we all knew our lines, and Mary, you looked so beautiful, and after that, I saw Devon and they were shouting bravo, bravo Dabby, hurray, you've escaped, you've sailed thousands and thousands of miles on the open sea and you've come back to your Devon, bravo Dabby, bravo.

Mary When are you doing this, Dabby?

Dabby Tonight.

Mary You can't.

Dabby I'll be in the play till the end, then in the confusion, when it's over, we can slip away. The tide is up, the night will be dark, everything's ready.

Mary The Lieutenant will be blamed, I won't let you.

Dabby If you say anything to the Lieutenant, I'll refuse to act in the play.

Arscott When I say my lines, I think of nothing else. Why can't you do the same?

Dabby Because it's only for one night. I want to grow old in Devon.

Mary They'll never let us do another play, I'm telling the Lieutenant.

All No, you're not.

Dabby Please, I want to go back to Devon.

Wisehammer I don't want to go back to England now. It's too small and they don't like Jews. Here, no one has more of a right than anyone else to call you a foreigner. I want to become the first famous writer.

Mary You can't become a famous writer until you're dead.

Wisehammer You can if you're the only one.

Sideway I'm going to start a theatre company. Who wants to be in it?

Wisehammer I will write you a play about justice.

Sideway Only comedies, my boy, only comedies.

Wisehammer What about a comedy about unrequited love?

Liz I'll be in your company, Mr Sideway.

Ketch And so will I. I'll play all the parts that have dignity and gravity.

Sideway I'll hold auditions tomorrow.

Dabby Tomorrow.

Duckling Tomorrow.

 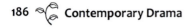

Mary Tomorrow.

Liz Tomorrow.

A silence. (Un ange passe.)

Mary Where are my shoes?

Ralph comes in.

Ralph Arscott, remember to address the soldiers when you talk of recruiting. Look at them: you are speaking to them. And don't forget, all of you, to leave a space for people to laugh.

Arscott I'll kill anyone who laughs at me.

Ralph They're not laughing at you, they're laughing at Farquhar's lines. You must expect them to laugh.

Arscott That's all right, but if I see Major Ross or any other officer laughing at me, I'll kill them.

Mary No more violence. By the way, Arscott, when you carry me off the stage as Jack Wilful, could you be a little more gentle? I don't think he'd be so rough with a young gentleman.

Ralph Where's Caesar?

Ketch I saw him walking towards the beach earlier. I thought he was practising his lines.

Arscott Caesar!

He goes out.

Wisehammer (*to Liz*) When I say 'Do you love fishing, Madam?', do you say something then? -

Ralph (*goes over to Duckling*) I am so sorry, Duckling. Harry was my friend.

Duckling I loved him. But now he'll never know that. I thought that if he knew he would become cruel.

Ralph Are you certain you don't want Dabby to take your part?

Duckling No! I will do it. I want to do it.

Pause.

He liked to hear me say my lines.

Ralph He will be watching from somewhere. (*He goes to Mary.*) How beautiful you look.

Mary I dreamt I had a necklace of pearls, and three children.

Ralph If we have a boy we will call him Harry.

Mary And if we have a girl?

Ralph She will be called Betsey Alicia.

Arscott comes in with Caesar who is drunk and dishevelled.

Arscott Lying on the beach, dead drunk.

Caesar (*to Ralph, pleading*) I can't. All these people. My ancestors are angry, they do not want me to be laughed at by all those people.

Ralph You wanted to be in this play and you will be in this play—.

Ketch I'm nervous too, but I've overcome it. You have to be brave to be an actor.

Caesar My ancestors will kill me.

He swoons. Arscott hits him.

Arscott You're going to ruin my first scene.

Caesar Please, Lieutenant, save me.

Ralph Caesar, if I were back home, I wouldn't be in this play either. My ancestors wouldn't be very pleased to see me here—But our ancestors are thousands of miles away.

Caesar I cannot be a disgrace to Madagascar.

Arscott You will be more of a disgrace if you don't come out with me on that stage. NOW.

Mary Think of us as your family.

Sideway (*to Ralph*) What do you think of this bow?

Ralph Caesar, I am your Lieutenant and I command you to go on that stage. If you don't, you will be tried and hanged for treason.

Ketch And I'll tie the rope in such a way you'll dangle there for hours full of piss and shit.

Ralph What will your ancestors think of that, Caesar?

Caesar cries but pulls himself together.

Ketch (*to Liz*) I couldn't have hanged you.

Liz No?

Ralph Dabby, have you got your chickens?

Dabby My chickens? Yes. Here.

Ralph Are you all right?

Dabby Yes. (*Pause.*) I was dreaming.

Ralph Of your future success?

Dabby Yes. Of my future success.

Ralph And so is everyone here, I hope. Now, Arscott.

Arscott Yes, Sir!

Ralph Calm.

Arscott I have been used to danger, Sir.

Sideway Here.

Liz What's that?

Sideway Salt. For good luck.

Ralph Where did you get that from?

Sideway I have been saving it from my rations. I have saved enough for each of us to have some.

They all take a little salt.

Wisehammer Lieutenant?

Ralph Yes, Wisehammer.

Wisehammer There's—There's—

Mary There's his prologue.

Ralph The prologue. I forgot.

Pause.

Let me hear it again.

Wisehammer
From distant climes o'er wide-spread seas we come,
Though not with much éclat or beat of drum,
True patriots all; for be it understood,
We left our country for our country's good;
No private views disgraced our generous zeal,
What urg'd our travels was our country's weal,
And none will doubt but that our emigration
Has prov'd most useful to the British nation.

Silence.

Ralph When Major Ross hears that, he'll have an apoplectic fit.

Mary I think it's very good.

Dabby So do I. And true.

Sideway It's very good, Wisehammer, it's very well written, but it's too—too political. It will be considered provocative.

Wisehammer You don't want me to say it.

Ralph Not tonight. We have many people against us.

Wisehammer I could tone it down. I could omit 'We left our country for our country's good.'

Dabby That's the best line.

Ralph It would be wrong to cut it.

Wisehammer I worked so hard on it.

Liz It rhymes.

Sideway We'll use it in the Sideway Theatre.

Ralph You will get much praise as Brazen, Wisehammer.

Wisehammer It isn't the same as writing.

Ralph The theatre is like a small republic, it requires private sacrifices for the good of the whole. That is something you should agree with, Wisehammer.

Pause.

And now, my actors, I want to say what a pleasure it has been to work with you. You are on your own tonight and you must do your utmost to provide the large audience out there with a pleasurable, intelligible and memorable evening.

Liz We will do our best, Mr Clark.

Mary I love this!

Ralph Arscott.

Arscott (*to Caesar*) You walk three steps ahead of me. If you stumble once, you know what will happen to you later? Move!

Ralph You're on.

Arscott is about to go on, then remembers.

Arscott Halberd! Halberd!

He is handed his halberd and goes up stage and off, preceded by Caesar beating the drum. Backstage, the remaining actors listen with trepidation to Kite's first speech.

'If any gentlemen soldiers, or others, have a mind to serve Her Majesty, and pull down the French King; if any prentices have severe masters, any children have undutiful parents; if any servants have too little wages or any husband too much wife; let them repair to the noble Sergeant Kite, at the Sign of the Raven, in this good town of Shrewsbury, and they shall receive present relief and entertainment'...

And to the triumphant music of Beethoven's Fifth Symphony and the sound of applause and laughter front the First Fleet audience, the first Australian performance of The Recruiting Officer begins.

Six Characters in Search of an Author
(1922)

By Luigi Pirandello (1867–1936)

INTRODUCTION

"I think," Luigi Pirandello once wrote, "that life is a very sad piece of buffoonery." We can hardly blame him. One of the defining experiences of his life came when his wife's loss of her family's fortune caused her to gradually lose her mind and become abusive and violent as she falsely accused Pirandello—her caretaker—of infidelity. Pirandello took from this ordeal an understanding of the subjectivity of existence: his wife's view of him, however inaccurate, was *her* reality, and no less real than his "true" self. This issue arises repeatedly in Pirandello's dramatic work, and most memorably in *Six Characters in Search of an Author*. The play begins as a piece of buffoonery. A rehearsal (of a Pirandello play, no less) is interrupted by a group of "people" who insist that their drama—as yet unwritten—be told. At the same time, the play's producer and actors think that they are being duped. However, the story ends in sadness: the drama for which the "CHARACTERS" were created is a lurid, disturbing, and violent family drama which the "professionals" of the theater are incapable of grasping, much less conveying. Ultimately the play calls into question the business of staging drama, and the very entity for which it is staged—the audience.

Much of the play's absurd humor relies on the misunderstanding between the terms "character" and "actor," as well as some pointed jabs at the business of theater itself. At first, the actors and producer have a difficult time grasping that they are confronted with SIX CHARACTERS and not SIX human beings. The CHARACTERS struggle to understand the situation they have entered. The LITTLE GIRL (all of the CHARACTERS, except for the corrupt Madame Pace, have titles instead of names) wonders what a stage is, and the

Stepdaughter tells her, "It's a place where you play at being serious." The Father accuses the producer and the actors of "making what isn't true, *seem* true … without having to … for fun." In order to give their story as much gravity as possible, the father and the stepdaughter want to play out the pivotal scene in their drama themselves and are confused by the company's insistence that the actors will play the scene from a "script" that the CHARACTERS will provide. The producer has the final say: "It's actors who do the acting here." When he witnesses the scene being played by actors, after having "played" it himself, the father complains: "I'm already beginning … I don't know how to express it … to hear my own words ringing false … as if they had another sound from the one I had meant to give them." These words impute a certain inadequacy to the theater: it is incapable, despite its claims of being "true to life," of conveying a story and leaving its truth intact.

Certainly, the idea of a fixed truth is central to the CHARACTERS' identities. In explaining the CHARACTERS' status, the father in a sense valorizes it, claiming to have a stronger sense of identity than a living person could have: "A character has a life which is truly his; marked with his own special characteristics … and as a result he is always somebody! Whilst a man … man in general … can quite well be nobody." So the CHARACTERS at least know the parameters of their existence, but they are also bound by them; the price of being "always somebody" in this sense is that the CHARACTERS can never be anyone or anything else and can never do anything other than attempt to act out the unfinished drama for which they have been created. This imprisonment is reinforced most starkly in the suffering of the Mother, which, despite having a clear motivation, has no temporal beginning or ending: "It's happening now! It happens all the time! … I am alive and I am present always." She lives in an eternal present-tense, with no concrete past or future and only a singular quality. "She is not a woman," the father reminds us. "She is a mother."

Despite these differences between the CHARACTERS and real human beings, the central crisis of the as-yet-unnamed play, the moment which the father is compelled to stage, is one that brings to mind a very human conception of identity.

"My drama," he states, "lies entirely in this one thing … in my being conscious that each one of us believes himself to be a single person. But it's not true … each one of us is many persons … many persons … according to all the possibilities of being that there are within us … with some people we are one person … with others we are somebody quite different … and all the time we are under the illusion of always being one and the same person for everybody … we believe that we are always this one person in whatever it is we may be doing. But it's not true! It's not true! And we see this very clearly when by some tragic chance we are, as it were, caught up whilst in the middle of doing something and find ourselves suspended in midair. And then we perceive that all of us was not in what we were doing, and that it would, therefore, be an atrocious injustice to us to judge us by that action alone."

Here, he claims to have a life, full of the "possibilities of being," in which his behavior, self-definition, and outward image can change from situation to situation. And because the stepdaughter has claimed the license to "judge" him based upon a moment of indiscretion, the father feels himself victimized by "an atrocious injustice." However, this is precisely the kind of judgment to which any of us might find ourselves subject. Very few people, if any, see every last action or facet of our individual lives, and so their perception of us is based upon the fragments that they *do* witness. As a result, any of us can be "mis"-read or as the father claims to be, "suspended" in the mind of another as what we appear to be at any inopportune moment.

Given the conflict of the father being fixed as a character but mutable like a person, the incredulity of the actors and producer seems valid. It is not unreasonable—given what they have seen at this rehearsal—for them to imagine themselves as the victims of a practical joke. But the "reality" and the seriousness of the CHARACTERS' claims is brought home in the sudden appearance of Madame Pace; in the Son's inability to leave the stage; and in the tragic outcomes of the Boy and the LITTLE GIRL. The company is witness to a series of incidents that fall outside the boundaries of what can be explained away as a prank.

In the end, then, the question would seem to be: what has this experience done to the actors and the producer? How has it changed them or made their lives different? Do they now think about what they do (performance) or what they have (existence) in a different way? This is an answer Pirandello refuses to give us. We are prompted by this to turn these questions upon ourselves. Do we see ourselves as having an intrinsic identity (existence) independent of others' perceptions? Or are we—as humans and not "always as somebody" like the father claims—but a set of "possibilities" depending on the situation (performance)? And finally—is one alternative more desirable than the other?

THE CHARACTERS

The Father
The Mother
The Stepdaughter
The Son
The Boy (non-speaking)
The LITTLE GIRL (non-speaking)
Madame Pace

THE ACTORS

The Producer
The Leading Actress
The Leading Actor
The Second Actress
The Young Actress
The Young Actor
Other Actors and Actresses (a variable number)
The Stage Manager
The Prompter
The Property Man
The Stage-Hand
The Producer's Secretary
The Doorkeeper
Other Theatre Staff

The action of the play takes place on the stage of a theatre. There are no act or scene divisions, but there are two interruptions: when the Producer and the CHARACTERS go to the office to write the scenario, giving the Actors a break in rehearsal, and when a stage-hand lowers the front curtain by mistake.

References to 'prompt-box', 'curtains' and 'letting down trees' will need to be altered if they are not appropriate to the theatre where the performance is taking place.

ACT ONE

When the audience enters, the curtain is already up and the stage is just as it would be during the day. There is no set; it is empty, in almost total darkness. This is so that from the beginning the audience will have the feeling of being present, not at a performance of a properly rehearsed play, but at a performance of a play that happens spontaneously. Two small sets of steps, one on the right and one on the left, lead up to the stage from the auditorium. On the stage, the top is off the PROMPTOR'S *box and is lying next to it. Downstage, there is a small table and a chair with arms for the* PRODUCER: *it is turned with its back to the audience.*

Also downstage there are two small tables, one a little bigger than the other, and several chairs, ready for the rehearsal if needed. There are more chairs scattered on both left and right for the ACTORS: *to one side at the back and nearly hidden is a piano.*

When the houselights go down the STAGE HAND *comes on through the back door. He is in blue overalls and carries a tool bag. He brings some pieces of wood on, comes to the front, kneels down and starts to nail them together.*

The STAGE MANAGER *rushes on from the wings.*

STAGE MANAGER. Hey! What are you doing?

STAGE HAND. What do you think I'm doing? I'm banging nails in.

STAGE MANAGER. Now? (*He looks at his watch.*) It's half-past ten already. The Producer will be here in a moment to rehearse.

STAGE HAND. I've got to do my work some time, you know.

STAGE MANAGER. Right—but not now.

STAGE HAND. When?

STAGE MANAGER. When the rehearsal's finished. Come on, get all this out of the way and let me set for the second act of 'The Rules of the Game'.

The STAGE HAND *picks up his tools and wood and goes off, grumbling and muttering. The* ACTORS *of the company come in through the door, men and women, first one then another, then two together and so on: there will be nine or ten, enough for the parts for the rehearsal of a play by Pirandello, 'The Rules of the Game', today's rehearsal. They come in, say their 'Good-mornings' to the* STAGE MANAGER *and each other. Some go off to the dressing-rooms; others, among them the* PROMPTOR *with the text rolled up under his arm, scatter about the stage waiting for the* PRODUCER *to start the rehearsal. Meanwhile, sitting or standing in groups, they chat together; some smoke, one complains about his part, another one loudly reads something from 'The Stage'. It would be as well if the* ACTORS *and* ACTRESSES *were dressed in colourful clothes, and this first scene should be improvised naturally and vivaciously. After a while somebody might sit down at the piano and play a song; the younger* ACTORS *and* ACTRESSES *start dancing.*

STAGE MANAGER (*clapping his hands to call their attention*). Come on everybody! Quiet please. The Producer's here.

The piano and the dancing both stop. The ACTORS *turn to look out into the theatre and through the door at the back comes the* PRODUCER; *he walks down the gangway between the seats and, calling 'Good-morning' to the* ACTORS, *climbs up one of the sets of stairs onto the stage. The* SECRETARY *gives him the post, a few magazines, a script. The* ACTORS *move to one side of the stage.*

PRODUCER. Any letters?

SECRETARY. No. That's all the post there is. (*Giving him the script.*)

PRODUCER. Put it in the office. (*Then looking round and turning to the* STAGE MANAGER.) I can't see a thing here. Let's have some lights please.

STAGE MANAGER. Right. (*Calling.*) Workers please!

> *In a few seconds the side of the stage where the* ACTORS *are standing is brilliantly lit with white light. The* PROMPTOR *has gone into his box and spread out his script.*

PRODUCER. Good. (*Clapping hands.*) Well then, let's get started. Anybody missing?

STAGE MANAGER (*heavily ironic*). Our leading lady.

PRODUCER. Not again! (*Looking at his watch.*) We're ten minutes late already. Send her a note to come and see me. It might teach her to be on time for rehearsals. (*Almost before he has finished, the* LEADING ACTRESS'S *voice is heard from the auditorium.*)

LEADING ACTRESS. Morning everybody. Sorry I'm late. (*She is very expensively dressed and is carrying a lap-dog. She comes down the aisle and goes up on to the stage.*)

PRODUCER. You're determined to keep us waiting, aren't you?

LEADING ACTRESS. I'm sorry. I just couldn't find a taxi anywhere. But you haven't started yet and I'm not on at the opening anyhow. (*Calling the* STAGE MANAGER, *she gives him the dog.*) Put him in my dressing-room for me will you?

PRODUCER. And she's even brought her lap-dog with her! As if we haven't enough lap-dogs here already. (*Clapping his hands and turning to the* PROMPTOR.) Right then, the second act of 'The Rules of the Game'. (*Sits in his arm-chair.*) Quiet please! Who's on?

> *The* ACTORS *clear from the front of the stage and sit to one side, except for three who are ready to start the scene—and the* LEADING ACTRESS. *She has ignored the* PRODUCER *and is sitting at one of the little tables.*

PRODUCER. Are you in this scene, then?

LEADING ACTRESS. No—I've just told you.

PRODUCER (*annoyed*). Then get off, for God's sake. (*The* LEADING ACTRESS *goes and sits with the others. To the* PROMPTOR.) Come on then, let's get going.

PROMPTOR (*reading his script*). 'The house of Leone Gala. A peculiar room, both dining-room and study.'

PRODUCER (*to the* STAGE MANAGER). We'll use the red set.

STAGE MANAGER (*making a note*). The red set—right. PROMPTOR (*still reading*). 'The table is laid and there is a desk with books and papers. Bookcases full of books and china cabinets full of valuable china. An exit at the back leads to Leone's bedroom. An exit to the left leads to the kitchen. The main entrance is on the right.'

PRODUCER. Right. Listen carefully everybody: there, the main entrance, there, the kitchen. (*To the* LEADING ACTOR *who plays Socrates.*) Your entrances and exits will be from there. (*To the* STAGE MANAGER.) We'll have the French windows there and put the curtains on them.

STAGE MANAGER (*making a note*). Right.

PROMPTOR (*reading*). 'Scene One. Leone Gala, Guido Venanzi, and Filippo, who is called Socrates.' (*To* PRODUCER.) Have I to read the directions as well?

PRODUCER. Yes, you have! I've told you a hundred times.

PROMPTOR (*reading*). 'When the curtain rises, Leone Gala, in a cook's hat and apron, is beating an egg in a dish with a little wooden spoon. Filippo is beating another and he is dressed as a cook too. Guido Venanzi is sitting listening.'

LEADING ACTOR. Look, do I really have to wear a cook's hat?

PRODUCER (*annoyed by the question*). I expect so! That's what it says in the script. (*Pointing to the script.*)

LEADING ACTOR. If you ask me it's ridiculous.

PRODUCER (*leaping to his feet furiously*). Ridiculous? It's ridiculous, is it? What do you expect me to do if nobody writes good plays any more and we're reduced to putting on plays by Pirandello? And if you can understand them you must be very clever. He writes them on purpose so nobody enjoys them, neither actors nor critics nor audience. (*The* ACTORS *laugh. Then crosses to* LEADING ACTOR *and shouts at him.*) A cook's hat and you beat eggs. But don't run away with the idea that that's all you are doing—beating eggs. You must be joking! You have to be symbolic of the shells of the eggs you are beating. (*The* ACTORS *laugh again and start making ironical comments to each other.*) Be quiet! Listen carefully while I explain. (*Turns back to* LEADING ACTOR.) Yes, the shells, because they are symbolic of the empty form of reason, without its content, blind instinct! You are reason and your wife is instinct: you are playing a game where you have been given parts and in which you are not just yourself but the puppet of yourself. Do you see?

LEADING ACTOR (*spreading his hands*). Me? No.

PRODUCER (*going back to his chair*). Neither do I! Come on, let's get going; you wait till you see the end! You haven't seen anything yet! (*Confidentially.*) By the way, I should turn almost to face the audience if I were you, about three-quarters face. Well, what with the obscure dialogue and the audience not being able to hear you properly in any case, the whole lot'll go to hell. (*Clapping hands again.*) Come on. Let's get going!

PROMPTOR. Excuse me, can I put the top back on the prompt-box? There's a bit of a draught.

PRODUCER. Yes, yes, of course. Get on with it.

The STAGE DOORKEEPER, *in a braided cap, has come into the auditorium, and he comes all the way down the aisle to the stage to tell the* PRODUCER *the* SIX CHARACTERS *have come, who, having come in after him, look about them a little puzzled and dismayed. Every effort must be made to create the effect that the* SIX CHARACTERS *are very different from the* ACTORS *of the company. The placings of the two groups, indicated in the directions, once the* CHARACTERS *are on the stage, will help this; so will using different coloured lights. But the most effective idea is to use masks for the* CHARACTERS, *masks specially made of a material that will not go limp with perspiration and light enough not to worry the actors who wear them: they should be made so that the eyes, the nose and the mouth are all free. This is the way to bring out the deep significance of the play. The* CHARACTERS *should not appear as ghosts, but as created realities, timeless creations of the imagination, and so more real and consistent than the changeable realities of the* ACTORS. *The masks are designed to give the impression of figures constructed by art, each one fixed forever in its own fundamental emotion; that is, Remorse for the* FATHER, *Revenge for the* STEPDAUGHTER, *Scorn for the* SON, *Sorrow for the* MOTHER. *Her mask should have wax tears in the corners of the eyes and down the cheeks like the sculptured or painted weeping Madonna in a church. Her dress should be of a plain material, in stiff folds, looking almost as if it were carved and not of an ordinary material you can buy in a shop and have made up by a dressmaker.*

The FATHER *is about fifty: his reddish hair is thinning at the temples, but he is not bald: he has a full moustache that almost covers his young-looking mouth, which often opens in an uncertain and empty smile. He is pale, with a high forehead: he has blue oval eyes, clear and sharp: he is dressed in light trousers and a dark jacket: his voice is sometimes rich, at other times harsh and loud.*

The MOTHER *appears crushed by an intolerable weight of shame and humiliation. She is wearing a thick black veil and is dressed simply in black; when she raises her veil she shows a face like wax, but not suffering, with her eyes turned down humbly.*

The STEPDAUGHTER, *who is eighteen years old, is defiant, even insolent. She is very beautiful, dressed in mourning as well, but with striking elegance. She is scornful of the timid, suffering, dejected air of her* YOUNG BROTHER, *a grubby little boy of fourteen, also dressed in black; she is full of a warm tenderness, on the other hand, for the* LITTLE SISTER, *a girl of about four, dressed in white with a black silk sash round her waist.*

The SON *is twenty-two, tall, almost frozen in an air of scorn for the* FATHER *and indifference to the* MOTHER: *he is wearing a mauve overcoat and a long green scarf round his neck.*

DOORMAN. Excuse me, sir.

PRODUCER (*angrily*). What the hell is it now?

DOORMAN. There are some people here—they say they want to see you, sir.

The PRODUCER *and the* ACTORS *are astonished and turn to look out into the auditorium.*

PRODUCER. But I'm rehearsing! You know perfectly well that no-one's allowed in during rehearsals. (*Turning to face out front.*) Who are you? What do you want?

FATHER (*coming forward, followed by the others, to the foot of one of the sets of steps*). We're looking for an author.

PRODUCER (*angry and astonished*). An author? Which author?

FATHER. Any author will do, sir.

PRODUCER. But there isn't an author here because we're not rehearsing a new play.

STEPDAUGHTER (*excitedly as she rushes up the steps*). That's better still, better still! We can be your new play.

ACTORS (*lively comments and laughter from the* ACTORS). Oh, listen to that, etc.

FATHER (*going up on the stage after the* STEPDAUGHTER). Maybe, but if there isn't an author here … (*To the* PRODUCER.) Unless you'd like to be …

Hand in hand, the MOTHER *and the* LITTLE GIRL, *followed by the* LITTLE BOY, *go up on the stage and wait. The* SON *stays sullenly behind.*

PRODUCER. Is this some kind of joke?

FATHER. Now, how can you think that? On the contrary, we are bringing you a story of anguish.

STEPDAUGHTER. We might make your fortune for you!

PRODUCER. Do me a favour, will you? Go away. We haven't time to waste on idiots.

FATHER (*hurt but answering gently*). You know very well, as a man of the theatre, that life is full of all sorts of odd things which have no need at all to pretend to be real because they are actually true.

PRODUCER. What the devil are you talking about?

FATHER. What I'm saying is that you really must be mad to do things the opposite way round: to create situations that obviously aren't true and try to make them seem to be really happening. But then I suppose that sort of madness is the only reason for your profession.

The ACTORS *are indignant.*

PRODUCER (*getting up and glaring at him*). Oh, yes? So ours is a profession of madmen, is it?

FATHER. Well, if you try to make something look true when it obviously isn't, especially if you're not forced to do it, but do it for a game. … Isn't it your job to give life on the stage to imaginary people?

PRODUCER (*quickly answering him and speaking for the* ACTORS *who are growing more indignant*). I should like you to know, sir, that the actor's profession is one of great distinction. Even if nowadays the new writers only give us dull plays to act and puppets to present instead of men, I'd have you know that it is our boast that we have given life, here on this stage, to immortal works.

The ACTORS, *satisfied, agree with and applaud the* PRODUCER.

FATHER (*cutting in and following hard on his argument*). There! You see? Good! You've given life! You've created living beings with more genuine life than people have who breathe and wear clothes! Less real, perhaps, but nearer the truth. We are both saying the same thing.

The ACTORS *look at each other, astonished.*

PRODUCER. But just a moment! You said before …

FATHER. I'm sorry, but I said that before, about acting for fun, because you shouted at us and said you'd no time to waste on idiots, but you must know better than anyone that Nature uses human imagination to lift her work of creation to even higher levels.

PRODUCER. All right then: but where does all this get us?

FATHER. Nowhere. I want to try to show that one can be thrust into life in many ways, in many forms: as a tree or a stone, as water or a butterfly—or as a woman. It might even be as a character in a play.

PRODUCER (*ironic, pretending to be annoyed*). And you, and these other people here, were thrust into life, as you put it, as CHARACTERS in a play?

FATHER. Exactly! And alive, as you can see.

The PRODUCER *and the* ACTORS *burst into laughter as if at a joke.*

FATHER. I'm sorry you laugh like that, because we carry in us, as I said before, a story of terrible anguish as you can guess from this woman dressed in black.

Saying this, he offers his hand to the MOTHER *and helps her up the last steps and, holding her still by the hand, leads her with a sense of tragic solemnity across the stage which is suddenly lit by a fantastic light.*

The LITTLE GIRL *and the* BOY *follow the* MOTHER: *then the* SON *comes up and stands to one side in the background: then the* STEPDAUGHTER *follows and leans against the proscenium arch: the* ACTORS *are astonished at first, but then, full of admiration for the 'entrance', they burst into applause—just as if it were a performance specially for them.*

PRODUCER (*at first astonished and then indignant*). My God! Be quiet all of you. (*Turns to the* CHARACTERS.) And you lot get out! Clear off! (*To the* STAGE MANAGER.) Jesus! Get them out of here.

STAGE MANAGER (*comes forward but stops short as if held back by something strange*). Go on out! Get out!

FATHER (*to* PRODUCER). Oh no, please, you see, we …

PRODUCER (*shouting*). We came here to work, you know.

LEADING ACTOR. We really can't be messed about like this.

FATHER (*resolutely, coming forward*). I'm astonished! Why don't you believe me? Perhaps you are not used to seeing the CHARACTERS created by an author spring into life up here on the stage face to face with each other. Perhaps it's because we're not in a script? (*He points to the* PROMPTOR's *box.*)

STEPDAUGHTER (*coming down to the* PRODUCER, *smiling and persuasive*). Believe me, sir, we really are SIX of the most fascinating CHARACTERS. But we've been neglected.

FATHER. Yes, that's right, we've been neglected. In the sense that the author who created us, living in his mind, wouldn't or couldn't make us live in a written play for the world of art. And that really is a crime sir, because whoever has the luck to be born a character can laugh even at death. Because a character will never die! A man will die, a writer, the instrument of creation: but what he has created will never die! And to be able to live for ever you don't need to have extraordinary gifts or be able to do miracles. Who was Sancho Panza? Who was Prospero? But they will live for ever because—living seeds—they had the luck to find a fruitful soil, an imagination which knew how to grow them and feed them, so that they will live for ever.

PRODUCER. This is all very well! But what do you want here? FATHER. We want to live, sir.

PRODUCER (*ironically*). For ever!

FATHER. No, no: only for a few moments—in you.

AN ACTOR. Listen to that!

LEADING ACTRESS. They want to live in us!

YOUNG ACTOR (*pointing to the* STEPDAUGHTER). I don't mind … so long as I get her.

FATHER. Listen, listen: the play is all ready to be put together and if you and your actors would like to, we can work it out now between us.

PRODUCER (*annoyed*). But what exactly do you want to do? We don't make up plays like that here! We present comedies and tragedies here.

FATHER. That's right, we know that of course. That's why we've come.

PRODUCER. And where's the script?

FATHER. It's in us, sir. (*The* ACTORS *laugh.*) The play is in us: we are the play and we are impatient to show it to you: the passion inside us is driving us on.

STEPDAUGHTER (*scornfully, with the tantalising charm of deliberate impudence*). My passion, if only you knew! My passion for him! (*She points at the* FATHER *and suggests that she is going to embrace him: but stops and bursts into a screeching laugh.*)

FATHER (*with sudden anger*). You keep out of this for the moment! And stop laughing like that!

STEPDAUGHTER. Really? Then with your permission, ladies and gentlemen; even though it's only two months since I became an orphan, just watch how I can sing and dance.

> *The* ACTORS, *especially the younger, seem strangely attracted to her while she sings and dances and they edge closer and reach out their hands to catch hold of her.[1] She eludes them, and when the* ACTORS *applaud her and the* PRODUCER *speaks sharply to her she stays still quite removed from them all.*

ACTOR 1: Very good! etc.

PRODUCER (*angrily*). Be quiet! Do you think this is a nightclub? (*Turns to* FATHER *and asks with some concern.*) Is she a bit mad?

FATHER. Mad? Oh no—it's worse than that.

STEPDAUGHTER (*suddenly running to the* PRODUCER). Yes. It's worse, much worse! Listen please! Let's put this play on at once, because you'll see that at a particular point I—when this darling LITTLE GIRL here—(*Taking the* LITTLE GIRL *by the hand from next to the* MOTHER *and crossing with her to the* PRODUCER.) Isn't she pretty? (*Takes her in her arms.*) Darling! Darling! (*Puts her down again and adds, moved very deeply but almost without wanting to.*) Well, this lovely LITTLE GIRL here, when God suddenly takes her from this poor Mother: and this little idiot here (*Turning to the* LITTLE BOY *and seizing him roughly by the sleeve.*) does the most stupid thing, like the half-wit he is,—then you will see me run away! Yes, you'll see me rush away!

---

1 Suggested songs: Eartha Kitt's *Old Fashioned Millionaire*; Theme Song from *The Moon is Blue*, *I'm Gonna Wash That Man Right Out Of My Hair* from *South Pacific*.

But not yet, not yet! Because, after all the intimate things there have been between him and me (*In the direction of the* FATHER, *with a horrible vulgar wink.*) I can't stay with them any longer, to watch the insult to this mother through that supercilious cretin over there. (*Pointing to the* SON.) Look at him! Look at him! Condescending, stand-offish, because he's the legitimate son, him! Full of contempt for me, for the boy and for the LITTLE GIRL: because we are bastards. Do you understand? Bastards. (*Running to the* MOTHER *and embracing her.*) And this poor mother—she—who is the mother of all of us—he doesn't want to recognise her as his own mother—and he looks down on her, he does, as if she were only the mother of the three of us who are bastards—the traitor. (*She says all this quickly, with great excitement, and after having raised her voice on the word 'bastards' she speaks quietly, half-spitting the word 'traitor'.*)

MOTHER (*with deep anguish to the* PRODUCER). Sir, in the name of these two little ones, I beg you ... (*Feels herself grow faint and sways.*) Oh, my God.

FATHER (*rushing to support her with almost all the* ACTORS *bewildered and concerned*). Get a chair someone ... quick, get a chair for this poor widow.

> One of the ACTORS *offers a chair: the others press urgently around. The* MOTHER, *seated now, tries to stop the* FATHER *lifting her veil.*

ACTORS. Is it real? Has she really fainted? etc.

FATHER. Look at her, everybody, look at her.

MOTHER. No, for God's sake, stop it.

FATHER. Let them look!

MOTHER (*lifting her hands and covering her face, desperately*). Oh, please, I beg you, stop him from doing what he is trying to do; it's hateful.

PRODUCER (*overwhelmed, astounded*). It's no use, I don't understand this any more. (*To the* FATHER.) Is this woman your wife?

FATHER (*at once*). That's right, she is my wife. PRODUCER. How is she a widow, then, if you're still alive?

> The ACTORS *are bewildered too and find relief in a loud laugh.*

FATHER (*wounded, with rising resentment*). Don't laugh! Please don't laugh like that! That's just the point, that's her own drama. You see, she had another man. Another man who ought to be here.

MOTHER. No, no! (*Crying out.*)

STEPDAUGHTER. Luckily for him he died. Two months ago, as I told you: we are in mourning for him, as you can see.

FATHER. Yes, he's dead: but that's not the reason he isn't here. He isn't here because— well just look at her, please, and you'll understand at once—hers is not a passionate drama of the love of two men, because she was incapable of love, she could feel nothing—except, perhaps a little gratitude (but not to me, to him). She's not a woman; she's a mother. And her drama—and, believe me, it's a powerful one—her drama is focused completely on these four children of the two men she had.

MOTHER. I had them? How dare you say that I had them, as if I wanted them myself? It was him, sir! He forced the other man on me. He made me go away with him!

STEPDAUGHTER (*leaping up, indignantly*). It isn't true!

MOTHER (*bewildered*). How isn't it true?

STEPDAUGHTER. It isn't true, it just isn't true.

MOTHER. What do you know about it?

STEPDAUGHTER. It isn't true. (*To the* PRODUCER.) Don't believe it! Do you know why she said that? She said it because of him, over there. (*Pointing to the* SON.) She tortures herself, she exhausts herself with worry and all because of the indifference of that son of hers. She wants to make him believe that she abandoned him when he was two years old because the Father made her do it.

MOTHER (*passionately*). He did! He made me! God's my witness. (*To the* PRODUCER.) Ask him if it isn't true. (*Pointing to the* FATHER.) Make him tell our son it's true. (*Turning to the* STEPDAUGHTER.) You don't know anything about it.

STEPDAUGHTER. I know that when my father was alive you were always happy and contented. You can't deny it.

MOTHER. No, I can't deny it.

STEPDAUGHTER. He was always full of love and care for you. (*Turning to the* LITTLE BOY *with anger.*) Isn't it true? Admit it. Why don't you say something, you little idiot?

MOTHER. Leave the poor boy alone! Why do you want to make me appear ungrateful? You're my daughter. I don't in the least want to offend your father's memory. I've already told him that it wasn't my fault or even to please myself that I left his house and my son.

FATHER. It's quite true. It was my fault.

LEADING ACTOR (*to other actors*). Look at this. What a show!

LEADING ACTRESS. And we're the audience.

YOUNG ACTOR. For a change.

PRODUCER (*beginning to be very interested*). Let's listen to them! Quiet! Listen!

He goes down the steps into the auditorium and stands there as if to get an idea of what the scene will look like from the audience's viewpoint.

SON (*without moving, coldly, quietly, ironically*). Yes, listen to his little scrap of philosophy. He's going to tell you all about the Daemon of Experiement.

FATHER. You're a cynical idiot, and I've told you so a hundred times. (*To the* PRODUCER *who is now in the stalls.*) He sneers at me because of this expression I've found to defend myself.

SON. Words, words.

FATHER. Yes words, words! When we're faced by something we don't understand, by a sense of evil that seems as if it's going to swallow us, don't we all find comfort in a word that tells us nothing but that calms us?

STEPDAUGHTER. And dulls your sense of remorse, too. That more than anything.

FATHER. Remorse? No, that's not true. It'd take more than words to dull the sense of remorse in me.

STEPDAUGHTER. It's taken a little money too, just a little money. The money that he was going to offer as payment, gentlemen.

The ACTORS *are horrified.*

SON (*contemptuously to his stepsister*). That's a filthy TRICK.

STEPDAUGHTER. A filthy TRICK? There it was in a pale blue envelope on the little mahogany table in the room behind the shop at Madame Pace's. You know Madame Pace, don't you? One of those Madames who sell 'Robes et Manteaux' so that they can attract poor girls like me from decent families into their workroom.

SON. And she's bought the right to tyrannise over the whole lot of us with that money— with what he was going to pay her: and luckily—now listen carefully—he had no reason to pay it to her.

STEPDAUGHTER. But it was close!

MOTHER (*rising up angrily*). Shame on you, daughter! Shame!

STEPDAUGHTER. Shame? Not shame, revenge! I'm desperate, desperate to live that scene! The room … over here the showcase of coats, there the divan, there the mirror, and the screen, and over there in front of the window, that little mahogany table with the pale blue envelope and the money in it. I can see it all quite clearly. I could pick it up! But you should turn your faces away, gentlemen: because I'm nearly naked! I'm not blushing any longer—I leave that to him. (*Pointing at the* FATHER.) But I tell you he was very pale, very pale then. (*To the* PRODUCER.) Believe me.

PRODUCER. I don't understand any more.

FATHER. I'm not surprised when you're attacked like that! Why don't you put your foot down and let me have my say before you believe all these horrible slanders she's so viciously telling about me.

STEPDAUGHTER. We don't want to hear any of your long winded fairy-stories.

FATHER. I'm not going to tell any fairy-stories! I want to explain things to him.

STEPDAUGHTER. I'm sure you do. Oh, yes! In your own special way.

The PRODUCER *comes back up on stage to take control.*

FATHER. But isn't that the cause of all the trouble? Words! We all have a world of things inside ourselves and each one of us has his own private world. How can we understand each other if the words I use have the sense and the value that I expect them to have, but whoever is listening to me inevitably thinks that those same words have a different sense and value, because of the private world he has inside himself too. We think we understand each other: but we never do. Look! All my pity, all my compassion for this woman (*Pointing to the* MOTHER.) she sees as ferocious cruelty.

MOTHER. But he turned me out of the house!

FATHER. There, do you hear? I turned her out! She really believed that I had turned her out.

MOTHER. You know how to talk. I don't. ... But believe me, sir, (*Turning to the* PRODUCER.) after he married me... I can't think why! I was a poor, simple woman.

FATHER. But that was the reason! I married you for your simplicity, that's what I loved in you, believing—(*He stops because she is making gestures of contradiction. Then, seeing the impossibility of making her understand, he throws his arms wide in a gesture of desperation and turns back to the* PRODUCER.) No, do you see? She says no! It's terrifying, sir, believe me, terrifying, her deafness, her mental deafness. (*He taps his forehead.*) Affection for her children, oh yes. But deaf, mentally deaf, deaf, sir, to the point of desperation.

STEPDAUGHTER. Yes, but make him tell you what good all his cleverness has brought us.

FATHER. If only we could see in advance all the harm that can come from the good we think we are doing.

The LEADING ACTRESS, *who has been growing angry watching the* LEADING ACTOR *flirting with the* STEPDAUGHTER, *comes forward and snaps at the* PRODUCER.

LEADING ACTRESS. Excuse me, are we going to go on with our rehearsal?

PRODUCER. Yes, of course. But I want to listen to this first.

YOUNG ACTOR. It's such a new idea.

YOUNG ACTRESS. It's fascinating.

LEADING ACTRESS. For those who are interested. (*She looks meaningfully at the* LEADING ACTOR.)

PRODUCER (*to the* FATHER). Look here, you must explain yourself more clearly. (*He sits down.*)

FATHER. Listen then. You see, there was a rather poor fellow working for me as my assistant and secretary, very loyal: he understood her in everything. (*Pointing to the* MOTHER.) But without a hint of deceit, you must believe that: he was good and simple, like her: neither of them was capable even of thinking anything wrong, let alone doing it.

STEPDAUGHTER. So instead he thought of it for them and did it too!

FATHER. It's not true! What I did was for their good—oh yes and mine too, I admit it! The time had come when I couldn't say a word to either of them without there immediately flashing between them a sympathetic look: each one caught the other's eye for advice, about how to take what I had said, how not to make me angry. Well, that was enough, as I'm sure you'll understand, to put me in a bad temper all the time, in a state of intolerable exasperation.

PRODUCER. Then why didn't you sack this secretary of yours?

FATHER. Right! In the end I did sack him! But then I had to watch this poor woman wandering about in the house on her own, forlorn, like a stray animal you take in out of pity.

MOTHER. It's quite true.

FATHER (*suddenly, turning to her, as if to stop her*). And what about the boy? Is that true as well?

MOTHER. But first he tore my son from me, sir.

FATHER. But not out of cruelty! It was so that he could grow up healthy and strong, in touch with the earth.

STEPDAUGHTER (*pointing to the* SON *jeeringly*). And look at the result!

FATHER (*quickly*). And is it my fault, too, that he's grown up like this? I took him to a nurse in the country, a peasant, because his mother didn't seem strong enough to me, although she is from a humble family herself. In fact that was what made me marry her. Perhaps it was superstitious of me; but what was I to do? I've always had this dreadful longing for a kind of sound moral healthiness.

The STEPDAUGHTER *breaks out again into noisy laughter.*

Make her stop that! It's unbearable.

PRODUCER. Stop it will you? Let me listen, for God's sake.

When the PRODUCER *has spoken to her, she resumes her previous position … absorbed and distant, a half-smile on her lips. The* PRODUCER *comes down into the auditorium again to see how it looks from there.*

FATHER. I couldn't bear the sight of this woman near me. (*Pointing to the* MOTHER.) Not so much because of the annoyance she caused me, you see, or even the feeling of being stifled, being suffocated that I got from her, as for the sorrow, the painful sorrow that I felt for her.

MOTHER. And he sent me away.

FATHER. With everything you needed, to the other man, to set her free from me.

MOTHER. And to set yourself free!

FATHER. Oh, yes, I admit it. And what terrible things came out of it. But I did it for the best, and more for her than for me: I swear it! (*Folds his arms: then turns suddenly to the* MOTHER.) I never lost sight of you did I? Until that fellow, without my knowing it, suddenly took you off to another town one day. He was idiotically suspicious of my interest in them, a genuine interest, I assure you, without any ulterior motive at all. I watched the new little family growing up round her with unbelievable tenderness, she'll confirm that. (*He points to the* STEPDAUGHTER.)

STEPDAUGHTER. Oh yes, I can indeed. I was a pretty LITTLE GIRL, you know, with plaits down to my shoulders and my little frilly knickers showing under my dress—so pretty—he used to watch me corning out of school. He came to see how I was maturing.

FATHER. That's shameful! It's monstrous.

STEPDAUGHTER. No it isn't! Why do you say it is?

FATHER. It's monstrous! Monstrous. (*He turns excitedly to the* PRODUCER *and goes on in explanation.*) After she'd gone away (*Pointing to the* MOTHER.), my house seemed empty. She'd been like a weight on my spirit but she'd filled the house with her presence. Alone in the empty rooms I wandered about like a lost soul. This boy here, (*Indicating the* SON.) growing up away from home—whenever he came back to the home—I don't know—but he didn't seem to be mine any more. We needed the mother between us, to link us together, and so he grew up by himself, apart, with no connection to me either through intellect or love. And then—it must seem odd, but it's true—first I was curious about and then strongly attracted to the little family that had come about because of what I'd done. And the thought of them began to fill all the emptiness that I felt around me. I needed, I really needed to believe that she was happy, wrapped up in the simple cares of her life, lucky because she was better off away from the complicated torments of a soul like mine. And to prove it, I used to watch that child coming out of school.

STEPDAUGHTER. Listen to him! He used to follow me along the street; he used to smile at me and when we came near the house he'd wave his hand—like this! I watched him, wide-eyed, puzzled. I didn't know who he was. I told my mother about him and she knew at once who it must be. (MOTHER *nods agreement.*) At first, she didn't let me go to school again, at any rate for a few days. But when I did go back, I saw him standing near the door again—looking ridiculous—with a brown paper bag in his hand. He came close and petted me: then he opened the bag and took out a beautiful straw hat with a hoop of rosebuds round it—for me!

PRODUCER. All this is off the point, you know.

SON (*contemptuously*). Yes … literature, literature.

FATHER. What do you mean, literature? This is real life: real passions.

PRODUCER. That may be! But you can't put it on the stage just like that.

FATHER. That's right you can't. Because all this is only leading up to the main action. I'm not suggesting that this part should be put on the stage. In any case, you can see for yourself, (*Pointing at the* STEPDAUGHTER.) she isn't a pretty LITTLE GIRL any longer with plaits down to her shoulders.

STEPDAUGHTER.—and with frilly knickers showing under her frock.

FATHER. The drama begins now: and it's new and complex.

STEPDAUGHTER (*coming forward, fierce and brooding*). As soon as my father died …

FATHER (*quickly, not giving her time to speak*). They were so miserable. They came back here, but I didn't know about it because of the Mother's stubbornness. (*Pointing to the* MOTHER.) She can't really write you know; but she could have got her daughter to write, or the boy, or tell me that they needed help.

MOTHER. But tell me, sir, how could I have known how he felt?

FATHER. And hasn't that always been your fault? You've never known anything about how I felt.

MOTHER. After all the years away from him and after all that had happened.

FATHER. And was it my fault if that fellow took you so far away? (*Turning back to the* PRODUCER.) Suddenly, overnight, I tell you, he'd found a job away from here without my knowing anything about it. I couldn't possibly trace them; and then, naturally I suppose, my interest in them grew less over the years. The drama broke out, unexpected and violent, when they came back: when I was driven in misery by the needs of my flesh, still alive with desire … and it is misery, you know, unspeakable misery for the man who lives alone and who detests sordid, casual affairs; not old enough to do without women, but not young enough to be able to go and look for one without shame! Misery? Is that what I called it. It's horrible, it's revolting, because there isn't a woman who will give her love to him any more. And when he realises this, he should do without. … It's easy to say though. Each of us, face to face with other men, is clothed with some sort of dignity, but we know only too well all the unspeakable things that go on in the heart. We surrender, we give in to temptation: but afterwards we rise up out of it very quickly, in a desperate hurry to rebuild our dignity, whole and firm as if it were a gravestone that would cover every sign and memory of our shame, and hide it from even our own eyes. Everyone's like that, only some of us haven't the courage to talk about it.

STEPDAUGHTER. But they've all got the courage to do it!

FATHER. Yes! But only in secret! That's why it takes more courage to talk about it! Because if a man does talk about it—what happens then?—everybody says he's a cynic. And it's simply not true; he's just like everybody else; only better perhaps, because he's not afraid to use his intelligence to point out the blushing shame of human bestiality, that man, the beast, shuts his eyes to, trying to pretend it doesn't exist. And what about woman—what is she like? She looks at you invitingly, teasingly. You take her in your arms. But as soon as she feels your arms round her she closes her eyes. It's the sign of her mission, the sign by which she says to a man, 'Blind yourself—I'm blind!'

STEPDAUGHTER. And when she doesn't close her eyes any more? What then? When she doesn't feel the need to hide from herself any more, to shut her eyes and hide her own shame. When she can see instead, dispassionately and dry-eyed this blushing shame of a man who has blinded himself, who is without love. What then? Oh, then what disgust, what utter disgust she feels for all these intellectual complications, for all this philosophy that points to the bestiality of man and then tries to defend him, to excuse him … I can't listen to him, sir. Because when a man says he needs to 'simplify' life like this—reducing it to bestiality—and throws away every human scrap of innocent desire, genuine feeling, idealism, duty, modesty, shame, then there's nothing more contemptible and nauseating than his remorse—crocodile tears!

PRODUCER. Let's get to the point, let's get to the point. This is all chat.

FATHER. Right then! But a fact is like a sack—it won't stand up if it's empty. To make it stand up, first you have to put in it all the reasons and feelings that caused it in the first place. I couldn't possibly have known that when that fellow died they'd come back here, that they were desperately poor and that the Mother had gone out to work as a dressmaker, nor that she'd gone to work for Madame Pace, of all people.

STEPDAUGHTER. She's a very high-class dressmaker—you must understand that. She apparently has only high-class customers, but she has arranged things carefully so that these high-class customers in fact serve her—they give her a respectable front

... without spoiling things for the other ladies at the shop, who are not quite so high-class at all.

MOTHER. Believe me, sir, the idea never entered my head that the old hag gave me work because she had an eye on my daughter ...

STEPDAUGHTER. Poor Mummy! Do you know what that woman would do when I took back the work that my mother had been doing? She would point out how the dress had been ruined by giving it to my mother to sew: she bargained, she grumbled. So, you see, I paid for it, while this poor woman here thought she was sacrificing herself for me and these two children, sewing dresses all night for Madame Pace.

The ACTORS *make gestures and noises of disgust.*

PRODUCER (*quickly*). And there one day, you met ...

STEPDAUGHTER (*pointing at the* FATHER). Yes, him. Oh, he was an old customer of hers! What a scene that's going to be, superb!

FATHER. With her, the mother, arriving—

STEPDAUGHTER (*quickly, viciously*).—Almost in time!

FATHER (*crying out*).—No, just in time, just in time! Because, luckily, I found out who she was in time. And I took them all back to my house, sir. Can you imagine the situation now, for the two of us living in the same house? She, just as you see her here: and I, not able to look her in the face.

STEPDAUGHTER. It's so absurd! Do you think it's possible for me, sir, after what happened at Madame Pace's, to pretend that I'm a modest little miss, well brought up and virtuous just so that I can fit in with his damned pretensions to a 'sound moral healthiness'?

FATHER. This is the real drama for me; the belief that we all, you see, think of ourselves as one single person: but it's not true: each of us is several different people, and all these people live inside us. With one person we seem like this and with another we seem very different. But we always have the illusion of being the same person for everybody and of always being the same person in everything we do. But it's not true! It's not true! We find this out for ourselves very clearly when by some terrible chance we're suddenly stopped in the middle of doing something and we're left dangling there, suspended. We realise then, that every part of us was not involved in what we'd been doing and that it would be a dreadful injustice of other people to judge us only by this one action as we dangle there, hanging in chains, fixed for all eternity, as if the whole of one's personality were summed up in that single, interrupted action. Now do you understand this girl's treachery? She accidentally found me somewhere I shouldn't have been, doing something I shouldn't have been doing!

She discovered a part of me that shouldn't have existed for her: and now she wants to fix on me a reality that I should never have had to assume for her: it came from a single brief and shameful moment in my life. This is what hurts me most of all. And you'll see that the play will make a tremendous impact from this idea of mine. But then, there's the position of the others. His … (*Pointing to the* SON.)

SON (*shrugging his shoulders scornfully*). Leave me out of it. I don't come into this.

FATHER. Why don't you come into this?

SON. I don't come into it and I don't want to come into it, because you know perfectly well that I wasn't intended to be mixed up with you lot.

STEPDAUGHTER. We're vulgar, common people, you see! He's a fine gentleman. But you've probably noticed that every now and then I look at him contemptuously, and when I do, he lowers his eyes—he knows the harm he's done me.

SON (*not looking at her*). I have?

STEPDAUGHTER. Yes, you. It's your fault, dearie, that I went on the streets! Your fault! (*Movement of horror from the* ACTORS.) Did you or didn't you, with your attitude, deny us —I won't say the intimacy of your home—but that simple hospitality that makes guests feel comfortable? We were intruders who had come to invade the country of your 'legitimacy'! (*Turning to the* PRODUCER.) I'd like you to have seen some of the little scenes that went on between him and me, sir. He says that I tyrannised over everyone. But don't you see? It was because of the way he treated us. He called it 'vile' that I should insist on the right we had to move into his house with my mother—and she's his mother too. And I went into the house as its mistress.

SON (*slowly coming forward*). They're really enjoying themselves, aren't they, sir? It's easy when they all gang up against me. But try to imagine what happened: one fine day, there is a son sitting quietly at home and he sees arrive as bold as brass, a young woman like this, who cheekily asks for his father, and heaven knows what business she has with him. Then he sees her come back with the same brazen look in her eye accompanied by that LITTLE GIRL there: and he sees her treat his father—without knowing why—in a most ambiguous and insolent way—asking him for money in a tone that leads one to suppose he really ought to give it, because he is obliged to do so.

FATHER. But I was obliged to do so: I owed it to your mother.

SON. And how was I to know that? When had I ever seen her before? When had I ever heard her mentioned? Then one day I see her come in with her (*Pointing at the* STEPDAUGHTER.), that boy and that LITTLE GIRL: they say to me, 'Oh, didn't you know? This is your mother, too.' Little by little I began to understand, mostly from her attitude (*Points to* STEPDAUGHTER.) why they'd come to live in the house so suddenly. I can't and I won't say what I feel, and what I think. I wouldn't even like to confess it to myself. So I can't take any active part in this. Believe me, sir, I am a character who has not been fully developed dramatically, and I feel uncomfortable, most uncomfortable, in their company. So please leave me out of it.

FATHER. What! But it's precisely because you feel like this …

SON (*violently exasperated*). How do you know what I feel? When have you ever bothered yourself about me?

FATHER. All right! I admit it! But isn't that a situation in itself? This withdrawing of yourself, it's cruel to me and to your mother: when she came back to the house, seeing you almost for the first time, not recognising you, but knowing that you're her own son. … (*Turning to point out the* MOTHER *to the* PRODUCER.) There, look at her: she's weeping.

STEPDAUGHTER (*angrily, stamping her foot*). Like the fool she is!

FATHER (*quickly pointing at the* STEPDAUGHTER *to the* PRODUCER). She can't stand that young man, you know. (*Turning and referring to the* SON.) He says that he doesn't come into it, but he's really the pivot of the action! Look here at this LITTLE BOY, who clings to his mother all the time, frightened, humiliated. And it's because of him over there! Perhaps this LITTLE BOY's problem is the worst of all: he feels an outsider, more than the others do; he feels so mortified, so humiliated just being in the house,—because it's charity, you see. (*Quietly.*) He's like his father: timid; he doesn't say anything …

PRODUCER. It's not a good idea at all, using him: you don't know what a nuisance children are on the stage.

FATHER. He won't need to be on the stage for long. Nor will the LITTLE GIRL— he's the first to go.

PRODUCER. That's good! Yes. I tell you all this interests me—it interests me very much. I'm sure we've the material here for a good play.

STEPDAUGHTER (*trying to push herself in*). With a character like me you have!

FATHER (*driving her off, wanting to hear what the* PRODUCER *has decided*). You stay out of it!

PRODUCER (*going on, ignoring the interruption*). It's new, yes.

FATHER. Oh, it's absolutely new!

PRODUCER. You've got a nerve, though, haven't you, coming here and throwing it at me like this?

FATHER. I'm sure you understand. Born as we are for the stage …

PRODUCER. Are you amateur actors?

FATHER. No! I say we are born for the stage because …

PRODUCER. Come on now! You're an old hand at this, at acting!

FATHER. No I'm not. I only act, as everyone does, the part in life that he's chosen for himself, or that others have chosen for him. And you can see that sometimes my own passion gets a bit out of hand, a bit theatrical, as it does with all of us.

PRODUCER. Maybe, maybe ... But you do see, don't you, that without an author ... I could give you someone's address ...

FATHER. Oh no! Look here! You do it.

PRODUCER. Me? What are you talking about?

FATHER. Yes, you. Why not?

PRODUCER. Because I've never written anything!

FATHER. Well, why not start now, if you don't mind my suggesting it? There's nothing to it. Everybody's doing it. And your job is even easier, because we're here, all of us, alive before you.

PRODUCER. That's not enough.

FATHER. Why isn't it enough? When you've seen us live our drama ...

PRODUCER. Perhaps so. But we'll still need someone to write it.

FATHER. Only to write it down, perhaps, while it happens in front of him—live—scene by scene. It'll be enough to sketch it out simply first and then run through it.

PRODUCER (*coming back up, tempted by the idea*). Do you know I'm almost tempted ... just for fun ... it might work.

FATHER. Of course it will. You'll see what wonderful scenes will come right out of it! I could tell you what they will be!

PRODUCER. You tempt me ... you tempt me! We'll give it a chance. Come with me to the office. (*Turning to the* ACTORS.) Take a break: but don't go far away. Be back in a quarter of an hour or twenty minutes. (*To the* FATHER.) Let's see, let's try it out. Something extraordinary might come out of this.

FATHER. Of course it will! Don't you think it'd be better if the others came too? (*Indicating the other* CHARACTERS.)

PRODUCER. Yes, come on, come on. (*Going, then turning to speak to the* ACTORS.) Don't forget; don't be late: back in a quarter of an hour.

The PRODUCER *and the* SIX CHARACTERS *cross the stage and go. The* ACTORS *look at each other in astonishment.*

LEADING ACTOR. Is he serious? What's he going to do?

YOUNG ACTOR. I think he's gone round the bend.

ANOTHER ACTOR. Does he expect to make up a play in five minutes?

YOUNG ACTOR. Yes, like the old actors in the commedia del'arte!

LEADING ACTRESS. Well if he thinks I'm going to appear in that sort of nonsense ...

YOUNG ACTOR. Nor me!

FOURTH ACTOR. I should like to know who they are.

THIRD ACTOR. Who do you think? They're probably escaped lunatics—or crooks.

YOUNG ACTOR. And is he taking them seriously?

YOUNG ACTRESS. It's vanity. The vanity of seeing himself as an author.

LEADING ACTOR. I've never heard of such a thing! If the theatre, ladies and gentlemen, is reduced to this …

FIFTH ACTOR. I'm enjoying it!

THIRD ACTOR. Really? We shall have to wait and see what happens next I suppose.

Talking, they leave the stage. Some go out through the back door, some to the dressing-rooms.
The Curtain stays up.
The interval lasts twenty minutes.

ACT TWO

The theatre warning-bell sounds to call the audience back. From the dressing-rooms, the door at the back and even from the auditorium, the ACTORS, *the* STAGE MANAGER, *the* STAGE HANDS, *the* PROMPTOR, *the* PROPERTY MAN *and the* PRODUCER, *accompanied by the* SIX CHARACTERS *all come back on to the stage.*
The house lights go out and the stage lights come on again.

PRODUCER. Come on, everybody! Are we all here? Quiet now! Listen! Let's get started! Stage manager?

STAGE MANAGER. Yes, I'm here.

PRODUCER. Give me that little parlour setting, will you? A couple of plain flats and a door flat will do. Hurry up with it!

The STAGE MANAGER *runs off to order someone to do this immediately and at the same time the* PRODUCER *is making arrangements with the* PROPERTY MAN, *the* PROMPTOR, *and the* ACTORS: *the two flats and the door flat are painted in pink and gold stripes.*

PRODUCER (*to* PROPERTY MAN). Go see if we have a sofa in stock.

PROPERTY MAN. Yes, there's that green one.

STEPDAUGHTER. No, no, not a green one! It was yellow, yellow velvet with flowers on it: it was enormous! And so comfortable!

PROPERTY MAN. We haven't got one like that.

PRODUCER. It doesn't matter! Give me whatever there is.

STEPDAUGHTER. What do you mean, it doesn't matter? It was Mme. Pace's famous sofa.

PRODUCER. It's only for a rehearsal! Please, don't interfere. (*To the* STAGE MANAGER.) Oh, and see if there's a shop window, will you—preferably a long, low one.

STEPDAUGHTER. And a little table, a little mahogany table for the blue envelope.

STAGE MANAGER (*to the* PRODUCER). There's that little gold one.

PRODUCER. That'll do—bring it.

FATHER. A mirror!

STEPDAUGHTER. And a screen! A screen, please, or I won't be able to manage, will I?

STAGE MANAGER. All right. We've lots of big screens, don't you worry.

PRODUCER (*to* STEPDAUGHTER). Then don't you want some coat-hangers and some clothes racks?

STEPDAUGHTER. Yes, lots of them, lots of them.

PRODUCER (*to the* STAGE MANAGER). See how many there are and have them brought up.

STAGE MANAGER. Right, I'll see to it.

> The STAGE MANAGER *goes off to do it: and while the* PRODUCER *is talking to the* PROMPTOR, *the* CHARACTERS *and the* ACTORS, *the* STAGE MANAGER *is telling the* SCENE SHIFTERS *where to set up the furniture they have brought.*

PRODUCER (*to the* PROMPTOR). Now you, go sit down, will you? Look, this is an outline of the play, act by act. (*He hands him several sheets of paper.*) But you'll need to be on your toes.

PROMPTOR. Shorthand?

PRODUCER (*pleasantly surprised*). Oh, good! You know shorthand?

PROMPTOR. I don't know much about prompting, but I do know about shorthand.

PRODUCER. Thank God for that anyway! (*He turns to a* STAGE HAND.) Go fetch me some paper from my office—lots of it—as much as you can find!

> The STAGE HAND *goes running off and then comes back shortly with a bundle of paper that he gives to the* PROMPTOR.

PRODUCER (*crossing to the* PROMPTOR). Follow the scenes, one after another, as they are played and try to get the lines down … at least the most important ones. (*Then turning to the* ACTORS.) Get out of the way everybody! Here, go over to the prompt side (*Pointing to stage left.*) and pay attention!

LEADING ACTRESS. But, excuse me, we …

PRODUCER (*anticipating her*). You won't be expected to improvise, don't worry!

LEADING ACTOR. Then what are we expected to do?

PRODUCER. Nothing! Just go over there, listen and watch. You'll all be given your parts later written out. Right now we're going to rehearse, as well as we can. And they will be doing the rehearsal. (*He points to the* CHARACTERS.)

FATHER (*rather bewildered, as if he had fallen from the clouds into the middle of the confusion on the stage*). We are? Excuse me, but what do you mean, a rehearsal?

PRODUCER. I mean a rehearsal—a rehearsal for the benefit of the actors. (*Pointing to the* ACTORS.)

FATHER. But if we are the characters …

PRODUCER. That's right, you're 'the characters': but characters don't act here, my dear chap. It's actors who act here. The characters are there in the script—(*Pointing to the* PROMPTOR.) that's when there is a script.

FATHER. That's the point! Since there isn't one and you have the luck to have the CHARACTERS alive in front of you …

PRODUCER. Great! You want to do everything yourselves, do you? To act your own play, to produce your own play!

FATHER. Well yes, just as we are.

PRODUCER. That would be an experience for us, I can tell you!

LEADING ACTOR. And what about us? What would we be doing then?

PRODUCER. Don't tell me you think you know how to act! Don't make me laugh! (*The* ACTORS *in fact laugh.*) There you are, you see, you've made them laugh. (*Then remembering.*) But let's get back to the point! We need to cast the play. Well, that's easy: it almost casts itself. (*To the* SECOND ACTRESS.) You, the mother. (*To the* FATHER.) You'll need to give her a name.

FATHER. Amalia.

PRODUCER. But that's the real name of your wife isn't it? We can't use her real name.

FATHER. But why not? That is her name. … But perhaps if this lady is to play the part … (*Indicating the* ACTRESS *vaguely with a wave of his hand.*) I think of her as Amalia … (*Pointing to the* MOTHER.) But do as you like … (*A little confused.*) I don't know what to say. … I'm already starting to … how can I explain it … to sound false, my own words sound like someone else's.

PRODUCER. Now don't worry yourself about it, don't worry about it at all. We'll work out the right tone of voice. As for the name, if you want it to be Amalia, then Amalia it shall be: or we can find another. For the moment we'll refer to the CHARACTERS like this: (*To the* YOUNG ACTOR, *the juvenile lead.*) you are The Son. (*To the* LEADING ACTRESS.) You, of course, are The Stepdaughter.

STEPDAUGHTER (*excitedly*). What did you say? That woman is me? (*Bursts into laughter.*)

PRODUCER (*angrily*). What are you laughing at?

LEADING ACTRESS (*indignantly*). Nobody has ever dared to laugh at me before! Either you treat me with respect or I'm walking out! (*Starting to go.*)

STEPDAUGHTER. I'm sorry. I wasn't really laughing at you.

PRODUCER (*to the* STEPDAUGHTER). You should feel proud to be played by ...

LEADING ACTRESS (*quickly, scornfully*). ... that woman!

STEPDAUGHTER. But I wasn't thinking about her, honestly. I was thinking about me: I can't see myself in you at all ... you're not a bit like me!

FATHER. Yes, that's right: you see, our meaning ...

PRODUCER. What are you talking about, 'our meaning'? Do you think you have exclusive rights to what you represent? Do you think it can only exist inside you? Not a bit of it!

FATHER. What? Don't we even have our own meaning?

PRODUCER. Not a bit of it! Whatever you mean is only material here, to which the actors give form and body, voice and gesture, and who, through their art, have given expression to much better material than what you have to offer: yours is really very trivial and if it stands up on the stage, the credit, believe me, will all be due to my actors.

FATHER. I don't dare to contradict you. But you for your part, must believe me—it doesn't seem trivial to us. We are suffering terribly now, with these bodies, these faces ...

PRODUCER (*interrupting impatiently*). Yes, well, the make-up will change that, make-up will change that, at least as far as the faces are concerned.

FATHER. Yes, but the voices, the gestures ...

PRODUCER. That's enough! You can't come on the stage here as yourselves. It is our actors who will represent you here: and let that be the end of it!

FATHER. I understand that. But now I think I see why our author who saw us alive as we are here now, didn't want to put us on the stage. I don't want to offend your actors. God forbid that I should! But I think that if I saw myself represented ... by I don't know whom ...

LEADING ACTOR (*rising majestically and coming forward, followed by a laughing group of* YOUNG ACTRESSES). By me, if you don't object.

FATHER (*respectfully, smoothly*). I shall be honoured, sir.

(*He bows.*) But I think, that no matter how hard this gentleman works with all his will and all his art to identify himself with me ... (*He stops, confused.*)

LEADING ACTOR. Yes, go on.

FATHER. Well, I was saying the performance he will give, even if he is made up to look like me … I mean with the difference in our appearance … (*All the* ACTORS *laugh.*) it will be difficult for it to be a performance of me as I really am. It will be more like—well, not just because of his figure—it will be more an interpretation of what I am, what he believes me to be, and not how I know myself to be. And it seems to me that this should be taken into account by those who are going to comment on us.

PRODUCER. So you are already worrying about what the critics will say, are you? And I'm still waiting to get this thing started! The critics can say what they like: and we'll worry about putting on the play. If we can! (*Stepping out of the group and looking around.*) Come on, come on! Is the scene set for us yet? (*To the* ACTORS *and* CHARACTERS.) Out of the way! Let's have a look at it. (*Climbing down off the stage.*) Don't let's waste any more time. (*To the* STEPDAUGHTER.) Does it look all right to you? Yes, an envelope for letters!

STEPDAUGHTER. What? That? I don't recognise it at all.

PRODUCER. Good God! Did you expect us to reconstruct the room at the back of Mme. Pace's shop here on the stage? (*To the* FATHER.) Did you say the room had flowered wallpaper?

FATHER. White, yes.

PRODUCER. Well it's not white: it's striped. That sort of thing doesn't matter at all! As for the furniture, it looks to me as if we have nearly everything we need. Move that little table a bit further downstage. (*A* STAGE HAND *does it. To the* PROPERTY MAN.) Go and fetch an envelope, pale blue if you can find one, and give it to that gentleman there. (*Pointing to the* FATHER.)

STAGE HAND. An envelope for letters?

PRODUCER)

FATHER)

STAGE HAND. Right. (*He goes off.*)

PRODUCER. Now then, come on! The first scene is the young lady's. (*The* LEADING ACTRESS *comes to the centre.*) No, no, not yet. I said the young lady's. (*He points to the* STEPDAUGHTER.) You stay there and watch.

STEPDAUGHTER (*adding quickly*). … how I bring it to life.

LEADING ACTRESS (*resenting this*). I shall know how to bring it to life, don't you worry, when I am allowed to.

PRODUCER (*his head in his hands*). Ladies, please, no more arguments! Now then. The first scene is between the young lady and Mme Pace. Oh! (*Worried, turning round and looking out into the auditorium.*) Where is Mme. Pace?

FATHER. She isn't here with us.

PRODUCER. So what do we do now?

FATHER. But she is real. She's real too!

PRODUCER. All right. So where is she?

FATHER. May I deal with this? (*Turns to the* ACTRESSES.) Would each of you ladies be kind enough to lend me a hat, a coat, a scarf or something?

ACTRESSES (*some are surprised or amused*). What? My scarf? A coat? What's he want my hat for? What are you wanting to do with them? (*All the* ACTRESSES *are laughing.*)

FATHER. Oh, nothing much, just hang them up here on the racks for a minute or two. Perhaps someone would be kind enough to lend me a coat?

ACTORS. Just a coat? Come on, more! The man must be mad.

AN ACTRESS. What for? Only my coat?

FATHER. Yes, to hang up here, just for a moment. I'm very grateful to you. Do you mind?

ACTRESSES (*taking off various hats, coats, scarves, laughing and going to hang them on the racks*). Why not? Here you are. I really think it's crazy. Is it to dress the set?

FATHER. Yes, exactly. It's to dress the set.

PRODUCER. Would you mind telling me what you are doing?

FATHER. Yes, of course: perhaps, if we dress the set better, she will be drawn by the articles of her trade and, who knows, she may even come to join us … (*He invites them to watch the door at the back of the set.*) Look! Look!

The door at the back opens and MME. PACE *takes a few steps downstage: she is a gross old harridan wearing a ludicrous carroty-coloured wig with a single red rose stuck in at one side, Spanish fashion: garishly made-up: in a vulgar but stylish red silk dress, holding an ostrich-feather fan in one hand and a cigarette between two fingers in the other. At the sight of this Apparition, the* ACTORS *and the* PRODUCER *immediately jump off the stage with cries of fear, leaping down into the auditorium and up the aisles. The* STEPDAUGHTER, *however, runs across to* MME. PACE, *and greets her respectfully, as if she were the mistress.*

STEPDAUGHTER (*running across to her*). Here she is! Here she is!

FATHER (*smiling broadly*). It's her! What did I tell you? Here she is!

PRODUCER (*recovering from his shock, indignantly*). What sort of TRICK is this?

LEADING ACTOR (*almost at the same time as the others*). What the hell is happening?

JUVENILE LEAD. Where on earth did they get that extra from?

YOUNG ACTRESS. They were keeping her hidden!

LEADING ACTRESS. It's a game, a conjuring TRICK!

FATHER. Wait a minute! Why do you want to spoil a miracle by being factual. Can't you see this is a miracle of reality, that is born, brought to life, lured here, reproduced, just for the sake of this scene, with more right to be alive here than you have? Perhaps it has more truth than you have yourselves. Which actress can improve on

Mme. Pace there? Well? That is the real Mme. Pace. You must admit that the actress who plays her will be less true than she is herself—and there she is in person! Look! My daughter recognised her straight away and went to meet her. Now watch—just watch this scene.

Hesitantly, the PRODUCER *and the* ACTORS *move back to their original places on the stage. But the scene between the* STEPDAUGHTER *and* MME. PACE *has already begun while the* ACTORS *were protesting and the* FATHER *explaining: it is being played under their breaths, very quietly, very naturally, in a way that is obviously impossible on stage. So when the* ACTORS' *attention is recalled by the* FATHER *they turn and see that* MME. PACE *has just put her hand under the* STEPDAUGHTER'S *chin to make her lift her head up: they also hear her speak in a way that is unintelligible to them. They watch and listen hard for a few moments, then they start to make fun of them.*

PRODUCER. Well?

LEADING ACTOR. What's she saying?

LEADING ACTRESS. Can't hear a thing!

JUVENILE LEAD. Louder! Speak up!

STEPDAUGHTER (*leaving* MME. PACE *who has an astonishing smile on her face, and coming down to the* ACTORS). Louder? What do you mean, 'Louder'? What we're talking about you can't talk about loudly. I could shout about it a moment ago to embarrass him (*Pointing to the* FATHER.) to shame him and to get my own back on him! But it's a different matter for Mme. Pace. It would mean prison for her.

PRODUCER. What the hell are you on about? Here in the theatre you have to make yourself heard! Don't you see that? We can't hear you even from here, and we're on the stage with you! Imagine what it would be like with an audience out front! You need to make the scene go! And after all, you would speak normally to each other when you're alone, and you will be, because we shan't be here anyway. I mean we're only here because it's a rehearsal. So just imagine that there you are in the room at the back of the shop, and there's no one to hear you.

The STEPDAUGHTER, *with a knowing smile, wags her finger and her head rather elegantly, as if to say no.*

PRODUCER. Why not?

STEPDAUGHTER (*mysteriously, whispering loudly*). Because there is someone who will hear if she speaks normally. (*Pointing to* MME. PACE.)

PRODUCER (*anxiously*). You're not going to make someone else appear are you?

The ACTORS *get ready to dive off the stage again,*

FATHER. No, no. She means me. I ought to be over there, waiting behind the door: and Mme. Pace knows I'm there, so excuse me will you: I'll go there now so that I shall be ready for my entrance.

He goes towards the back of the stage.

PRODUCER (*stopping him*). No, no wait a minute! You must remember the stage conventions! Before you can go on to that part ...

STEPDAUGHTER (*interrupts him*). Oh yes, let's get on with that part. Now! Now! I'm dying to do that scene. If he wants to go through it now, I'm ready!

PRODUCER (*shouting*). But before that we must have, clearly stated, the scene between you and her. (*Pointing to* MME. PACE.) Do you see?

STEPDAUGHTER. Oh God! She's only told me what you already know, that my mother's needlework is badly done again, the dress is spoilt and that I shall have to be patient if I want her to go on helping us out of our mess.

MME. PACE (*coming forward, with a great air of importance*). Ah, yes, sir, for that I do not wish to make a profit, to make advantage.

PRODUCER (*half frightened*). What? Does she really speak like that?

All the ACTORS *burst out laughing.*

STEPDAUGHTER (*laughing too*). Yes, she speaks like that, half in Spanish, in the silliest way imaginable!

MME. PACE. Ah it is not good manners that you laugh at me when I make myself to speak, as I can, English, senor.

PRODUCER. No, no, you're right! Speak like that, please speak like that, madam. It'll be marvellous. Couldn't be better! It'll add a little touch of comedy to a rather crude situation. Speak like that! It'll be great!

STEPDAUGHTER. Great! Why not? When you hear a proposition made in that sort of accent, it'll almost seem like a joke, won't it? Perhaps you'll want to laugh when you hear that there's an 'old senor' who wants to 'amuse himself with me'—isn't that right, Madame?

MME. PACE. Not so old ... but not quite young, no? But if he is not to your taste ... he is, how you say, discreet!

The MOTHER *leaps up, to the astonishment and dismay of the* ACTORS *who had not been paying any attention to her, so that when she shouts out they are startled and then smilingly restrain her: however she has already snatched off* MME. PACE's *wig and flung it on the floor.*

MOTHER. You witch! Witch! Murderess! Oh, my daughter!

STEPDAUGHTER (*running across and taking hold of the* MOTHER). No! No! Mother! Please!

FATHER (*running across to her as well*). Calm yourself, calm yourself! Come and sit down.

MOTHER. Get her away from here!

STEPDAUGHTER (*to the* PRODUCER *who has also crossed to her*). My mother can't bear to be in the same place with her.

FATHER (*also speaking quietly to the* PRODUCER). They can't possibly be in the same place! That's why she wasn't with us when we first came, do you see! If they meet, everything's given away from the very beginning.

PRODUCER. It's not important, that's not important! This is only a first run-through at the moment! It's all useful stuff, even if it is confused. I'll sort it all out later. (*Turning to the* MOTHER *and taking her to sit down on her chair.*) Come on my dear, take it easy, take it easy: come and sit down again.

STEPDAUGHTER. Go on, Mme. Pace.

MME. PACE (*offended*). Oh no, thank-you! I no longer do nothing here with your mother present.

STEPDAUGHTER. Get on with it, bring in this 'old senor' who wants to 'amuse himself with me'! (*Turning majestically to the others.*) You see, this next scene has got to be played out—we must do it now. (*To* MME. PACE.) Oh, you can go!

MME. PACE. Ah, I go, I go—I go! Most probably I go!

She leaves banging her wig back into place, glaring furiously at the ACTORS *who applaud her exit, laughing loudly.*

STEPDAUGHTER (*to the* FATHER). Now you come on! No, you don't need to go off again! Come back! Pretend you've just come in! Look, I'm standing here with my eyes on the ground, modestly—well, come on, speak up! Use that special sort of voice, like somebody who has just come in. 'Good afternoon, my dear.'

PRODUCER (*off the stage by now*). Look here, who's the director here, you or me? (*To the* FATHER *who looks uncertain and bewildered.*) Go on, do as she says: go upstage—no, no don't bother to make an entrance. Then come down stage again.

The FATHER *does as he is told, half mesmerised. He is very pale but already involved in the reality of his recreated life, smiles as he draws near the back of the stage, almost if he genuinely is not aware of the drama that is about to sweep over him. The* ACTORS *are immediately intent on the scene that is beginning now.*

The Scene

FATHER (*coming forward with a new note in his voice*). Good afternoon, my dear.

STEPDAUGHTER (*her head down trying to hide her fright*). Good afternoon.

FATHER (*studying her a little under the brim of her hat which partly hides her face from hint and seeing that she is very young, he exclaims to himself a little complacently and a little guardedly because of the danger of being compromised in a risky adventure*). Ah … but … tell me, this won't be the first time, will it? The first time you've been here?

STEPDAUGHTER. No, sir.

FATHER. You've been here before? (*And after the* STEPDAUGHTER *has nodded an answer.*) More than once? (*He waits for her reply: tries again to look at her under the brim of her hat: smiles: then says.*) Well then … it shouldn't be too. … May I take off your hat?

STEPDAUGHTER (*quickly, to stop him, unable to conceal her shudder of fear and disgust*). No, don't! I'll do it!

She takes it off unsteadily.

The MOTHER *watches the scene intently with the* SON *and the two smaller children who cling close to her all the time: they make a group on one side of the stage opposite the* ACTORS. *She follows the words and actions of the* FATHER *and the* STEPDAUGHTER *in this scene with a variety of expressions on her face—sadness, dismay, anxiety, horror: sometimes she turns her face away and sobs.*

MOTHER. Oh God! Oh God!

FATHER (*he stops as if turned to stone by the sobbing: then he goes on in the same tone of voice*). Here, give it to me. I'll hang it up for you. (*He takes the hat in his hand.*) But such a pretty, dear little head like yours should have a much smarter hat than this! Would you like to help me choose one, then, from these hats of Madame's hanging up here? Would you?

YOUNG ACTRESS (*interrupting*). Be careful! Those are our hats!

PRODUCER (*quickly and angrily*). For God's sake, shut up! Don't try to be funny! We're rehearsing! (*Turns back to the* STEPDAUGHTER.) Please go on, will you, from where you were interrupted.

STEPDAUGHTER (*going on*). No, thank you, sir.

FATHER. Oh, don't say no to me please! Say you'll have one—to please me. Isn't this a pretty one—look! And then it will please Madame too, you know. She's put them out here on purpose, of course.

STEPDAUGHTER. No, look, I could never wear it.

FATHER. Are you thinking of what they would say at home when you went in wearing a new hat? Goodness me! Don't you know what to do? Shall I tell you what to say at home?

STEPDAUGHTER (*furiously, nearly exploding*). That's not why! I couldn't wear it because ... as you can see: you should have noticed it before. (*Indicating her black dress.*)

FATHER. You're in mourning! Oh, forgive me. You're right, I see that now. Please forgive me. Believe me, I'm really very sorry.

STEPDAUGHTER (*gathering all her strength and making herself overcome her contempt and revulsion*). That's enough. Don't go on, that's enough. I ought to be thanking you and not letting you blame yourself and get upset. Don't think any more about what I told you, please. And I should do the same. (*Forcing herself to smile and adding.*) I should try to forget that I'm dressed like this.

PRODUCER (*interrupting, turning to the* PROMPTOR *in the box and jumping up on the stage again*). Hold it, hold it! Don't put that last line down, leave it out. (*Turning to the* FATHER *and the* STEPDAUGHTER.) It's going well! It's going well! (*Then to the* FATHER *alone.*) Then we'll put in there the bit that we talked about. (*To the* ACTORS.) That scene with the hats is good, isn't it?

STEPDAUGHTER. But the best bit is coming now! Why can't we get on with it?

PRODUCER. Just be patient, wait a minute. (*Turning and moving across to the* ACTORS.) Of course, it'll all have to be made a lot more light-hearted.

LEADING ACTOR. We shall have to play it a lot quicker, I think.

LEADING ACTRESS. Of course: there's nothing particularly difficult in it. (*To the* LEADING ACTOR.) Shall we run through it now?

LEADING ACTOR. Yes right. ... Shall we take it from my entrance? (*He goes to his position behind the door upstage.*)

PRODUCER (*to the* LEADING ACTRESS). Now then, listen, imagine the scene between you and Mme. Pace is finished. I'll write it up myself properly later on. You ought to be over here I think—(*She goes the opposite way.*) Where are you going now?

LEADING ACTRESS. Just a minute, I want to get my hat—(*She crosses to take her hat from the stand.*)

PRODUCER. Right, good, ready now? You are standing here with your head down.

STEPDAUGHTER (*very amused*). But she's not dressed in black!

LEADING ACTRESS. Oh, but I shall be, and I'll look a lot better than you do, darling.

PRODUCER (*to the* STEPDAUGHTER). Shut up, will you! Go over there and watch! You might learn something! (*Clapping his hands.*) Right! Come on! Quiet please! Take it from his entrance.

He climbs off stage so that he can see better. The door opens at the back of the set and the LEADING ACTOR *enters with the lively, knowing air of an ageing rouet. The playing of the following scene by the* ACTORS *must seem from the very beginning to be something quite different from the earlier scene, but without having the faintest air of parody in it.*

Naturally the STEPDAUGHTER *and the* FATHER, *unable to see themselves in the* LEADING ACTOR *and* LEADING ACTRESS, *hearing their words said by them, express their reactions in different ways, by gestures, or smiles or obvious protests so that we are aware of their suffering, their astonishment, their disbelief.*

The PROMPTOR'*s voice is heard clearly between every line in the scene, telling the* ACTORS *what to say next.*

LEADING ACTOR. Good afternoon, my dear.
FATHER (*immediately, unable to restrain himself*). Oh, no!

The STEPDAUGHTER, *watching the* LEADING ACTOR *enter this way, bursts into laughter.*

PRODUCER (*furious*). Shut up, for God's sake! And don't you dare laugh like that! We're never going to get anywhere at this rate.
STEPDAUGHTER (*coming to the front*). I'm sorry, I can't help it! The lady stands exactly where you told her to stand and she never moved. But if it were me and I heard someone say good afternoon to rue in that way and with a voice like that I should burst out laughing—so I did.
FATHER (*coming down a little too*). Yes, she's right, the whole manner, the voice …
PRODUCER. To hell with the manner and the voice! Get out of the way, will you, and let me watch the rehearsal!
LEADING ACTOR (*coming down stage*). If I have to play an old man who has come to a knocking shop—
PRODUCER. Take no notice, ignore them. Go on please! It's going well, it's going well! (*He waits for the* ACTOR *to begin again*). Right, again!
LEADING ACTOR. Good afternoon, my dear.
LEADING ACTRESS. Good afternoon.

LEADING ACTOR (*copying the gestures of the* FATHER, *looking under the brim of the hat, but expressing distinctly the two emotions, first, complacent satisfaction and then anxiety*). Ah! But tell me ... this won't be the first time I hope.

FATHER (*instinctively correcting him*). Not 'I hope'—'will it', 'will it'.

PRODUCER. Say 'will it'—and it's a question.

LEADING ACTOR (*glaring at the* PROMPTOR). I distinctly heard him say 'I hope'.

PRODUCER. So what? It's all the same, 'I hope' or 'isn't it'. It doesn't make any difference. Carry on, carry on. But perhaps it should still be a little bit lighter; I'll show you—watch me! (*He climbs up on the stage again, and going back to the entrance, he does it himself.*) Good afternoon, my dear.

LEADING ACTRESS. Good afternoon.

PRODUCER. Ah, tell me ... (*He turns to the* LEADING ACTOR *to make sure that he has seen the way he has demonstrated of looking under the brim of the hat.*) You see—surprise ... anxiety and self-satisfaction. (*Then, starting again, he turns to the* LEADING ACTRESS.) This won't be the first time, will it? The first time you've been here? (*Again turns to the* LEADING ACTOR, *questioningly.*) Right? (*To the* LEADING ACTRESS.) And then she says, 'No, sir'. (*Again to* LEADING ACTOR.) See what I mean? More subtlety. (*And he climbs off the stage.*)

LEADING ACTRESS. No, sir.

LEADING ACTOR. You've been here before? More than once?

PRODUCER. No, no, no! Wait for it, wait for it. Let her answer first. 'You've been here before?'

> *The* LEADING ACTRESS *lifts her head a little, her eyes closed in pain and disgust, and when the* PRODUCER *says 'Now' she nods her head twice.*

STEPDAUGHTER (*involuntarily*). Oh, my God! (*And she immediately claps her hand over her mouth to stifle her laughter.*)

PRODUCER. What now?

STEPDAUGHTER (*quickly*). Nothing, nothing!

PRODUCER (*to* LEADING ACTOR). Come on, then, now it's you.

LEADING ACTOR. More than once? Well then, it shouldn't be too. ... May I take off your hat?

> *The* LEADING ACTOR *says this last line in such a way and adds to it such a gesture that the* STEPDAUGHTER, *even with her hand over her mouth trying to stop herself laughing, can't prevent a noisy burst of laughter.*

LEADING ACTRESS (*indignantly turning*). I'm not staying any longer to be laughed at by that woman!

LEADING ACTOR. Nor am I! That's the end—no more!

PRODUCER (*to* STEPDAUGHTER, *shouting*). Once and for all, will you shut up! Shut up!

STEPDAUGHTER. Yes, I'm sorry … I'm sorry.

PRODUCER. You're an ill-mannered little bitch! That's what you are! And you've gone too far this time!

FATHER (*trying to interrupt*). Yes, you're right, she went too far, but please forgive her …

PRODUCER (*jumping on the stage*). Why should I forgive her? Her behaviour is intolerable!

FATHER. Yes, it is, but the scene made such a peculiar impact on us …

PRODUCER. Peculiar? What do you mean peculiar? Why peculiar?

FATHER. I'm full of admiration for your actors, for this gentleman (*To the* LEADING ACTOR.) and this lady. (*To the* LEADING ACTRESS.) But, you see, well … they're not us!

PRODUCER. Right! They're not! They're actors!

FATHER. That's just the point—they're actors. And they are acting our parts very well, both of them. But that's what's different. However much they want to be the same as us, they're not.

PRODUCER. But why aren't they? What is it now?

FATHER. It's something to do with … being themselves, I suppose, not being us.

PRODUCER. Well we can't do anything about that! I've told you already. You can't play the parts yourselves.

FATHER. Yes, I know, I know …

PRODUCER. Right then. That's enough of that. (*Turning back to the* ACTORS.) We'll rehearse this later on our own, as we usually do. It's always a bad idea to have rehearsals with authors there! They're never satisfied. (*Turns back to the* FATHER *and the* STEPDAUGHTER.) Come on, let's get on with it; and let's see if it's possible to do it without laughing.

STEPDAUGHTER. I won't laugh any more, I won't really. My best bit's coming up now, you wait and see!

PRODUCER. Right: when you say 'Don't think any more about what I told you, please. And I should do the same'. (*Turning to the* FATHER.) then you come in immediately with the line 'I understand, ah yes, I understand' and then you ask …

STEPDAUGHTER (*interrupting*). Ask what? What does he ask?

PRODUCER. Why you're in mourning.

STEPDAUGHTER. No! No! That's not right! Look: when I said that I should try not to think about the way I was dressed, do you know what he said? 'Well then, let's take it off, we'll take it off at once, shall we, your little black dress.'

PRODUCER. That's great! That'll be wonderful! That'll bring the house down!

STEPDAUGHTER. But it's the truth!

PRODUCER. The truth! Do me a favour will you? This is the theatre you know! Truth's all very well up to a point but …

STEPDAUGHTER. What do you want to do then?

PRODUCER. You'll see! You'll see! Leave it all to me.

STEPDAUGHTER. No. No I won't. I know what you want to do! Out of my feeling of re-vulsion, out of all the vile and sordid reasons why I am what I am, you want to make a sugary little sentimental romance. You want him to ask me why I'm in mourning and you want me to reply with the tears running down my face that it is only two months since my father died. No. No. I won't have it! He must say to me what he really did say. 'Well then, let's take it off, we'll take it off at once, shall we, your little black dress.' And I, with my heart still grieving for my father's death only two months before, I went behind there, do you see? Behind that screen and with my fingers trembling with shame and loathing I took off the dress, unfastened my bra …

PRODUCER (*his head in his hands*). For God's sake! What are you saying!

STEPDAUGHTER (*shouting excitedly*). The truth! I'm telling you the truth!

PRODUCER. All right then. Now listen to me. I'm not denying it's the truth. Right. And believe me I understand your horror, but you must see that we can't really put a scene like that on the stage.

STEPDAUGHTER. You can't? Then thanks very much. I'm not stopping here.

PRODUCER. No, listen …

STEPDAUGHTER. No, I'm going. I'm not stopping. The pair of you have worked it all out together, haven't you, what to put in the scene. Well, thank you very much! I understand everything now! He wants to get to the scene where he can talk about his spiritual torments but I want to show you my drama! Mine!

PRODUCER (*shaking with anger*). Now we're getting to the real truth of it, aren't we? Your drama—yours! But it's not only yours, you know. It's drama for the other people as well! For him (*Pointing to the* FATHER.) and for your mother! You can't have one character coming on like you're doing, trampling over the others, taking over the play. Everything needs to be balanced and in harmony so that we can show what has to be shown! I know perfectly well that we've all got a life inside us and that we all want to parade it in front of other people. But that's the difficulty, how to present only the bits that are necessary in relation to the other CHARACTERS: and in the small amount we show, to hint at all the rest of the inner life of the character!

I agree, it would be so much simpler, if each character, in a soliloquy or in a lecture could pour out to the audience what's bubbling away inside him. But that's not the way we work. (*In an indulgent, placating tone.*) You must restrain yourself, you see. And believe me, it's in your own interests: because you could so easily make a bad impression, with all this uncontrollable anger, this disgust and exasperation. That seems a bit odd, if you don't mind my saying so, when you've admitted that you'd been with other men at Mme. Pace's and more than once.

STEPDAUGHTER. I suppose that's true. But you know, all the other men were all him as far as I was concerned.

PRODUCER (*not understanding*). Uum—? What? What are you talking about?

STEPDAUGHTER. If someone falls into evil ways, isn't the responsibility for all the evil which follows to be laid at the door of the person who caused the first mistake? And in my case, it's him, from before I was even born. Look at him: see if it isn't true.

PRODUCER. Right then! What about the weight of remorse he's carrying? Isn't that important? Then, give him the chance to show it to us.

STEPDAUGHTER. But how? How on earth can he show all his long-suffering remorse, all his moral torments as he calls them, if you don't let him show his horror when he finds me in his arms one fine day, after he had asked me to take my dress off, a black dress for my father who had just died: and he finds that I'm the child he used to go and watch as she came out of school, me, a woman now, and a woman he could buy. (*She says these last words in a voice trembling with emotion.*)

> The MOTHER, *hearing her say this, is overcome and at first gives way to stifled sobs: but then she bursts out into uncontrollable crying. Everyone is deeply moved. There is a long pause.*

STEPDAUGHTER (*as soon as the* MOTHER *has quietened herself she goes on, firmly and thoughtfully*). At the moment we are here on our own and the public doesn't know about us. But tomorrow you will present us and our story in whatever way you choose, I suppose. But wouldn't you like to see the real drama? Wouldn't you like to see it explode into life, as it really did?

PRODUCER. Of course, nothing I'd like better, then I can use as much of it as possible.

STEPDAUGHTER. Then persuade my mother to leave.

MOTHER (*rising and her quiet weeping changing to a loud cry*). No! No! Don't let her! Don't let her do it!

PRODUCER. But they're only doing it for me to watch—only for me, do you see?

MOTHER. I can't bear it, I can't bear it!

PRODUCER. But if it's already happened, I can't see what's the objection.

MOTHER. No! It's happening now, as well: it's happening all the time. I'm not acting my suffering! Can't you understand that? I'm alive and here now but I can never forget that terrible moment of agony, that repeats itself endlessly and vividly in my mind. And these two little children here, you've never heard them speak have you? That's because they don't speak any more, not now. They just cling to me all the time: they help to keep my grief alive, but they don't really exist for themselves any more, not for themselves. And she (*Indicating the* STEPDAUGHTER.) … she has gone away, left me completely, she's lost to me, lost … you see her here for one reason only: to keep perpetually before me, always real, the anguish and the torment I've suffered on her account.

FATHER. The eternal moment, as I told you, sir. She is here (*Indicating the* STEPDAUGH-TER.) to keep me too in that moment, trapped for all eternity, chained and suspended in that one fleeting shameful moment of my life. She can't give up her role and you cannot rescue me from it.

PRODUCER. But I'm not saying that we won't present that bit. Not at all! It will be the climax of the first act, when she (*He points to the* MOTHER.) surprises you.

FATHER. That's right, because that is the moment when I am sentenced: all our suffering should reach a climax in her cry. (*Again indicating the* MOTHER.)

STEPDAUGHTER. I can still hear it ringing in my ears! It was that cry that sent me mad! You can have me played just as you like: it doesn't matter! Dressed, too, if you want, so long as I can have at least an arm—only an arm—bare, because, you see, as I was standing like this (*She moves across to the* FATHER *and leans her head on his chest.*) with my head like this and my arms round his neck, I saw a vein, here in my arm, throbbing: and then it was almost as if that throbbing vein filled me with a shivering fear, and I shut my eyes tightly like this, like this and buried my head in his chest. (*Turning to the* MOTHER.) Scream, Mummy, scream. (*She buries her head in the* FATHER'*S chest, and with her shoulders raised as if to try not to hear the scream, she speaks with a voice tense with suffering.*) Scream, as you screamed then!

MOTHER (*coming forward to pull them apart*). No! She's my daughter! My daughter! (*Tearing her from him.*) You brute, you animal, she's my daughter! Can't you see she's my daughter?

PRODUCER (*retreating as far as the footlights while the* ACTORS *are full of dismay*). Marvellous! Yes, that's great! And then curtain, curtain!

FATHER (*running downstage to him, excitedly*). That's it, that's it! Because it really was like that!

PRODUCER (*full of admiration and enthusiasm*). Yes, yes, that's got to be the curtain line! Curtain! Curtain!

At the repeated calls of the PRODUCER, *the* STAGE MANAGER *lowers the curtain, leaving on the apron in front, the* PRODUCER *and the* FATHER.

PRODUCER (*looking up to heaven with his arms raised*). The idiots! I didn't mean now! The bloody idiots—dropping it in on us like that! (*To the* FATHER, *and lifting up a corner of the curtain.*) That's marvellous! Really marvellous! A terrific effect! We'll end the act like that! It's the best tag line I've heard for ages. What a First Act ending! I couldn't have done better if I'd written it myself!

They go through the curtain together.

ACT THREE

When the curtain goes up we see that the STAGE MANAGER *and* STAGE HANDS *have struck the first scene and have set another, a small garden fountain.*

From one side of the stage the ACTORS *come on and from the other the* CHARACTERS. *The* PRODUCER *is standing in the middle of the stage with his hand over his mouth, thinking.*

PRODUCER (*after a short pause, shrugging his shoulders*). Well, then: let's get on to the second act! Leave it all to me, and everything will work out properly.

STEPDAUGHTER. This is where we go to live at his house (*Pointing to the* FATHER.) in spite of the objections of him over there. (*Pointing to the* SON.)

PRODUCER (*getting impatient*). All right, all right! But leave it all to me, will you?

STEPDAUGHTER. Provided that you make, it clear that he objected!

MOTHER (*from the corner, shaking her head*). That doesn't matter! The worse it was for us, the more he suffered from remorse.

PRODUCER (*impatiently*). I know, I know! I'll take it all into account. Don't worry!

MOTHER (*pleading*). To set my mind at rest, sir, please do make sure it's clear that I tried all I could—

STEPDAUGHTER (*interrupting her scornfully and going on*).—to pacify me, to persuade me that this despicable creature wasn't worth making trouble about! (*To the* PRODUCER.) Go on, set her mind at rest, because it's true, she tried very hard. I'm having a whale of a time now! You can see, can't you, that the meeker she was and the more she tried to worm her way into his heart, the more lofty and distant he became! How's that for a dramatic situation!

PRODUCER. Do you think that we can actually begin the Second Act?

STEPDAUGHTER. I won't say another word! But you'll see that it won't be possible to play everything in the garden, like you want to do.

PRODUCER. Why not?

STEPDAUGHTER (*pointing to the* SON). Because to start with, he stays shut up in his room in the house all the time! And then all the scenes for this poor little devil of a boy happen in the house. I've told you once.

PRODUCER. Yes, I know that! But on the other hand we can't put up a notice to tell the audience where the scene is taking place, or change the set three or four times in each Act.

LEADING ACTOR. That's what they used to do in the good old days.

PRODUCER. Yes, when the audience was about as bright as that little girl over there!

LEADING ACTRESS. And it makes it easier to create an illusion.

FATHER (*leaping up*). An illusion? For pity's sake don't talk about illusions! Don't use that word, it's especially hurtful to us!

PRODUCER (*astonished*). And why, for God's sake?

FATHER. It's so hurtful, so cruel! You ought to have realized that!

PRODUCER. What else should we call it? That's what we do here—create an illusion for the audience …

LEADING ACTOR. With our performance …

PRODUCER. A perfect illusion of reality!

FATHER. Yes, I know that, I understand. But on the other hand, perhaps you don't understand us yet. I'm sorry! But you see, for you and for your actors what goes on here on the stage is, quite rightly, well, it's only a game.

LEADING ACTRESS (*interrupting indignantly*). A game! How dare you! We're not children! What happens here is serious!

FATHER. I'm not saying that it isn't serious. And I mean, really, not just a game but an art, that tries, as you've just said, to create the perfect illusion of reality.

PRODUCER. That's right!

FATHER. Now try to imagine that we, as you see us here, (*He indicates himself and the other* CHARACTERS.) that we have no other reality outside this illusion.

PRODUCER (*astonished and looking at the* ACTORS *with the same sense of bewilderment as they feel themselves*). What the hell are you talking about now?

FATHER (*after a short pause as he looks at them, with a faint smile*). Isn't it obvious? What other reality is there for us? What for you is an illusion you create, for us is our only reality. (*Brief pause. He moves towards the* PRODUCER *and goes on.*) But it's not only true for us, it's true for others as well, you know. Just think about it. (*He looks intently into the* PRODUCER'S *eyes.*) Do you really know who you are? (*He stands pointing at the* PRODUCER.)

PRODUCER (*a little disturbed but with a half smile*). What? Who I am? I am me!

FATHER. What if I told you that that wasn't true: what if I told you that you were me?

PRODUCER. I would tell you that you were mad!

The ACTORS *laugh.*

FATHER. That's right, laugh! Because everything here is a game! (*To the* PRODUCER.) And yet you object when I say that it is only for a game that the gentleman there (*Pointing to the* LEADING ACTOR.) who is 'himself' has to be 'me', who, on the contrary, am 'myself'. You see, I've caught you in a trap.

The ACTORS *start to laugh.*

PRODUCER. Not again! We've heard all about this a little while ago.

FATHER. No, no. I didn't really want to talk about this. I'd like you to forget about your game, (*Looking at the* LEADING ACTRESS *as if to anticipate what she will say.*) I'm sorry—your artistry! Your art!—that you usually pursue here with your actors; and I am going to ask you again in all seriousness, who are you?

PRODUCER (*turning with a mixture of amazement and annoyance, to the* ACTORS). Of all the bloody nerve! A fellow who claims he is only a character comes and asks me who I am!

FATHER (*with dignity but without annoyance*). A character, my dear sir, can always ask a man who he is, because a character really has a life of his own, a life full of his own specific qualities, and because of these he is always 'someone'. While a man—I'm not speaking about you personally, of course, but man in general—well, he can be an absolute 'nobody'.

PRODUCER. All right, all right! Well, since you've asked me, I'm the Director, the Producer—I'm in charge! Do you understand?

FATHER (*half smiling, but gently and politely*). I'm only asking to try to find out if you really see yourself now in the same way that you saw yourself, for instance, once upon a time in the past, with all the illusions you had then, with everything inside and outside yourself as it seemed then—and not only seemed, but really was! Well then, look back on those illusions, those ideas that you don't have any more, on all those things that no longer seem the same to you. Don't you feel that not only this stage is falling away from under your feet but so is the earth itself, and that all these realities of today are going to seem tomorrow as if they had been an illusion?

PRODUCER. So? What does that prove?

FATHER. Oh, nothing much. I only want to make you see that if we (*Pointing to himself and the other* CHARACTERS.) have no other reality outside our own illusion, perhaps you ought to distrust your own sense of reality: because whatever is a reality today, whatever you touch and believe in and that seems real for you today, is going to be—like the reality of yesterday—an illusion tomorrow.

PRODUCER (*deciding to make fun of him*). Very good! So now you're saying that you as well as this play you're going to show me here, are more real than I am?

FATHER (*very seriously*). There's no doubt about that at all.

PRODUCER. Is that so?

FATHER. I thought you'd realised that from the beginning.

PRODUCER. More real than I am?

FATHER. If your reality can change between today and tomorrow—

PRODUCER. But everybody knows that it can change, don't they? It's always changing! Just like everybody else's!

FATHER (*crying out*). But ours doesn't change! Do you see? That's the difference! Ours doesn't change, it can't change, it can never be different, never, because it is already determined, like this, for ever, that's what's so terrible! We are an eternal reality. That should make you shudder to come near us.

PRODUCER (*jumping up, suddenly struck by an idea, and standing directly in front of the* FATHER). Then I should like to know when anyone saw a character step out of his part and make a speech like you've done, proposing things, explaining things. Tell me when, will you? I've never seen it before.

FATHER. You've never seen it because an author usually hides all the difficulties of creating. When the CHARACTERS are alive, really alive and standing in front of their author, he has only to follow their words, the actions that they suggest to him: and he must want them to be what they want to be: and it's his bad luck if he doesn't do what they want! When a character is born he immediately assumes such an independence even of his own author that everyone can imagine him in scores of situations that his author hadn't even thought of putting him in, and he sometimes acquires a meaning that his author never dreamed of giving him.

PRODUCER. Of course I know all that.

FATHER. Well, then. Why are you surprised by us? Imagine what a disaster it is for a character to be born in the imagination of an author who then refuses to give him life in a written script. Tell me if a character, left like this, suspended, created but without a final life, isn't right to do what we are doing now, here in front of you. We spent such a long time, such a very long time, believe me, urging our author, persuading him, first me, then her, (*Pointing to the* STEPDAUGHTER.) then this poor Mother …

STEPDAUGHTER (*coming down the stage as if in a dream*). It's true, I would go, would go and tempt him, time after time, in his gloomy study just as it was growing dark, when he was sitting quietly in an armchair not even bothering to switch a light on but leaving the shadows to fill the room: the shadows were swarming with us, we had come to tempt him. (*As if she could see herself there in the study and is annoyed by the presence of the* ACTORS.) Go away will you! Leave us alone! Mother there, with that son of hers—me with the little girl—that poor little kid always on his own—and then me with him (*Pointing to the* FATHER.) and then at last, just me, on my own, all on my own, in the shadows. (*She turns quickly as if she wants to cling on to the vision she has of herself, in the shadows.*) Ah, what scenes, what scenes we suggested to him! What a life I could have had! I tempted him more than the others!

FATHER. Oh yes, you did! And it was probably all your fault that he did nothing about it! You were so insistent, you made too many demands.

STEPDAUGHTER. But he wanted me to be like that! (*She comes closer to the* PRODUCER *to speak to him in confidence.*) I think it's more likely that he felt discouraged about the theatre and even despised it because the public only wants to see ... PRODUCER. Let's get on, for God's sake, let's get on. Come to the point will you?

STEPDAUGHTER. I'm sorry, but if you ask me, we've got too much happening already, just with our entry into his house. (*Pointing to the* FATHER.) You said that we couldn't put up a notice or change the set every five minutes.

PRODUCER. Right! Of course we can't! We must combine things, group them together in one continuous flowing action: not the way you've been wanting, first of all seeing your little brother come home from school and wander about the house like a lost soul, hiding behind the doors and brooding on some plan or other that would—what did you say it would do?

STEPDAUGHTER. Wither him ... shrivel him up completely.

PRODUCER. That's good! That's a good expression. And then you 'can see it there in his eyes, getting stronger all the time'—isn't that what you said?

STEPDAUGHTER. Yes, that's right. Look at him! (*Pointing to him as he stands next to his* MOTHER.)

PRODUCER. Yes, great! And then, at the same time, you want to show the LITTLE GIRL playing in the garden, all innocence. One in the house and the other in the garden—we can't do it, don't you see that?

STEPDAUGHTER. Yes, playing in the sun, so happy! It's the only pleasure I have left, her happiness, her delight in playing in the garden: away from the misery, the squalor of that sordid flat where all four of us slept and where she slept with me—with me! Just think of it! My vile, contaminated body close to hers, with her little arms wrapped tightly round my neck, so lovingly, so innocently. In the garden, whenever she saw me, she would run and take my hand. She never wanted to show me the big flowers, she would run about looking for the 'little weeny' ones, so that she could show them to me; she was so happy, so thrilled! (*As she says this, tortured by the memory, she breaks out into a long desperate cry, dropping her head on her arms that rest on a little table. Everybody is very affected by her. The* PRODUCER *comes to her almost paternally and speaks to her in a soothing voice.*)

PRODUCER. We'll have the garden scene, we'll have it, don't worry: and you'll see, you'll be very pleased with what we do! We'll play all the scenes in the garden! (*He calls out to a* STAGE HAND *by name.*) Hey …, let down a few bits of tree, will you? A couple of cypresses will do, in front of the fountain. (*Someone drops in the two cypresses and a* STAGE HAND *secures them with a couple of braces and weights.*)

PRODUCER (*to the* STEPDAUGHTER). That'll do for now, won't it? It'll just give us an idea. (*Calling out to a* STAGE HAND *by name again.*) Hey, … give me something for the sky will you?

STAGE HAND. What's that?

PRODUCER. Something for the sky! A small cloth to come in behind the fountain. (*A white cloth is dropped from the flies.*) Not white! I asked for a sky! Never mind: leave it! I'll do something with it. (*Calling out.*) Hey lights! Kill everything will you? Give me a bit of moonlight—the blues in the batten and a blue spot on the cloth. … (*They do.*) That's it! That'll do! (*Now on the scene there is the light he asked for, a mysterious blue light that makes the* ACTORS *speak and move as if in the garden in the evening under a moon. To the* STEPDAUGHTER.) Look here now: the little boy can come out here in the garden and hide among the trees instead of hiding behind the doors in the house. But it's going to be difficult to find a little girl to play the scene with you where she shows you the flowers. (*Turning to the* LITTLE BOY.) Come on, come on, son, come across here. Let's see what it'll look like. (*But the* BOY *doesn't move.*) Come on will you, come on. (*Then he pulls him forward and tries to make him hold his head up, but every time it falls down again on his chest.*) There's something very odd about this lad. …What's wrong with him? My God, he'll have to say something sometime! (*He comes over to him again, puts his hand on his shoulder and pushes him between the trees.*) Come a bit nearer: let's have a look. Can you hide a bit more? That's it. Now pop your head out and look round. (*He moves away to look at the effect and as the* BOY *does what he has been told to do, the* ACTORS *watch impressed and a little disturbed.*) Ahh, that's good, very good. …(*He turns to the* STEPDAUGHTER.) How about having the little girl, surprised to see him there, run across. Wouldn't that make him say something?

STEPDAUGHTER (*getting up*). It's no use hoping he'll speak, not as long as that creature's there. (*Pointing to the* SON.) You'll have to get him out of the way first.

SON (*moving determinedly to one of the sets of steps leading off the stage*). With pleasure!
I'll go now! Nothing will please me better!

PRODUCER (*stopping him immediately*). Hey, no! Where are you going? Hang on!

> The MOTHER *gets up, anxious at the idea that he is really going and instinctively raising her arms as if to hold him back, but without moving from where she is.*

SON (*at the footlights, to the* PRODUCER *who is restraining him there*). There's no reason why I should be here! Let me go will you? Let me go!

PRODUCER. What do you mean there's no reason for you to be here?

STEPDAUGHTER (*calmly, ironically*). Don't bother to stop him. He won't go!

FATHER. You have to play that terrible scene in the garden with your mother.

SON (*quickly, angry and determined*). I'm not going to play anything! I've said that all along! (*To the* PRODUCER.) Let me go will you?

STEPDAUGHTER (*crossing to the* PRODUCER). It's all right. Let him go. (*She moves the* PRODUCER's *hand from the* SON. *Then she turns to the* SON *and says.*) Well, go on then! Off you go!

> The SON *stays near the steps but as if pulled by some strange force he is quite unable to go down them: then to the astonishment and even the dismay of the* ACTORS, *he moves along the front of the stage towards the other set of steps down into the auditorium: but having got there, he again stays near and doesn't actually go down them. The* STEPDAUGHTER *who has watched him scornfully but very intently, bursts into laughter.*

STEPDAUGHTER. He can't, you see? He can't! He's got to stay here! He must. He's chained to us for ever! No, I'm the one who goes, when what must happen does happen, and I run away, because I hate him, because I can't bear the sight of him any longer. Do you think it's possible for him to run away? He has to stay here with that wonderful father of his and his mother there. She doesn't think she has any other son but him. (*She turns to the* MOTHER.) Come on, come on, Mummy, come on! (*Turning back to the* PRODUCER *to point her out to him.*) Look, she's going to try to stop him. … (*To the* MOTHER, *half compelling her, as if by some magic power.*) Come on, come on. (*Then to the* PRODUCER *again.*) Imagine how she must feel at showing her affection for him in front of your actors! But her longing to be near him is so strong that— look! She's going to go through that scene with him again! (*The* MOTHER *has now actually come close to the* SON *as the* STEPDAUGHTER *says the last line: she gestures to show that she agrees to go on.*)

SON (*quickly*). But I'm not! I'm not! If I can't get away then I suppose I shall have to stay here; but I repeat that I will not have any part in it.

FATHER (*to the* PRODUCER, *excitedly*). You must make him!

SON. Nobody's going to make me do anything!

FATHER. I'll make you!

STEPDAUGHTER. Wait! Just a minute! Before that, the little girl has to go to the fountain. (*She turns to take the* LITTLE GIRL, *drops on her knees in front of her and takes her face between her hands.*) My poor little darling, those beautiful eyes, they look so bewildered. You're wondering where you are, aren't you? Well, we're on a stage, my darling! What's a stage? Well, it's a place where you pretend to be serious. They put on plays here. And now we're going to put on a play. Seriously! Oh, yes! Even you. ... (*She hugs her tightly and rocks her gently for a moment.*) Oh, my little one, my little darling, what a terrible play it is for you! What horrible things have been planned for you! The garden, the fountain. ... Oh, yes, it's only a pretend fountain, that's right. That's part of the game, my pretty darling: everything is pretends here. Perhaps you'll like a pretends fountain better than a real one: you can play here then. But it's only a game for the others; not for you, I'm afraid, it's real for you, my darling, and your game is in a real fountain, a big beautiful green fountain with bamboos casting shadows, looking at your own reflection, with lots of baby ducks paddling about, shattering the reflections. You want to stroke one! (*With a scream that electrifies and terrifies everybody.*) No, Rosetta, no! Your mummy isn't watching you, she's over there with that selfish bastard! Oh, God, I feel as if all the devils in hell were tearing me apart inside. ... And you ... (*Leaving the* LITTLE GIRL *and turning to the* LITTLE BOY *in the usual way.*) What are you doing here, hanging about like a beggar? It'll be your fault too, if that little girl drowns; you're always like this, as if I wasn't paying the price for getting all of you into this house. (*Shaking his arm to make him take his hand out of his pocket.*) What have you got there? What are you hiding? Take it out, take your hand out! (*She drags his hand out of his pocket and to everyone's horror he is holding a revolver. She looks at him for a moment, almost with satisfaction: then she says, grimly.*) Where on earth did you get that? (*The* BOY, *looking frightened, with his eyes wide and empty, doesn't answer.*) You idiot, if I'd been you, instead of killing myself, I'd have killed one of those two: either or both, the father and the son. (*She pushes him towards the cypress trees where he then stands watching; then she takes the* LITTLE GIRL *and helps her to climb in to the fountain, making her lie so that she is hidden: after that she kneels down and puts her head and arms on the rim of the fountain.*)

PRODUCER. That's good! It's good! (*Turning to the* STEPDAUGHTER.) And at the same time ...

SON (*scornfully*). What do you mean, at the same time? There was nothing at the same time! There wasn't any scene between her and me. (*Pointing to the* MOTHER.) She'll tell you the same thing herself, she'll tell you what happened.

> The SECOND ACTRESS *and the* JUVENILE LEAD *have left the group of* ACTORS *and have come to stand nearer the* MOTHER *and the* SON *as if to study them so as to play their parts.*

MOTHER. Yes, it's true. I'd gone to his room …

SON. Room, do you hear? Not the garden!

PRODUCER. It's not important! We've got to reorganise the events anyway. I've told you that already.

SON (*glaring at the* JUVENILE LEAD *and the* SECOND ACTRESS). What do you want?

JUVENILE LEAD. Nothing. I'm just watching.

SON (*turning to the* SECOND ACTRESS). You as well! Getting ready to play her part are you? (*Pointing to the* MOTHER.)

PRODUCER. That's it. And I think you should be grateful-they're paying you a lot of attention.

SON. Oh, yes, thank you! But haven't you realised yet that you'll never be able to do this play? There's nothing of us inside you and you actors are only looking at us from the outside. Do you think we could go on living with a mirror held up in front of us that didn't only freeze our reflection for ever, but froze us in a reflection that laughed back at us with an expression that we didn't even recognise as our own?

FATHER. That's right! That's right!

PRODUCER (*to* JUVENILE LEAD *and* SECOND ACTRESS). Okay. Go back to the others.

SON. It's quite useless. I'm not prepared to do anything.

PRODUCER. Oh, shut up, will you, and let me listen to your mother. (*To the* MOTHER.) Well, you'd gone to his room, you said.

MOTHER. Yes, to his room. I couldn't bear it any longer. I wanted to empty my heart to him, tell him about all the agony that was crushing me. But as soon as he saw me come in …

SON. Nothing happened. I got away! I wasn't going to get involved. I never have been involved. Do you understand?

MOTHER. It's true! That's right!

PRODUCER. But we must make up the scene between you, then. It's vital!

MOTHER. I'm ready to do it! If only I had the chance to talk to him for a moment, to pour out all my troubles to him.

FATHER (*going to the* SON *and speaking violently*). You'll do it! For your Mother! For your Mother!

SON (*more than ever determined*). I'm doing nothing!

FATHER (*taking hold of his coat collar and shaking him*). For God's sake, do as I tell you! Do as I tell you! Do you hear what she's saying? Haven't you any feelings for her?

SON (*taking hold of his* FATHER). No I haven't! I haven't! Let that be the end of it!

> *There is a general uproar. The* MOTHER *frightened out of her wits, tries to get between them and separate them.*

MOTHER. Please stop it! Please!

FATHER (*hanging on*). Do as I tell you! Do as I tell you!

SON (*wrestling with him and finally throwing him to the ground near the steps. Everyone is horrified*). What's come over you? Why are you so frantic? Do you want to parade our disgrace in front of everybody? Well, I'm having nothing to do with it! Nothing! And I'm doing what our author wanted as well—he never wanted to put us on the stage.

PRODUCER. Then why the hell did you come here?

SON (*pointing to the* FATHER). He wanted to, I didn't.

PRODUCER. And aren't you here now?

SON. He was the one who wanted to come and he dragged all of us here with him and agreed with you in there about what to put in the play: and that meant not only what had really happened, as if that wasn't bad enough, but what hadn't happened as well.

PRODUCER. All right, then, you tell me what happened. You tell me! Did you rush out of your room without saying anything?

SON (*after a moment's hesitation*). Without saying anything. I didn't want to make a scene.

PRODUCER (*needling him*). What then? What did you do then? SON (*he is now the centre of everyone's agonised attention and he crosses the stage*). Nothing. … I went across the garden. … (*He breaks off gloomy and absorbed.*)

PRODUCER (*urging him to say more, impressed by his reluctance to speak*). Well? What then? You crossed the garden?

SON (*exasperated, putting his face into the crook of his arm*). Why do you want me to talk about it? It's horrible! (*The* MOTHER *is trembling with stifled sobs and looking towards the fountain.*)

PRODUCER (*quietly, seeing where she is looking and turning to the* SON *with growing apprehension*). The little girl?

SON (*looking straight in front, out to the audience*). There, in the fountain …

FATHER (*on the floor still, pointing with pity at the* MOTHER). She was trailing after him!

PRODUCER (*to the* SON, *anxiously*). What did you do then?

SON (*still looking out front and speaking slowly*). I dashed across. I was going to jump in and pull her out. … But something else caught my eye: I saw something behind the tree that made my blood run cold: the little boy, he was standing there with a mad look in his eyes: he was standing looking into the fountain at his little sister, floating there, drowned.

> The STEPDAUGHTER *is still bent at the fountain hiding the* LITTLE GIRL, *and she sobs pathetically, her sobs sounding like an echo. There is a pause.*

SON (*continued*). I made a move towards him: but then …

> *From behind the trees where the* LITTLE BOY *is standing there is the sound of a shot.*

MOTHER (*with a terrible cry she runs along with the* SON *and all the* ACTORS *in the midst of a great general confusion*). My son! My son! (*And then from out of the confusion and crying her voice comes out.*) Help! Help me!

PRODUCER (*amidst the shouting he tries to clear a space whilst the* LITTLE BOY *is carried by his feet and shoulders behind the white skycloth.*) Is he wounded? Really wounded? (*Everybody except the* PRODUCER *and the* FATHER *who is still on the floor by the steps, has gone behind the skycloth and stays there talking anxiously. Then independently the* ACTORS *start to come back into view.*

LEADING ACTRESS (*coming from the right, very upset*). He's dead! The poor boy! He's dead! What a terrible thing!

LEADING ACTOR (*coming back from the left and smiling*). What do you mean, dead? It's all make-believe. It's a sham! He's not dead. Don't you believe it!

OTHER ACTORS FROM THE RIGHT. Make-believe? It's real! Real! He's dead!

OTHER ACTORS FROM THE LEFT. No, he isn't He's pretending! It's all make-believe.

FATHER (*running off and shouting at them as he goes*). What do you mean, make-believe? It's real! It's real, ladies and gentlemen! It's reality! (*And with desperation on his face he too goes behind the skycloth.*)

PRODUCER (*not caring any more*). Make-believe?! Reality?! Oh, go to hell the lot of you! Lights! Lights! Lights!

> *At once all the stage and auditorium is flooded with light. The* PRODUCER *heaves a sigh of relief as if he has been relieved of a terrible weight and they all look at each other in distress and with uncertainty.*

PRODUCER. God! I've never known anything like this! And we've lost a whole day's work! (*He looks at the dock.*) Get off with you, all of you! We can't do anything now! It's too late to start a rehearsal. (*When the* ACTORS *have gone, he calls out.*) Hey, lights! Kill everything! (*As soon as he has said this, all the lights go out completely and leave him in the pitch dark.*) For God's sake!! You might have left the workers! I can't see where I'm going!

Suddenly, behind the sky cloth, as if because of a bad connection, a green light comes up to throw on the cloth a huge sharp shadow of the CHARACTERS, *but without the* LITTLE BOY *and the* LITTLE GIRL. *The* PRODUCER, *seeing this, jumps off the stage, terrified. At the same time the flood of light on them is switched off and the stage is again bathed in the same blue light as before. Slowly the* SON *comes on from the right, followed by the* MOTHER *with her arms raised towards him. Then from the left, the* FATHER *enters.*

They come together in the middle of the stage and stand there as if transfixed. Finally from the left the STEPDAUGHTER *comes on and moves towards the steps at the front: on the top step she pauses for a moment to look back at the other three and then bursts out in a raucous laugh, dashes down the steps and turns to look at the three figures still on the stage. Then she runs out of the auditorium and we can still hear her manic laughter out into the foyer and beyond.*

After a pause the curtain falls slowly.

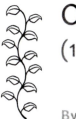

Oleanna
(1992)

By **David Mamet** (1947–)

INTRODUCTION

*O*leanna is one of David Mamet's best-known and most controversial plays. Set in the office of a university professor, the play has a cast of only two characters: Carol, a student, and John, a professor twice her age. In the play, a meeting to discuss a grade escalates into a conflict that threatens to destroy John's life.

Despite the play's apparent economy, the dramatic universe depicted by Mamet in *Oleanna* is a battlefield on which students and teachers battle for control of a university's curriculum. Carol points out that the inequity of power—normally professors' ability to assign a value to students' work, but in this case the power Carol seizes at John's expense—makes open and honest communication impossible. But between the cause (power differential) and effect (dishonesty), there is an intermediate stage: the necessary adoption of roles for professors and students, and the accompanying behavioral routines.

In the play's first scene, Carol comes off as a genuinely confused student, doing poorly in John's class and concerned about her grade. Her appeals to John come in the form of claims to conformity, which reveal John's inability, or refusal, to conform to his role. "I'm doing what I'm told," Carol pleads. "I did, I did everything that, I read your *book*, you told me to buy your book and read it. Everything you *say* I … I do." John, apparently sensing that Carol is looking for more help than he can provide, tells her, "I'm not your *father*." Obviously, he is stating a fact, but he is also asserting his role: he is her professor, and will do no more than that job allows. Strangely, he later abandons this position: "We're going to take off the artificial *stricture* of 'Teacher,' and

'Student,'" he tells Carol. In an attempt to assuage her fear, he tells her, "We'll start the whole course over." These words prove to be his undoing.

When Carol notifies the tenure committee (currently in the process of deciding John's tenure case) about her meeting with John, she seizes upon the ambiguity of John's words and gestures (especially as they would be perceived by individuals not present at the meeting) to cast him as a renegade, which, ironically, is precisely what John fancies himself to be. "That's my job," John says to Carol. "To provoke you." His scholarly book, which calls the process of education "hazing," includes the description of John as a "maveRICK." He admits that he finds teaching "artificial," something that leaves Carol bemused. "You say that higher education is a joke," she complains. "And treat it as such, you treat it as such." John, having admitted that he loves lecturing to his classes, "the aspect of *performance*," as he calls it, finds that Carol is willing to use this as ammunition as well: "You feel yourself empowered... you say so yourself. To *strut*... to *posture*... to 'perform'... and confess to a taste to play the Patriarch in your class. To grant *this*. To deny *that*."

We find, however, that Carol is performing as well, perhaps in more than one sense. In the first scene, she tries to elicit John's sympathy by describing the pain of putting on a show in class: "I'm *smiling* in class, I'm *smiling*, the whole time," she complains. "What are you *talking* about? What is everyone *talking* about? I don't *understand*." The picture she paints is one of a hapless young woman, hiding her embarrassment behind a façade of comprehension and conformity. As we learn later, this may or may not have been true. By the end of the play, we learn that Carol is a member of an unspecified "Group" ("those who suffer what I suffer") that has either sent her on a mission to entrap John or has parlayed her genuine predicament into political leverage. We never actually find out whether Carol is a mastermind or an unwitting pawn, and we are uncertain as to which facet of her (the pitiable underachiever in the first scene or the domineering ideologue in the last) is closer to her "genuine" self.

Mamet has been accused of "stacking the deck" in this play, of manipulating readers and audiences into seeing John as the victim of a sinister plot. It is useful, however, to consider the opposite point of view, not just in the interest of even-handedness, but of objectivity as well. John may claim that he is not an "exploiter," not a patriarch, and not a sexist, but the violence of his words and actions at the end of the play is reprehensible, no matter how audiences have responded to it (some audiences have boisterously and crudely voiced their support for John). He may give lip service to the idea of treating students as equals, but ultimately, this is a lie: "I'm a teacher. I am a teacher. Eh? It's my *name* on the door, and I teach the class, and that's what I do. I've got a book with my name on it." Ultimately, his judgment needs to be questioned. Why does he tell Carol that he "likes" her, when there is no evidence that he does? Why does he consider it ethical or appropriate to rewrite the rules of the class, secretly, for just one student? Why *must* he use an episode from his sexual past as an illustrative example in his first conversation with Carol? John makes errors that a first-year graduate assistant would know to avoid. Regardless of the extent to which we may think his ruinous ending is unjust, we must consider the ways in which he contributes to his own downfall. His admitted discomfort with his role causes his deviations from it, and is therefore at least partially responsible for the consequences.

CHARACTERS

CAROL A woman of twenty
JOHN A man in his forties

The play takes place in John's office.

ONE

JOHN is *talking on the phone,* CAROL *is seated across the desk from him.*

JOHN (*on phone*): And what about the land. (*Pause*) The land. And what about the land? (*Pause*) What about it? (*Pause*) No. I don't understand. Well, yes, I'm I'm … … no, I'm *sure* it's signif … I'm sure it's significant. (*Pause*) Because it's significant to mmmmmm … … did you call Jerry? (*Pause*) Because … no, no, no, no, no. What did they say …? Did you speak to the *real* estate … where *is* she …? Well, well, all right. Where are her notes? Where are the notes we took with her. (*Pause*) I thought you were? No. No, I'm sorry, I didn't mean that, I just thought that I saw you, when we were there … what …? I thought I saw you with a *pencil* WHY NOW? is what I'm say … well, that's why I say "call Jerry." Well, I can't right now, be … no, I *didn't* schedule any … Grace: I *didn't* … I'm well aware … Look: Look. Did you call Jerry? Will you call Jerry …? Because I can't now. I'll be there, I'm sure I'll be there in fifteen, in twenty. I intend to. No, we aren't *going* to lose the, we aren't *going* to lose the house. Look: Look, I'm not minimizing it. The "easement." Did she say "easement"? (*Pause*) What did she *say; is* it a "term of art," are we *bound* by it … I'm sorry … (*Pause*) are: we: yes. *Bound* by … Look: (*He checks his watch.*) before the other side *goes home,* all right? "a term of art." Because: that's right (*Pause*) The yard for the boy. Well, that's the whole … Look: I'm going to meet you there … (*He checks his watch.*) Is the realtor there? All right, tell her to show you the basement again. Look at the *this* because ... Bec ... I'm leaving in, I'm leaving in ten or fifteen ... Yes. No, no, I'll meet you at the new ... That's a good. If he thinks it's necc ... you tell Jerry to meet ... All right? We *aren't* going to lose the deposit. All right? I'm sure it's going to be ... (*Pause*) I hope so. (*Pause*) I love you, too. (*Pause*) I love you, too. As soon as ... I will.

(*He hangs up.*) (*He bends over the desk and makes a note.*) (*He looks up.*) (*To* CAROL:)
I'm sorry ...

CAROL: (*Pause*) What is a "term of art"?

JOHN: (*Pause*) I'm sorry ...?

CAROL: (*Pause*) What is a "term of art"?

JOHN: Is that what you want to talk about?

CAROL: ... to talk about ...?

JOHN: Let's take the mysticism out of it, shall we? Carol? (*Pause*) Don't you think? I'll tell you: when you have some "thing." Which must be broached. (*Pause*) Don't you think ...? (*Pause*)

CAROL: ... don't I think ...?

JOHN: Mmm?

CAROL: ... did I ...?

JOHN: ... what?

CAROL: Did .... did I .... did I say something wr ...

JOHN: (*Pause*) No. I'm sorry. No. You're right. I'm very sorry. I'm somewhat rushed. As you see. I'm sorry. You're right. (*Pause*) What is a "term of art"? It seems to mean a *term*, which has come, through its use, to mean something *more specific* than the words would, to someone *not acquainted* with them ... indicate. That, I believe, is what a "term of art," would mean. (*Pause*)

CAROL: You don't know what it means ...?

JOHN: I'm not sure that I know what it means. It's one of those things, perhaps you've had them, that, you look them up, or have someone explain them to you, and you say "aha," and, you immediately *forget* what ...

CAROL: You don't do that.

JOHN: ... I ...?

CAROL: You don't do ...

JOHN: ... I don't, what ...?

CAROL: ... for ...

JOHN: ... I don't for ...

CAROL: ... no ...

JOHN: ... forget things? Everybody does that.

CAROL: No, they don't.

JOHN: They don't ...

CAROL: No.

JOHN: (*Pause*) No. Everybody does that.

CAROL: Why would they do that ...?

JOHN: Because. I don't know. Because it doesn't interest them.

CAROL: No.

JOHN: I think so though. (*Pause*) I'm sorry that I was distracted.

CAROL: You don't have to say that to me.

JOHN: You paid me the compliment, or the "obeisance"—all right—of coming in here ... All right. *Carol.* I find that I am at a *standstill*. I find that I ...

CAROL: ... what ...

JOHN: ... one moment. In regard to your ... to your ...

CAROL: Oh, oh. You're buying a new house!

JOHN: No, let's get on with it.

CAROL: "get on"? (*Pause*)

JOHN: I know how ... *believe* me. I know how ... potentially *humiliating* these ... I have no desire to ... I have no desire other than to help you. But: (*He picks up some papers on his desk.*) I won't even say "but." I'll say that as I go back over the ...

CAROL: I'm just, I'm just trying to ...

JOHN: ... no, it will not do.

CAROL: ... what? What will ...?

JOHN: No. I see I see what you it ... (*He gestures to the papers.*) but your work ...

CAROL: I'm just: I sit in class I ... (*She holds up her notebook.*) I take notes ...

JOHN (*simultaneously with* "notes"): Yes. I understand. What I am trying to *tell* you is that some, some basic ...

CAROL: ... I ...

JOHN: ... one moment: some basic missed communi ...

CAROL: I'm doing what I'm told. I bought your book, I read your ...

JOHN: No, I'm sure you ...

CAROL: No, no, no. I'm doing what I'm told. It's *difficult* for me. It's *difficult* ...

JOHN: ... but ...

CAROL: I don't ... lots of the *language* ...

JOHN: ... please ...

CAROL: The *language,* the "things" that you say ...

JOHN: I'm sorry. No. I don't think that that's true.

CAROL: It *is* true. I ...

JOHN: I think …

CAROL: It *is* true.

JOHN: … I …

CAROL: Why would I …?

JOHN: I'll tell you why: you're an incredibly bright girl.

CAROL: … I …

JOHN: You're an incredibly … you have no problem with the … Who's kidding who?

CAROL: … I …

JOHN: No. No. I'll tell you why. I'll tell …. I think you're *angry*, I …

CAROL: … why would I …

JOHN: … wait one moment. I …

CAROL: It *is* true. I have *problems* …

JOHN: … every …

CAROL: … I come from a different *social* …

JOHN: … ev …

CAROL: a different economic …

JOHN: … Look:

CAROL: No. I: when I *came* to this school:

JOHN: Yes. Quite … (*Pause*)

CAROL: … does that mean nothing …?

JOHN: … but look: look …

CAROL: … I …

JOHN: (*Picks up paper.*) Here: Please: Sit down. (*Pause*) Sit down. (*Reads from her paper.*) "I think that the ideas contained in this work express the author's feelings in a way that he intended, based on his results." What can that mean? Do you see? What …

CAROL: I, the best that I …

JOHN: I'm saying, that perhaps this course …

CAROL: No, no, no, you can't, you can't … I have to …

JOHN: … how …

CAROL: … I have to pass it …

JOHN: Carol, I:

CAROL: I *have* to pass this course, I …

JOHN: Well.

CAROL: … don't you …

JOHN: Either the …

CAROL: … I …

JOHN: … either the, I… either the *criteria* for judging progress in the class are …

CAROL: No, no, no, no, I have to pass it.

JOHN: Now, look: I'm a human being, I …

CAROL: I did what you told me. I did, I did everything that, I read your *book,* you told me to buy your book and read it. Everything you *say* I … (*She gestures to her notebook.*) (*The phone rings.*) I do. … Ev …

JOHN: … look:

CAROL: … everything I'm told …

JOHN: Look. Look. I'm not your *father.* (*Pause*)

CAROL: What?

JOHN: I'm.

CAROL: Did I say you were my father?

JOHN: … no …

CAROL: Why did you say that …?

JOHN: I …

CAROL: … why …?

JOHN: … in class I … (*He picks up the phone.*) (*Into phone:*) Hello. I can't talk now. Jerry? Yes? I underst … I can't talk now. I know … I know … Jerry. I can't *talk* now. Yes I. Call me back in … Thank you. (*He hangs up.*) (*To* CAROL:) What do you want me to do? We are two people, all right? Both of whom have subscribed to …

CAROL: No no …

JOHN: … certain arbitrary …

CAROL: No. You have to help me.

JOHN: Certain institutional … you tell me what you want me to do …. You tell me what you want me to …

CAROL: How can I go back and tell them the *grades* that I …

JOHN: … what can I do …?

CAROL: *Teach* me. *Teach* me.

JOHN: … I'm trying to teach you.

CAROL: I read your book. I read it. I don't under …

JOHN: … you don't understand it.

CAROL: No.

JOHN: Well, perhaps it's not well *written* …

CAROL: (*simultaneously with* "written"): No. No. No. I want to *understand* it.

JOHN: What don't you understand? (*Pause*)

CAROL: *Any* of it. What you're trying to say. When you talk about …

JOHN: … yes …? (*She consults her notes.*)

CAROL: "Virtual warehousing of the young" …

JOHN: "Virtual warehousing of the young." If we artificially prolong adolescence …

CAROL: … and about "The Curse of Modern Education."

JOHN: … well …

CAROL: I don't …

JOHN: Look. It's just a *course,* it's just a *book,* it's just a …

CAROL: No. No. There are *people* out there. People who came *here.* To know something they didn't *know.* Who *came* here. To be *helped.* To be *helped.* So someone would *help* them. To *do* something. To *know* something. To get, what do they say? "To get on in the world." How can I do that if I don't, if I fail? But I don't *understand.* I don't *understand.* I don't understand what anything means … and I walk around. From morning 'til night: with this one thought in my head. I'm *stupid.*

JOHN: No one thinks you're stupid.

CAROL: No? What am I …?

JOHN: I …

CAROL: … what am I, then?

JOHN: I think you're angry. Many people are. I have a *telephone* call that I have to make. And an *appointment,* which is rather *pressing;* though I sympathize with your concerns, and though I wish I had the time, this was not a previously scheduled meeting and I …

CAROL: … you think I'm nothing …

JOHN: … have an appointment with a *realtor,* and with my wife and …

CAROL: You think that I'm stupid.

JOHN: No, I certainly don't.

CAROL: You said it.

JOHN: No. I did not.

CAROL: You did.

JOHN: When?

CAROL: … you …

JOHN: No. I never did, or never would say that to a student, and …

CAROL: You said, "What can that mean?" (*Pause*) "What can that mean?" … (*Pause*)

JOHN: … and what did that mean to you …?

CAROL: That meant I'm stupid. And I'll never learn. That's what that meant. And you're right.

JOHN: … I …

CAROL: But then. But then, what am I doing here …?

JOHN: … if you thought that I …

CAROL: … when nobody wants me, and …

JOHN: … if you interpreted …

CAROL: Nobody *tells* me anything. And I *sit* there ... in the *corner*. In the *back*. And everybody's talking about "this" all the time. And "concepts," and "precepts" and, and, and, and, and, WHAT IN THE WORLD ARE YOU *TALKING* ABOUT? And I read your book. And they said "Fine, go in that class." Because you talked about responsibility to the young. I DON'T KNOW WHAT IT MEANS AND I'M *FAILING* ...

JOHN: May ...

CAROL: No, you're right. "Oh, hell" I failed. Flunk me out of it. It's garbage. Everything I do. "The ideas contained in this work express the author's feelings." That's right. That's right. I know I'm stupid. I know what I am. (*Pause*) I know what I am, Professor. You don't have to tell me. (*Pause*) It's pathetic. Isn't it?

JOHN: ... Aha ... (*Pause*) Sit down. Sit down. Please. (*Pause*) Please sit down.

CAROL: Why?

JOHN: I want to talk to you.

CAROL: Why?

JOHN: Just sit down. (*Pause*) Please. Sit down. Will you, please ...? (*Pause. She does so.*) Thank you.

CAROL: What?

JOHN: I want to tell you something.

CAROL: (*Pause*) What?

JOHN: Well, I know what you're talking about.

CAROL: No. You don't.

JOHN: I think I do. (*Pause*)

CAROL: How can you?

JOHN: I'll tell you a story about myself. (*Pause*) Do you mind? (*Pause*) I was raised to think myself stupid. That's what I want to tell you. (*Pause*)

CAROL: What do you mean?

JOHN: Just what I said. I was brought up, and my earliest, and most persistent memories are of being told that I was stupid. "You have such *intelligence*. Why must you behave so *stupidly?*" Or, "Can't you *understand?* Can't you *understand?*" And I could *not* understand. I could *not* understand.

CAROL: What?

JOHN: The simplest problem. Was beyond me. It was a mystery.

CAROL: What was a mystery?

JOHN: How people learn. How I could learn. Which is what I've been speaking of in class. And of *course* you can't hear it. Carol. Of *course* you can't. (*Pause*) I used to speak of "real people," and wonder what the *real* people did. The *real* people. Who were they? *They* were the people other than myself. The *good* people. The *capable* people. The people who could do the things, I could not do: learn, study, retain … all that *garbage*—which is what I have been talking of in class, and that's *exactly* what I have been talking of—If you are told ….Listen to this. If the young child is told he cannot understand. Then he takes it as a *description* of himself. What am I? I am *that which can not understand.* And I saw you out there, when we were speaking of the concepts of …

CAROL: I can't understand any of them.

JOHN: Well, then, that's *my* fault. That's not your fault. And that is not verbiage. That's what I firmly hold to be the truth. And I am sorry, and I owe you an apology.

CAROL: Why?

JOHN: And I suppose that I have had some *things* on my mind …. We're buying a *house,* and …

CAROL: People said that you were stupid …?

JOHN: Yes.

CAROL: When?

JOHN: I'll tell you when. Through my life. In my childhood; and, perhaps, they stopped. But I heard them continue.

CAROL: And what did they say?

JOHN: They said I was incompetent. Do you see? And when I'm tested the, the, the *feelings* of my youth about the *very subject of learning* come up. And I … I become, I feel "unworthy," and "unprepared." …

CAROL: … yes.

JOHN: … eh?

CAROL: … yes.

JOHN: And I feel that I must fail. (*Pause*)

CAROL: … but then you *do* fail (*Pause*) You have to. (*Pause*) Don't you?

JOHN: A *pilot.* Flying a plane. The pilot is flying the plane. He thinks: Oh, my *God,* my mind's been drifting! Oh, my God! What kind of a cursed imbecile am I, that I, with this so precious cargo *of Life* in my charge, would allow my attention to wander. Why was I born? How deluded are those who put their trust in me, … et cetera, so on, and he crashes the plane.

CAROL: (*Pause*) He could just …

JOHN: That's right.

CAROL: He could say:

JOHN: My attention *wandered* for a moment …

CAROL: … uh huh …

JOHN: I had a *thought* I did not like … but now:

CAROL: … but now it's …

 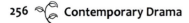

JOHN: That's what I'm telling you. It's time to put my attention ... see: it is not: this is what I learned. It is Not Magic. Yes, Yes. *You.* You are going to be frightened. When faced with what may or may not be but which you are going to perceive as a test. You will become frightened. And you will say: "I am incapable of ... " and everything *in* you will think these two things. "I must. But I can't." And you will think: Why was I born to be the laughingstock of a world in which everyone is better than I? In which I am entitled to nothing. Where I can not learn.

(*Pause*)

CAROL: Is that ... (*Pause*) Is that what I have ...?

JOHN: Well. I don't know if I'd put it that way. Listen: I'm talking to you as I'd talk to my son. Because that's what I'd like him to have that I never had. I'm talking to you the way I wish that someone had talked to me. I don't know how to do it, other than to be *personal,* ... but ...

CAROL: Why would you want to be personal with me?

JOHN: Well, you see? That's what I'm saying. We can only interpret the behavior of others through the screen we ... (*The phone rings.*) Through ... (*To phone:*) Hello ...? (*To* CAROL:) Through the screen we create. (*To phone:*) Hello. (*To* CAROL:) Excuse me a moment. (*To phone:*) Hello? No, I can't talk nnn ... I know I did. In a few ... I'm ... is he coming to the ... yes, I talked to him. We'll meet you at the No, because I'm with a *student.* It's going to be fff ... This is important, too. I'm with a *student,* Jerry's going to ... Listen: the sooner I get off, the sooner I'll be down, all right. I love you. Listen, listen, I said "I love you," it's going to work *out* with the, because I feel that it is, I'll be right down. All right? Well, then it's going to take as long as it takes. (He *hangs up.*) (*To* CAROL:) I'm sorry.

CAROL: What was that?

JOHN: There are some problems, as there usually are, about the final agreements for the new house.

CAROL: You're buying a new house.

JOHN: That's right.

CAROL: Because of your promotion.

JOHN: Well, I suppose that that's right.

CAROL: Why did you stay here with me?

JOHN: Stay here.

CAROL: Yes. When you should have gone.

JOHN: Because I like you.

CAROL: You like me.

JOHN: Yes.

CAROL: Why?

JOHN: Why? Well? Perhaps we're similar. (*Pause*) Yes. (*Pause*)

CAROL: You said "everyone has problems."

JOHN: Everyone has problems.

CAROL: Do they?

JOHN: Certainly.

CAROL: You do?

JOHN: Yes.

CAROL: What are they?

JOHN: Well. (*Pause*) Well, you're perfectly right. (*Pause*) If we're going to take off the Artificial *Stricture,* of "Teacher," and "Student," why should *my* problems be any more a mystery than your own? Of *course* I have problems. As you saw.

CAROL: … with what?

JOHN: With my *wife* … with *work* …

CAROL: With work?

JOHN: Yes. And, and, perhaps my problems are, do you see? *Similar* to yours.

CAROL: Would you tell me?

JOHN: All right. (*Pause*) I came *late* to teaching. And I found it Artificial. The notion of "I know and you do not"; and I saw an *exploitation* in the education process. I told you. I hated school, I hated teachers. I hated everyone who was in the position of a "boss" because I *knew*—I didn't *think,* mind you, I *knew* I was going to fail. Because I was a fuckup. I was just no goddamned good. When I … late in life … (*Pause*) When I *got out from under* … when I worked my way out of the need to fail. When I …

CAROL: How do you do that? (*Pause*)

JOHN: You have to look at what you are, and what you feel, and how you act. And, finally, you have to look at how you act. And say: If that's what I *did,* that must be how I think of myself.

CAROL: I don't understand.

JOHN: If I fail all the time, it must be that I think of myself as a failure. If I do not want to think of myself as a failure, perhaps I should begin by *succeeding* now and again. Look. The tests, you see, which you encounter, in school, in college, in life, were designed, in the most part, for idiots. *By* idiots. There is no need to fail at them. They are not a test of your worth. They are a test of your ability to retain and spout back misinformation. Of *course* you fail them. They're *nonsense.* And I …

CAROL: … no …

JOHN: Yes. They're *garbage*. They're a *joke*. Look at me. Look at me. The Tenure Committee. The Tenure Committee. Come to judge me. The Bad Tenure Committee.

The "Test." Do you see? They put me to the test. Why, they had people voting on me I wouldn't employ to wax my car. And yet, I go before the Great Tenure Committee, and I have an urge, to vomit, to, to, to puke my badness on the table, to show them: "I'm no good. Why would you pick me?"

CAROL: They granted you tenure.

JOHN: Oh no, they announced it, but they haven't *signed*. Do you see? "At any moment ... "

CAROL: ... mmm ...

JOHN: "They might not *sign*" ... I might not ... the *house* might not go through ... Eh? Eh? They'll find out my "dark secret." (*Pause*)

CAROL: ... what is it ...?

JOHN: There *isn't* one. But *they* will find an index of my badness ...

CAROL: Index?

JOHN: A " ... pointer." A "Pointer." You see? Do you see? I *understand* you. I. Know. That. Feeling. Am I entitled to my job, and my nice *home,* and my *wife,* and my *family,* and so on. This is what I'm saying: That theory of education which, that *theory:*

CAROL: I ... I ... (*Pause*)

JOHN: What?

CAROL: I ...

JOHN: What?

CAROL: I want to know about my grade. (*Long pause*)

JOHN: Of course you do.

CAROL: Is that bad?

JOHN: No.

CAROL: Is it bad that I asked you that?

JOHN: No.

CAROL: Did I upset you?

JOHN: No. And I apologize. Of *course* you want to know about your grade. And, of course, you can't concentrate on anyth ... (*The telephone starts to ring.*) Wait a moment.

CAROL: I should go.

JOHN: I'll make you a deal.

CAROL: No, you have to ...

JOHN: Let it ring. I'll make you a deal. You stay here. We'll start the whole course over. I'm going to say it was not you, it was I who was not paying attention. We'll start the whole course over. Your grade is an "A." Your final grade is an "A." (*The phone stops ringing.*)

CAROL: But the class is only half over …

JOHN (*simultaneously with* "over"): Your grade for the whole term is an "A." If you will come back and meet with me. A few more times. Your grade's an "A." Forget about the paper. You didn't like it, you didn't like writing it. It's not important. What's important is that I awake your interest, if I can, and that I answer your questions. Let's start over. (*Pause*)

CAROL: Over. With what?

JOHN: Say this is the beginning.

CAROL: The beginning.

JOHN: Yes.

CAROL: Of what?

JOHN: Of the class.

CAROL: But we can't start over.

JOHN: I say we can. (*Pause*) I say we can.

CAROL: But I don't believe it.

JOHN: Yes, I know that. But it's true. What is The Class but you and me? (*Pause*)

CAROL: There are rules.

JOHN: Well. We'll break them.

CAROL: How can we?

JOHN: We won't tell anybody.

CAROL: Is that all right?

JOHN: I say that it's fine.

CAROL: Why would you do this for me?

JOHN: I like you. Is that so difficult for you to …

CAROL: Um …

JOHN: There's no one here but you and me. (*Pause*)

CAROL: All right. I did not understand. When you referred …

JOHN: All right, yes?

CAROL: When you referred to hazing.

JOHN: Hazing.

CAROL: You wrote, in your book. About the comparative … the comparative … (*She checks her notes.*)

JOHN: Are you checking your notes …?

CAROL: Yes.

JOHN: Tell me in your own …

CAROL: I want to make sure that I have it right.

JOHN: No. Of course. You want to be exact.

CAROL: I want to know everything that went on.

JOHN: … that's good.

CAROL: … so I …

JOHN: That's very good. But I was suggesting, many times, that that which we wish to retain is retained oftentimes, I think, *better* with less expenditure of effort.

CAROL: (*Of notes*) Here it is: you wrote of *hazing*.

JOHN: … that's correct. Now: I said "hazing." It means ritualized annoyance. We shove this book at you, we say read it. Now, you say you've read it? I think that you're *lying*. I'll *grill* you, and when I find you've lied, you'll be disgraced, and your life will be ruined. It's a sick game. Why do we do it? Does it educate? In no sense. Well, then, what is higher education? It is something- other-than-useful.

CAROL: What is "something-other-than-useful?"

JOHN: It has become a ritual, it has become an article of faith. That all must be subjected to, or to put it differently, that all are entitled to Higher Education. And my point …

CAROL: You disagree with that?

JOHN: Well, let's address that. What do you think?

CAROL: I don't know.

JOHN: What do you think, though? (*Pause*)

CAROL: I don't know.

JOHN: I spoke of it in class. Do you remember my example?

CAROL: Justice.

JOHN: Yes. Can you repeat it to me? (*She looks down at her notebook.*) Without your notes? I ask you as a favor to me, so that I can see if my idea was interesting.

CAROL: You said "justice" …

JOHN: Yes?

CAROL: … that all are entitled … (*Pause*) I … I … I …

JOHN: Yes. To a speedy trial. To a fair trial. But they needn't be given a trial *at all* unless they stand accused. Eh? Justice is their right, should they choose to avail themselves of it, they should have a fair trial. It does not follow, of necessity, a person's life is incomplete without a trial in it. Do you see? My point is a confusion between equity and *utility* arose. So we confound the *usefulness* of higher education with our, granted, right to equal access to the same. We, in effect, create a *prejudice* toward it, completely independent of...

CAROL: … that it is prejudice that we should go to school?

JOHN: Exactly. (*Pause*)

CAROL: How can you say that? How …

JOHN: Good. Good, *Good*. That's right! Speak up! What is a prejudice? An unreasoned belief. We are all subject to it. None of us is not. When it is threatened, or opposed, we feel anger, and feel, do we not? As you do now. Do you not? Good.

CAROL: … but how can you …

JOHN: … let us examine. Good.

CAROL: How …

JOHN: Good. Good. When …

CAROL: I'M SPEAKING … (*Pause*)

JOHN: I'm sorry.

CAROL: How can you …

JOHN: … I beg your pardon.

CAROL: That's all right.

JOHN: I beg your pardon.

CAROL: That's all right.

JOHN: I'm sorry I interrupted you.

CAROL: That's all right.

JOHN: You were saying?

CAROL: I was saying … I was saying … (*She checks her notes.*) How can you say in a class. Say in a college class, that college education is prejudice?

JOHN: I said that our predilection for it …

CAROL: Predilection …

JOHN: … you know what that means.

CAROL: Does it mean "liking"?

JOHN: Yes.

CAROL: But how can you say that? That College …

JOHN: … that's my *job*, don't you know.

CAROL: What is?

JOHN: To provoke you.

CAROL: No.

JOHN: Oh. Yes, though.

CAROL: To provoke me?

JOHN: That's right.

CAROL: To make me mad?

JOHN: That's right. To force you …

CAROL: … to make me mad is your job?

JOHN: To force you to ... listen: (*Pause*) Ah. (*Pause*) When I was young somebody told me, are you ready, the rich copulate less often than the poor. But when they do, they take more of their clothes off. Years. Years, mind you, I would compare experiences of my own to this dictum, saying, aha, this fits the norm, or ah, this is a variation from it. What did it mean? Nothing. It was some jerk thing, some school kid told me that took up room inside my head. (*Pause*)

Somebody told you, and you hold it as an article of faith, that higher education is an unassailable good. This notion is so dear to you that when I question it you become angry. Good. Good, I say. Are not those the very things which we should question? I say college education, since the war, has become so a matter of course, and such a fashionable necessity, for those either of or aspiring to to the new vast middle class, that we espouse it, as a matter of right and have ceased to ask, "What is it good for?" (*Pause*)

What might be some reasons for pursuit of higher education?

One: A love of learning.
Two: The wish for mastery of a skill.
Three: For economic betterment.
(*Stops. Makes a note.*)

CAROL: I'm keeping you.
JOHN: One moment. I have to make a note ...
CAROL: It's something that I said?
JOHN: No, we're buying a house.
CAROL: You're buying the new house.
JOHN: To go with the tenure. That's right. Nice *house,* close to the *private school* ... (*He continues making his note.*) ... We were talking of economic *betterment* (CAROL *writes in her notebook.*) ... I was thinking of the School Tax. (*He continues writing.*) (*To himself:*) ... *where is it written* that I have to send my child to public school ... Is it a law that I have to improve the City Schools at the expense of my own interest? And, is this not simply *The White Man's Burden?* Good. And (*Looks up to* CAROL) ... does this interest you?
CAROL: No. I'm taking notes ...
JOHN: You don't have to take notes, you know, you can just listen.
CAROL: I want to make sure I remember it. (*Pause*)
JOHN: I'm not lecturing you, I'm just trying to tell you some things I think.

CAROL: What do you think?

JOHN: Should all kids go to college? *Why* ...

CAROL: (*Pause*) To learn.

JOHN: But if he does not learn.

CAROL: If the child does not learn?

JOHN: Then why is he in college? Because he was told it was his "right"?

CAROL: Some might find college instructive.

JOHN: I would hope so.

CAROL: But how do they feel? Being told they are wasting their time?

JOHN: I don't think I'm telling them that.

CAROL: You said that education was "prolonged and systematic hazing."

JOHN: Yes. It can be so.

CAROL: ... if education is so *bad,* why do you do it?

JOHN: I do it because I love it. (*Pause*) Let's .... I suggest you look at the demographics, wage-earning capacity, college- and non-college-educated men and women, 1855 to 1980, and let's see if we can wring some worth from the statistics. Eh? And ...

CAROL: No.

JOHN: What?

CAROL: I can't understand them.

JOHN: ... you ...?

CAROL: ... the "charts." The *Concepts,* the ...

JOHN: "Charts" are simply ...

CAROL: When I leave here ...

JOHN: Charts, do you see ...

CAROL: No, I can't ...

JOHN: You can, though.

CAROL: NO, NO—I DON'T UNDERSTAND. DO YOU SEE??? I DON'T *UNDERSTAND* ...

JOHN: What?

CAROL: *Any* of it. *Any* of it. I'm *smiling* in class, I'm *smiling,* the whole time. What are you *talking* about? What is everyone *talking* about? I don't *understand.* I don't know what it *means,* I don't know what it means to *be* here ... you tell me I'm intelligent, and then you tell me I should not be *here,* what do you *want* with me? What does it *mean?* Who should I *listen* to ... I ...

(*He goes over to her and puts his arm around her shoulder.*)

NO! (*She walks away from him.*)

JOHN: Sshhhh.

CAROL: No, I don't under …

JOHN: Sshhhhh.

CAROL: I don't know what you're *saying* …

JOHN: Sshhhhh. It's all right.

CAROL: … I have no …

JOHN: Sshhhhh. Sshhhhh. Let it go a moment (*Pause*) Sshhhhh … let it go. (*Pause*) Just let it go. (*Pause*) Just let it go. It's all right. (*Pause*) Sshhhhh. (*Pause*) I understand … (*Pause*) What do you feel?

CAROL: I feel bad.

JOHN: I know. It's all right.

CAROL: I … (*Pause*)

JOHN: What?

CAROL: I …

JOHN: What? Tell me.

CAROL: I don't understand you.

JOHN: I know. It's all right.

CAROL: I …

JOHN: What? (*Pause*) What? *Tell* me.

CAROL: I can't tell you.

JOHN: No, you must.

CAROL: I can't.

JOHN: No. Tell me. (*Pause*)

CAROL: I'm bad. (*Pause*) Oh, God. (*Pause*)

JOHN: It's all right.

CAROL: I'm …

JOHN: It's all right

CAROL: I can't talk about this.

JOHN: It's all right. Tell me.

CAROL: Why do you want to know this?

JOHN: I don't want to know. I want to know whatever you …

CAROL: I always …

JOHN: … good …

CAROL: I always … all my life … I have never told anyone this …

JOHN: Yes. Go on. (*Pause*) Go on.

CAROL: All of my life … (*The phone rings.*) (*Pause.* JOHN *goes to the phone and picks it up.*)

JOHN (*into phone*): I can't talk now. (*Pause*) What? (*Pause*) Hmm. (*Pause*) All right, I … I. Can't. Talk. Now. No, no, no, I *Know* I did, but …. What? Hello. What? She *what?* She *can't,* she said the agreement is void? How, how is the agreement *void?* *That's Our House.*

I have the *paper;* when we come down, next week, with the payment, and the paper, that house is … wait, wait, wait, wait, wait, wait, wait: Did Jerry … is Jerry there? (*Pause*) Is *she* there …? Does she have a *lawyer …?* How the *hell,* how the *Hell.* That is … it's a question, you said, of the *easement.* I don't underst … it's not the *whole agreement.* It's just the *easement?* why would she? Put, put, put, *Jerry* on. (*Pause*) Jer, *Jerry:* What the *Hell* … that's my *house.* That's … Well, I'm, no, no, no, I'm *not* coming ddd … List, *Listen, screw* her. You *tell* her. You, listen: I want you to take *Grace?* you take Grace, and get out of that house. You *leave* her there. Her and her lawyer, and you *tell* them, we'll see them in court next … no. No, Leave her there, leave her to *stew* in it: You tell her, we're *getting* that house, and we are going to … No. I'm *not* coming down. I'll be damned if I'll sit in the same rrr … the next, you tell her the next time I *see* her is in court … I … (*Pause*) What? (*Pause*) What? I don't understand. (*Pause*) Well, what about the house? (*Pause*) There isn't any problem with the hhh … (*Pause*) No, no, no, that's all right. All ri … All right … (*Pause*) Of course. Tha … Thank you. No, I will. Right away. (He *hangs up.*) (*Pause*)

CAROL: What is it? (*Pause*)

JOHN: It's a surprise party.

CAROL: It is.

JOHN: Yes.

CAROL: A party for you.

JOHN: Yes.

CAROL: Is it your birthday?

JOHN: No.

CAROL: What is it?

JOHN: The tenure announcement.

CAROL: The tenure announcement.

JOHN: They're throwing a party for us in our new house.

CAROL: Your new house.

JOHN: The house that we're buying.

CAROL: You have to go.

JOHN: It seems that I do.

CAROL: (*Pause*) They're proud of you.

JOHN: Well, there are those who would say it's a form of aggression.

CAROL: What is?

JOHN: A surprise.

TWO

JOHN *and* CAROL *seated across the desk from each other.*

JOHN: You see, (*pause*) I love to teach. And flatter myself I am *skilled* at it. And I love the, the aspect of *performance*. I think I must confess that.

When I found I loved to teach I swore that I would not become that cold, rigid automaton of an instructor which I had encountered as a child.

Now, I was not unconscious that it was given me to err upon the other side. And, so, I asked and *ask* myself if I engaged in heterodoxy, I will not say "gratuitously" for I do not care to posit orthodoxy as a given good—but, "to the detriment of, of my students." (*Pause*)

As I said. When the possibility of tenure opened, and, of course, I'd long pursued it, I was, of course *happy*, and *covetous* of it.

I asked myself if I was wrong to covet it. And thought about it long, and, I hope, truthfully, and saw in myself several things in, I think, no particular order. (*Pause*)

That I *would* pursue it. That I *desired* it, that I was not pure of longing for security, and that that, perhaps, was not reprehensible in me. That I had duties *beyond* the school, and that my duty to my home, for instance, was, or should be, if it were not, of an equal weight. That tenure, and security, and yes, and *comfort*, were not, of themselves, to be scorned; and were even worthy of honorable pursuit. And that it was given me. Here, in this place, which I enjoy, and in which I find comfort, to assure myself of—as far as it rests in The Material—a continuation of that joy and comfort. In exchange for what? Teaching. Which I love.

What was the price of this security? To obtain *tenure*. Which tenure the committee is in the process of granting me. And on the basis of which I contracted to purchase a house. Now, as you don't have your own family, at this point, you may not know what that means. But to me it is important. A home. A Good Home. To raise my family. Now: The Tenure Committee will meet. This is the process, and a *good* process. Under which the school has functioned for quite a long time. They will meet, and hear your complaint—which you have the right to make; and they will dismiss it. They will *dismiss* your complaint; and, in the intervening period, I will lose my house. I will not be able to close on my house. I will lose my *deposit,* and the home I'd picked out for my wife and son will go by the boards. Now: I see I have angered you. I understand your anger at teachers. I was angry with mine. I felt hurt and humiliated by them. Which is one of the reasons that I went into education.

CAROL: What do you want of me?

JOHN: (*Pause*) I was hurt. When I received the report. Of the tenure committee. I was shocked. And I was hurt. No, I don't mean to subject you to my weak sensibilities. All right. Finally, I didn't understand. Then I thought: is it not always at those points at which we reckon ourselves unassailable that we are most vulnerable and … (*Pause*) Yes. All right. You find me pedantic. Yes. I am. By nature, by *birth,* by profession, I don't know … I'm always looking for a *paradigm* for …

CAROL: I don't know what a paradigm is.

JOHN: It's a model.

CAROL: Then why can't you use that word? (*Pause*)

JOHN: If it is important to you. Yes, all right. I was looking for a model. To continue: I feel that one point …

CAROL: I …

JOHN: One second … upon which I am unassailable is my unflinching concern for my students' dignity. I asked you here to … in the spirit of *investigation,* to ask you … to ask … (*Pause*) What have I done to you? (*Pause*) And, and, I suppose, how I can make amends. Can we not settle this now? It's pointless, really, and I want to know.

CAROL: What you can do to force me to retract?

JOHN: That is not what I meant at all.

CAROL: To bribe me, to convince me …

JOHN: … No.

CAROL: To retract …

JOHN: That is not what I meant at all. I think that you know it is not.

CAROL: That is not what I know. I *wish* I …

JOHN: I do not want to … you wish what?

CAROL: No, you said what amends can you make. To force me to retract.

JOHN: That is not what I said.

CAROL: I have my notes.

JOHN: Look. Look. The Stoics say …

 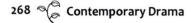

CAROL: The Stoics?

JOHN: The Stoical Philosophers say if you remove the phrase "I have been injured," you have removed the injury. Now: Think: I know that you're upset Just tell me. Literally. Literally: what wrong have I done you?

CAROL: Whatever you have done to me—to the extent that you've done it to *me,* do you know, rather than to me as a *student,* and, so, to the student body, is contained in my report. To the tenure committee.

JOHN: Well, all right. (*Pause*) Let's see. (*He reads.*) I find that I am sexist. That I am *elitist.* I'm not sure I know what that means, other than it's a derogatory word, meaning "bad." That I .... That I insist on wasting time, in nonprescribed, in self-aggrandizing and theatrical *diversions* from the prescribed *text* ... that these have taken both sexist and pornographic forms ... here we find listed ... (*Pause*) Here we find listed ... instances " ... closeted with a student" ... "Told a rambling, sexually explicit story, in which the frequency and attitudes of fornication of the poor and rich are, it would seem, the central point ... moved to *embrace* said student and ... all part of a pattern ... " (*Pause*)

(*He reads.*) That I used the phrase "The White Man's Burden" ... that I told you how I'd asked you to my room because I quote like you. (*Pause*)

(*He reads.*) "He said he 'liked' me. That he 'liked being with me.' He'd let me write my examination paper over, if I could come back oftener to see him in his office." (*Pause*) (*To* CAROL:) It's *ludicrous.* Don't you know that? It's not *necessary.* It's going to *humiliate* you, and it's going to cost me my *house,* and ...

CAROL: It's *"ludicrous ... "*?

(JOHN *picks up the report and reads again.*)

JOHN: "He told me he had problems with his wife; and that he wanted to take off the artificial stricture of Teacher and Student. He put his arm around me ... "

CAROL: Do you deny it? Can you deny it ...? Do you see? (*Pause*) Don't you see? You don't see, do you?

JOHN: I don't see ...

CAROL: You think, you think you can deny that these things happened; or, if they *did,* if they *did,* that they meant what you *said* they meant. Don't you see? You drag me in here, you drag us, to listen to you "go on"; and "go on" about this, or that, or we don't "express" ourselves very well. We don't say what we mean. Don't we? Don't we? We *do* say what we mean. And you say that "I don't understand you … ": Then *you* … (*Points.*)

JOHN: "Consult the Report"?

CAROL: … that's right.

JOHN: You see. You see. Can't you …. You see what I'm saying? Can't you tell me in your own words?

CAROL: Those are my own words. (*Pause*)

JOHN: (*He reads.*) "He told me that if I would stay alone with him in his office, he would change my grade to an A." (*To* CAROL:) What have I done to you? Oh. My God, are you so hurt?

CAROL: What I "feel" is irrelevant. (*Pause*)

JOHN: Do you know that I tried to help you?

CAROL: What I know I have reported.

JOHN: I would like to help you now. I would. Before this escalates.

CAROL: (*simultaneously with* "escalates"): You see. I don't think that I need your help. I don't think I need anything you have.

JOHN: I feel …

CAROL: I don't *care* what you feel. Do you see? DO YOU SEE? You can't *do* that anymore. You. Do. Not. Have. The Power. Did you misuse it? *Someone* did. Are you part of that group? *Yes. Yes.* You Are. You've *done* these things. And to say and to say, "Oh. Let me help you with your problem … "

JOHN: Yes. I understand. I understand. You're *hurt*. You're *angry*. Yes. I think your *anger* is *betraying* you. Down a path which helps no one.

CAROL: I don't *care* what you think.

JOHN: You don't? (*Pause*) But you talk *of rights*. Don't you see? I have rights too. Do you see? I have a *house* … part of the *real* world; and The Tenure Committee, Good Men and True …

CAROL: … Professor …

JOHN: … Please: *Also* part of that world: you understand? This is my *life*. I'm not a *bogeyman*. I don't "stand" for something, I …

CAROL: … Professor …

JOHN: … I …

CAROL: Professor. I came here as a *favor*. At your personal request. Perhaps I should not have done so. But I did. On my behalf, and on behalf of my group. And you speak of the tenure committee, one of whose members is a woman, as you know. And though you might call it Good Fun, or An Historical Phrase, or An Oversight, or, All of the Above, to refer to the committee as Good Men and True, it is a demeaning remark. It is a sexist remark, and to overlook it is to countenance continuation of that method of thought. It's a remark …

JOHN: OH COME ON. Come on. … Sufficient to deprive a family of …

CAROL: Sufficient? Sufficient? Sufficient? Yes. It is a *fact* … and that story, which I quote, is *vile* and classist, and manipulative and pornographic. It …

JOHN: … it's pornographic …?

CAROL: What gives you the *right*. Yes. To speak to a *woman* in your private … Yes. Yes. I'm sorry. I'm sorry. You feel yourself empowered … you say so yourself. To *strut*. To *posture*. To "perform." To "Call me in here … " Eh? You say that higher education is a joke. And treat it as such, you *treat* it as such. And *confess* to a taste to play the *Patriarch* in your class. To grant *this*. To deny *that*. To embrace your students.

JOHN: How can you assert. How can you stand there and …

CAROL: How can you *deny* it. You did it to me. *Here*. You *did* …. You *confess*. You love the Power. To *deviate*. To *invent*, to transgress … to *transgress* whatever norms have been established for us. And you think it's charming to "question" in yourself this taste to mock and destroy. But you should question it. Professor. And you pick those things which you feel *advance* you: publication, *tenure*, and the steps to get them you call "harmless rituals." And you perform those steps. Although you say it is hypocrisy. But to the aspirations of your students. Of *hardworking students*, who come here, who *slave* to come here—you have no idea what it cost me to come to this school—you *mock* us. You call education "hazing," and from your so-protected, so-elitist seat you hold our confusion as a *joke*, and our hopes and efforts with it. Then you sit there and say "what have I done?" And ask me to understand that *you* have aspirations too. But I tell you. I tell you. That you are vile. And that you are exploitative. And if you possess one ounce of that inner honesty you describe in your book, you can look in yourself and see those things that I see. And you can find revulsion equal to my own. Good day. (*She prepares to leave the room.*)

JOHN: Wait a second, will you, just one moment. (*Pause*) Nice day today.

CAROL: What?

JOHN: You said "Good day." I think that it is a nice day today.

CAROL: *Is* it?

JOHN: Yes, I think it is.

CAROL: And why is that important?

JOHN: Because it is the essence of all human communication. I say something conventional, you respond, and the information we exchange is not about the "weather," but that we both agree to converse. In effect, we agree that we are both human. (*Pause*)

I'm not a ... "exploiter," and you're not a ... "deranged," what? *Revolutionary* ... that we may, that we may have ... positions, and that we may have ... desires, which are in *conflict*, but that we're just human. (*Pause*) That means that sometimes we're *imperfect*. (*Pause*) Often we're in conflict ... (*Pause*) *Much* of what we do, you're right, in the name of "principles" is *self-serving* ... much of what we do is *conventional*. (*Pause*) You're right. (*Pause*) You said you came in the class because you wanted to learn about *education*. I don't know that I can teach you about education. But I know that I can tell you what I *think* about education, and then *you* decide. And you don't have to fight with me. *I'm* not the subject. (*Pause*) And where I'm *wrong* ... perhaps it's not your job to "fix" me. I don't want to fix *you*. I would like to tell you what I *think*, because that *is* my job, conventional as it is, and flawed as I may be. And then, if you can show me some better *form*, then we can proceed from there. But, just like "nice day, isn't it ...?" I don't think we can proceed until we accept that each of us is human. (*Pause*) And we still can have difficulties. We *will* have them ... that's all right too. (*Pause*) Now:

CAROL: ... wait ...

JOHN: Yes. I want to hear it.

CAROL: ... the ...

JOHN: Yes. Tell me frankly.

CAROL: ... my position ...

JOHN: I want to hear it. In your own words. What you want. And what you feel.

CAROL: ... I ...

JOHN: ... yes ...

CAROL: My Group.

JOHN: Your "Group" ...? (*Pause*)

CAROL: The people I've been talking to ...

JOHN: There's no shame in that. Everybody needs advisers. Everyone needs to expose themselves. To various points of view. It's not wrong. It's essential. Good, Good. Now: You and I.. (*The phone rings.*)

You and I ...

(*He hesitates for a moment, and then picks it up.*) (*Into phone*) Hello. (*Pause*) Um ... no, I know they do. (*Pause*) I know she does. Tell her that I ... can I call you back? ... Then tell her that I think it's going to be fine. (*Pause*) Tell her just, just hold on. I'll ... can I get back to you? ... Well ... no, no, no, we're *taking* the house ... we're ... no, no, nn ... no, she will nnn, it's not a *question* of refunding the dep ... no ... it's not a *question* of the deposit ... will you call Jerry? Babe, baby, will you just call Jerry? Tell him, nnn ... tell him they, well, they're to keep the deposit, because the deal, be ... because the deal is going to go *through* ... because I know ... be ...

will you please? Just *trust* me. Be … well, I'm dealing with the complaint. Yes. Right *Now.* Which is why I … yes, no, no, it's really, I can't *talk* about it now. Call Jerry, and I can't talk now. Ff … fine. Gg … good-bye. (*Hangs up.*) (*Pause*) I'm sorry we were interrupted.

CAROL: No …

JOHN: I … I was saying:

CAROL: You said that we should agree to talk about my complaint.

JOHN: That's correct.

CAROL: But we *are* talking about it.

JOHN: Well, that's correct too. You see? This is the *gist* of education.

CAROL: No, no. I mean, we're talking about it at the Tenure Committee Hearing. (*Pause*)

JOHN: Yes, but I'm saying: we can talk about it *now,* as easily as …

CAROL: No. I think that we should stick to the process …

JOHN: … wait a …

CAROL: … the "conventional" process. As you said. (*She gets up.*) And you're right, I'm sorry if I was, um, if I was "discourteous" to you. You're right.

JOHN: Wait, wait a …

CAROL: I really should go.

JOHN: Now, look, granted. I have an interest. In the status quo. All right? Everyone does. But what I'm saying is that the *committee* …

CAROL: Professor, you're right. Just don't impinge on me. We'll take our differences, and …

JOHN: You're going to make a … look, look, look, you're going to …

CAROL: I shouldn't have come here. They told me …

JOHN: One moment. No, No. There are *norms,* here, and there's no reason. Look: I'm trying to *save* you …

CAROL: No one *asked* you to … you're trying to save *me?* Do me the courtesy to …

JOHN: I *am* doing you the courtesy, I'm talking *straight* to you. We can settle this *now.* And I want you to sit *down* and …

CAROL: You must excuse me … (*She starts to leave the room.*)

JOHN: Sit down, it seems we each have a …. Wait one moment. Wait one moment … just do me the courtesy to … (*He restrains her from leaving.*)

CAROL: LET ME GO.

JOHN: I have no desire to *hold* you. I just want to *talk* to you...

CAROL: LET ME GO. LET ME GO. WOULD SOMEBODY *HELP* ME? WOULD SOMEBODY *HELP* ME PLEASE …?

THREE

(*At rise,* CAROL *and* JOHN *are seated.*)

JOHN: I have asked you here. (*Pause*) I have asked you here against, against my …

CAROL: I was most surprised you asked me.

JOHN: … against my better *judgment,* against …

CAROL: I was most surprised …

JOHN: … against the … yes. I'm sure.

CAROL: … If you would like me to leave, I'll leave. I'll go right now … (*She rises.*)

JOHN: Let us begin *correctly?* may we? I feel …

CAROL: That is what I wished to do. That's why I came here, but now …

JOHN: … I feel …

CAROL: But now perhaps you'd like me to leave …

JOHN: I don't want you to leave. I asked you to come …

CAROL: I didn't have to come here.

JOHN: No. (*Pause*) Thank you.

CAROL: All right. (*Pause*) (*She sits down.*)

JOHN: Although I feel that it *profits,* it would *profit* you something, to …

CAROL: … what I …

JOHN: If you would hear me out, if you would hear me out.

CAROL: I came here to, the court officers told me not to come.

JOHN: … the "court" officers …?

CAROL: I was shocked that you asked.

JOHN: … wait …

CAROL: Yes. But I did *not* come here to hear what it "profits" me.

JOHN: The "court" officers …

CAROL: … no, no, perhaps I should leave … (*She gets up.*)

JOHN: Wait.

CAROL: No. I shouldn't have …

JOHN: … wait. Wait. Wait a moment.

CAROL: Yes? What is it you want? (*Pause*) What is it you want?

JOHN: I'd like you to stay.

CAROL: You want me to stay.

JOHN: Yes.

CAROL: You do.

JOHN: Yes. (*Pause*) Yes. I would like to have you hear me out. If you would. (*Pause*) Would you please? If you would do that I would be in your debt. (*Pause*) (*She sits.*) Thank You. (*Pause*)

CAROL: What is it you wish to tell me?

JOHN: All right. I cannot … (*Pause*) I cannot help but feel you are owed an apology. (*Pause*) (*Of papers in his hands*) I have read. (*Pause*) And reread these accusations.

CAROL: What "accusations"?

JOHN: The, the tenure comm … what other accusations …?

CAROL: The tenure committee …?

JOHN: Yes.

CAROL: Excuse me, but those are not accusations. They have been *proved.* They are facts.

JOHN: … I …

CAROL: No. Those are not "accusations."

JOHN: … those?

CAROL: … the committee (*The phone starts to ring.*) the committee has …

JOHN: … All right …

CAROL: … those are not accusations. The Tenure Committee.

JOHN: ALL RIGHT. ALL RIGHT. ALL RIGHT. (*He picks up the phone.*) Hello. Yes. No. I'm here. Tell Mister … No, I can't talk to him now … I'm sure he has, but I'm fff … I know … No I have no time t … tell Mister … tell Mist … tell Jerry that *I'm fine* and that I'll call him right aw … (*Pause*) My wife … Yes. I'm sure she has. Yes, thank you. Yes, I'll call her too. I cannot talk to you now. (*He hangs up.*) (*Pause*) All right. It was good of you to come. Thank you. I have studied. I have spent some time studying the indictment.

CAROL: You will have to explain that word to me.

JOHN: An "indictment" …

CAROL: Yes.

JOHN: Is a "bill of particulars." A …

CAROL: All right. Yes.

JOHN: In which is alleged …

CAROL: No. I cannot allow that. I cannot allow that. Nothing is alleged. Everything is proved …

JOHN: Please, wait a sec …

CAROL: I cannot *come* to allow …

JOHN: If I may … If I may, from whatever you feel is "established," by …

CAROL: The issue here is not what I "feel." It is not my "feelings," but the feelings of women. And men. Your superiors, who've been "polled," do you see? To whom *evidence* has been presented, who have *ruled,* do you see? Who have weighed the testimony and the evidence, and have *ruled,* do you see? That you are *negligent.* That you are *guilty,* that you are found *wanting,* and in *error;* and are *not,* for the reasons so-told, to be given tenure. That you are to be disciplined. For facts. For *facts.* Not "alleged," what is the word? But *proved.* Do you see? By *your own actions.*

That is what the tenure committee has said. That is what my lawyer said. For what you did in class. For what you did *in this office.*

JOHN: They're going to discharge me.

CAROL: As full well they should. You don't understand? You're angry? What has *led* you to this place? Not your sex. Not your race. Not your class. YOUR OWN ACTIONS. And you're *angry.* You *ask* me here. What *do* you want? You want to "charm" me. You want to "convince" me. You want me to recant. I will *not* recant. Why should I …? What I say is right. You tell me, you are going to tell me that you have a wife and child. You are going to say that you have a career and that you've worked for twenty years for this. Do you know what you've *worked* for? *Power.* For *power.* Do you understand? And you sit there, and you tell me *stories.* About your *house,* about all the private *schools,* and about *privilege,* and how you are entitled. To *buy,* to *spend,* to *mock,* to *summon.* All your stories. All your silly weak *guilt,* it's all about *privilege;* and you won't know it. Don't you see? You worked twenty years for the right to *insult* me. And you feel entitled to be *paid* for it. Your Home. Your Wife … Your sweet "deposit" on your house …

JOHN: Don't you have feelings?

CAROL: That's my point. You see? Don't you have feelings? Your final argument. What is it that has no feelings. *Animals.* I don't take your side, you question if I'm Human.

JOHN: Don't you have feelings?

CAROL: I have a responsibility. I …

JOHN: … to …?

CAROL: To? This institution. To the *students.* To my *group.*

JOHN: … your "group." …

CAROL: Because I speak yes not for myself. But for the group; for those who suffer what I suffer. On behalf of whom even if I, were, inclined, to what, forgive? Forget? What? Overlook your …

JOHN: … my behavior?

CAROL: … it would be wrong.

JOHN: Even if you were inclined to "forgive" me.

CAROL: It would be wrong.

JOHN: And what would transpire.

CAROL: Transpire?

JOHN: Yes.

CAROL: "Happen?"

JOHN: Yes.

CAROL: Then *say* it. For Christ's sake. Who the *hell* do you think that you are? You want a post. You want unlimited power. To do and to say what you want. As it pleases you—Testing, Questioning, Flirting …

JOHN: I never …

CAROL: Excuse me, one moment will you?

(*She reads from her notes.*)

The twelfth: "Have a good day dear."

The fifteenth: "Now, don't *you* look fetching … "

April seventeenth: "If you girls would come over here … " I saw you. I saw you, Professor. For two semesters sit there, stand there and exploit our, as you thought, "paternal prerogative," and what is that but rape; I swear to God. You asked me in here to explain something to me, as a child, that I did not understand. But I came to explain something to you. You Are Not God. You ask me why I came? I came here to instruct you.

(*She produces his book.*)

And your book? You think you're going to show me some "light"? You *"maverick."* Outside of tradition. No, no, (*She reads from the book's liner notes.*) *"of* that fine tradition of *inquiry.* Of Polite *skepticism"* … and you say you believe in free intellectual discourse. YOU BELIEVE IN NOTHING. YOU BELIEVE IN NOTHING AT ALL.

JOHN: I believe in freedom of thought.

CAROL: Isn't that fine. *Do* you?

JOHN: Yes. I do.

CAROL: Then why do you question, for one moment, the committee's decision refusing your tenure? Why do you question your suspension? You believe in what *you call* freedom of thought. Then, fine. *You* believe in freedom-of-thought *and* a home, and, *and* prerogatives for your kid, *and* tenure. And I'm going to tell you. You believe *not* in "freedom of thought," but in an elitist, in, in a protected hierarchy which rewards you. And for whom you are the clown. And you mock and exploit the system which pays your rent. You're wrong. I'm not wrong. You're wrong. You think that I'm full of hatred. I know what you think I am.

JOHN: Do you?

CAROL: You think I'm a, of course I do. You think I am a frightened, repressed, confused, I don't know, abandoned young thing of some doubtful sexuality, who wants, power and revenge. (*Pause*) *Don't* you? (*Pause*)

JOHN: Yes. I do. (*Pause*)

CAROL: Isn't that better? And I feel that that is the first moment which you've treated me with respect. For you told me the truth. (*Pause*) I did not come here, as you are assured, to gloat. Why would I want to gloat? I've profited nothing from your, your, as you say, your "misfortune." I came here, as you did me the honor to *ask* me here, I came here to *tell* you something.

(*Pause*) That I think … that I think you've been wrong. That I think you've been terribly wrong. Do you hate me now? (*Pause*)

JOHN: Yes.

CAROL: Why do you hate me? Because you think me wrong? No. Because I have, you think, *power* over you. Listen to me. Listen to me, Professor. (*Pause*) It is the power that you hate. So deeply that, that any atmosphere of free discussion is impossible. It's not "unlikely." It's *impossible*. Isn't it?

JOHN: Yes.

CAROL: *Isn't* it …?

JOHN: Yes. I suppose.

CAROL: Now. The thing which you find so cruel is the selfsame process of selection I, and my group, go through *every day of our lives*. In admittance to school. In our tests, in our class rankings …. Is it unfair? I can't tell you. But, if it is fair. Or even if it is "unfortunate but necessary" for us, then, by God, so must it be for you. (*Pause*) You write of your "responsibility to the young." Treat us with respect, and that will *show* you your responsibility. You write that education is just hazing. (*Pause*) But we worked to get to this school. (*Pause*) And some of us. (*Pause*) Overcame prejudices. Economic, sexual, you cannot begin to imagine. And endured humiliations I *pray* that you and those you love never will encounter. (*Pause*) To gain admittance here. To pursue that same dream of security *you* pursue. We, who, who are, at any moment, in danger of being deprived of it. By …

JOHN: … by …?

CAROL: By the administration. By the teachers. By *you*. By, say, one low grade, that keeps us out of graduate school; by one, say, one capricious or inventive answer on our parts, which, perhaps, you don't find amusing. Now you *know*, do you see? What it is to be subject to that power. (*Pause*)

JOHN: I don't understand. (*Pause*)

CAROL: My charges are not trivial. You see that in the haste, I think, with which they were accepted. A *joke* you have told, with a sexist tinge. The language you use, a verbal or physical caress, yes, yes, I know, you say that it is meaningless. I understand. I differ from you. To lay a hand on someone's shoulder.

JOHN: It was devoid of sexual content.

CAROL: I say it was not. I SAY IT WAS NOT. Don't you begin to *see* …? Don't you begin to understand? IT'S NOT FOR YOU TO SAY.

JOHN: I take your point, and I see there is much good in what you refer to.

CAROL: … do you think so …?

JOHN: … but, and this is not to say that I cannot change, in those things in which I am deficient … But, the …

CAROL: Do you hold yourself harmless from the charge of sexual exploitativeness …? (*Pause*)

JOHN: Well, I … I … I … You know I, as I said. I … think I am not too old to *learn,* and I *can* learn, I …

CAROL: Do you hold yourself innocent of the charge of …

JOHN: … wait, wait, wait … All right, let's go back to …

CAROL: YOU FOOL. Who do you think I am? To come here and be taken in by a *smile.* You little yapping fool. You think I want "revenge." I don't want revenge. I WANT UNDERSTANDING.

JOHN: … *do* you?

CAROL: I do. (*Pause*)

JOHN: What's the use. It's over.

CAROL: Is it? What is?

JOHN: My job.

CAROL: Oh. Your job. That's what you want to talk about. (*Pause*) (*She starts to leave the room. She steps and turns back to him.*) All right. (*Pause*) What if it were possible that my Group withdraws its complaint. (*Pause*)

JOHN: What?

CAROL: That's right. (*Pause*)

JOHN: Why.

CAROL: Well, let's say as an act of friendship.

JOHN: An act of friendship.

CAROL: Yes. (*Pause*)

JOHN: In exchange for what.

CAROL: Yes. But I don't think, "exchange." Not "in exchange." For what do we derive from it? (*Pause*)

JOHN: "Derive."

CAROL: Yes.

JOHN: (*Pause*) Nothing. (*Pause*)

CAROL: That's right. We derive nothing. (*Pause*) Do you see that?

JOHN: Yes.

CAROL: That is a little word, Professor. "Yes." "I see that." But you will.

JOHN: And you might speak to the committee …?

CAROL: To the committee?

JOHN: Yes.

CAROL: Well. Of course. That's on your mind. We might.

JOHN: "If" what?

CAROL: "Given" what. Perhaps. I think that that is more friendly.

JOHN: GIVEN WHAT?

CAROL: And, believe me, I understand your rage. It is not that I don't feel it. But I do not see that it is deserved, so I do not resent it …. All right. I have a list.

JOHN: … a list.

CAROL: Here is a list of books, which we …

JOHN: … a list of books …?

CAROL: That's right. Which we find questionable.

JOHN: What?

CAROL: Is this so bizarre …?

JOHN: I can't believe …

CAROL: It's not necessary you believe it.

JOHN: Academic freedom …

CAROL: Someone chooses the books. If you can choose them, others can. "What are you, "God"?

JOHN: … no, no, the "dangerous." …

CAROL: You have an agenda, we have an agenda. I am not interested in your feelings or your motivation, but your actions. If you would like me to speak to the Tenure Committee, here is my list. You are a Free Person, you decide. (*Pause*)

JOHN: Give me the list. (*She does so. He reads.*)

CAROL: I think you'll find …

JOHN: I'm capable of reading it. Thank you.

CAROL: We have a number of *texts* we need re …

JOHN: I see that.

CAROL: We're amenable to …

JOHN: Aha. Well, let me look over the … (He *reads.*)

CAROL: I think that …

JOHN: LOOK. I'm reading your demands. All right?! (He *reads*) (*Pause*) You want to ban my book?

CAROL: We do not …

JOHN (*Of list*): It says here …

CAROL: … We want it removed from inclusion as a representative example of the university.

JOHN: Get out of here.

CAROL: If you put aside the issues of personalities.

JOHN: Get the fuck out of my office.

CAROL: No, I think I would reconsider.

JOHN: … you think you can.

CAROL: We can and we *will.* Do you want our support? That is the only quest …

JOHN: … to ban my *book* …?

CAROL: … that is correct …

JOHN: … this … this is a *university* … we …

CAROL: … and we have a statement … which we need you to … (*She hands him a sheet of paper.*)

JOHN: No, no. It's out of the question. I'm sorry. I don't know what I was thinking of. I want to tell you something. I'm a teacher. I am a teacher. Eh? It's my *name* on the door, and I teach the class, and that's what I do. I've got a book with my name on it. And my son will *see* that *book* someday. And I have a respon … No, I'm sorry I have a *responsibility … to myself,* to my *son,* to my *profession.* … I haven't been *home* for two days, do you know that? Thinking this out.

CAROL: … you haven't?

JOHN: I've been, no. If it's of interest to you. I've been in a *hotel. Thinking.* (*The phone starts ringing.*) *Thinking* …

CAROL: … you haven't been home?

JOHN: … *thinking,* do you see.

CAROL: Oh.

JOHN: And, and, I owe you a debt, I see that now. (*Pause*) You're *dangerous,* you're *wrong* and it's my *job* … to say no to you. That's my job. You are absolutely right. You want to ban my book? Go to *hell,* and they can do whatever they want to me.

CAROL: … you haven't been home in two days …

JOHN: I think I told you that.

CAROL: … you'd better get that phone. (*Pause*) I think that you should pick up the phone. (*Pause*)

(JOHN *picks up the phone.*)

JOHN (*on phone*): Yes. (*Pause*) Yes. Wh … I. I. I had to be away. All ri … did they wor … did they worry ab … No. I'm all right, now, Jerry. I'm f … I got a little turned *around*, but I'm *sitting* here and … I've got it figured out. I'm fine. I'm fine don't worry about me. I got a little bit mixed up. But I am not sure that it's not a blessing. It cost me my job? Fine. Then the job was not worth having. Tell Grace that I'm coming home and everything is fff … (*Pause*) What? (*Pause*) What? (*Pause*) What do you *mean?* WHAT? Jerry … Jerry. They … Who, who, what can they do …? (*Pause*) NO. (*Pause*) NO. They can't do th … What do you mean? (*Pause*) But how … (*Pause*) She's, she's, she's *here* with me. To … Jerry. I don't underst … (*Pause*) (*He hangs up.*) (*To* CAROL:) What does this mean?

CAROL: I thought you knew.

JOHN: What. (*Pause*) What does it mean. (*Pause*)

CAROL: You tried to rape me. (*Pause*) According to the law. (*Pause*)

JOHN: … what …?

CAROL: You tried to rape me. I was leaving this office, you "pressed" yourself into me. You "pressed" your body into me.

JOHN: … I …

CAROL: My Group has told your lawyer that we may pursue criminal charges.

JOHN: … no …

CAROL: … under the statute. I am told. It was battery.

JOHN: … no …

CAROL: Yes. And attempted rape. That's right. (*Pause*)

JOHN: I think that you should go.

CAROL: Of course. I thought you knew.

JOHN: I have to talk to my lawyer.

CAROL: Yes. Perhaps you should.

(*The phone rings again*) (*Pause*)

JOHN: (*Picks up phone. Into phone:*) Hello? I … Hello …? I … Yes, he just called. No … I. I can't talk to you now, Baby. (*To* CAROL:) Get out.

CAROL: … your wife …?

JOHN: … who it is is no concern of yours. *Get* out. (*To phone:*) No, no, it's going to be all right. I. I can't talk now, Baby. (*To* CAROL:) Get out of here.

CAROL: I'm going.

JOHN: Good.

CAROL (*exiting*): … and don't call your wife "baby."

JOHN: What?

CAROL: Don't call your wife baby. You heard what I said.

(CAROL *starts to leave the room.* JOHN *grabs her and begins to beat her.*)

JOHN: You vicious little bitch. You think you can come in here with your political correctness and destroy my life?

(*He knocks her to the floor.*)

After how I treated you …? You should be … *Rape you …?* Are you kidding me …?

(*He picks up a chair, raises it above his head, and advances on her*)

I wouldn't touch you with a ten-foot pole. You little *cunt …*

(*She cowers on the floor below him. Pause. He looks down at her. He lowers the chair. He moves to his desk, and arranges the papers on it. Pause. He looks over at her.*)

… well …

(*Pause. She looks at him.*)

CAROL: Yes. That's right.

(*She looks away from him, and lowers her head. To herself:*) … yes. That's right.

END

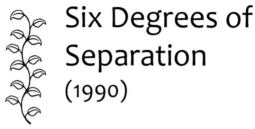

Six Degrees of Separation (1990)

By John Guare (1938–)

INTRODUCTION

In 1983, David Hampton, a 19-year old black man from a middle-class family in Buffalo, used his personal charm and an invented life story to wheedle his way into upper-crust Manhattan society. Claiming he was the disenfranchised son of actor Sidney Poitier, he talked his way into the homes of Ivy League professors and television executives, accepting meals, clothes, and money before his real identity was discovered. When Hampton died in 2003, his attorney said that his famous act was "performance art on the world's smallest possible stage, usually involving an audience of only one or two."

John Guare, in converting this "odd news" item into a play in 1990, seems to have chosen a story ready-made for the stage. A young man acts, pretending to be the son of yet another actor, and ingratiates himself to a series of affluent, well-educated adults who are themselves vulnerable to thespian temptation—the promise of bit roles in a film version of the musical *Cats*.

If it is too much to suggest that Hampton's story (Guare renames him "Paul") is not the focus of *Six Degrees of Separation*, we must acknowledge that Guare makes it compete for our attention with the story of Flan and Ouisa Kittredge, the play's two other main characters (and its narrators). We meet the Kittredges first and experience the story from their perspective. An exclusive focus on Paul would ask us to understand why he would pretend to be someone he is not in order to attain things he otherwise could not have—but such a request would hardly serve as the basis of an interesting play precisely because that impulse is ridiculously *easy* to understand. What is harder to grasp, and what the play demands that we grasp, is why Flan and Ouisa so willingly accept Paul into their home, and the emptiness in their lives that makes them susceptible to this prank.

Paul's initial foray into the Kittredges' home, purporting to be a mugging victim who knows their children from school, turns out to be useful to Flan, helping him broker a covert deal for a Cezanne painting. Flan is an art dealer who acts as a liaison between buyers and sellers who wish to keep their artifacts off the open market; not only does he keep the actual, tangible artifacts at arm's length, but as it turns out he does not even finance the deals himself, relying instead on the help of co-investors. One of these, his friend "Geoffrey," happens to be in town on the night Paul stabs himself to convince Flan and Ouisa to take him in. Ouisa admits that she and Flan were performing for Geoffrey, in a sense: "We weren't auditioning," she tries to claim, "but I kept thinking two million dollars." Once inside, Paul regales Flan, Ouisa, and Geoffrey with tales of a stolen thesis (purportedly on "the death of the imagination") and cooks a fabulous meal for them. Ultimately Flan succeeds in ensuring Geoffrey's investment.

Paul becomes a sort of adopted child to Flan and Ouisa, which is ironic, given that they already have two children, Tess and Woody. Since Paul's shirt had blood on it when he first entered, the Kittredges give him a new shirt—Woody's shirt. At the end of the play, Flan and Ouisa turn Tess away so they can negotiate Paul's surrender to the police over the phone. Tess tells them, angrily, "I'm going to ruin my life and get married and throw away everything you want me to be because it's the only way to hurt you."

For his part, Paul pretends to be an insider, specifically Flan's neglected son, in conning a young couple from Utah. He teaches Rick and Elizabeth how to speak like an upper-crust person, just as Trent, an actual friend of Woody and Tess, coached Paul to do in the first place. This series of performances and coaching sessions, the passing on of acting technique, results not only in the deception of Flan and Ouisa, but in the financial and personal ruin of Rick and Elizabeth.

Larkin, a friend of Flan and Ouisa and also one of Paul's dupes, muses, "We let him into our lives … you'd think we'd be satisfied with our accomplishments." Clearly, their own lives are insufficiently fulfilling. Paul exposes the void that Flan and Ouisa have been trying to cover up, or which they had been pretending did not exist. They latched onto Paul's fantastic tale, played along to an extent, because their reality was inadequate. As Paul says in Ouisa's dream, "the imagination is the place we are all trying to get to."

A painting revolves slowly high over the stage. The painting is by Kandinsky. He has painted on either side of the canvas in two, different styles. One side is geometric and somber. The other side is wild and vivid. The painting stops its revolve and opts for the geometric side.

A couple runs on stage, in nightdress, very agitated, FLANDERS KITTREDGE *is 44.* LOUISA KITTREDGE *is 43. They are very attractive. They speak to us.*

OUISA: Tell them!

FLAN: I am shaking.

OUISA: You have to do *something!*

FLAN: It's awful.

OUISA: Is anything gone?

FLAN: How can I look? I'm shaking.

OUISA (*To us*): Did he take anything?

FLAN: Would you concentrate on yourself?

OUISA: I want to know if anything's gone?

FLAN (*To us*): We came in the room.

OUISA: I went in first. You didn't see what I saw.

FLAN: Calm down.

OUISA: We could have been killed.

FLAN: The silver Victorian inkwell.

OUISA: How can you think of *things?* We could have been murdered .

(*An actor appears for a moment holding up an ornate Victorian inkwell capped by a silver beaver.*)

FLAN: There's the inkwell. Silver beaver. Why?

OUISA: Slashed—our throats slashed.

(*Another actor appears for a moment holding up a framed portrait of a dog, say, a pug.*)

FLAN: And there's the watercolor. Our dog.

OUISA: Go to bed at night happy and then murdered. Would we have woken up?

FLAN: Now I lay me down to sleep—the most terrifying words—just think of it—

OUISA: I pray the Lord my soul to keep—

FLAN: The nightmare part—If I should die before I wake—

OUISA: If I should die—I pray the Lord my soul to take—
FLAN AND OUISA: Oh.
OUISA: It's awful.
FLAN: We're alive.

(FLAN *stops, frightened suddenly, listening.*)

FLAN: Hello?

(*He holds her.*)

FLAN: Hello!
OUISA (*Whispers*): You don't call out Hello unless—
FLAN: I think we'd tell if someone else were here.
OUISA: We didn't all night. Oh, it was awful awful awful awful.

(*They pull off their robes and are smartly dressed for dinner.*)

FLAN (*To us*): We were having a wonderful evening last night.
OUISA (*To us*): A friend we hadn't seen for many years came by for dinner.
FLAN (*Portentously*): A friend from South Africa—
OUISA: Don't say it so portentously.
FLAN (*Bright*): A friend from South Africa.
OUISA: Don't be ga-ga.
FLAN (*To us*): I'm an art dealer. Private sales. Purchases.
OUISA (*To us*): We knew our friend from South Africa
FLAN: through our children when they all lived in New York.
OUISA: They had gone back to South Africa.
FLAN: He was here in New York briefly on business and asked us to ask him for dinner.
OUISA: He's King Midas rich. Literally. Gold mines.
FLAN: Seventy thousand workers in just one gold mine.
OUISA: But he is always short of cash because his government won't let its people—
FLAN: its white people—
OUISA: —its white people take out any money. So it's like taking in a War Baby.
FLAN: When he called it was like a bolt from the blue as I had a deal coming up and was short by
OUISA: two million.

FLAN: The figure is superfluous.

OUISA: I hate when you use the word "superfluous." I mean, he needed two million and we hadn't seen Geoffrey in a long time and while Geoffrey might not have the price of a dinner he easily might have two million dollar.

FLAN: The currents last night were very churny.

OUISA: We weren't sucking up. We like Geoffrey.

FLAN: It's that awful thing of having truly rich folk for friends.

OUISA: Face it. The money does get in the—

FLAN: Only if you let it. The fact of the money shouldn't get in—

OUISA: Having a rich friend is like drowning and your friend makes life boats. But the friend gets very touchy if you say one word: life boat. Well, that's two words. We were afraid our South African friend might say "You only love me for my life boats?" But we *like* Geoffrey.

FLAN: It wasn't a life-threatening evening.

OUISA: Rich people can do something for you even if you're not sure what it is you want them to do.

FLAN: Hardly a life boat evening—

OUISA (*Sing-song*): Portentous.

FLAN: But when he called and asked us to take him for dinner, he made a sudden pattern in life's little tea leaves because who wants to go to banks? Geoffrey called and our tempests settled into showers and life was manageable. What more can you want?

   (GEOFFREY *is there, an elegant, impeccably British South African, slightly older than* OUISA *and* FLAN. FLAN *passes drinks.*)

GEOFFREY: Listen. (*They do.*)

   It always amazes me when New York is so quiet.

OUISA: With the kids away, we get used to a lower noise quotient.

FLAN: Geoffrey, you have to move out of South Africa. You'll be killed. Why do you stay in South Africa?

GEOFFREY: One has to stay there to educate the black workers and we'll know we've been successful when they kill us.

FLAN: Planning the revolution that will destroy you.

OUISA: Putting your life on the line.

GEOFFREY: You don't think of it like that. I wish you'd come visit.

OUISA: But we'd visit you and sit in your gorgeous house planning trips into the townships demanding to see the poorest of the poor. "Are you sure they're the worst off? I mean, we've come all this way. We don't want to see people just mildly victimized by apartheid. We demand shock." It doesn't seem right sitting on the East Side talking about revolution.

FLAN: Only small murky cafes for Pepe le Moko here.

OUISA: No. La Pasionaria. I will come to South Africa and build barricades and lean against them, singing.

FLAN: And the people would follow.

OUISA: "Follow Follow Follow." What's that song?

FLAN: The way Gorbachev cheered on the striking coal miners in the Ukraine—yes, you must strike—it is your role in history to dismantle this system. Russia and Poland—you can't believe the developments in the world—*The Fantasticks,* "Follow Follow Follow."

OUISA: China.

FLAN and OUISA (*Despair*): Oh.

GEOFFREY: Oy vay China. As my grandmother would say.

(*They all laugh.*)

Our role in history. And we offer ourselves up to it.

FLAN: That is your role in history. Not our role.

OUISA: A role in history. To say that so easily.

FLAN (*To* GEOFFREY): Do you want another drink before we go out?

OUISA: The phrase—striking coal miners—I see all these very striking coal miners modelling the fall fashions—

GEOFFREY: Where should we?

FLAN: There's good Szechuan. And Hunan

OUISA: The sign painter screwed up the sign. Instead of The Hunan Wok, he painted The Human Wok.

GEOFFREY: God! The restaurants! New York has become the Florence of the sixteenth century: Genius on every corner.

OUISA: I don't think genius has kissed the Human Wok.

GEOFFREY: The new Italian looked cheery.

FLAN and OUISA: Good.

FLAN: We made reservations.

OUISA: They wrap ravioli up like salt water taffy.

FLAN: Six on a plate for a few hundred dollars.

GEOFFREY: You have to come to South Africa so I can pay you back. I'll take you on my plane into the Okavango Swamps—

OUISA: Did you hear—to take back to Johannesburg. Out in East Hampton

FLAN: last weekend

OUISA: a guy goes into one of the better food stores—

FLAN: Dean and DeLuca—

OUISA: one of the Dean and DeLuca look alikes. Gets a pack of cigarettes and an ice cream bar. Goes up front. Sees there's a line at the register. Slaps down two twenty dollar bills and goes out.

FLAN: We sent it to the *Times*.

OUISA: They have the joke page of things around New York.

FLAN: They send you a bottle of champagne.

(*They all laugh brightly.*)

OUISA (*To us*): We weren't auditioning but I kept thinking Two million dollars two million dollars.

FLAN (*To us*): It's like when people say 'Don't think about elephants' and all you can think about is elephants elephants.

OUISA (*To us*): Two million dollars two million dollars.

(*They laugh brightly. The doorbell rings.*)

OUISA (*To* FLAN): Whatever you do, don't think about elephants.

(OUISA *goes.*)

GEOFFREY: Elephants?

FLAN: Louisa is a Dada manifesto.

GEOFFREY: Tell me about the Cezanne?

FLAN: Mid-period. Landscape of a dark green forest. In the far distance you see the sunlight. One of his first uses of a pale color being forced to carry the weight of the picture. The experiment that would pay off in the apples. A burst of color asked to carry so much. The Japanese don't like anything about it except it's a Cezanne—

(*A young black man—*PAUL—*enters, supported by* THE DOORMAN, PAUL *is in his early twenties, very handsome, very preppy. He has been beaten badly. Blood seeps through his white Brooks Brothers shirt.*
OUISA *follows at a loss.*
THE DOORMAN *helps* PAUL *to the sofa and stands at the door warily.*)

PAUL: I'm so sorry to bother you, but I've been hurt and I've lost everything and I didn't know where to go. Your children—I'm a friend of—

OUISA (*To us*): And he mentioned our daughter's name.

FLAN (*To us*): And the school where they went.

OUISA (*To* FLAN): Harvard. You can say Harvard.

FLAN (*To us*): We don't want to get into libel.

PAUL: I was mugged. Out there. In Central Park. By the statue of that Alaskan husky. I was standing there trying to figure out why there is a statue of a dog who saved lives in the Yukon in Central Park and I was standing there trying to puzzle it out when—

OUISA: Are you okay?

PAUL: They took my money and my briefcase. I said my thesis is in there—

FLAN: His shirt's bleeding.

OUISA: His shirt is not bleeding. *He's* bleeding.

PAUL (*A wave of nausea*): I get this way around blood.

FLAN: Not on the rug.

PAUL: I don't mind the money. But in this age of mechanical reproduction they managed to get the only copy of my thesis.

FLAN: Eddie, get the doctor—

PAUL: No! I'll survive.

FLAN: You'll be fine.

(FLAN *helps* PAUL *out of the room.* THE DOORMAN *goes.*)

OUISA (*To us*): We bathed him. We did First Aid.

GEOFFREY (*Leaving*): It's been wonderful seeing you—

OUISA (*Very cheery*): No no no! Stay!—

(*To us*) Two million dollars two million dollars—

GEOFFREY: My time is so short—before I leave America, I really should see—

FLAN (*Calling from the hall*): Where are the bandages!?—

OUISA: The Red Cross advises: Press edges of the wound firmly together, wash area with water—

GEOFFREY: May I use your phone?

OUISA: You darling old poop—just sit back—this'll only take mo—

(*Calling*) Flan, go into Woody's room and get him a clean shirt.

Geoffrey have you seen the new book on Cezanne?

(*To us*) I ran down the hall to get the book on Cezanne, got the gauze from my bathroom, gave the Cezanne to Flan who wanted the gauze, gave the gauze to Geoffrey who wanted Cezanne. Two million dollars two million dollars—

(FLAN *comes back in the room.*)

FLAN: He's going to be fine.

OUISA (*To us*): And peace was restored.

(PAUL *enters, slightly recovered, wearing a clean pink shirt. He winces as he pulls on his blazer.*)

PAUL: Your children said you were kind. All the kids were sitting around the dorm one night dishing the shit out of their parents. But your kids were silent and said, No, not our parents. Not Flan and Ouisa. Not the Kittredges. The Kittredges are kind. So after the muggers left, I looked up and saw these Fifth Avenue apartments. Mrs. Onassis lives there. I know the Babcocks live over there. The Auchinclosses live there. But you lived here. I came here.

OUISA: Can you believe what the kids said?

FLAN (*To us*): We mentioned our kids names.

OUISA: We can mention our kids' names. Our children are not going to sue us for using their names.

PAUL: But your kids—I love them. Talbot and Woody mean the world to me.

FLAN: He lets you call him Woody? Nobody's called him Woody in years.

PAUL: They described this apartment in detail. The Kandinsky!—that's a double. One painted on either side.

FLAN: We flip it around for variety.

PAUL: It's wonderful.

FLAN (*To us*): Wassily Kandinsky. Born 1866 Moscow. Blue Rider Exhibition 1914. He said "It is clear that the choice of object that is one of the elements in the harmony of form must be decided only by a corresponding vibration in the human soul." Died 1944 France.

PAUL: It's the way they said it would be.

OUISA (*To us*): Geoffrey had been silent up to now.

GEOFFREY: Did you bitch your parents?

PAUL: As a matter of fact. No. Your kids and I ... we both liked our parents ... loved our—look, am I getting in the way? I burst in here, hysterical. Blood. I didn't mean to—

FLAN and OUISA: No!

OUISA: Tell us about our children.

FLAN (*To us*): Three. Two at Harvard. Another girl at Groton.

OUISA: How is Harvard?

PAUL: Well, fine. It's just there. Everyone's in a constant state of luxurious despair and constant discovery and paralysis.

OUISA (*To us*): We asked him where home was.

FLAN (*To us*): Out West, he said.

PAUL: Although I've lived all over. My folks are divorced. He's remarried. He's doing a movie.

OUISA: He's in the movies?

PAUL: He's directing this one but he does act.

FLAN: What's he directing?

PAUL: *Cats.*

OUISA: Someone is directing a film of *Cats?*

FLAN: Don't be snooty.

PAUL: You've seen it? T.S. Eliot—

FLAN: Well, yes. Years ago.

OUISA: A benefit for some disease or school—

FLAN: Surely they can't make the movie of *Cats.*

OUISA: Of course they can.

PAUL: They're going to try. My father'll be here auditioning—

OUISA: Cats?

PAUL: He's going to use people.

OUISA: What a courageous stand!

PAUL: They thought of lots of ways to go. Animation.

FLAN: Animation would be nice.

PAUL: But he found a better way. As a matter of fact, he turned it down at first. He went to tell the producers—as a courtesy—all the reasons why you couldn't make a movie of *Cats* and in going through all the reasons why you couldn't make a movie of *Cats,* he suddenly saw how you could make a movie of *Cats*—

OUISA: Eureka in the bathtub. How wonderful.

FLAN: May we ask who—

OUISA (*To us*): And it was here we pulled up—ever so slightly—pulled up closer—

FLAN (*To us*): And he told us.

OUISA (*To us*): He named the greatest black star in movies. Sidney—

FLAN: Don't say it. We're trying to keep this abstract. Plus libel laws.

OUISA: Sidney Poitier! There. I don't care. We have to have truth. (*To us*) He started out as a lawyer and is terrified of libel. I'm not.

(PAUL *steps forward cheerily.*)

PAUL (*To us*): Sidney Poitier, the future Jackie Robinson of films, was born the twenty-fourth of February 1927 in Miami during a visit his parents made to

Florida—legally?—to sell tomatoes they had grown on their farm in the Bahamas. He grew up on Cat Island, "so poor they didn't even own dirt" he has said. Neglected by his family, my father would sit on the shore, and, as he told me many times, "conjure up the kind of worlds that were on the other side and what I'd do in them." He arrived in New York City from the Bahamas in the winter of 1943 at age fifteen and a half and lived in the pay toilet of the bus station across from the old Madison Square Garden at Fiftieth and Eighth Avenue. He moved to the roof of the Brill Building, commonly known as Tin Pan Alley, and washed dishes at the Turf Restaurant for $4.11 a night. He taught himself to read by reading the newspaper. In the black newspaper, the theater page was opposite the want ad page. Among his 42 films are *No Way Out*, 1950; *Cry the Beloved Country*, 1952; *Blackboard Jungle*, 1955; *The Defiant Ones*, 1958; *Raisin in the Sun*, 1961; *Lilies of the Field*, 1963; *In the Heat of the Night*, 1967; *To Sir With Love*, 1967; *Shoot to Kill*, 1988; and, of course, *Guess Who's Coming to Dinner*. He won the Oscar for *Lilies of the Field* and was twice named top male box-office star in the country. My father made no films from 1977 to 1987 but worked as director and author. Dad said to me once, "I still don't fully understand how all that came about in the sequence it came about."

(PAUL *returns to the sofa.*)

PAUL: Dad's not in till tomorrow at the Sherry. I came down from Cambridge. Thought I'd stay at some fleabag for adventure. Orwell. Down and Out. I really don't know New York. I know Rome and Paris and Los Angeles a lot better.

OUISA: We're going out to dinner. You'll come.

PAUL: Out to dinner?

FLAN: Out to dinner.

PAUL: But why go out to dinner?

OUISA: Because we have reservations and oh my god what time is it? Have we lost the reservations and we don't have a damn thing in the house and it's sixteenth-century Florence and there's genius on every block.

GEOFFREY: Don't mock.

(*She kisses* GEOFFREY.)

PAUL: You must have something in the fridge.

FLAN: A frozen steak from the Ice Age.

PAUL: Why spend a hundred dollars on a bowl of rice? Let me into the kitchen. Cooking calms me. What I'd like to do is calm down, pay back your kids—

OUISA (*To us*): He mentioned our kids names—

FLAN (*To us*): Two. Two at Harvard. A daughter at Groton.

PAUL: who've been wonderful to me.

OUISA: They've never mentioned you.

FLAN: What are they supposed to say? We've become friends with the son of Sidney Poitier, barrier breaker of the fifties and sixties?

GEOFFREY: Your father means a great deal in South Africa.

OUISA (*To us*): Even Geoffrey was touched.

PAUL: I'm glad of that. Dad and I went to Russia once to a film festival and he was truly amazed how much his presence meant—

OUISA: Oh no! Tell us stories of movie stars tying up their children and being cruel.

PAUL: I wish.

GEOFFREY: You wish?

PAUL: If I wanted to write a book about him, I really couldn't. No one would want to read it. He's decent. I admire him.

OUISA: He's married to an actress who was in one of—she's white? Am I right?

PAUL: That is not my mother. That is his second wife. He met Joanna making *The Lost Man*. He left my mother, who had stuck by him in the lean years. I had just been born. *The Lost Man* is the only film of my father's I can't bring myself to see.

OUISA: Oh, I'm sorry. We didn't mean to—

PAUL (*Bright*): No! We're all good friends now. His kids from that marriage. Us—the old kids. I'd love to get in that kitchen.

FLAN (*To* OUISA): What should we do?

OUISA (*To us*): It's Geoffrey's only night in New York.

GEOFFREY: I vote stay in.

OUISA, FLAN and PAUL: Good!

(PAUL *goes off to the kitchen.*)

OUISA (*To us*): We moved into the kitchen.

FLAN (*To us*): We watched him cook.

OUISA (*To us*): We watched him cook and chop.

FLAN (*To us*): He sort of did wizardry—

OUISA (*To us*): An old jar of sun-dried tomatoes—

FLAN (*To us*): Leftovers—tuna fish—olives—onions—

(PAUL *returns with three dishes heaped with food.*)

PAUL: Here's dinner. All ready.

OUISA: Shall we move into the dining room?

PAUL: No, let's stay in here. It's nice in here.

(OUISA, FLAN *and* GEOFFREY *take plates skeptically.*)

OUISA: Have you declared your major yet?

PAUL: You're like all parents. What's your major?

FLAN: Geoffrey, Harvard has all those great titles the students give courses.

OUISA: The Holocaust and Ethics—

FLAN: Krauts and Doubts.

(*They eat. Surprise. It's delicious.*)

GEOFFREY: This is the best pasta I've ever—

PAUL: My father insisted we learn to cook.

FLAN: Isn't he from Jamaica? There's a taste of—

GEOFFREY: The islands.

PAUL: Yes. Before he made it, he ran four restaurants in Harlem. You have good buds!

GEOFFREY: See? Good buds. I've never been complimented on my buds—

PAUL (*To* GEOFFREY): You're from—

GEOFFREY: Johannesburg.

(*Pause*)

PAUL: My dad took me to a movie shot in South Africa. The camera moved from this vile rioting in the streets to a villa where people picked at lunch on a terrace, the only riot the flowers and the birds—gorgeous plumage and petals. And I didn't understand. And Dad said to me, "You meet these young blacks who are having a terrible time. They've had a totally inadequate education and yet in '76—the year of the Soweto riots—they took on a tremendous political responsibility. It just makes you wonder at the maturity that is in them. It makes you realize that the 'crummy childhood' theory, that everything can be blamed in a Freudian fashion on the fact that you've had a bad upbringing, just doesn't hold water." Is everything okay?

(FLAN, OUISA *and* GEOFFREY *are mesmerized, and then resume eating.*)

FLAN, OUISA and GEOFFREY (*While eating*): Mmmmmm … yes.

GEOFFREY: What about being black in America?

PAUL: My problem is I've never felt American. I grew up in Switzerland. Boarding school. Villa Rosey.

OUISA: There is a boarding school in Switzerland that takes you at age eighteen months.

PAUL: That's not me. I've never felt people liked me for my connections. Movie star kid problems. None of those. May I?

FLAN: Oh, please.

(PAUL *pours a brandy.*)

PAUL: But I never knew I was black in that racist way till I was sixteen and came back here. Very protected. White servants. After the divorce we moved to Switzerland, my mother, brother and I. I don't feel American, I don't even feel black. I suppose that's very lucky for me even though Freud says there's no such thing as luck. Just what you make.

OUISA: Does Freud say that? I think we're lucky having this dinner. Isn't this the finest time? A toast to you.

GEOFFREY: To *Cats*!

FLAN: Blunt question. What's he like?

OUISA: Let's not be star fuckers.

FLAN: I'm not a star fucker.

PAUL: My father, being an actor, has no real identity You say to him, Pop, what's new? And he says, "I got an interesting script today. I was asked to play a lumberjack up in the Yukon. Now, I've been trained as a preacher, but my church fell apart. My wife says we have to get money to get through this winter. And I sign up as part of this team where all my beliefs are challenged. But I hold firm. In spite of prejudice. Because I want to get back to you. Out of this forest, back to the church …" And my father is in tears and I say Pop, this is not a real event, this is some script that was sent to you. And my father says "I'm trying it out to see how it fits on me." But he has no life—he has no memory—only the scripts producers send him in the mail through his agents. That's his past.

OUISA (*To us*): I just loved the kid so much. I wanted to reach out to him.

FLAN (*To us*): And then we asked him what his thesis was on,

GEOFFREY: The one that was stolen. Please?

PAUL: Well …

A substitute teacher out on Long Island was dropped from his job for fighting with a student. A few weeks later, the teacher returned to the classroom, shot the student unsuccessfully, held the class hostage and then shot himself. Successfully. This fact caught my eye: last sentence. *Times.* A neighbor described him as a nice boy. Always reading *Catcher in the Rye.*

The nitwit—Chapman—who shot John Lennon said he did it because he wanted to draw the attention of the world to *The Catcher in the Rye* and the reading of that book would be his defense.

And young Hinckley, the whiz kid who shot Reagan and his press secretary, said if you want my defense all you have to do is read *Catcher in the Rye.* It seemed to be time to read it again.

FLAN: I haven't read it in years.

(OUISA *shushes* FLAN.)

PAUL: I borrowed a copy from a young friend of mine because I wanted to see what she had underlined and I read this book to find out why this touching, beautiful, sensitive story published in July 1951 had turned into this manifesto of hate.

I started reading. It's exactly as I remembered. Everybody's a phoney. Page two: "My brother's in Hollywood being a prostitute." Page three: "What a phony slob his father was." Page nine: "People never notice anything."

Then on page twenty-two my hair stood up. Remember Holden Caulfield—the definitive sensitive youth—wearing his red hunter's cap. "A deer hunter hat? Like hell it is. I sort of closed one eye like I was taking aim at it. This is a people-shooting hat I shoot people in this hat."

Hmmm, I said. This book is preparing people for bigger moments in their lives than I ever dreamed of. Then on page eighty-nine: "I'd rather push a guy out the window or chop his head off with an ax than sock him in the jaw. I hate fist fights ... what scares me most is the other guy's face ..."

I finished the book. It's a touching story, comic because the boy wants to do so much and can't do anything. Hates all phoniness and only lies to others. Wants everyone to like him, is only hateful, and is completely self-involved. In other words, a pretty accurate picture of a male adolescent.

And what alarms me about the book—not the book so much as the aura about it—is this: The book is primarily about paralysis. The boy can't function. And at the end, before he can run away and start a new life, it starts to rain and he folds.

Now there's nothing wrong in writing about emotional and intellectual paralysis. It may indeed, thanks to Chekhov and Samuel Beckett, be the great modern theme.

The extraordinary last lines of *Waiting For Godot*— "Let's go." "Yes, let's go." Stage directions: They do not move.

But the aura around this book of Salinger's—which perhaps should be read by everyone *but* young men—is this: It mirrors like a fun house mirror and amplifies like a distorted speaker one of the great tragedies of our times—the death of the imagination.

Because what else is paralysis?

The imagination has been so debased that imagination—being imaginative—rather than being the lynchpin of our existence now stands as a synonym for something outside ourselves like science fiction or some new use for tangerine slices on raw pork chops—what an imaginative summer recipe—and *Star Wars!* So imaginative! And *Star Trek*—so imaginative! And *Lord of the Rings*—all those dwarves—so *imaginative*—The imagination has moved out of the realm of being our link, our most personal link, with our inner lives and the world outside that world—this world we share. What is schizophrenia but a horrifying state where what's in here doesn't match up with what's out there?

Why has imagination become a synonym for style?

I believe that the imagination is the passport we create to take us into the real world.

I believe the imagination is another phrase for what is most uniquely *us*.

Jung says the greatest sin is to be unconscious.

 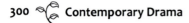

Our boy Holden says "What scares me most is the other guy's face—it wouldn't be so bad if you could both be blindfolded—most of the time the faces we face are not the other guys' but our own faces. And it's the worst kind of yellowness to be so scared of yourself you put blindfolds on rather than deal with yourself ..."

To face ourselves. That's the hard thing. The imagination.

That's God's gift to make the act of self-examination bearable.

(*Pause*)

OUISA: Well, indeed.

(*Pause*)

FLAN: I hope your muggers read every word.
OUISA: Darling.
GEOFFREY: I'm going to buy a copy of *Catcher in the Rye* at the airport and read it.
OUISA: Cover to cover.
PAUL: I'll test you. I should be going.
FLAN: Where will you stay?
OUISA: Not some flea bag.
PAUL: I get into the Sherry tomorrow morning. It's not so far off. I can walk around. I don't think they'll mug me twice in one evening.
OUISA: You'll stay here tonight.
PAUL: No! I have to be there at seven.
OUISA: We'll get you up.
PAUL: I have to be at the hotel at seven sharp or Dad will have a fit.
OUISA: Up at six-fifteen, which is any moment now, and we have that wedding in Roxbury—
FLAN: There's an alarm in that room.
PAUL: If it's any problem—
FLAN: It's only a problem if you leave.
PAUL: Six-fifteen? I'll tiptoe out.
FLAN: And we want to be in *Cats*.
OUISA: Flan!
PAUL: It's done.

GEOFFREY: I'll fly back. With my wife.

OUISA: Pushy. Both of you.

PAUL: He's not. Dad said I could be in charge of the extras. You'd just be extras. That's all I can promise.

FLAN: In cat suits?

PAUL: No. You can be humans.

FLAN: That's very important. It has to be in our contracts. Weare humans.

GEOFFREY: We haven't got any business done tonight.

FLAN: Forget it. It was only an evening at home.

OUISA: Whatever you do, don't think about elephants.

PAUL: Did I intrude?

FLAN and OUISA: No!

PAUL: I'm sorry—oh Christ—

GEOFFREY (*To* FLAN): There's all ways of doing business. Flanders, walk me to the elevator.

OUISA: Love to Diana.

(*To us*) We embraced. And Flan and Geoffrey left—

(FLAN *and* GEOFFREY *go.*
Pause. PAUL *and* OUISA *look at each other. Is it uncomfortable? Then:*)

PAUL: Let me clean up—

OUISA: No! Leave it for—

PAUL: Nobody comes in on Sunday.

OUISA: Yvonne will be in on Tuesday.

PAUL: You'll have every bug in Christendom—

(*They both reach for the dishes.*)

OUISA: Let me—

(PAUL *takes the dishes.*)

PAUL: No. You watch. It gives me a thrill to be looked at.

(*Pause,* PAUL *goes off.*)

OUISA (*To us, amazed*): He washed up.

(FLAN *returns, amazed.*)

FLAN: He's in.

OUISA: He's in?

FLAN: He's in for two million.

OUISA: Two million!

FLAN: He says the Cezanne is a great investment. We should get it for six million and sell it to the Tokyo bunch for ten.

OUISA: Happy days! Oh god!

(PAUL *returns.*)

PAUL: Two million dollars?

OUISA: Figure it out. He doesn't have the price of a dinner but he can cough up two million dollars and the Japs will go ten! Break all those dishes! Two million! Go to ten! And we put up nothing?

FLAN: He sold that Hockney print I know he bought for a hundred bucks fifteen years ago for thirty-four thousand dollars. Sotheby took their cut, sure, but still—Two million! Wildest dreams. Paul, I should give you a commission.

PAUL: Your kids said you were an art dealer. But you don't have a gallery. I don't understand—

FLAN: People want to sell privately. Not go through a gallery.

OUISA: A divorce. Taxes. Publicity.

FLAN: People come to me looking for a certain school of painting.

OUISA: A modern. Impressionist. Renaissance.

FLAN: But don't want museums to know where it is.

OUISA: Japanese.

FLAN: I've got Japanese looking for a Cezanne. I have a syndicate that will buy the painting. There is a great second-level Cezanne coming up for sale in a very messy divorce.

OUISA: Wife doesn't want hubby to know she owns a Cezanne.

FLAN: I needed an extra two million. Geoffrey called. Invited him here for dinner.

OUISA: Tonight was a very nervous very casual very big thing.

PAUL: I couldn't tell—

OUISA: All the better.

PAUL: I'm glad I helped—

OUISA: You were wonderful!

PAUL: I'm so pleased I was wonderful. All this *and* a pink shirt.

OUISA: Keep it. Look at the time.

PAUL: It's going to be time for me to get up.

FLAN: Then we'll say our good-nights now.

PAUL: Oh Christ. Regretfully. I'll tiptoe.

(FLAN *takes out his wallet.*)

FLAN: Take fifty dollars.

OUISA: Give him fifty dollars.

PAUL: Don't need it.

OUISA: Suppose your father's plane is late?

FLAN: A strike. Air controllers.

OUISA: Walking-around money. I wouldn't want my kids to be stuck in the street without a nickel.

FLAN: And you saved us a fortune. Do you know what our bill would've been at that little Eye-tie store front?

OUISA: And we picked up two million dollars. One billionth of a percent commission is—

FLAN: Fifty dollars.

(FLAN *hands him the money.* PAUL *hesitates, then takes it.*)

PAUL: But I'll get it back to you tomorrow. I want my father to meet you.

OUISA: We'd love to. Bring him up for dinner.

PAUL: Could I?

FLAN: You see how easy it is.

OUISA: Sure. If Paul does the cooking. (*They all laugh.*)

FLAN, OUISA and PAUL: Good night.

(FLAN *points* PAUL *to his room.*)

FLAN: Second door on the right.

(PAUL *goes.* FLAN *and* OUISA *get ready for bed, pulling on their robes.*)

FLAN: I want to get on my knees and thank God—money—

OUISA: Who said when artists dream they dream of money? I must be such an artist. Bravo. Bravo.

FLAN: I don't want to lose our life here. I don't want all the debt to pile up and crush us.

OUISA: It won't. We're safe.

FLAN: For a while. We almost lost it. If I didn't get this money, OUISA:, I would've lost the Cezanne. It would've gone. I had nowhere to get it.

OUISA: Why don't you tell me how much these things mean? You wait till the last minute—

FLAN: I don't want to worry you.

OUISA: Not worry me? I'm your partner.

(*They embrace.*)

FLAN: There is a God.

OUISA: And his name is—

FLAN: Geoffrey?

OUISA: Sidney

(FLAN *goes.* OUISA *curls up on the sofa.*)

OUISA (*To us*): I dreamt of Sidney Poitier and his rise to acclaim. I dreamt that Sidney Poitier sat at the edge of my bed and I asked him what troubled him. Sidney? What troubles you? Is it right to make a movie of *Cats?*

(PAUL *appears as* SIDNEY POITIER *in dinner clothes.*)

PAUL/SIDNEY: I'll tell you why I have to make a movie of *Cats.* I know what *Cats* is, LOUISA:. May I call you LOUISA:? I have no illusions about the merits of *Cats.* But the world has been too heavy with all the right-to-lifers. Protect the lives of the unborn. Constitutional amendments. Marches! When does life begin? Or the converse. The end of life. The right to die. Why is life at this point in the twentieth century so focused on the very beginning of life and the very end of life? What about the eighty years we have to live between those two inexorable bookends?

OUISA: And you can get all that into *Cats?*

PAUL/SIDNEY: I'm going to try.

OUISA: Thank you. Thank you. You shall.

(*Darkness. Then* FLAN *appears.*)

FLAN (*To us*): This is what I dreamt. I didn't dream so much as realize this. I felt so close to the paintings. I wasn't just selling them like pieces of meat. I remembered why I loved paintings in the first place—what had got me into this—and I thought—dreamed—remembered— how easy it is for a painter to *lose* a painting. He can paint and paint—work on a canvas for months and one day he loses it—just loses the structure—loses the sense of it—you lose the painting.

When the kids were little, we went to a parents' meeting at their school and I asked the teacher why all her students were geniuses in the second grade? Look at the first grade. Blotches of green and black. Look at the third grade. Camouflage. But the second grade—your grade. Matisses everyone. You've made my child a Matisse. Let me study with you. Let me into second grade! What is your secret? And this is what she said: "Secret? I don't have any secret. I just know when to take their drawings away from them."

I dreamt of color. I dreamt of our son's pink shirt. I dreamt of pinks and yellows and the new van Gogh that MOMA got and the "Irises" that sold for 53.9 million and, wishing a van Gogh was mine, I looked at my English hand-lasted shoes and thought of van Gogh's tragic shoes. I remembered me as I was. A painter losing a painting. But a South African awaiting revolution came to dinner. We were safe.

(*Darkness,* OUISA *appears.*)

OUISA (*To us*): And it was six AM and I woke up so happy looking at my clean kitchen, all the more memorable because the previous evening had left no traces, and the paper was at the front door and I sat in the kitchen happily doing the crossword puzzle in ink. Everybody does it in ink. I never met one person who didn't say they did it in ink. And I'm doing the puzzle and I see the time and it's nearly seven and PAUL: had to meet his father and I didn't want him to be late and was he healthy after his stabbing?

I went down the hall to the room where we had put him. The hall is eighteen feet long. I stopped in front of the door. Paul? (*She calls into the darkness.*)
PAUL'S VOICE (*Moaning*): Yes Yes
OUISA: Paul??
PAUL'S VOICE (*Moaning*): Yes Yes
OUISA: Are you all right?
OUISA (*To us*): I opened the door and turned on the light.

OUISA (*Screams*): Flan!!!

> (*The stage is blindingly bright.*
> PAUL, *startled, sits up in bed.*
> *A naked guy stands up on the bed.*)

HUSTLER: What the fuck is going on here? Who the fuck are you?!
OUISA: Flan!
FLAN: What is it?

> (FLAN *appears from the dark, tying his robe around him.* THE HUSTLER, *naked but for white socks, comes into the room.*)

HUSTLER: Hey! How ya doin'?
FLAN: Oh my God!
OUISA (*A scream*): Ahhh!

> (THE HUSTLER *stretches out on the sofa.*)

HUSTLER: I gotta get some sleep—

> (PAUL *runs into the room pulling on his clothes.*)

PAUL: I can explain.

> (PAUL *tosses* THE HUSTLER'S *clothes onto the sofa.*)

OUISA: You went out after we went to sleep and picked up this thing?
PAUL: I am so sorry.
FLAN: You brought this thing into our house! Thing! Thing! Get out! Get out of my house!

> (FLAN *tips the sofa, hurling* THE HUSTLER *onto the floor.* THE HUSTLER *leaps at* FLAN *threateningly.*)

OUISA: Stop it! He might have a gun!
HUSTLER: I might have a gun. I might have a knife.
OUISA: He has a gun! He has a knife!

(THE HUSTLER *chases* OUISA *around the room.*)

PAUL: I can explain!

FLAN: Give me my fifty dollars.

PAUL: I spent it.

OUISA: Get out!

FLAN: Take your clothes. Go back to sleep in the gutter.

(*He flings* THE HUSTLER'S *clothes into the hall.* THE HUSTLER *viciously grabs* FLAN *by the lapels of his robe.*)

HUSTLER: Fuck you!

(THE HUSTLER *throws* FLAN *back, picks up his clothes and leaves,* FLAN *catches his breath.* OUISA *is terrified.*)

PAUL: Please. Don't tell my father. I don't want him to know. I haven't told him. He doesn't know I got so lonely. I got so afraid. My dad coming. I had the money. I went out after we went to sleep and I brought him back. I couldn't be alone. You had so much. I couldn't be alone. I was so afraid.

OUISA: Just go.

PAUL: I'm so sorry.

(PAUL *goes.*
FLAN *and* OUISA, *at a loss, straighten out the pillows on the sofa. They are exhausted.*)

OUISA (*To us*): And that's that.

FLAN: I am shaking.

OUISA: You have to do *something!*

FLAN: It's awful.

OUISA: Is anything gone?

FLAN: How can I look? I'm shaking.

OUISA: Did he take anything?

FLAN: Would you concentrate on yourself?

OUISA: I want to know if anything's gone?

FLAN: Calm down.

OUISA: We could have been killed.

FLAN: The silver Victorian inkwell.

OUISA: How can you think of *things?* We could have been murdered.

(*An actor appears for a moment holding up an ornate Victorian inkwell capped by a silver beaver.*)

FLAN: There's the inkwell. Silver beaver. Why?

OUISA: Slashed—our throats slashed.

(*Another actor appears for a moment holding up a framed portrait of a dog, say, a pug.*)

FLAN: And there's the watercolor. Our dog.

OUISA: Go to bed at night happy and then murdered. Would we have woken up?

FLAN: We're alive.

OUISA: We called our kids.

FLAN: No answer.

(*The phone rings. They clutch each other.*)

OUISA: It's him!

(FLAN *goes to the phone.*)

OUISA: Don't pick it up!

(FLAN *does.*
GEOFFREY *appears.*)

GEOFFREY: Flanders, I'm at the airport. Look, I've been thinking. Those Japs really want the Cezanne. They'll pay. You can depend on me for an additional overcall of two-fifty.

FLAN: Two hundred and fifty thousand?

GEOFFREY: And I was thinking for South Africa. What about a Black American Film Festival? With this Spike Lee you have now and of course get Poitier down to be the president of the jury and I know Cosby and I love this Eddie Murphy and my wife went fishing in Norway with Diana Ross and her new Norwegian husband. And also they must have some *new* blacks—

FLAN: Yes. It sounds a wonderful idea.
GEOFFREY: I'll call him at the Sherry—
FLAN: No! We'll call!
GEOFFREY: They're calling my plane—And again last night—
FLAN: No need to thank. See you shortly.
GEOFFREY: The banks.
FLAN: My lawyer.
GEOFFREY: Exactly.
FLAN: Safe trip.

> (GEOFFREY *goes.*
> *Another couple in their forties,* KITTY *and* LARKIN, *appear.* OUISA *and* FLAN *take off their robes and are dressed for day.*)

OUISA: Do we have a story to tell you!
KITTY: Do we have a story to tell you!
OUISA (*To us*): Our two and their son are at Harvard together.

> (KITTY *and* LARKIN *are pleased about this.*)

FLAN: Let me tell you our story.
LARKIN: When did your story happen?
FLAN: Last night. We are still zonked.
KITTY: We win. Our story happened Friday night. So we go first.
LARKIN: We're going to be in the movies.
KITTY: We are going to be in the movie of *Cats*.

> (OUISA *and* FLAN *look at each other.*)

OUISA: You tell your story first.
LARKIN: Friday night we were home, the doorbell rang—
KITTY: I am not impressed but it was the son of—
OUISA and FLAN (*To us*): You got it.
KITTY: The kid was mugged. We had to go out. We left him. He was so charming. His father was taking the red eye. He couldn't get into the hotel till seven AM. He stayed with us.

> (*She is very pleased.*)

LARKIN: In the middle of the night, we heard somebody screaming Burglar! Burglar! We came out in the hall. Paul is chasing this naked blonde thief down the corridor. The blond thief runs out, the alarm goes off. The kid saved our lives.

FLAN: That was no burglar.

OUISA: You had another house guest.

(KITTY *and* LARKIN *laugh.*)

LARKIN: We feel so guilty. Paul could've been killed by that intruder. He was very understanding—

OUISA: Was anything missing from your house?

LARKIN: Nothing.

FLAN: Did you give him money?

KITTY: Twenty-five dollars until his father arrived.

FLAN (*To us*): We told them our story.

KITTY and LARKIN: Oh.

OUISA: Have you talked to your kids?

KITTY: Can't get through.

(OUISA *makes a phone call.*)

OUISA: Sherry Netherlands. I'd like—

LARKIN (*To us*): She gave the name.

KITTY: Sidney Poitier must be registered.

(*The doorbell rings.* FLAN *goes.*)

OUISA: No! I'm not a fan. This is not a fan call. We know he's there. His son is a friend of—

(*Click. The Sherry's hung up.*)

LARKIN: He must be there under another name.

(*Another phone call.*)

OUISA: Hi. Celebrity Service? I'm not sure how you work.

KITTY: Greta Garbo used the name Harriet Brown.

OUISA: You track down celebrities? Am I right?

LARKIN: Everybody must have known she was Greta Garbo.

OUISA: I'm trying to find out how one would get in touch with
—No, I'm not a press agent—No, I'm not with anyone—My husband. Flanders Kittredge. (*Click.*) Celebrity Service doesn't give out information over the phone.

LARKIN: Try the public library.

KITTY: Try *Who's Who.*

(FLAN *returns carrying an elaborate arrangement of flowers.* FLAN *reads the card.*)

FLAN: "To thank you for a wonderful time. Paul Poitier."

(FLAN *reaches into the bouquet. He takes out a pot of jam.*)

FLAN: A pot of jam?

LARKIN: A pot of jam.

(*They back off as if it might explode.*)

KITTY; I think we should call the police.

(*A* DETECTIVE *appears.*)

DETECTIVE: What are the charges?

OUISA: He came into our house.

FLAN: He cooked us dinner.

OUISA: He told us the story of *Catcher in the Rye.*

FLAN: He said he was the son of Sidney Poitier.

DETECTIVE: Was he?

OUISA: We don't know.

FLAN: We gave him fifty dollars.

KITTY: We gave him twenty-five.

LARKIN: Shhhh!

OUISA: He picked up a hustler.

FLAN: He left.

KITTY: He chased the burglar out of our house.

OUISA: He didn't steal anything.

LARKIN: We looked and looked.

KITTY: Top to bottom. Nothing gone.

(THE DETECTIVE *closes his notebook.*)

OUISA: Granted this does not seem major now.

DETECTIVE: Look. We're very busy.

FLAN: You can't chuck us out.

DETECTIVE: Come up with charges. Then I'll do something.

(THE DETECTIVE *goes.*)

OUISA (*To us*): Our kids came down from Harvard.

(*Their children,* WOODY *and* TESS, *and* KITTY *and* LARKIN'S *boy,* BEN, *enter, groaning.*)

FLAN: —the details he knew—how would he know about the painting? Although I think it's a very fine Kandinsky.

OUISA: And none of you know this fellow? He has this wild quality—yet a real elegance and a real concern and a real consideration—

TESS: Well, Mom, you should have let him stay. You should have divorced all your children and just let this dreamboat stay. Plus he sent you flowers.

FLAN: And jam.

THE KIDS: Oooooo.

OUISA: I wish I knew how to get hold of his father. Just to see if there is any truth in it.

LARKIN: Who knows Sidney Poitier so we could just call him up and ask him?

KITTY (*Eager*): I have a friend who does theatrical law, I bet he—

LARKIN: What friend?

KITTY: Oh, it's nobody.

LARKIN: I want to know.

KITTY (*Screams*): Nobody!

LARKIN: Whatever's going on anywhere, I do not want to know. I don't want to know. I don't want to know …

KITTY (*Overlapping*): Nobody. Nobody. Nobody …

BEN: Dad. Mom. Please. For once. Please?

(BEN, KITTY, LARKIN *go in anguish.*)

FLAN: Tess, when you see your little sister, don't tell her that he and the, uh, hustler, used her bed.

TESS: You put him in that bed. I'm not going to get involved with any conspiracy.

FLAN: It's not a conspiracy. It's a *family.*

> (TESS *and* FLAN *growl at each other.*
> *Darkness.*
> OUISA, *alone, stretches out on the sofa.*
> PAUL *appears wearing the pink shirt.*)

PAUL: The imagination. That's our out. Our imagination teaches us our limits and then how to grow beyond those limits. The imagination says Listen to me. I am your darkest voice. I am your 4 AM voice. I am the voice that wakes you up and says this is what I'm afraid of. Do not listen to me at your peril. The imagination is the noon voice that sees clearly and says yes, this is what I want for my life. It's there to sort out your nightmare, to show you the exit from the maze of your nightmare, to transform the nightmare into dreams that become your bedrock. If we don't listen to that voice, it dies. It shrivels. It vanishes.

> (PAUL *takes out a switchblade and opens it.*)

The imagination is not our escape. On the contrary, the imagination is the place we are all trying to get to.

> (PAUL *lifts his shirt and stabs himself.*
> OUISA *sits up and screams.*
> PAUL *is gone.*
> *The phone rings. It's* THE DETECTIVE.)

DETECTIVE: I got a call that might interest you.

> (DR. FINE *appears, a very earnest professional man in his 50s.*)

DR. FINE (*To us*): I was seeing a patient. I'm an obstetrician at New York Hospital. The nurse opened my office door and said there's a friend of your son's here …

> (PAUL *appears.*)

DR. FINE (*To us*): I treated the kid. He was more scared than hurt.
A knife wound, a few bruises.

PAUL: I don't know how to thank you, sir. My father is coming here.

(*The four parents appear.*)

FLAN and OUISA and KITTY and LARKIN: He's making a film of *Cats.*

DR. FINE: And he told me the name of a matinee idol of my youth. Somebody who had really forged ahead and made new paths for blacks just by the strength of his own talent. Strangely, I had identified with him before I started medical school. I mean, I'm a Jew. My grandparents were killed in the war. I had this sense of self-hatred, of fear. And this kid's father—the bravery of his films—had given me a direction, a confidence. Simple as that. We're always paying off debts.

Then my beeper went off. A patient in her tenth month of labor. Her water finally broke. I gave him the keys.

(PAUL *catches the keys.*)

PAUL: Doug told me all about your brownstone. How you got it at a great price because there had been a murder in it and for a while people thought it had a curse but you were a scientific man and were courageous!

DR. FINE: Well, yes! Courageous!
I ran off to the delivery room. Twins! Two boys.
I thought of my son. I dialed my boy at Dartmouth.
Amazingly he was in his room. Doing *what* I hate to ask.

(DOUG, *20, appears.*)

DR. FINE: So you accuse me of having, no interest in your life, not doing for friends, being a rotten father. Well, you should be very happy.

DOUG: The son of who? Dad, I never heard of him. Dad, as usual, you are a real cretin. You gave him the keys? You gave a complete stranger who happens to mention my name the keys to our house? Dad, sometimes it is so obvious to me why Mom left. I am so embarrassed to know you. You gave the keys to a stranger who shows up at your office? Mother told me you beat her! Mom told me you were a rotten lover and drank so much your body smelled of cheap white wine. Mom said sleeping with you was like sleeping with a salad made of bad dressing. Why you had to bring me into the world!

DR. FINE: There are two sides to every story—

DOUG: You're an idiot! You're an idiot!

(DOUG *goes into the dark, screaming.*)

DR. FINE: I went home—courageously—with a policeman.

(A POLICEMAN *accompanies* DR. FINE. PAUL *appears wearing a silk robe, carrying a snifter of brandy.*)

DR. FINE: Arrest him!

PAUL: Pardon?

DR. FINE: Breaking and entering.

PAUL: Breaking and entering?

DR. FINE: You're an impostor.

PAUL: Officer, your honor, your eminence, DR. FINE *gave* me the keys to his brownstone. Isn't that so?

DR. FINE: My son doesn't know you.

PAUL: This man gave me the keys to the house. Isn't that so?

POLICEMAN (*Screams*): Did you give him the key to the house?

DR. FINE: Yes! But under false pretenses. This fucking black kid crack addict came into my office lying—

PAUL: I have taken this much brandy but can pour the rest back into the bottle. And I've used electricity listening to the music, but I think you'll find that nothing's taken from the house.

(PAUL *goes.*)

DR. FINE: I want you to arrest this fraud.

(*The* POLICEMAN *walks away.*
DOUG *returns.*)

DOUG: A cretin. A creep! No wonder mother left you!

(DOUG *goes.*

Pause.)

DR. FINE: Two sides. Every story.

(OUISA *holds up a book.*)

OUISA: I went down to the Strand. I got Sidney Poitier's autobiography (*Reads:*) "Back in
New York with Juanita and the children, I began to become aware that our marriage,
while working on some levels, was falling apart in other fundamental areas."

FLAN: There's a picture of him and his four—daughters. No sons. Four daughters. The
book's called *This Life.*

DR. FINE: Published by Knopf.

KITTY: 1980.

LARKIN: Out of print.

KITTY: Oh dear.

OUISA: This kid bulldozing his way into our lives.

LARKIN: We let him in our lives. I run a foundation. You're a dealer. You're a doctor.
You'd think we'd be satisfied with our achievements.

FLAN: Agatha Christie would ask, what do we all have in common?

OUISA: It seems the common thread linking us all is an overwhelming need to be in the
movie of *Cats.*

KITTY: Our kids. Struggling through their lives.

LARKIN: I don't want to know anything about the spillover of their lives.

OUISA: All we have in common is our children went to boarding school together.

FLAN (*To* DR. FINE): How come we never met?

DR. FINE: His mother had custody. I lived out West. After he graduated from high
school, she moved West. I moved East.

LARKIN: I think we should drop it right here.

KITTY: Are you afraid Ben is mixed up in this fraud?

LARKIN: I don't want to know too much about my kid.

KITTY: You think Ben is hiding things from us? I tell you, I'm getting to the bottom of
this. My son has no involvements with any black frauds. Doctor, you said something
about crack?

LARKIN: I don't want to know.

DR. FINE: It just leaped out of my mouth. No proof. Oh dear god, no proof.

FLAN: We'll take a vote. Do we pursue this to the end no matter what we find out about
our kids?

OUISA: I vote yes.

DR. FINE: I trust Doug. Yes.

LARKIN: No.

KITTY: Yes.

FLAN: Yes.

(KITTY *looks through the Poitier autobiography.*)

KITTY: Listen to the last page, "… making it better for our children. Protecting them. From what? The truth is what we were protecting those little people from … there is a lot to worry about and I'd better start telling the little bastards—start worrying!" The end.

(KITTY *closes the book in dismay. All the children,* TESS, WOODY, BEN, DOUG, *enter, groaning.*)

FLAN: It's obvious. It's somebody you went to high school with, since you each go to different colleges.

OUISA: He knows the details about our lives.

FLAN: Who in your high school, part of your gang, has become homosexual or is deep into drugs?

TESS: That's like, about fifteen people.

LARKIN: I don't want to know.

TESS: I find it really insulting that you would assume that it has to be a guy. This movie star's son could have had a relationship with a girl in high school—

BEN: That's your problem in a nutshell. You're so limited.

TESS: That's why I'm going to Afghanistan. To climb mountains.

OUISA: You are not climbing mountains.

FLAN: We have not invested all this money in you to scale the face of K-2.

TESS: Is that all I am? An investment?

OUISA: All right. Track down everybody in your high school class. Male. Female. Whatever. Not just homosexuals. Drug addicts. The kid might be a drug dealer.

DOUG: Why do you look at me when you say that? Do you think I'm an addict? A drug pusher? I really resent the accusations.

DR. FINE: No one is accusing you of anything.

LARKIN: I don't want to know. I don't want to know. I don't want to know.

FLAN: Nobody is accusing anyone of anything. I'm asking you to go on a detective search and find out from your high school class if anyone has met a black kid pretending to be a movie star's son.

BEN: He promised you parts in *Cats?*

OUISA: It wasn't just that. It was fun.

TESS: You went to *Cats.* You said it was an all-time low in a lifetime of theater-going.

OUISA: Film is a different medium.

TESS: You said Aeschylus did not invent theater to have it end up a bunch of chorus kids wondering which of them will go to Kitty Kat Heaven.

OUISA: I don't remember saying that.

FLAN: No, I think that was *Starlight Express*—

TESS: Well, maybe he'll make a movie of *Starlight Express* and you can all be on roller skates—

DOUG: This is so humiliating.

BEN: This is so pathetic.

TESS: This is so racist.

OUISA: This is *not* racist!

DOUG: How can I get in touch with anybody in high school? I've outgrown them.

KITTY: How can you outgrow them? You graduated a year ago!

OUISA: Here is a copy of your yearbook. I want you to get the phone numbers of everybody in your class. You all went to the same boarding school. You can phone from here.

DR. FINE: You can charge it to my phone.

OUISA: Call everyone in your class and ask them if they know—

DOUG: Never!

TESS: This is the KGB.

DR. FINE: You're on the phone all the time. Now I ask you to make calls all over the country and you become reticent.

TESS: This is the entire McCarthy period.

WOODY: I just want to get one thing straight.

FLAN: Finally, we hear from the peanut gallery.

WOODY: You gave him my pink shirt? You gave a complete stranger my pink shirt? That pink shirt was a Christmas present from *you.* I treasured that shirt. I loved that shirt. My collar size has grown a full size from weight lifting. And you saw my arms had grown, you saw my neck had grown. And you bought me that shirt for my new body. I loved that shirt. The first shirt for my new body And you gave that shirt away. I can't believe it. I hate it here. I hate this house. I hate you.

DOUG: You never do anything for me.

TESS: You've never done anything but tried to block me.

BEN: I'm only this pathetic extension of your eighth-rate personality.

DOUG: Social Darwinism pushed beyond all limits.

WOODY: You gave away my pink shirt?

TESS: You want me to be everything you weren't.

DOUG: You said drugs and looked at me.

(*The parents leave, speechless, defeated. The kids look through their high school yearbook.* TESS *spots a face.*)

TESS: Trent Conway.

ALL THE KIDS: Trent Conway.

(TRENT CONWAY *appears.*)

TESS: Trent Conway. Look at those beady eyes staring out at me. Trent Conway. He's at MIT.

(*To us*)

So I went to MIT. He was there in his computer room and I just pressed him and pressed him and pressed him. I had a tape recorder strapped to me.

(*Darkness*)

TRENT'S VOICE TAPED: Yes, I knew Paul.

TESS'S VOICE TAPED: But what happened between you?

TRENT'S VOICE TAPED: It was …. It was …

(*The lights come up slowly.* PAUL *and* TRENT *appear. Rain. Distant thunder. Jazz playing somewhere off.* PAUL *is dressed in jeans and a tank top, high-top sneakers.*)

TRENT: This is the way you must speak. Hear my accent. Hear my voice. Never say you're going horseback riding. You say you're going riding. And don't say couch. Say sofa. And you say *bodd-ill.* It's bottle. Say bottle of beer.

PAUL: Bodd-ill a bee-ya.

TRENT: Bottle of beer.

(PAUL *sits on the sofa. He pulls out a thick address book from under him.*)

PAUL: What's this?

TRENT: My address book.

PAUL: All these names. Addresses. Tell me about these people

(TRENT *sits beside him.*)

TRENT: I want you to come to bed with me.

PAUL (*Fierce*): Tell me about these people, man!

TRENT: I just want to look at you. Sorry.

(PAUL *is hypnotized by the address book.*)

PAUL: Are these all rich people?

TRENT: No. Hand to mouth on a higher plateau.

PAUL: I think it must be very hard to be with rich people. You have to have money. You have to give them presents.

TRENT: Not at all. Rich people do something nice for you, you give them a pot of jam.

PAUL: That's what pots of jam are for?

TRENT: Orange. Grapefruit. Strawberry. But fancy. They have entire stores filled with fancy pots of jam wrapped in cloth. English. Or French.

PAUL: I'll tell you what I'll do. I pick a name. You tell me about them. Where they live. Secrets. And for each name you get a piece of clothing.

TRENT: All right.

PAUL: Kittredge. Talbot and Woodrow.

TRENT: Talbot, called Tess, was anorexic and was in a hospital for a while.

(PAUL *takes off a shoe and kicks it to* TRENT.)

PAUL: Their parents.

TRENT: Ouisa and Flan, for Flanders, Kittredge. Rhode Island, I believe. Newport, but not along the ocean. The street behind the ocean. He's an art dealer. They have a Kandinsky.

PAUL: A Kan—what—ski?

TRENT: Kandinsky. A double-sided Kandinsky.

(PAUL *kicks off his other shoe.* TRENT *catches it joyously.*)

TRENT: I feel like Scheherazade!

(He embraces PAUL *with fierce tenderness.)*

I don't want you to leave me, Paul. I'll go through my address book and tell you about family after family. You'll never not fit in again. We'll give you a new identity. I'll make you the most eagerly sought-after young man in the East. And then I'll come into one of these homes one day—and you'll be there and I'll be presented to you. And I'll pretend to meet you for the first time and our friendship will be witnessed by my friends, our parents' friends. If it all happens under their noses, they can't judge me. They can't disparage you. I'll make you a guest in their houses. Ask me another name. I'd like to try for the shirt.

*(*PAUL *kisses* TRENT.*)*

PAUL: That's enough for today.

*(*PAUL *takes his shoes and the address book and goes.*
TRENT *turns to* TESS.*)*

TRENT: Paul stayed with me for three months. We went through the address book letter by letter. Paul vanished by the L's. He took the address book with him. Well, he's already been in all your houses. Maybe I will meet him again. I sure would like to.

TESS: His past? His real name?

TRENT: I don't know anything about him. It was a rainy night in Boston. He was in a doorway. That's all.

TESS: He took stuff from you?

TRENT: Besides the address book? He took my stereo and sport jacket and my word processor and my laser printer. And my skis. And my TV.

TESS: Will you press charges?

TRENT: No.

TESS: It's a felony.

TRENT: Why do they want to find him?

TESS: They say to help him. If there's a crime, the cops will get involved.

TRENT: Look, we must keep in touch. We were friends for a brief bit in school. I mean we were really good friends.

TESS: Won't you press charges?

TRENT: Please.

(They go.

OUISA *appears*.)

OUISA (*To us*): Tess played me the tapes.
TESS'S VOICE TAPED: Won't you press charges?
TRENT'S VOICE TAPED: Please.
OUISA (*To us*): Can you believe it? Paul learned all that in three months. Three months! Who would have thought it? Trent Conway, the Henry Higgins of our time. Paul looked at those names and said I am Columbus. I am Magellan. I will sail into this new world.

I read somewhere that everybody on this planet is separated by only six other people. Between us and everybody else on this planet. The president of the United States. A gondolier in Venice. Fill in the names. I find that A] tremendously comforting that we're so close and B] like Chinese water torture that we're so close. Because you have to find the right six people to make the connection. It's not just big names. It's *anyone*. A native in a rain forest. A Tierra del Fuegan. An Eskimo. I am bound to everyone on this planet by a trail of six people. It's a profound thought. How Paul found us. How to find the man whose son he pretends to be. Or perhaps *is* his son, although I doubt it. How every person is a new door, opening up into other worlds. between me and everyone else on this planet. But to find the right six people.

(FLAN *appears*.)

FLAN (*To us*): We didn't hear for a while. We went about our lives.

(*The* DOORMAN *appears*.)

OUISA (*To us*): And then one day our doorman, whom we tip very well at Christmas and any time he does something nice for us—our doorman spit at my husband, J. Flanders Kittredge. I mean, spit at him.

(*The* DOORMAN *spits at* FLAN.)

DOORMAN: Your son! I know all about your son.
FLAN: What about my son?
DOORMAN: Not the little shit who lives here. The other son. The secret son. The Negro son you deny.

(*The* DOORMAN *spits at* FLAN *again.*)

FLAN: The Negro son?

DOORMAN: The black son you make live in Central Park.

OUISA (*To us*): The next chapter. Rick and Elizabeth and Paul sit on the grass in Central Park.

> (RICK, ELIZABETH *and* PAUL *run on laughing in Central Park.* RICK, *a nice young guy in his mid-twenties, plays the guitar energetically. He and* PAUL *and* ELIZABETH, *a beautiful girl in her mid-twenties, are having a great time singing a cheery song, say James Taylor's "Shower The People," until* RICK *hits the wrong chord. They try to break down the harmony.* RICK *can't for the life of him find the right chord.* THE THREE OF THEM *laugh.* PAUL *is wearing the pink shirt.*)

PAUL: Tell me about yourselves.

RICK: We're here from Utah.

PAUL: Do they have any black people in Utah?

RICK: Maybe two. Yes, the Mormons brought in two.

ELIZABETH: We came to be actors.

RICK: She won the all-state competition for comedy and drama.

PAUL: My gosh!

ELIZABETH: "The quality of mercy is not strained.
  It droppeth like the gentle rain from heaven."

RICK: And we study and we wait tables.

ELIZABETH: Because you have to have technique.

PAUL: Like the painters. Cezanne looked for the rules behind the spontaneity of Impressionism.

RICK: Cez—That's a painter?

ELIZABETH: We don't know anything about painting.

PAUL: My dad loves painting. He has a Kandinsky but he loves Cezanne the most. He lives up there.

RICK: What?

PAUL: He lives up there. Count six windows over. John Flanders Kittredge. His chums call him Flan. I was the child of Flan's hippie days. His radical days. He went down South as a freedom marcher, to register black voters—his friends were killed. Met my mother. Registered her and married her in a fit of sentimental righteousness and knocked her up with me and came back here and abandoned her. Went to Harvard. He's now a fancy art dealer. Lives up there. Count six windows over. Won't see me.

The new wife—the white wife—The Louisa Kittredge Call Me Ouisa Wife—the mother of the new children wife—

RICK: Your brothers and sisters?

PAUL (*Bitter*): They go to Andover and Exeter and Harvard and Yale. The awful thing is my father started out good. My mother says there is a good man inside J. Flanders Kittredge.

ELIZABETH: He'll see you if he was that good. He can't forget you entirely.

PAUL: I call him. He hangs up.

RICK: Go to his office—

PAUL: He doesn't have an office. He works out of there. They won't even let me in the elevator.

RICK: Dress up as a messenger.

ELIZABETH: Say you have a masterpiece for him.
"I got the Mona Lisa waitin' out in the truck."

PAUL: I don't want to embarrass him. Look, this is so fucking tacky. (*Pause*) You love each other?

ELIZABETH: A lot.

(RICK *and* ELIZABETH *touch each other's hands.*)

PAUL: I hope we can meet again.

(PAUL *turns to go.*)

RICK: Where do you live?

PAUL: Live? I'm home.

ELIZABETH: You're not out on the streets?

PAUL: You're such assholes. Where would I live?

RICK: Stay with us.

ELIZABETH: We just have a railroad flat in a tenement—

RICK: It's over a roller disco. The last of the roller discos but it's quiet by five AM and a great narrow space—

ELIZABETH: A railroad loft and we could give you a corner. The tub's in the kitchen but there's light in the morning—

RICK (*To us*): And he did!

(*The light changes to the loft.*)

PAUL: This is the way you must speak. Hear my accent. Hear my voice. Never say you're going horseback riding. You say you're going riding. And don't say couch. Say sofa. And you say bodd-ill. It's bottle. Say bottle of beer.

RICK: Bodd-ill a bee-ya.

PAUL: Bottle of beer. And never be afraid of rich people You know what they love? A fancy pot of jam. That's all. Get yourself a patron. That's what you need. You shouldn't be waiting tables. You're going to wake up one day and the temporary job you picked up to stay alive is going to be your full-time life.

(ELIZABETH *embraces* PAUL *gratefully.*)

PAUL: You've given me courage. I'm going to try and see him right now.

(PAUL *goes.*
RICK *and* ELIZABETH *lay on their backs and dream.*)

RICK: I'll tell you all the parts I want to do. Vanya in *Uncle Vanya.*

ELIZABETH: Masha in *Three Sisters.* No, Irina first. The young one who yearns for love. Then Masha who loves. Then the oldest one, Olga, who never knows love.

RICK: I'd like a shot at Laertes. I think it's a much better part.

(ELIZABETH *gazes in a mirror.*)

ELIZABETH: Do you think it'll hurt me?

RICK: What'll hurt you?

ELIZABETH: My resemblance to Liv Ullmann.

(PAUL *runs in.*)

PAUL: HE WROTE ME! I WROTE HIM AND HE WROTE ME BACK!!! He's going to give me a thousand dollars! And that's just for starters! He sold a Cezanne to the Japanese and made millions and he can give me money without her knowing it.

ELIZABETH: I knew it!

PAUL: I'm moving out of here!

ELIZABETH: You can't!

RICK: No!

PAUL: But I am going to give you the money to put on a showcase of any play you want and you'll be in it and agents will come see you and you'll be seen and you'll be started. And when you win your Oscars—both of you—you'll look in the camera and thank me—

ELIZABETH: I want to thank Paul Kittredge.

RICK: Thanks, Paul!

PAUL: One hitch, I'm going to meet him in Maine. He's up there visiting his parents in Dark Harbor. My grandparents whom I've never met. He's finally going to tell my grandparents about me. He's going to make up for lost time. He's going to give me money. I can go back home. Get my momma that beauty parlor she's wanted all her life. One problem. How am I going to get to Maine? The wife checks all the bills. He has to account for the money She handles the purse strings. Where the hell am I going to get two hundred and fifty dollars to get to Maine?

ELIZABETH: How long would you need it for?

PAUL: I'll be gone a week. But I could wire it back to you.

RICK (*Quiet*): We could lend it to him for a week.

ELIZABETH (*Quiet*): We can't. If something happens—

RICK (*Quiet*): You're like his stepmother. These women holding on to all the purse strings.

ELIZABETH: No. We worked too hard to save that. I'm sorry.

I'll meet you both after work. If your father loves you, he'll get you the ticket up there.

(*She goes.*)

RICK (*To us*): We stopped by the bank. I withdrew the money He took it.

PAUL: Let's celebrate!

(ELIZABETH *appears.*)

ELIZABETH (*To us*): I went to a money machine to get twenty dollars and I couldn't get anything. The machine devoured my card. I called up the emergency number and the voice said my account was closed. They had withdrawn all the money and closed the account. I went to that apartment on Fifth Avenue. I told the doorman: I want my money. I work tables. I work hard. I saved. I'm here trying to get to meet people. I am stranded. Who do I know to go to? "The quality of mercy is not strained?" Fuck you, quality of mercy.

(*She goes.*
RICK *appears.*)

RICK (*To us*): He told me he had some of his own money and he wanted to treat me. We went to a store that rented tuxedos and we dressed to the nines. We went to the Rainbow Room. We danced. High over New York City. I swear. He stood up and held out my chair and we danced and there was a stir. Nothing like this ever happened in Utah. And we danced. And I'll tell you nothing like that must have ever happened at the Rainbow Room because we were asked to leave. I tell you. It was so funny.

And we walked out and walked home and I knew Elizabeth was waiting for me and I would have to explain about the money and calm her down because we'll get it back but I forgot because we took a carriage ride in the park and he asked me if he could fuck me and I had never done anything like that and he did and it was fantastic. It was the greatest night I ever had and before we got home he kissed me on the mouth and he vanished.

Later I realized he had no money of his own. He had spent my money—our money—on that night at the Rainbow Room.

How am I going to face Elizabeth? What have I done? What did I let him do to me? I wanted experience. I came here to have experience. But I didn't come here to do this or lose that or be this or do this to Elizabeth. I didn't come here to be *this*. My father said I was a fool and I can't have him be right. What have I done?

> (*He goes into the dark.*
> LARKIN *and* KITTY *appear.*)

LARKIN: Kitty and I were at a roller disco two clients opened.
KITTY: And it was Valentine's Day
LARKIN: and we came out and we saw a body on the street.
KITTY: My legs were still shaky from the roller skating which I have not done in I hate to tell you how many years and we knew the body had just landed there in that clump
LARKIN: because the blood seeping out had not reached the gutter yet.
KITTY: You could see the blood just oozing out slowly towards the curb.
LARKIN: The boy had jumped from above.
KITTY: The next day we walked through the park by Gracie Mansion
LARKIN: and it was cold and we saw police putting a jacket on a man sitting on a bench.

KITTY: Only we got closer and it wasn't a sweater.

LARKIN: It was a body bag. A homeless person had frozen during the night.

KITTY: Was it that cold?

LARKIN: Sometimes there are periods where you see death everywhere.

(*Darkness,* OUISA *and* FLAN *appear in their robes with* THE DETECTIVE *and* ELIZABETH.)

DETECTIVE: This young girl came forward with the story. She told me the black kid was your son, lived here. It all seemed to come into place. What I'm saying is she'll press charges.

ELIZABETH: I want him dead. He took all our money. He took my life. Rick's dead! You bet your life I'll press charges.

OUISA: We haven't seen him since that night.

DETECTIVE: Find him. We have a case.

FLAN: I'll release it to the papers. I have friends. I can call the *Times.*

OUISA (*To us*): Which is what happened.

FLAN (*To us*): The paper of note—the *Times*—ran a story on so-called smart, sophisticated, tough New Yorkers being boondoggled by a confidence man now wanted by the police. Who says New Yorkers don't have a heart? They promised it would either run in the Living section or the Home section.

KITTY (*To us*): The story ran.

DR. FINE (*To us*): In the B section front page.

DETECTIVE (*To us*): Smart New Yorkers.

LARKIN (*To us*): We never heard from Sidney Poitier.

OUISA (*To us*): Six degrees. Six degrees.

(*They all go except for* OUISA *and* FLAN, *who pull off their robes, they are dressing for the evening.*)

OUISA (*To us*): We are bidding tonight on an Henri Matisse.

FLAN (*To us*): We will go as high as—

OUISA: Don't tell all the family secrets—

FLAN (*To us*): Well over twenty-five million.

OUISA (*To us*): Out of which he will keep—

FLAN (*To us*): I'll have to give most of it away, but the good part is it gives me a credibility in this new market. I mean, a David fucking Hockney print sold for a hundred bucks fifteen years ago went for thirty-four thousand dollars! A print! A flower. You know Geoffrey. Our South African—

OUISA (*To us*): —it's a black-tie auction—Sotheby's—

FLAN: I know we'll get it.

OUISA (*Noting the time*): Flan—

FLAN: I know the Matisse will be mine—for a few hours. Then off to Tokyo. Or Saudi.

(FLAN *leaves as* OUISA *phones* TESS.)

OUISA (*To* TESS): I'm totally dolled up. The black. Have you seen it? I have to tell you the sign I saw today. Cruelty-free cosmetics. A store was selling cruelty-free cosmetics.

TESS: Mother, that is such a beautiful thing. Do you realize the agony cosmetic companies put rabbits through to test eye shadow?

OUISA: Dearest, I know that. I'm only talking about the phrase. Cruelty-free cosmetics should take away all evidence of time and cellulite and—

TESS: Mother, I'm getting married.

OUISA: I thought you were going to Afghanistan.

TESS: I am going to get married and then go to Afghanistan.

OUISA: One country at a time. You are not getting married.

TESS: Immediately so deeply negative—

OUISA: I know everyone you know and you are not marrying any of them.

TESS: The arrogance that you would assume you know everyone I know. The way you say it: I know everyone you know—

OUISA: Unless you met them in the last two days—you can't hold a secret.

(*The other line rings.*)

Wait—I'm putting you on hold—

TESS: No one ever calls on that number.

OUISA: Wait. Hold on.

TESS: Mother!

OUISA: Hello?

(PAUL *appears, frightened.*)

PAUL: Hello.

OUISA: Paul?

PAUL: I saw the story in the paper. I didn't know the boy killed himself. He gave me the money.

OUISA: Let me put you on hold. I'm talking to my child—

PAUL: If you put me on hold, I'll be gone and you'll never hear from me again.

(OUISA *pauses.* TESS *fades into black.*)

OUISA: You have to turn yourself in. The boy committed suicide. You stole the money. The girl is pressing charges. They're going to get you. Why not turn yourself in and you can get off easier. You can strike a bargain. Learn when you're trapped. You're so brilliant. You have such promise. You need help.

PAUL: Would you help me?

OUISA: What would you want me to do?

PAUL: Stay with you.

OUISA: That's impossible.

PAUL: Why?

OUISA: My husband feels you betrayed him.

PAUL: Do you?

OUISA: You were lunatic! And picking that drek off the street. Are you suicidal? Do you have AIDS? Are you infected?

PAUL: I do not have it. It's a miracle. But I don't. Do you feel I betrayed you? If you do, I'll hang up and never bother you again—

OUISA: Where have you been?

PAUL: Travelling.

OUISA: You're not in trouble? I mean, more trouble?

PAUL: No, I only visited you. I didn't like the first people so much. They went out and just left me alone. I didn't like the doctor. He was too eager to please. And he left me alone. But you. You and your husband. We all stayed together.

OUISA: What did you want from us?

PAUL: Everlasting friendship.

OUISA: Nobody has that.

PAUL: You do.

OUISA: What do you think we are?

PAUL: You're going to tell me secrets? You're not what you appear to be? You have no secrets. Trent Conway told me what your kids have told him over the years.

OUISA: What have the kids told him about us?

PAUL: I don't tell that. I save that for blackmail.

OUISA: Then perhaps I'd better hang up.

PAUL (*Panic*): No! I went to a museum! I liked Toulouse-Lautrec!

OUISA: As well you should.

PAUL: I read *The Andy Warhol Diaries.*

OUISA: Ahh, you've become an aesthete.

PAUL: Are you laughing at me?

OUISA: No. I read them too.

PAUL: I read *The Agony and the Ecstasy,* by Irving Stone, about Michelangelo painting the Sistine Chapel.

OUISA: You're ahead of me there.

PAUL: Have you seen the Sistine Chapel?

OUISA: Oh yes. Even gone to the top of it in a rickety elevator to watch the men clean it.

PAUL: You've been to the top of the Sistine Chapel?

OUISA: Absolutely. Stood right under the hand of God touching the hand of man. The workman said "Hit it. Hit it. It's only a fresco." I did. I slapped God's hand.

PAUL: You did?

OUISA: And you know what they clean it with? All this technology. Q-tips and water.

PAUL: No!

OUISA: Clean away the years of grime and soot and paint-overs. Q-tips and water changing the history of Western Art. Vivid colors.

PAUL: Take me to see it?

OUISA: Take you to see it? Paul, they think you might have murdered someone! You stole money!

(FLAN *appears, needing help with his studs.*)

FLAN: Honey could you give me a hand with—

OUISA (*Mouths to* FLAN) It's Paul.

(FLAN *goes to the other phone.*)

FLAN: I'll call that detective.

(*The other line rings.* TESS *appears.*)

TESS: Dad! We were cut off. I'm getting marr—

FLAN: Darling, could you call back—

TESS: I'm getting married and going to Afghanistan—

FLAN: We cannot talk about this now—

TESS: I'm going to ruin my life and get married and throw away everything you want me to be because it's the only way to hurt you!

> (TESS *goes.*
> THE DETECTIVE *appears.*)

FLAN: I've got that kid on the line.

DETECTIVE: Find out where he is.

> (THE DETECTIVE *goes.*)

FLAN (*Mouths to* OUISA): Find out where he is???

PAUL: Who's there?

OUISA: Look, why don't you come here. Where are you?

PAUL: I come there and you'll have the cops waiting.

OUISA: You have to trust us.

PAUL: Why?

OUISA: Because—we like you.

FLAN (*Mouths*): Where is he?

PAUL: Who's there?

OUISA: It's—

FLAN: I'm not here.

OUISA: It's Flan.

PAUL: Are you in tonight? I could come and make a feast for you.

OUISA: We're going out now. But you could be here when we come back.

FLAN: Are you nuts! Tell a crook we're going out. The house is empty.

PAUL: Where are you going?

OUISA: To Sotheby's.

> (FLAN *grabs the phone.*)

FLAN: The key's under the mat!

PAUL: Hi! Can I come to Sotheby's?

> (FLAN *hands the phone back to* OUISA.)

OUISA: Hi.

PAUL: I said hi to Flan.

OUISA: Paul says hi.

FLAN: Hi.

OUISA: Sotheby's.

PAUL: That's wonderful! I'll come!

OUISA: You can't.

PAUL: Why? I was helpful last time—

FLAN: Thank him—he was very help—

(OUISA *hands* FLAN *the phone.*)

FLAN: Paul? You were helpful getting me this contract—

PAUL: Really! I was thinking maybe that's what I should do is what you do—in art but making money out of art and meeting people and not working in an office—

FLAN: You only see the glam side of it. There's a whole grotty side that—

PAUL: I could learn the grotty—

FLAN: You have to have art history. You have to have language. You have to have economics—

PAUL: I'm fast. I could do it. Do your kids want to—

FLAN: No, it's not really a profession you hand down from generation to gen—what the hell am I talking career counselling to you! You embarrassed me in my building! You stole money. There is a warrant out for your arrest!

(OUISA *wrests the phone away.*)

OUISA: Don't hang up! Paul? Are you there? Paul? (*To* FLAN) You made him hang up—

PAUL: I'm here.

OUISA: You are! Who are you? What's your real name?

PAUL: If you let me stay with you, I'll tell you. That night was the happiest night I ever had.

OUISA (*To* FLAN): It was the happiest night he ever had.

FLAN: Oh please. I am not a bullshitter but never bullshit a bullshitter.

(FLAN *goes.*)

OUISA: Why?

PAUL: You let me use all the parts of myself that night—

OUISA: It was magical. That Salinger stuff—

PAUL: Graduation speech at Groton two years ago.

OUISA: Your cooking—

PAUL: Other people's recipes. Did you see Donald Barthelme's obituary? He said collage was the art form of the twentieth century.

OUISA: Everything is somebody else's.

PAUL: Not your children. Not your life.

OUISA: Yes, You got me there. That is mine. It is no one else's.

PAUL: You don't sound happy.

OUISA: There's so much you don't know. You are so smart and so stupid—

PAUL (*Furious*): Never say I'm stupid—

OUISA: Have some flexibility. You're stupid not to recognize what you could be.

PAUL: What could I be?

OUISA: So much.

PAUL: With you behind me?

OUISA: Perhaps. You liked that night? I've thought since that you spent all your time laughing at us.

PAUL: No.

OUISA: That you had brought that awful hustling thing back to show us your contempt—

PAUL: I was so happy I wanted to add sex to it. Don't you do that?

(*Pause*)

OUISA: No.

PAUL: I'll tell you my name.

OUISA: Please?

PAUL: It's Paul Poitier-Kittredge. It's a hyphenated name.

(*Pause*)

OUISA: Paul, you need help. Go to the police. Turn yourself in. You'll be over it all the sooner. You can start.

PAUL: Start what?

OUISA: Your life.

PAUL: Will you help me?

(OUISA *pauses, and makes a decision.*)

OUISA: I will help you. But you have to go to the police and go to jail and—

PAUL: Will you send me books and polaroids of you and cassettes? And letters?

OUISA: Yes.

PAUL: Will you visit me?

OUISA: I will visit you.

PAUL: And when you do, you'll wear your best clothes and knock em dead?

OUISA: I'll knock em dead. But you've got to be careful in prison. You have to use condoms.

PAUL: I won't have sex in prison. I only have sex when I'm happy.

OUISA: Go to the police.

PAUL: Will you take me?

OUISA: I'll give you the name of the detective to see—

PAUL: I'll be treated with care if you take me to the police. If they don't know you're special, they kill you.

OUISA: I don't think they kill you.

PAUL: Mrs. Louisa Kittredge, I am black.

OUISA: I will deliver you to them with kindness and affection.

PAUL: And I'll plead guilty and go to prison and serve a few months.

OUISA: A few months tops.

PAUL: Then I'll come out and work for you and learn—

OUISA: We'll work that out.

PAUL: I want to know now.

OUISA: Yes. You'll work for us.

PAUL: Learn all the trade. Not just the grotty part.

OUISA: Top to bottom.

PAUL: And live with you.

OUISA: No.

PAUL: Your kids are away.

OUISA: You should have your own place.

PAUL: You'll help me find a place?

OUISA: We'll help you find a place.

PAUL: I have no furniture.

OUISA: We'll help you out.

PAUL: I made a list of things I liked in the museum. Philadelphia Chippendale.

OUISA (*Bursts out laughing*): Believe it or not, we have two Philadelphia Chippendale chairs—

PAUL: I'd rather have one nice piece than a room full of junk.

OUISA: Quality. Always. You'll have all that. Philadelphia Chippendale.

PAUL: All I have to do is go to the police.

OUISA: Make it all history. Put it behind you.

PAUL: Tonight.

OUISA: It can't be tonight. I will take you tomorrow. We have an auction tonight at Sotheby's—

PAUL: Bring me?

OUISA: I can't. It's black tie.

PAUL: I have black tie from a time I went to the Rainbow Room. Have you ever been to the Rainbow Room?

OUISA: Yes.

PAUL: What time do you have to be there?

OUISA: Eight o'clock.

PAUL: It's five-thirty now. You could come get me now and take me to the police tonight and then go to Sotheby's—

OUISA: We're going to drinks before at the Pierre.

PAUL: Japanese?

OUISA: Germans.

PAUL: You're just like my father.

OUISA: Which father?

PAUL: Sidney!

(*Pause*)

OUISA: Paul. He's not your father. And Flanders is not your father.

(FLAN *comes in, dressed.*)

FLAN: Oh fuck. We have drinks with the Japanese at six- fifteen—Get off that fucking phone. Is it that kid? Get him out of our life! Get off that phone or I'll rip it out of the wall!

(OUISA *looks at* FLAN.)

OUISA (*To* PAUL): Paul, I made a mistake. It is not the Germans. We will come right now and get you. Where are you? Tell me? I'll take you to the police. They will treat you with dignity

PAUL: I'm in the lobby of the Waverly movie theater on Sixth Avenue and Third Street.

OUISA: We'll be there in half an hour.

PAUL: I'll give you fifteen minutes grace time.

OUISA: We'll be there, Paul. We love you.

PAUL: Ouisa. I love you. Ouisa Kittredge. Hey? Bring a pink shirt.

OUISA: We'll have a wonderful life.

> (*She hangs up.*
> PAUL *goes into the dark.*)

OUISA: We can skip the shmoozing. Pick the boy up, take him to the police and be at Sotheby's before eight.

> (THE DETECTIVE *appears.*)

FLAN: He's at the Waverly Theater. Sixth Avenue and Third Street. The lobby.

OUISA: We promised we would bring him to you. He's special. Remember that he's special. Honor our promise.

> (THE DETECTIVE *nods and goes.*)

OUISA (*To us*): We go. Traffic on the FDR.

FLAN (*To us*): We get there. I run into the theater. No one.

OUISA: A young man. Black. Have you seen him?

FLAN (*To us*): The girl in the box office said the police were there, had arrested a young man. Dragged him kicking, screaming into a squad car. He was a kid waiting for his family. We could never get through or find out.

OUISA (*To us*): We weren't family.

FLAN (*To us*): That detective was transferred.

OUISA (*To us*): And we didn't know Paul's name.

We called the precinct.
Another precinct had made the arrest.
Why? Were there other charges?
We couldn't find out.

We weren't family.
We didn't know Paul's name.

We called the district attorney's office.
We weren't family.
We didn't know Paul's name.

I called the Criminal Courts.
I wasn't family.
I didn't know Paul's name.

FLAN: Why does it mean so much to you?

OUISA: He wanted to be us. Everything we are in the world, this paltry thing—our life—he wanted it. He stabbed himself to get in here. He envied us. We're not enough to be envied.

FLAN: Like the papers said. We have hearts.

OUISA: Having a heart is not the point. We were hardly taken in. We believed him—for a few hours. He did more for us in a few hours than our children ever did. He wanted to be your child. Don't let that go. He sat out in that park and said that man is my father. He's in trouble and we don't know how to help him.

FLAN: Help him? He could've killed me. And you.

OUISA: You were attracted to him—

FLAN: Cut me out of that pathology! You are on your own—

OUISA: Attracted by youth and his talent and the embarrassing prospect of being in the movie version of *Cats*. Did you put that in your *Times* piece? And we turn him into an anecdote to dine out on. Or dine in on. But it was an experience. I will not turn him into an anecdote. How do we fit what happened to us into life without turning it into an anecdote with no teeth and a punch line you'll mouth over and over for years to come. "Tell the story about the imposter who came into our lives—" "That reminds me of the time this boy—." And we become these human juke boxes spilling out these anecdotes. But it was an experience. How do we *keep* the experience?

FLAN (*To us*): That's why I love paintings. Cezanne. The problems he brought up are the problems painters are still dealing with. Color. Structure. Those are problems.

OUISA: There is color in my life, but I'm not aware of any structure.

FLAN (*To us*): Cezanne would leave blank spaces in his canvasses if he couldn't account for the brush stroke, give a reason for the color.

OUISA: Then I am a collage of unaccounted-for brush strokes. I am all random. God, Flan, how much of your life can you account for?

FLAN: Are you drunk? The Cezanne sale went through. We are rich. Geoffrey's rich. Tonight there's a Matisse we'll get and next month there's a Bonnard and after that—

(*She considers him.*)

OUISA: These are the times I would take a knife and dig out your heart. Answer me? How much of your—
FLAN: —life can I account for! *All!* I am a gambler!

(*Pause*)

OUISA: We're a terrible match.
OUISA (*To us*): Time passes.
OUISA: I read today that a young man committed suicide in Riker's Island. Tied a shirt around his neck and hanged himself. Was it the pink shirt? This burst of color? The pink shirt. Was it Paul? Who are you? We never found out who you are?
FLAN: I'm sure it's not him. He'll be back. We haven't heard the last of him. The imagination. He'll find a way.
FLAN (*To us*): We have to go. An auction.
FLAN: I'll get the elevator.

(FLAN *goes.*)

OUISA (*To us*): But if it was the pink shirt. Pink. A burst of pink. The Sistine Chapel. They've cleaned it and it's all these colors.
FLAN'S VOICE: Darling—

(OUISA *starts to go. She looks up.* PAUL *is there, wearing the pink shirt.*)

PAUL: The Kandinsky. It's painted on two sides.

(*He glows for a moment and is gone.*
She considers. She smiles.
The Kandinsky begins its slow revolve.)

THE END

Topdog/Underdog
(2001)

By Suzan-Lori Parks (1963–)

INTRODUCTION

Top dog/Underdog is a play involving a pair of brothers christened Lincoln and Booth by their father as "*a joke.*" There is some irony, of course, in Suzan-Lori Parks' use of these two names in a theatrical presentation. Abraham Lincoln, as we all know, was assassinated while watching a play (*Our American Cousin*, which was being performed in Ford's Theatre in Washington, D.C.). What is less widely known is that his assassin, John Wilkes Booth, was a popular actor, the son of British Shakespearean actor Junius Brutus Booth and the brother of Edwin Booth, one of the most significant American actors of the 19th century.

Beyond this symbolism (and foreshadowing), Parks also utilizes the image of Lincoln here for the second time in her career. In an earlier work, *The America Play*, a character named The Foundling Father recounts his career as a Lincoln impersonator. He would sit, pretending to watch a play, while paying spectators would "shoot" him with fake firearms. Despite being black, he was told that he bore a strong resemblance to Abraham Lincoln, and was so compelled to "play" Lincoln that he abandoned his family in pursuit of this dream.

In *Top dog/Underdog*, Lincoln's low-paying arcade job, impersonating his namesake in the same manner, is a fallback position—he even admits that he makes less by impersonating Abraham Lincoln than a white man would make in the same job. Booth never stops reminding Lincoln about his more glamorous past as a street hustler—a master of 3-card Monte. Booth's taunting is meant to convince Lincoln to return to this life because Booth wants to be a part of it.

Superficially, Booth is trying to rebrand himself as an affluent "player" (even going so far as to rename himself 3-Card) in order to regain the affection of his sometime girlfriend, Grace. But in reality, Booth is searching for an identity, perhaps even trying to steal Lincoln's. While perfectly adept at shoplifting, Booth carries out his "work" in secret while Lincoln is used to enjoy a sort of celebrity status. As the play shows us, the 3-card Monte hustle involves more than manual skill: it is a full-fledged performance— complete with banter, facial expressions, and interactive skills too nuanced for Booth to master but still handled with complete virtuosity by Lincoln. Booth is in turn enraged that he cannot mimic his brother, and disgusted that Lincoln is only willing to "pretend to be [his] old self."

Lincoln insists, "There's more to me than some cheap hustle," but the play's only indication of what that might be comes when Lincoln chooses to drink instead of rehearsing his assassination routine. The siblings' father is described as a drunk; perhaps this is a trait that has been passed on. Even more powerful, however, is the lure of the cards, which Lincoln studies "like an alcoholic would study a drink." Lincoln abandons his former profession after an associate, Lonny, is shot and killed, but the con is so much a part of him that he loses his sexual potency when he stops hustling and regains it only in the wake of his relapse. In giving Lincoln physiological symptoms to accompany his withdrawal, Parks suggests to us that the 3-card Monte performance is real to Lincoln in a way it can never be to Booth.

Booth's attempt to assume Lincoln's persona is doomed to fall short, leaving him with an unresolved resentment over something he thinks Lincoln stole from him. As she was preparing to leave Lincoln and Booth, their mother tells Booth—the younger brother—to look after Lincoln—something he perceives as an inappropriate role reversal: "I told her I was the little brother and the big brother should look out after the little brother." Booth longed to play a supporting role in Lincoln's con game when it was still running but Lincoln denied Booth this place by keeping him at arm's length from his "crew," and continues to remind Booth of his inferior skills. It is this latter tendency—sharply reinforced in the final card game between the brothers—that lays bare the chilling void of empathy in their relationship. This Lincoln and Booth, unlike the Lincoln and Booth of history, are not two strangers thrown together by the forces of history. They have been chained together from the beginning, barely concealing their mutual disdain and contempt until the façade can no longer be maintained.

THE PLAYERS

Lincoln, the topdog
Booth (aka 3-Card) the underdog

AUTHOR'S NOTES: From the "Elements of Style"

I'm continuing the use of my slightly unconventional theatrical elements.
Here's a road map.

- (Rest)
  Take a little time, a pause, a breather; make a transition

- A Spell
  An elongated and heightened *(Rest)*. Denoted by repetition of figures' names with
  no dialogue. Has sort of an architectural look:

  Lincoln
  Booth
  Lincoln
  Booth

This is a place where the figures experience their pure true simple state. While no action
or stage business is necessary, directors should fill this moment as they best see fit.

- [Brackets in the text indicate optional cuts for production.]

- (Parentheses around dialogue indicate softly spoken passages (asides; sotto voce)).

SCENE ONE

Thursday evening.
A seedily furnished rooming house room.
A bed, a reclining chair, a small wooden chair,
some other stuff but not much else.
Booth, a black man in his early 30s, practices his
3-card monte scam on the classic setup:
3 playing cards and the cardboard playing board
atop 2 mismatched milk crates.

His moves and accompanying patter are, for the most part, studied and awkward.

Booth: Watch me close watch me close now: who-see-thuh-red-card-who-see-thuh-red-card? I-see-thuh-red-card. Thuh-red-card-is-thuh-winner. Pick-thuh-red-card-you-pick-uh-winner. Pick-uh-black-card-you-pick-uh-loser. Theres-thuh-loser, yeah, theres-thuh-black-card, theres-thuh-other-loser-and-theres-thuh-red-card, thuh-winner.

(*Rest*)

Watch me close watch me close now: 3-Card-throws-thuh-cards-lightning-fast. 3-Card-thats-me-and-Ima-last. Watch-me-throw-cause-here-I-go. One-good-pickll-get-you-in, 2-good-picks-and-you-gone-win. See-thuh-red-card-see-thuh-thuh-red-card-who-see-thuh-red-card?

(*Rest*)

Dont touch my cards, man, just point to thuh one you want. You-pick-that-card-you-pick-a-loser, yeah, that-cards-a-loser. You-pick-that-card-thats-thuh-other-loser. You-pick-that-card-you-pick-a-winner. Follow that card. You gotta chase that card. You-pick-thuh-dark-deuce-thats-a-loser-other-dark-deuces-thuh-other-loser, red-deuce, thuh-deuce-of-heartsll-win-it-all. Follow thuh red card.

(*Rest*)

Ima show you thuh cards: 2 black cards but only one heart. Now watch me now. Who-sees-thuh-red-card-who-knows- where-its-at? Go on, man, point to thuh card. Put yr money down cause you aint no clown. No? Ah you had thuh card, but you didnt have thuh heart.

(*Rest*)

You wanna bet? 500 dollars? Shoot. You musta been watching 3-Card real close. Ok. Lay the cash in my hand cause 3-Cards thuh man. Thank you, mister. This card you say?

(*Rest*)

Wrong! Sucker! Fool! Asshole! Bastard! I bet yr daddy heard how stupid you was and drank himself to death just cause he didnt wanna have nothing to do witchu! I bet yr mama seen you when you comed out and she walked away from you with thuh afterbirth still hanging from out twixt her legs, sucker! Ha Ha Ha! And 3-Card, once again, wins all thuh money!!

(*Rest*)

What? Cops looking my way? Fold up thuh game, and walk away. Sneak outa sight. Set up on another corner.

(*Rest*)

Yeah.

 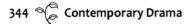

(Rest)

Having won the imaginary loot and dodged the
imaginary cops, Booth sets up his equipment and
starts practicing his scam all over again.
Lincoln comes in quietly. He is a black man in his later 30s.
He is dressed in an antique frock coat and wears
a top hat and fake beard, that is, he is dressed to look
like Abraham Lincoln. He surreptitiously walks into
the room to stand right behind Booth,
who, engrossed in his cards,
does not notice Lincoln right away.

Booth: Watch me close watch me close now: who-see-thuh-red-who-see-thuh-red-card? I-see-thuh-red-card. Thuh-red-card-is-thuh-winner, Pick-thuh-red-card-you-pick-uh-winner. Pick-uh-black-card-you-pick-uh-loser. Theres-thuh loser-yeah-theres-thuh-black-card, theres-thuh-other-loser-and-theres-thuh-red-card, thuh-winner. Don't touch my cards, man, don't—

(Rest)

Dont do that shit. Dont do that shit. Dont do that shit!

Booth, sensing someone behind him, whirls around,
pulling a gun from his pants. While the presence of
Lincoln doesnt surprise him, the Lincoln costume does.

Booth: And woah, man dont *ever* be doing that shit! Who thuh fuck you think you is coming in my shit all spooked out and shit. You pull that one more time I'll shoot you!

Lincoln: I only had a minute to make the bus.

Booth: Bullshit.

Lincoln: Not completely. I mean, its either bull or shit, but not a complete lie so it aint bullshit, right?

(Rest)

Put yr gun away.

Booth: Take off the damn hat at least.

Lincoln takes off the stovepipe hat.
Booth puts his gun away.

Lincoln: Its cold out there. This thing kept my head warm.

Booth: I dont like you wearing that bullshit, that shit that bull that disguise that getup that motherdisfuckinguise anywhere in the vicinity of my humble abode.

> Lincoln takes off the beard.

Lincoln: Better?

Booth: Take off the damn coat too. Damn, man. Bad enough you got to wear that shit all day you come up in here wearing it. What my women gonna say?

Lincoln: What women?

Booth: I got a date with Grace tomorrow. Shes in love with me again but she dont know it yet. Aint no man can love her the way I can. She sees you in that getup its gonna reflect bad on me. She coulda seen you coming down the street. Shit. Could be standing outside right now taking her ring off and throwing it on the sidewalk.

> Booth takes a peek out the window.

Booth: I got her this ring today. Diamond. Well, diamond-esque, but it looks just as good as the real thing. Asked her what size she wore. She say 7 so I go boost a size 6 and a half, right? Show it to her and she loves it and I shove it on her finger and its a tight fit right, so she cant just take it off on a whim, like she did the last one I gave her. Smooth, right?

> Booth takes another peek out the window.

Lincoln: She out there?

Booth: Nope. Coast is clear.

Lincoln: You boosted a ring?

Booth: Yeah. I thought about spending my inheritance on it but—take off that damn coat, man, you make me nervous standing there looking like a spook, and that damn face paint, take it off. You should take all of it off at work and leave it there.

Lincoln: I dont bring it home someone might steal it.

Booth: At least *take it off* there, then.

Lincoln: Yeah.

(*Rest*)

> Lincoln takes off the frock coat and
> applies cold cream, removing the whiteface.

Lincoln: I was riding the bus. Really I only had a minute to make my bus and I was sitting in the arcade thinking should I change into my street clothes or should I make the bus? Nobody was in there today anyway. Middle of week middle of winter. Not like on weekends. Weekends the place is packed. So Im riding the bus home. And this kid asked me for my autograph. I pretended I didnt hear him at first. I'd had a long day. But he kept asking. Theyd just done Lincoln in history class and he knew all about him, he'd been to the arcade but, I dunno, for some reason he was tripping cause there was Honest Abe right beside him on the bus. I wanted to tell him to go fuck hisself. But then I got a look at him. A little rich kid. Born on easy street, you know the type. So I waited until I could tell he really wanted it, the autograph, and I told him he could have it for 10 bucks. I was gonna say 5, cause of the Lincoln connection but something in me made me ask for 10.

Booth: But he didnt have a 10. All he had was a penny. So you took the penny.

Lincoln: All he had was a *20*. So I took the 20 and told him to meet me on the bus tomorrow and Honest Abe would give him the change.

Booth: Shit.

Lincoln: Shit is right.

(*Rest*)

Booth: Whatd you do with thuh 20?

Lincoln Bought drinks at Luckys. A round for everybody. They got a kick out of the getup.

Booth You shoulda called me down.

Lincoln: Next time, bro.

(*Rest*)

You making bookshelves? With the milk crates, you making bookshelves?

Booth: Yeah, big bro, Im making bookshelves.

Lincoln: Whats the cardboard part for?

Booth: Versatility.

Lincoln: Oh.

Booth: I was thinking we dont got no bookshelves we dont got no dining room table so Im making a sorta modular unit you put the books in the bottom and the table top on top. We can eat and store our books. We could put the photo album in there.

> Booth gets the raggedy family photo album
> and puts it in the milk crate.

Booth: Youd sit there, Id sit on the edge of the bed. Gathered around the dinner table. Like old times.

Lincoln: We just gotta get some books but thats great, Booth, thats real great.

Booth: Dont be calling me Booth no more, K?

Lincoln: You changing yr name?

Booth: Maybe.

Lincoln

Booth:

Lincoln: What to?

Booth: Im not ready to reveal it yet.

Lincoln: You already decided on something?

Booth: Maybe.

Lincoln: You gonna call yrself something african? That be cool. Only pick something thats easy to spell and pronounce, man, cause you know, some of them african names, I mean, ok, Im down with the power to the people thing, but, no ones gonna hire you if they cant say yr name. And some of them fellas who got they african names, no one can say they names and they cant say they names neither. I mean, you dont want yr new handle to obstruct yr employment possibilities.

Booth:

Lincoln

Booth: You bring dinner?

Lincoln: "Shango" would be a good name. The name of the thunder god. If you aint decided already Im just throwing it in the pot. I brought chinese.

Booth: Lets try the table out.

Lincoln: Cool.

> They both sit at the new table.
> The food is far away near the door.

Lincoln

Booth:

Lincoln: I buy it you set it up. Thats the deal. Thats the deal, right?

Booth: You like this place?

Lincoln: Ssallright.

Booth: But a little cramped sometimes, right?

Lincoln: You dont hear me complain. Although that recliner sometimes Booth, man— no Booth, right—man, Im too old to be sleeping in that chair.

Booth: Its my place. You dont got a place. Cookie, she threw you out. And you cant seem to get another woman. Yr lucky I let you stay.

Lincoln: Every Friday you say *mi casa es su casa.*

Booth: Every Friday you come home with yr paycheck. Today is Thursday and I tell you brother, its a long way from Friday to Friday. All kinds of things can happen. All kinds of bad feelings can surface and erupt while yr little brother waits for you to bring in yr share.

(*Rest*)

I got my Thursday head on, Link. Go get the food.

Lincoln doesnt budge.

Lincoln: You dont got no running water in here, man.

Booth: So?

Lincoln: You dont got no toilet you dont got no sink.

Booth: Bathrooms down the hall.

Lincoln: You living in thuh Third World, fool! Hey, I'll get thuh food.

Lincoln goes to get the food.
He sees a stray card on the floor and
examines it without touching it. He brings the food over,
putting it nicely on the table.

Lincoln: You been playing cards?

Booth: Yeah.

Lincoln: Solitaire?

Booth: Thats right. Im getting pretty good at it.

Lincoln: Thats soup and thats sauce. I got you the meat and I got me the skrimps.

Booth: I wanted the skrimps.

Lincoln: You said you wanted the meat. This morning when I left you said you wanted the meat.

(*Rest*)

Here man, take the skrimps. No sweat.

They eat. Chinese food from styrofoam containers,
cans of soda, fortune cookies. Lincoln eats slowly
and carefully, Booth eats ravenously.

Lincoln: Yr getting good at solitaire?

Booth: Yeah. How about we play a hand after eating?

Lincoln: Solitaire?

Booth: Poker or rummy or something.

Lincoln: You know I dont touch thuh cards, man.

Booth: Just for fun.

Lincoln: I dont touch thuh cards.

Booth: How about for money?

Lincoln: You dont got no money. All the money you got I bring in here.

Booth: I got my inheritance.

Lincoln: Thats like saying you dont got no money cause you aint never gonna do nothing with it so its like you dont got it.

Booth: At least I still got mines. You blew yrs.

Lincoln:

Booth:

Lincoln: You like the skrimps?

Booth: Ssallright.

Lincoln: Whats yr fortune?

Booth: "Waste not want not." Whats yrs?

Lincoln: "Your luck will change!"

> Booth finishes eating. He turns his back to Lincoln
> and fiddles around with the cards, keeping them
> on the bed, just out of Lincolns sight.
> He mutters the 3-card patter under his breath.
> His moves are still clumsy. Every once and a while
> he darts a look over at Lincoln who
> does his best to ignore Booth.

Booth: (((((Watch me close watch me close now: who-see-thuh-red-card-who-see-thuh-red-card? I-see-thuh-red-card. Thuh-red-card-is-thuh-winner. Pick-thuh-red-card-you-pick-uh-winner. Pick-uh-black-card-and-you-pick-uh-loser. Theres-thuh-loser, yeah, theres-thuh-black-card, theres-thuh-other-loser-and-theres-thuh-red-card, thuh-winner! Cop C, Stick, Cop C! Go on—))))

Lincoln ((Shit.))

Booth: (((((((One-good-pickll-get-you-in, 2-good-picks-and-you-gone-win. Dont touch my cards, man, just point to thuh one you want. You-pick-that-card-you-pick-uh-loser, yeah, that- cards-uh-loser. You-pick-that-card-thats-thuh-other-loser. You-pick-that-card-you-pick-uh-winner. Follow-that-card. You-gotta-chase-that-card!)))))))

Lincoln: You wanna hustle 3-card monte, you gotta do it right, you gotta break it down. Practice it in smaller bits. Yr trying to do the whole thing at once thats why you keep fucking it up.

Booth: Show me.

Lincoln: No. Im just saying you wanna do it you gotta do it right and if you gonna do it right you gotta work on it in smaller bits, thatsall.

Booth: You and me could team up and do it together. We'd clean up, Link.

Lincoln: I'll clean up—bro.

> Lincoln cleans up. As he clears the food, Booth goes back
> to using the "table" for its original purpose.

Booth: My new names 3-Card. 3-Card, got it? You wanted to know it so now you know it. 3-card monte by 3-Card. Call me 3-Card from here on out.

Lincoln: 3-Card. Shit.

Booth: Im getting everybody to call me 3-Card. Grace likes 3-Card better than Booth. She says 3-Cards got something to it. Anybody not calling me 3-Card gets a bullet.

Lincoln: Yr too much, man.

Booth: Im making a point.

Lincoln: Point made, 3-Card. Point made.

> Lincoln picks up his guitar. Plays at it.

Booth: Oh come on, man we could make money you and me. Throwing down the cards. 3-Card and Link: look out! We could clean up you and me. You would throw the cards and I'd be yr Stickman. The one in the crowd who looks like just an innocent passerby, who looks like just another player, like just another customer, but who gots intimate connections with you, the Dealer, the one throwing the cards, the main man. I'd be the one who brings in the crowd, I'd be the one who makes them want to put they money down, you do yr moves and I do mines. You turn yr head and I turn the card—

Lincoln: It aint as easy as all that. Theres—

Booth: We could be a team, man. Rake in the money! Sure thered be some cats out there with fast eyes, some brothers and sisters who would watch real close and pick the right card, and so thered be some days when we would lose money, but most of the days we would come out on top! Pockets bulging, plenty of cash! And the ladies would be thrilling! You could afford to get laid! Grace would be all over me again.

Lincoln: I thought you said she was all over you.

Booth: She is she is. Im seeing her tomorrow but today we gotta solidify the shit twixt you and me. Big brother Link and little brother Booth—

Lincoln: 3-Card.

Booth: Yeah. Scheming and dreaming. No one throws the cards like you, Link. And with yr moves and my magic, and we get Grace and a girl for you to round out the posse. We'd be golden, bro! Am I right?

Lincoln

Lincoln

Booth: Am I right?

Lincoln: I dont touch thuh cards, 3-Card. I dont touch thuh cards no more.

Lincoln

Booth

Lincoln

Booth

Booth: You know what Mom told me when she was packing to leave? You was at school motherfucker you was at school. You got up that morning and sat down in yr regular place and read the cereal box while Dad read the sports section and Mom brought you yr dick toast and then you got on the damn school bus cause you didnt have the sense to do nothing else you was so into yr own shit that you didnt have the sense to feel nothing else going on. I had the sense to go back cause I was feeling something going on man, I was feeling something changing. So I—

Lincoln: Cut school that day like you did almost every day—

Booth: She was putting her stuff in bags. She had all them nice suitcases but she was putting her stuff in bags.

(Rest)

Packing up her shit. She told me to look out for you. I told her I was the little brother and the big brother should look out after the little brother. She just said it again. That I should look out for you. Yeah. So who gonna look out for me. Not like you care. Here I am interested in an economic opportunity, willing to work hard, willing to take risks and all you can say you shiteating motherfucking pathetic limpdick uncle tom, all you can tell me is how you dont do no more what I be wanting to do. Here I am trying to earn a living and you standing in my way. YOU STANDING IN MY WAY, LINK!

Lincoln: Im sorry.

Booth: Yeah, you sorry all right.

Lincoln: I cant be hustling no more, bro.

Booth: What you do all day aint no hustle?

Lincoln: Its honest work.

Booth: Dressing up like some crackerass white man, some dead president and letting people shoot at you sounds like a hustle to me.

Lincoln: People know the real deal. When people know the real deal it aint a hustle.

Booth: We do the card game people will know the real deal. Sometimes we will win sometimes they will win. They fast they win, we faster we win.

Lincoln: I aint going back to that, bro. I aint going back.

Booth: You play Honest Abe. You aint going back but you going all the way back. Back to way back then when folks was slaves and shit.

Lincoln: Dont push me.

Booth

Lincoln

Booth: You gonna have to leave.

Lincoln: I'll be gone tomorrow.

Booth: Good. Cause this was only supposed to be a temporary arrangement.

Lincoln: I will be gone tomorrow.

Booth: Good.

> Booth sits on his bed. Lincoln, sitting in his easy chair
> with his guitar, plays and sings.

Lincoln:
My dear mother left me, my fathers gone away
My dear mother left me and my fathers gone away
I dont got no money, I dont got no place to stay.
My best girl, she threw me out into the street
My favorite horse, they ground him into meat
Im feeling cold from my head down to my feet.
My luck was bad but now it turned to worse
My luck was bad but now it turned to worse
Dont call me up a doctor, just call me up a hearse.

Booth: You just made that up?

Lincoln: I had it in my head for a few days.

Booth: Sounds good.

Lincoln: Thanks.

(*Rest*)

Daddy told me once why we got the names we do.

Booth: Yeah?

Lincoln: Yeah.

(*Rest*)

He was drunk when he told me, or maybe I was drunk when he told me. Anyway he told me, may not be true, but he told me. Why he named us both. Lincoln and Booth.

Booth: How come. How come, man?
Lincoln: It was his idea of a joke.

> Both men relax back as the lights fade.

SCENE TWO

> Friday evening.
> The very next day.
> Booth comes in looking like he is
> bundled up against the cold.
> He makes sure his brother isnt home, then stands
> in the middle of the room. From his big coat sleeves
> he pulls out one new shoe then another,
> from another sleeve come two more shoes.
> He then slithers out a belt from each sleeve.
> He removes his coat. Underneath he wears a very nice
> new suit. He removes the jacket and pants
> revealing another new suit underneath. The suits still have
> the price tags on them. He takes two neckties
> from his pockets and two folded shirts
> from the back of his pants. He pulls a magazine
> from the front of his pants. Hes clearly
> had a busy day of shoplifting.
> He lays one suit out on Lincolns easy chair.
> The other he lays out on his own bed.
> He goes out into the hall returning with a folding screen
> which he sets up between the bed and
> the recliner creating 2 separate spaces.
> He takes out a bottle of whiskey and two glasses,
> setting them on the two stacked milk crates.
> He hears footsteps and sits down in the
> small wooden chair reading the magazine.
> Lincoln, dressed in street clothes, comes in.

Lincoln: Taaaaadaaaaaaaa!
Booth: Lordamighty, Pa, I smells money!
Lincoln: Sho nuff, Ma. Poppas brung home thuh bacon.

Booth: Bringitherebringitherebringithere.

> With a series of very elaborate moves
> Lincoln brings the money over to Booth.

Booth: Put it in my hands, Pa!
Lincoln: I want ya tuh smells it first, Ma!
Booth: Put it neath my nose then, Pa!
Lincoln: Take yrself a good long whiff of them greenbacks.
Booth: Oh lordamighty Ima faint, Pa! Get me muh med-sin!

> Lincoln quickly pours two large glasses of whiskey.

Lincoln: Dont die on me, Ma!
Booth: Im fading fast, Pa!
Lincoln: Thinka thuh children, Ma! Thinka thuh farm!
Booth: 1-2-3.

> Both men gulp down their drinks simultaneously.

Lincoln and Booth: AAAAAAAAAAAAAAAAAAAAH!

> Lots of laughing and slapping on the backs.

Lincoln: Budget it out man budget it out.
Booth: You in a hurry?
Lincoln: Yeah. I wanna see how much we got for the week.
Booth: You rush in here and dont even look around. Could be a fucking A-bomb in the middle of the floor you wouldnt notice. Yr wife, Cookie—
Lincoln: X-wife—
Booth: —could be in my bed you wouldnt notice—
Lincoln: She was once—
Booth: Look the fuck around please.

> Lincoln looks around and sees the new suit on his chair.

Lincoln: Wow.
Booth: Its yrs.
Lincoln: Shit.

Booth: Got myself one too.

Lincoln: Boosted?

Booth: Yeah I boosted em. Theys stole from a big-ass department store. That store takes in more money in one day than we will in our whole life. I stole and I stole generously. I got one for me and I got one for you. Shoes belts shirts ties socks in the shoes and everything. Got that screen too.

Lincoln: You all right, man.

Booth: Just cause I aint good as you at cards dont mean I cant do nothing.

Lincoln: Lets try em on.

> They stand in their separate sleeping spaces,
> Booth near his bed, Lincoln near his recliner,
> and try on their new clothes.

Booth: Ima wear mine tonight. Gracell see me in this and *she* gonna ask me tuh marry *her*.

(*Rest*)

I got you the blue and I got me the brown. I walked in there and walked out and they didnt as much as bat an eye. Thats how smooth lil bro be, Link.

Lincoln: You did good. You did real good 3-Card.

Booth: All in a days work.

Lincoln: They say the clothes make the man. All day long I wear that getup. But that dont make me who I am. Old black coat not even real old just fake old. Its got worn spots on the elbows, little raggedy places thatll break through into holes before the winters out. Shiny strips around the cuffs and the collar. Dust from the cap guns on the left shoulder where they shoot him, where they shoot me I should say but I never feel like they shooting me. The fella who had the gig before I had it wore the same coat. When I got the job they had the getup hanging there waiting for me. Said thuh fella before me just took it off one day and never came back.

(*Rest*)

Remember how Dads clothes used to hang in the closet?

Booth: Until you took em outside and burned em.

(*Rest*)

He had some nice stuff. What he didnt spend on booze he spent on women. What he didnt spend on them two he spent on clothes. He had some nice stuff. I would look at his stuff and calculate thuh how long it would take till I was big enough to fit it. Then you went and burned it all up.

Lincoln: I got tired of looking at em without him in em.

(*Rest*)

They said thuh fella before me—he took off the getup one day, hung it up real nice, and never came back. And as they offered me thuh job, saying of course I would have to wear a little makeup and accept less than what they would offer a—another guy—

Booth: Go on, say it. "White." Theyd pay you less than theyd pay a white guy.

Lincoln: I said to myself thats exactly what I would do: wear it out and then leave it hanging there and not come back. But until then, I would make a living at it. But it dont make me. Worn suit coat, not even worn by the fool that Im supposed to be playing, but making fools out of all those folks who come crowding in for they chance to play at something great. Fake beard. Top hat. Dont make me into no Lincoln. I was Lincoln on my own before any of that.

> The men finish dressing. They style and profile.

Booth: Sharp, huh?

Lincoln: Very sharp.

Booth: You look sharp too, man. You look like the real you. Most of the time you walking around all bedraggled and shit. You look good. Like you used to look back in thuh day when you had Cookie in love with you and all the women in the world was eating out of yr hand.

Lincoln: This is real nice, man. I dont know where Im gonna wear it but its real nice.

Booth: Just wear it around. Itll make you feel good and when you feel good yll meet someone nice. Me I aint interested in meeting no one nice, I mean, I only got eyes for Grace. You think she'll go for me in this?

Lincoln: I think thuh tie you gave me'll go better with what you got on.

Booth Yeah?

Lincoln: Grace likes bright colors dont she? My ties bright, yrs is too subdued.

Booth: Yeah. Gimmle yr tie.

Lincoln: You gonna take back a gift?

Booth: I stole the damn thing didnt I? Gimmie yrs! I'll give you mines.

> They switch neckties. Booth is pleased.
> Lincoln is *more* pleased.

Lincoln: Do thuh budget.

Booth: Right. Ok lets see: we got 314 dollars. We put 100 aside for the rent. 100 a week times 4 weeks makes the rent and—

Lincoln and Booth: —we dont want thuh rent spent.

Booth: That leaves 214. We put aside 30 for the electric leaving 184. We put aside 50 for thuh phone leaving 134.

Lincoln: We dont got a phone.

Booth: We pay our bill theyll turn it back on.

Lincoln: We dont need no phone.

Booth: How you gonna get a woman if you dont got a phone? Women these days are more cautious, more whaddacallit, more circumspect. You go into a club looking like a fast daddy, you get a filly to give you her numerophono and gone is the days when she just gives you her number and dont ask for yrs.

Lincoln: Like a woman is gonna call me.

Booth: She dont wanna call you she just doing a preliminary survey of the property. Shit, Link, you dont know nothin no more.

(*Rest*)

She gives you her number and she asks for yrs. You give her yr number. The phone number of yr home. Thereby telling her 3 things: 1) you got a home, that is, you aint no smooth talking smooth dressing *homeless* joe; 2) that you is in possession of a telephone and a working telephone number which is to say that you got thuh cash and thuh wherewithal to acquire for yr self the worlds most revolutionary communication apparatus and you together enough to pay yr bills!

Lincoln: Whats 3?

Booth: You give her yr number you telling her that its cool to call if she should so please, that is, that you aint got no wife or wife approximation on the premises.

(*Rest*)

50 for the phone leaving 134. We put aside 40 for "med-sin."

Lincoln: The price went up. 2 bucks more a bottle.

Booth: We'll put aside 50, then. That covers the bills. We got 84 left. 40 for meals together during the week leaving 44. 30 for me 14 for you. I got a woman I gotta impress tonight.

Lincoln: You didnt take out for the phone last week.

Booth: Last week I was depressed. This week things is looking up. For both of us.

Lincoln: Theyre talking about cutbacks at the arcade. I only been there 8 months, so—

Booth: Dont sweat it man we'll find something else.

Lincoln: Not nothing like this. I like the job. This is sit down, you know, easy work. I just gotta sit there all day. Folks come in kill phony Honest Abe with the phony pistol. I can sit there and let my mind travel.

Booth: Think of women.

Lincoln: Sometimes.

(*Rest*)

All around the whole arcade is buzzing and popping. Thuh whirring of thuh duckshoot, baseballs smacking the back wall when someone misses the stack of cans, some woman getting happy cause her fella just won the ring toss. The Boss playing the barker talking up the fake freaks. The smell of the ocean and cotton candy and rat shit. And in thuh middle of all that, I can just sit and let my head go quiet. Make up songs, make plans. Forget.

(*Rest*)

You should come down again.

Booth: Once was plenty, but thanks.

(*Rest*)

Yr Best Customer, he come in today?

Lincoln: Oh, yeah, he was there.

Booth: He shoot you?

Lincoln: He shot Honest Abe, yeah.

Booth: He talk to you?

Lincoln: In a whisper. Shoots on the left whispers on the right.

Booth: Whatd he say this time?

Lincoln: "Does thuh show stop when no ones watching or does thuh show go on?"

Booth: Hes getting deep,

Lincoln: Yeah.

Booth: Whatd he say, that one time? "Yr only yrself—"

Lincoln: "—when no ones watching," yeah.

Booth: Thats deep shit.

(*Rest*)

Hes a brother, right?

Lincoln: I think so.

Booth: He know yr a brother?

Lincoln: I dunno. Yesterday he had a good one. He shoots me, Im playing dead, and he leans in close then goes: "God aint nothing but a parasite."

Booth: Hes one *deep* black brother.

Lincoln: Yeah. He makes the day interesting.

Booth: (*Rest*)

Thats a fucked-up job you got.

Lincoln: Its a living.

Booth: But you aint living,

Lincoln: Im alive aint I?

(*Rest*)

One day I was throwing the cards. Next day Lonny died. Somebody shot him. I knew I was next, so I quit. I saved my life.

(*Rest*)

The arcade gig is the first lucky break Ive ever had. And Ive actually grown to like the work. And now theyre talking about cutting me.

Booth: You was lucky with thuh cards.

Lincoln: Lucky? Aint nothing lucky about cards. Cards aint luck. Cards is work. Cards is skill. Aint never nothing lucky about cards.

(*Rest*)

I dont wanna lose my job.

Booth: Then you gotta jazz up yr act. Elaborate yr moves, you know. You was always too stiff with it. You cant just sit there! Maybe, when they shoot you, you know, leap up flail yr arms then fall down and wiggle around and shit so they gotta shoot you more than once. Blam Blam Blam! Blam!

Lincoln: Help me practice. I'll sit here like I do at work and you be like one of the tourists.

Booth: No thanks.

Lincoln: My paychecks on the line, man.

Booth: I got a date. Practice on yr own.

(*Rest*)

I got a rendezvous with Grace. Shit she so sweet she makes my teeth hurt.

(*Rest*)

Link, uh, howbout slipping me an extra 5 spot. Its the biggest night of my life.

Lincoln

Booth

> Lincoln gives Booth a 5er.

Booth Thanks.

Lincoln: No sweat.

Booth: Howabout I run through it with you when I get back. Put on yr getup and practice till then.

Lincoln: Sure.

> Booth leaves. Lincoln stands there alone.
> He takes off his shoes, giving them a shine.
> He takes off his socks and his fancy suit,
> hanging it neatly over the little wooden chair.

He takes his getup out of his shopping bag. He puts it on,
slowly, like an actor preparing for a great role:
frock coat, pants, beard, top hat, necktie.
He leaves his feet bare. The top hat has an elastic band
which he positions securely underneath his chin.
He picks up the white pancake makeup
but decides against it.
He sits. He pretends to get shot,
flings himself on the floor and thrashes around.
He gets up, considers giving the new moves another try,
but instead pours himself a big glass of whiskey
and sits there drinking.

SCENE THREE

Much later that same Friday evening. The recliner
is reclined to its maximum horizontal position
and Lincoln lies there asleep.
He wakes with a start. He is horrific,
bleary eyed and hungover, in his full Lincoln regalia.
He takes a deep breath, realizes where he is
and reclines again, going back to sleep.
Booth comes in full of swagger. He slams the door
trying to wake his brother who is dead to the world.
He opens the door and slams it again. This time Lincoln
wakes up, as hungover and horrid as before.
Booth swaggers about, his moves are exaggerated,
rooster-like. He walks round and round Lincoln making sure his brother sees him.

Lincoln: You hurt yrself?
Booth: I had me "an evening to remember."
Lincoln: You look like you hurt yrself.
Booth: Grace Grace Grace. *Grace.* She wants me back. She wants me back so bad she wiped her hand over the past where we wasnt together just so she could say we aint never been apart. She wiped her hand over our breakup. She wiped her hand over her childhood, her teenage years, her first boyfriend, just so she could say that she been mine since the dawn of time.

Lincoln: Thats great, man.

Booth: And all the shit I put her through: she wiped it clean. And the women I saw while I was seeing her—

Lincoln: Wiped clean too?

Booth: Mister Clean, Mister, Mister Clean!

Lincoln: Whered you take her?

Booth: We was over at her place. I brought thuh food. Stopped at the best place I could find and stuffed my coat with only the best. We had candlelight, we had music we had—

Lincoln: She let you do it?

Booth: Course she let me do it.

Lincoln: She let you do it without a rubber?

Booth: —Yeah.

Lincoln: Bullshit.

Booth: I put my foot down—and she *melted.* And she was—huh—she was something else. I dont wanna get you jealous, though.

Lincoln: Go head, I dont mind.

Booth: (*Rest*)

Well, you know what she looks like.

Lincoln: She walks on by and the emergency room fills up cause all the guys get whiplash from lookin at her.

Booth: Thats right thats right. Well—she comes to the door wearing nothing but her little nightie, eats up the food I'd brought like there was no tomorrow and then goes and eats on me. (*Rest*)

Lincoln: Go on.

Booth: I dont wanna make you feel bad, man.

Lincoln: Ssallright. Go on.

Booth (*Rest*)

Well, uh, you know what shes like. Wild. Goodlooking. So sweet my teeth hurt.

Lincoln Sexmachine.

Booth Yeah.

Lincoln: Hotsy-Totsy.

Booth Yeah.

Lincoln: Amazing Grace.

Booth: Amazing Grace! Yeah. Thats right. She let me do her how I wanted. And no rubber.

(*Rest*)

LincolnGo on.

Booth: You dont wanna hear the mushy shit

Lincoln: Sure I do.

Booth: You hate mushy shit. You always hated thuh mushy shit.

Lincoln: Ive changed. Go head. You had "an evening to remember," remember? I was just here alone sitting here. Drinking. Go head. Tell Link thuh stink.

(*Rest*)

Howd ya do her?

Booth: Dogstyle.

Lincoln: Amazing Grace.

Booth: In front of a mirror.

Lincoln: So you could see her. Her face her breasts her back her ass. Graces got a great ass.

Booth: Its all right.

Lincoln: Amazing Grace!

> Booth goes into his bed area and takes off his suit,
> tossing the clothes on the floor.

Booth: She said next time Ima have to use a rubber. She let me have my way this time but she said that next time I'd have to put my boots on.

Lincoln: Im sure you can talk her out of it.

Booth: Yeah.

(*Rest*)

What kind of rubbers you use, I mean, when you was with Cookie.

Lincoln: We didnt use rubbers. We was married, man.

Booth: Right. But you had other women on the side. What kind you use when you was with them?

Lincoln: Magnums.

Booth: Thats thuh kind I picked up. For next time. Grace was real strict about it.

> While Booth sits on his bed fiddling with his
> box of condoms, Lincoln sits in his chair
> and resumes drinking.

Lincoln: Im sure you can talk her out of it. You put yr foot down and she'll melt.

Booth: She was real strict. Sides I wouldnt wanna be taking advantage of her or nothing. Putting my foot down and her melting all over thuh place.

Lincoln: Magnums then.

(*Rest*)

Theyre for "the larger man."

Booth: Right. Right.

> Lincoln keeps drinking as Booth, sitting in the privacy
> of his bedroom, fiddles with the condoms,
> perhaps trying to put one on.

Lincoln: Thats right.

Booth: Graces real different from them fly-by-night gals I was making do with. Shes in school. Making something of herself. Studying cosmetology. You should see what she can do with a womans hair and nails.

Lincoln: Too bad you aint a woman.

Booth: What?

Lincoln: You could get yrs done for free, I mean.

Booth: Yeah. She got this way of sitting. Of talking. Everything she does is. Shes just so hot.

(*Rest*)

We was together 2 years. Then we broke up. I had my little employment difficulty and she needed time to think.

Lincoln: And shes through thinking now.

Booth: Thats right.

Lincoln

Booth

Lincoln: Whatcha doing back there?

Booth: Resting. That girl wore me out.

Lincoln: You want some med-sin?

Booth: No thanks.

Lincoln: Come practice my moves with me, then.

Booth: Lets hit it tomorrow, K?

Lincoln: I been waiting. I got all dressed up and you said if I waited up—come on, man, they gonna replace me with a wax dummy.

Booth: No shit.

Lincoln: Thats what theyre talking about. Probably just talk, but— come on, man, I even lent you 5 bucks.

Booth: Im tired.

Lincoln: You didnt get shit tonight.

Booth: You jealous, man. You just jail-us.

Lincoln: You laying over there yr balls blue as my boosted suit. Laying over there waiting for me to go back to sleep or black out so I wont hear you rustling thuh pages of yr fuck book.

Booth: Fuck you, man.

Lincoln: I was over there looking for something the other week and theres like 100 fuck books under yr bed and theyre matted together like a bad fro, bro, cause you spunked in the pages and didnt wipe them off.

Booth: Im hot. I need constant sexual release. If I wasnt taking care of myself by myself I would be out there running around on thuh town which costs cash that I dont have so I would be doing worse: I'd be out there doing who knows what, shooting people and shit. Out of a need for unresolved sexual release. I'm a hot man. I aint apologizing for it. When I dont got a woman, I gotta make do. Not like you, Link. When you dont got a woman you just sit there. Letting yr shit fester. Yr dick, if it aint falled off yet, is hanging there between yr legs, little whiteface shriveled-up blank-shooting grub worm. As goes thuh man so goes thuh mans dick. Thats what I say. Least my shits intact.
(*Rest*)
You a limp dick jealous whiteface motherfucker whose wife dumped him cause he couldnt get it up and she told me so. Came crawling to me cause she needed a man.
(*Rest*)
I gave it to Grace good tonight. So goodnight.

Lincoln(*Rest*)
Goodnight

Lincoln

Booth

Lincoln

Booth

Lincoln

Booth

> Lincoln sitting in his chair. Booth lying in bed.
> Time passes.
> Booth peeks out to see if Lincoln is asleep.
> Lincoln is watching for him.

Lincoln: You can hustle 3-card monte without me you know.

Booth: Im planning to.

Lincoln: I could contact my old crew. You could work with them. Lonny aint around no more but theres the rest of them. Theyre good.

Booth: I can get my own crew. I dont need yr crew. Buncha has-beens. I can get my own crew.

Lincoln: My crews experienced. We usedta pull down a thousand a day. Thats 7 G a week. That was years ago. They probably do twice, 3 times that now.

Booth: I got my own connections, thank you.

Lincoln: Theyd take you on in a heartbeat. With my say. My say still counts with them. They know you from before, when you tried to hang with us but—wernt ready yet. They know you from then, but I'd talk you up. I'd say yr my bro, which they know, and I'd say youd been working the west coast. Little towns. Mexican border. Taking tourists. I'd tell them you got moves like I dreamed of having. Meanwhile youd be working out yr shit right here, right in this room, getting good and getting better every day so when I did do the reintroductions youd have some marketable skills. Youd be passable.

Booth: I'd be more than passable, I'd be the be all end all.

Lincoln: Youd be the be all end all. And youd have my say. If yr interested.

Booth: Could do.

Lincoln: Youd have to get a piece. They all pack pistols, bro.

Booth: I *got* a piece.

Lincoln: Youd have to be packing something more substantial than that pop gun, 3-Card. These hustlers is upper echelon hustlers they pack upper echelon heat, not no Saturday night shit, now.

Booth: Whata you know of heat? You aint hung with those guys for 6, 7 years. You swore off em. Threw yr heat in thuh river and you "Dont touch thuh cards." I know more about heat than you know about heat.

Lincoln: Im around guns every day. At the arcade. Theyve all been reworked so they only fire caps but I see guns every day. Lots of guns.

Booth: What kinds?

Lincoln: You been there, you seen them. Shiny deadly metal each with their own deadly personality.

Booth: Maybe I *could* visit you over there. I'd boost one of them guns and rework it to make it shoot for real again. What kind you think would best suit my personality?

Lincoln: You aint stealing nothing from the arcade.

Booth: I go in there and steal if I want to go in there and steal I go in there and steal.

Lincoln: It aint worth it. They dont shoot nothing but blanks.

Booth: Yeah, like you. Shooting blanks.

(*Rest*)

(*Rest*)

You ever wonder if someones gonna come in there with a real gun? A real gun with real slugs? Someone with uh axe tuh grind or something?

Lincoln: No.

Booth: Someone who hates you come in there and guns you down and gets gone before anybody finds out.

Lincoln: I dont got no enemies.

Booth: Yr X.

Lincoln: Cookie dont hate me.

Booth: Yr Best Customer? Some miscellaneous stranger?

Lincoln: I cant be worrying about the actions of miscellaneous strangers.

Booth: But there they come day in day out for a chance to shoot Honest Abe.

(*Rest*)

Who are they mostly?

Lincoln: I dont really look.

Booth: You must see something.

Lincoln: Im supposed to be staring straight ahead. Watching a play, like Abe was.

Booth: All day goes by and you never ever take a sneak peek at who be pulling the trigger.

> Pulled in by his own curiosity, Booth has come out
> of his bed area to stand on the dividing line
> between the two spaces.

Lincoln: Its pretty dark. To keep thuh illusion of thuh whole thing.

(*Rest*)

But on thuh wall opposite where I sit theres a little electrical box, like a fuse box. Silver metal. Its got uh dent in it like somebody hit it with they fist. Big old dent so everything reflected in it gets reflected upside down. Like yr looking in uh spoon. And thats where I can see em. The assassins.

(*Rest*)

Not behind me yet but I can hear him coming. Coming in with his gun in hand, thuh gun he already picked out up front when he paid his fare. Coming on in. But not behind me yet. His dress shoes making too much noise on the carpet, the carpets too thin, Boss should get a new one but hes cheap. Not behind me yet. Not behind me yet. Cheap lightbulb just above my head.

(*Rest*)

And there he is. Standing behind me. Standing in position. Standing upside down. Theres some feet shapes on the floor so he knows just where he oughta stand. So he wont miss. Thuh gun is always cold. Winter or summer thuh gun is always cold. And when the gun touches me he can feel that Im warm and he knows Im alive. And if

Im alive then he can shoot me dead. And for a minute, with him hanging back there behind me, its real. Me looking at him upside down and him looking at me looking like Lincoln. Then he shoots.

(*Rest*)

I slump down and close my eyes. And he goes out thuh other way. More come in. Uh whole day full. Bunches of kids, little good for nothings, in they school uniforms. Businessmen smelling like two for one martinis. Tourists in they theme park t-shirts trying to catch it on film. Housewives with they mouths closed tight, shooting more than once.

(*Rest*)

They all get so into it. I do my best for them. And now they talking about replacing me with uh wax dummy. Itll cut costs.

Booth: You just gotta show yr boss that you can do things a wax dummy cant do. You too dry with it. You gotta add spicy shit.

Lincoln: Like what.

Booth: Like when they shoot you, I dunno, scream or something.

Lincoln: Scream?

> Booth plays the killer without using his gun.

Booth: Try it. I'll be the killer. Bang!

Lincoln: Aaaah!

Booth: Thats good.

Lincoln: A wax dummy can scream. They can put a voicebox in it and make it like its screaming.

Booth: You can curse. Try it. Bang!

Lincoln: Motherfucking cocksucker!

Booth: Thats good, man.

Lincoln: They aint going for that, though.

Booth: You practice rolling and wiggling on the floor?

Lincoln: A little.

Booth: Lemmie see. Bang!

> Lincoln slumps down, falls on the floor
> and silently wiggles around.

Booth: You look more like a worm on the sidewalk. Move yr arms. Good, Now scream or something.

Lincoln: Aaaah! Aaaaah! Aaaah!

Booth: A little tougher than that, you sound like yr fucking.

Lincoln: Aaaaaah!

Booth: Hold yr head or something, where I shotcha. Good. And look at me! I am the assassin! *I am Booth!!* Come on man this is life and death! Go all out!

Lincoln goes all out.

Booth: Cool, man thats cool. Thats enough.

Lincoln Whatdoyathink?

Booth: I dunno, man. Something about it. I dunno. It was looking too real or something.

Lincoln: They dont want it looking too real. I'd scare the customers. Then I'd be out for sure. Yr trying to get me fired.

Booth: Im trying to help. Cross my heart.

Lincoln: People are funny about they Lincoln shit. Its historical. People like they historical shit in a certain way. They like it to unfold the way they folded it up. Neatly like a book. Not raggedy and bloody and screaming. You trying to get me fired.
(Rest)
I am uh brother playing Lincoln. Its uh stretch for anyones imagination. And it aint easy for me neither. Every day I put on that shit, I leave my own shit at the door and I put on that shit and I go out there and I make it work. I make it look easy but its hard. That shit is hard. But it works. Cause I work it. And you trying to get me fired.
(Rest)
I swore off them cards. Took nowhere jobs. Drank. Then Cookie threw me out. What thuh fuck was I gonna do? I seen that "Help Wanted" sign and I went up in there and I looked good in the getup and agreed to the whiteface and they really dug it that me and Honest Abe got the same name.
(Rest)
Its a sit down job. With benefits. I dont wanna get fired. They wont give me a good reference if I get fired.

Booth: Iffen you was tuh get fired, then, well—then you and me could—hustle the cards together. We'd have to support ourselves somehow.
(Rest)
Just show me how to do the hook part of the card hustle, man. The part where the Dealer looks away but somehow he sees—

Lincoln: I couldnt remember if I wanted to.

Booth: Sure you could.

Lincoln: No.
(*Rest*)
Night, man.
Booth: Yeah.

> Lincoln stretches out in his recliner.
> Booth stands over him waiting for him to get up,
> to change his mind. But Lincoln is fast asleep.
> Booth covers him with a blanket then goes to his bed,
> turning off the lights as he goes. He quietly rummages
> underneath his bed for a girlie magazine which,
> as the lights fade, he reads with great interest.

SCENE FOUR

> Saturday.
> Just before dawn.
> Lincoln gets up. Looks around.
> Booth is fast asleep, dead to the world.

Lincoln: No fucking running water.

> He stumbles around the room looking for something
> which he finally finds: a plastic cup, which he uses as a urinal.
> He finishes peeing and finds an out of the way place
> to stow the cup. He claws at his Lincoln getup,
> removing it and tearing it in the process.
> He strips down to his t-shirt and shorts.

Lincoln: Hate falling asleep in this damn shit. Shit. Ripped the beard. I can just hear em tomorrow. Busiest day of the week. They looking me over to make sure Im presentable. They got a slew of guys working but Im the only one they look over every day. "Yr beards ripped, pal. Sure, well getcha new one but its gonna be coming outa yr pay." Shit. I should quit right then and there. I'd yank off the beard, throw it on the ground and stomp it, then go strangle the fucking boss. Thatd be good. My hands around his neck and his bug eyes bugging out. You been ripping me off since I took this job and now Im gonna have to take it outa *yr* pay, motherfucker. Shit.
(*Rest*)

Sit down job. With benefits.

(*Rest*)

Hustling. Shit, I was good. I was great. Hell I was the be all end all. I was throwing cards like throwing cards was made for me. Made for me and me alone. I was the best anyone ever seen. Coast to coast. Everybody said so. And I never lost. Not once. Not one time. Not never. Thats how much them cards was mines. I was the be all end all. I was that good.

(*Rest*)

Then you woke up one day and you didnt have the taste for it no more. Like something in you knew—. Like something in you knew it was time to quit. Quit while you was still ahead. Something in you was telling you—. But hells no. Not Link thuh stink. So I went out there and threw one more time. What thuh fuck. And Lonny died.

(*Rest*)

Got yrself a good job. And when the arcade lets you go yll get another good job. I dont gotta spend my whole life hustling. Theres more to Link than that. More to me than some cheap hustle. More to life than cheating some idiot out of his paycheck or his life savings.

(*Rest*)

Like that joker and his wife from out of town. Always wanted to see the big city. I said you could see the bigger end of the big city with a little more cash. And if they was fast enough, faster than me, and here I slowed down my moves I slowed em way down and my Lonny, my right hand, my Stickman, spanish guy who looked white and could draw a customer in like nothing else, Lonny could draw a fly from fresh shit, he could draw Adam outa Eve just with that look he had, Lonny always got folks playing.

(*Rest*)

Somebody shot him. They dont know who. Nobody knows nobody cares.

(*Rest*)

We took that man and his wife for hundreds. No, thousands. We took them for everything they had and everything they ever wanted to have. We took a father for the money he was gonna get his kids new bike with and he cried in the street while we vanished. We took a mothers welfare check, she pulled a knife on us and we ran. She threw it but her aim werent shit. People shopping. Greedy. Thinking they could take me and they got took instead.

(*Rest*)

Swore off thuh cards. Something inside me telling me—.

But I was good.

Lincoln

Lincoln

He sees a packet of cards.
He studies them like an alcoholic would study a drink.
Then he reaches for them, delicately picking them up
and choosing 3 cards.

Lincoln: Still got my moves. Still got my touch. Still got my chops. Thuh feel of it. And I aint hurting no one, God. Link is just here hustling hisself.
(*Rest*)
Lets see whatcha got.

He stands over the monte setup. Then he bends over it
placing the cards down and moving them around.
Slowly at first, aimlessly,
as if hes just making little ripples in water.
But then the game draws him in.
Unlike Booth, Lincolns patter and moves are
deft, dangerous, electric.

Lincoln: ((((Lean in close and watch me now: who see thuh black card who see thuh black card I see thuh black card black cards thuh winner pick thuh black card thats thuh winner pick thuh red card thats thuh loser pick thuh other red card thats thuh other loser pick thuh black card you pick thuh winner. Watch me as I throw thuh cards. Here we go.)))
(*Rest*)
(((Who see thuh black card who see thuh black card? You pick thuh red card you pick a loser you pick that red card you pick a loser you pick thuh black card thuh deuce of spades you pick a winner who sees thuh deuce of spades thuh one who sees it never fades watch me now as I throw thuh cards. Red losers black winner follow thuh deuce of spades chase thuh black deuce. Dark deuce will get you thuh win.)))

Even though Lincoln speaks softly, Booth wakes and,
unbeknownst to Lincoln, listens intently.

(*Rest*)
Lincoln: ((10 will get you 20, 20 will get you 40.))
(*Rest*)

((Ima show you thuh cards: 2 red cards but only one spade. Dark winner in thuh center and thuh red losers on thuh sides. Pick uh red card you got a loser pick thuh other red card you got a loser pick thuh black card you got a winner. One good pickll get you in, 2 good picks and you gone win. Watch me come on watch me now.))

(*Rest*)

((Who sees thuh winner who knows where its at? You do? You sure? Go on then, put yr money where yr mouth is. Put yr money down you aint no clown. No? Ah, you had thuh card but you didnt have thuh heart.))

(*Rest*)

((Watch me now as I throw thuh cards watch me real close. Ok, man, you know which card is the deuce of spades? Was you watching Links lighting fast express? Was you watching Link cause he the best? So you sure, huh? Point it out first, then place yr bet and Linkll show you yr winner.))

(*Rest*)

((500 dollars? You thuh man of thuh hour you thuh man with thuh power. You musta been watching Link real close. You must be thuh man who know thuh most. Ok. Lay the cash in my hand cause Link the man. Thank you, mister. This card you say?))

(*Rest*)

((Wrong! Ha!))

(*Rest*)

((Thats thuh show. We gotta go.))

> Lincoln puts the cards down.
> He moves away from the monte setup.
> He sits on the edge of his easy chair,
> but he can't take his eyes off the cards.

> Intermission

SCENE FIVE

> Several days have passed.
> Its now Wednesday night.
> Booth is sitting in his brand-new suit.
> The monte setup is nowhere in sight.
> In its place is a table with two nice chairs.
> The table is covered with a lovely tablecloth
> and there are nice plates, silverware,

champagne glasses and candles.
All the makings of a very romantic dinner for two.
The whole apartment in fact takes its cue from the table.
Its been cleaned up considerably.
New curtains on the windows,
a doily-like object on the recliner.
Booth sits at the table darting his eyes around,
making sure everything is looking good.

Booth: Shit.

He notices some of his girlie magazines visible from
underneath his bed. He goes over and
nudges them out of sight. He sits back down.
He notices that theyre still visible. He goes over and nudges
them some more, kicking at them finally. Then he takes the
spread from his bed and pulls it down, hiding them.
He sits back down. He gets up.
Checks the champagne on much melted ice.
Checks the food.

Booth: Foods getting cold, Grace!! Dont worry man, she'll get here, she'll get here.

He sits back down.
He goes over to the bed. Checks it for springiness.
Smoothes down the bedspread. Double-checks 2 matching
silk dressing gowns, very expensive, marked "His" and "Hers."
Lays the dressing gowns across the bed again.
He sits back down. He cant help but notice the visibility of
the girlie magazines again. He goes to the bed,
kicks them fiercely; then on his hands and
knees shoves them. Then he begins to get under the bed
to push them, but he remembers his nice clothing
and takes off his jacket. After a beat
he removes his pants and, in this half-dressed way,
he crawls under the bed to give those telltale
magazines a good and final shove.
Lincoln comes in.

At first Booth, still stripped down to his underwear, thinks its his date. When he realizes its his brother, he does his best to keep Lincoln from entering the apartment. Lincoln wears his frock coat and carries the rest of his getup in a plastic bag.

Lincoln: You in the middle of it?

Booth: What the hell you doing here?

Lincoln: If yr in thuh middle of it I can go. Or I can just be real quiet and just—sing a song in my head or something.

Booth: The casas off limits to you tonight.

Lincoln: You know when we lived in that 2-room place with the cement backyard and the frontyard with nothing but trash in it, Mom and Pops would do it in the middle of the night and I would always hear them but I would sing in my head, cause, I dunno, I couldnt bear to listen.

Booth: You gotta get out of here.

Lincoln: I would make up all kinds of songs. Oh, sorry, yr all up in it. No sweat, bro. No sweat. Hey, Grace, howyadoing?!

Booth: She aint here yet, man. Shes running late. And its a good thing too cause I aint all dressed yet. Yr gonna spend thuh night with friends?

Lincoln: Yeah.

Booth waits for Lincoln to leave. Lincoln stands his ground.

Lincoln: I lost my job.

Booth Hunh.

Lincoln: I come in there right on time like I do every day and that motherfucker gives me some song and dance about cutbacks and too many folks complaining.

Booth: Hunh.

Lincoln: Showd me thuh wax dummy—hes buying it right out of a catalog.

(*Rest*)

I walked out still wearing my getup.

(*Rest*)

I could go back in tomorrow. I could tell him I'll take another pay cut. Thatll get him to take me back

Booth: Link. Yr free. Dont go crawling back. Yr free at last! Now you can do anything you want. Yr not tied down by that job. You can—you can do something else. Something that pays better maybe.

Lincoln: You mean Hustle.

Booth: Maybe. Hey, Graces on her way. You gotta go.

Lincoln flops into his chair.
Booth is waiting for him to move. Lincoln doesnt budge.

Lincoln: I'll stay until she gets here. I'll act nice. I wont embarrass you.

Booth: You gotta go.

Lincoln: What time she coming?

Booth: Shes late. She could be here any second.

Lincoln: I'll meet her. I met her years ago. I'll meet her again.

(*Rest*)

How late is she?

Booth: She was supposed to be here at 8.

Lincoln: Its after 2 a.m. Shes—shes late.

(*Rest*)

Maybe when she comes you could put the blanket over me and I'll just pretend like Im not here.

(*Rest*)

I'll wait. And when she comes I'll go. I need to sit down. I been walking around all day.

Booth

Lincoln

Booth goes to his bed and dresses hurriedly.

Booth: Pretty nice, right? The china thuh silver thuh crystal.

Lincoln: Its great.

(*Rest*)

Boosted?

Booth Yeah.

Lincoln: Thought you went and spent yr inheritance for a minute, you had me going I was thinking shit, Booth—3-Card—that 3-Cards gone and spent his inheritance and the gal is—late.

Booth: Its boosted. Every bit of it.

(*Rest*)

Fuck this waiting bullshit.

Lincoln: She'll be here in a minute. Dont sweat it.

Booth Right.

Booth comes to the table. Sits. Relaxes as best he can.

Booth: How come I got a hand for boosting and I dont got a hand for throwing cards? Its sorta the same thing—you gotta be quick—and slick. Maybe yll show me yr moves sometime.

Lincoln

Booth

Lincoln

Booth

Lincoln: Look out the window. When you see Grace coming. I'll go.

Booth: Cool. Cause youd jinx it, youd really jinx it. Maybe you being here has jinxed it already. Naw. Shes just a little late. You aint jinxed nothing.

Booth sits by the window,
glancing out, watching for his date.
Lincoln sits in his recliner. He finds the whiskey bottle,
sips from it. He then rummages around,
finding the raggedy photo album.
He looks through it.

Lincoln: There we are at that house. Remember when we moved in?

Booth: No.

Lincoln: You were 2 or 3.

Booth: I was 5.

Lincoln: I was 8. We all thought it was the best fucking house in the world.

Booth: Cement backyard and a frontyard full of trash, yeah, dont be going down memory lane man, yll jinx thuh vibe I got going in here. Gracell be walking in here and wrinkling up her nose cause you done jinxed up thuh joint with yr raggedy recollections.

Lincoln: We had some great times in that house, bro. Selling lemonade on thuh corner, thuh treehouse out back, summers spent lying in thuh grass and looking at thuh stars.

Booth: We never did none of that shit.

Lincoln: But we had us some good times. That row of nails I got you to line up behind Dads car so when he backed out the driveway to work—

Booth: He came back that night, only time I ever seen his face go red, 4 flat tires and yelling bout how thuh white man done sabotaged him again.

Lincoln: And neither of us flinched. Neither of us let on that itd been us.

Booth: It was at dinner, right? What were we eating?

Lincoln Food.

Booth: We was eating pork chops, mashed potatoes and peas. I remember cause I had to look at them peas real hard to keep from letting on. And I would glance over at you, not really glancing not actually turning my head, but I was looking at you out thuh corner of my eye. I was sure he was gonna find us out and then he woulda whipped us good. But I kept glancing at you and you was cool, man. Like nothing was going on. You was cooooool.

(*Rest*)

What time is it?

Lincoln: After 3.

(*Rest*)

You should call her. Something mighta happened.

Booth: No man, Im cool. Shell be here in a minute. Patience is a virtue. She'll be here.

Lincoln: You look sad.

Booth: Nope. Im just, you know, Im just—

Lincoln: Cool.

Booth: Yeah. Cool.

> Booth comes over, takes the bottle of whiskey and
> pours himself a big glassful. He returns to the
> window looking out and drinking.

Booth: They give you a severance package, at thuh job?

Lincoln: A weeks pay.

Booth: Great.

Lincoln: I blew it. Spent it all.

Booth: On what?

Lincoln: —. Just spent it.

(*Rest*)

It felt good, spending it. Felt really good. Like back in thuh day when I was really making money. Throwing thuh cards all day and strutting and rutting all night. Didnt have to take no shit from no fool, didnt have to worry about getting fired in favor of some damn wax dummy. I was thuh shit and they was my fools.

(*Rest*)

Back in thuh day.

(*Rest*)

(*Rest*)

Why you think they left us, man?

Booth: Mom and Pops? I dont think about it too much.

Lincoln: I dont think they liked us.

Booth: Naw. That aint it.

Lincoln: I think there was something out there that they liked more than they liked us and for years they was struggling against moving towards that more liked something. Each of them had a special something that they was struggling against. Moms had hers. Pops had his. And they was struggling. We moved out of that nasty apartment into a house. A whole house. It wernt perfect but it was a house and theyd bought it and they brought us there and everything we owned, figuring we could be a family in that house and them things, them two separate things each of them was struggling against, would just leave them be. Them things would see thuh house and be impressed and just leave them be. Would see thuh job Pops had and how he shined his shoes every night before he went to bed, shining them shoes whether they needed it or not, and thuh thing he was struggling against would see all that and just let him be, and thuh thing Moms was struggling against, it would see the food on the table every night and listen to her voice when she'd read to us sometimes, the clean clothes, the buttons sewed on all right and it would just let her be. Just let us all be, just regular people living in a house. That wernt too much to ask.

Booth: Least we was grown when they split.

Lincoln: 16 and 13 aint grown.

Booth: 16s grown. Almost. And I was ok cause you were there.

(*Rest*)

Shit man, it aint like they both one day both, together packed all they shit up and left us so they could have fun in thuh sun on some tropical island and you and me would have to grub in thuh dirt forever. They didnt leave together. That makes it different. She left. 2 years go by. Then he left. Like neither of them couldnt handle it no more. She split then he split. Like thuh whole family mortgage bills going to work thing was just too much. And I dont blame them. You dont see me holding down a steady job. Cause its bullshit and I know it. I seen how it cracked them up and I aint going there.

(*Rest*)

It aint right me trying to make myself into a one woman man just because she wants me like that. One woman rubber-wearing motherfucker. Shit. Not me. She gonna walk in here looking all hot and shit trying to see how much she can get me to sweat, how much she can get me to give her before she gives me mines. Shit.

Lincoln

Booth

Lincoln: Moms told me I shouldnt never get married.

Booth: She told me thuh same thing.

Lincoln: They gave us each 500 bucks then they cut out.

Booth: Thats what Im gonna do. Give my kids 500 bucks then cut out. Thats thuh way to do it.

Lincoln: You dont got no kids.

Booth: Im gonna have kids then Im gonna cut out.

Lincoln: Leaving each of yr offspring 500 bucks as yr splitting.

Booth: Yeah.

(*Rest*)

Just goes to show Mom and Pops had some agreement between them.

Lincoln: How so.

Booth: Theyd stopped talking to eachother. Theyd stopped *screwing* eachother. But they had an agreement. Somewhere in there when it looked like all they had was hate they sat down and did thuh "split" budget.

(*Rest*)

When Moms splits she gives me 5 hundred-dollar bills rolled up and tied up tight in one of her nylon stockings. She tells me to put it in a safe place, to spend it only in case of an emergency, and not to tell nobody I got it, not even you. 2 years later Pops splits and before he goes—

Lincoln: He slips me 10 fifties in a clean handkerchief: "Hide this somewheres good, dont go blowing it, dont tell no one you got it, especially that Booth."

Booth: Theyd been scheming together all along. They left separately but they was in agreement. Maybe they arrived at the same place at the same time, maybe they renewed they wedding vows, maybe they got another family.

Lincoln: Maybe they got 2 new kids. 2 boys. Different than us, though. Better.

Booth Maybe.

> Their glasses are empty. The whiskey bottle is empty too.
> Booth takes the champagne bottle from the ice tub.
> He pops the cork and pours drinks for
> his brother and himself.

Booth: I didnt mind them leaving cause you was there. Thats why Im hooked on us working together. If we could work together it would be like old times. They split and we got that room downtown. You was done with school and I stopped going. And we had to run around doing odd jobs just to keep the lights on and the heat going and thuh child protection bitch off our backs. It was you and me against thuh world, Link. It could be like that again.

Lincoln

Booth

Lincoln

Booth

Lincoln: Throwing thuh cards aint as easy as it looks.

Booth: I aint stupid.

Lincoln: When you hung with us back then, you was just on thuh sidelines. Thuh perspective from thuh sidelines is thuh perspective of a customer. There was all kinds of things you didnt know nothing about.

Booth: Lonny would entice folks into thuh game as they walked by. Thuh 2 folks on either side of ya looked like they was playing but they was only pretending tuh play. Just tuh generate excitement. You was moving thuh cards as fast as you could hoping that yr hands would be faster than yr customers eyes. Sometimes you won sometimes you lost what else is there to know?

Lincoln: Thuh customer is actually called the "Mark." You know why?

Booth: Cause hes thuh one you got yr eye on. You mark him with yr eye.

Lincoln

Lincoln

Booth: Im right, right?

Lincoln: Lemmie show you a few moves. If you pick up these yll have a chance.

Booth: Yr playing.

Lincoln: Get thuh cards and set it up.

Booth: No shit.

Lincoln: Set it up set it up.

> In a flash, Booth clears away the romantic table setting
> by gathering it all up in the tablecloth and tossing it aside.
> As he does so he reveals the "table" underneath:
> the 2 stacked monte milk crates
> and the cardboard playing surface.
> Lincoln lays out the cards. The brothers are ready.
> Lincoln begins to teach Booth in earnest.

Lincoln: Thuh deuce of spades is thuh card tuh watch.

Booth: I work with thuh deuce of hearts. But spades is cool.

Lincoln: Theres thuh Dealer, thuh Stickman, thuh Sides, thuh Lookout and thuh Mark. I'll be thuh Dealer.

Booth: I'll be thuh Lookout. Lemmie be thuh Lookout, right? I'll keep an eye for thuh cops. I got my piece on me.

Lincoln: You got it on you right now?

Booth: I always carry it.

Lincoln: Even on a date? In yr own home?

Booth: You never know, man.

(*Rest*)

So Im thuh Lookout.

Lincoln: Gimmie yr piece.

> Booth gives Lincoln his gun. Lincoln moves
> the little wooden chair to face right in front of the setup.
> He then puts the gun on the chair.

Lincoln: We dont need nobody standing on the corner watching for cops cause there aint none.

Booth: I'll be thuh Stickman, then.

Lincoln: Stickman knows the game inside out. You aint there yet. But you will be. You wanna learn good, be my Sideman. Playing along with the Dealer, moving the Mark to lay his money down. You wanna learn, right?

Booth: I'll be thuh Side.

Lincoln: Good.

(*Rest*)

First thing you learn is what is. Next thing you learn is what aint. You dont know what is you dont know what aint, you dont know shit.

Booth: Right.

Lincoln

Booth

Booth: Whatchu looking at?

Lincoln: Im sizing you up.

Booth: Oh yeah?!

Lincoln: Dealer always sizes up thuh crowd.

Booth: Im yr Side, Link, Im on yr team, you dont go sizing up yr own team. You save looks like that for yr Mark.

Lincoln: Dealer always sizes up thuh crowd. Everybody out there is part of the crowd. His crew is part of the crowd, he himself is part of the crowd. Dealer always sizes up thuh crowd.

> Lincoln looks Booth over some more then
> looks around at an imaginary crowd.

Booth: Then what then what?
Lincoln: Dealer dont wanna play.
Booth: Bullshit man! Come on you promised!
Lincoln: Thats thuh Dealers attitude. He *acts* like he dont wanna play. He holds back and thuh crowd, with their eagerness to see his skill and their willingness to take a chance, and their greediness to win his cash, the larceny in their hearts, all goad him on and push him to throw his cards, although of course the Dealer has been wanting to throw his cards all along. Only he dont never show it.
Booth: Thats some sneaky shit, Link.
Lincoln: It sets thuh mood. You wanna have them in yr hand before you deal a hand, K?
Booth: Cool.— K.
Lincoln: Right.
Lincoln
Booth
Booth: You sizing me up again?
Lincoln: Theres 2 parts to throwing thuh cards. Both parts are fairly complicated. Thuh moves and thuh grooves, thuh talk and thuh walk, thuh patter and thuh pitter pat, thuh flap and thuh rap: what yr doing with yr mouth and what yr doing with yr hands.
Booth: I got thuh words down pretty good.
Lincoln: You need to work on both.
Booth: K.
Lincoln: A goodlooking walk and a dynamite talk captivates their entire attention. The Mark focuses with 2 organs primarily: his eyes and his ears. Leave one out you lose yr shirt. Captivate both, yr golden.
Booth: So them times I seen you lose, them times I seen thuh Mark best you, that was a time when yr hands werent fast enough or yr patter werent right.
Lincoln: You could say that.
Booth: So, there was plenty of times—

> Lincoln moves the cards around.

Lincoln: You see what Im doing? Dont look at my hands, man, look at my eyes. Know what is and know what aint.

Booth: What is?

Lincoln: My eyes.

Booth: What aint?

Lincoln: My hands. Look at my eyes not my hands. And you standing there thinking how thuh fuck I gonna learn how tuh throw thuh cards if I be looking in his eyes? Look into my eyes and get yr focus. Dont think about learning how tuh throw thuh cards. Dont think about nothing. Just look into my eyes. Focus.

Booth: Theyre red.

Lincoln: Look into my eyes.

Booth: You been crying?

Lincoln: Just look into my eyes, fool. Now. Look down at thuh cards. I been moving and moving and moving them around. Ready?

Booth: Yeah.

Lincoln: Ok, Sideman, thuh Marks got his eye on you. Yr gonna show him its easy.

Booth: K.

Lincoln: Pick out thuh deuce of spades. Dont pick it up just point to it.

Booth: This one, right?

Lincoln: Dont ask thuh Dealer if yr right, man, point to yr card with confidence.

> Booth points.

Booth: That one.
(*Rest*)
Flip it over, man.

> Lincoln flips over the card. It is in fact
> the deuce of spades. Booth struts around gloating
> like a rooster. Lincoln is mildly crestfallen.

Booth: Am I right or am I right?! Make room for 3-Card! Here comes thuh champ!

Lincoln: Cool. Stay focused. Now we gonna add the second element. Listen.

> Lincoln moves the cards and
> speaks in a low hypnotic voice.

Lincoln: Lean in close and watch me now: who see thuh black card who see thuh black card I see thuh black card black cards thuh winner pick thuh black card thats thuh winner pick thuh red card thats thuh loser pick thuh other red card thats thuh other loser pick thuh black card you pick thuh winner. Watch me as I throw thuh cards. Here we go.
(*Rest*)
Who see thuh black card who see thuh black card? You pick thuh red card you pick a loser you pick that red card you pick a loser you pick thuh black card thuh deuce of spades you pick a winner who sees thuh deuce of spades thuh one who sees it never fades watch me now as I throw thuh cards. Red losers black winner follow thuh deuce of spades chase thuh black deuce. Dark deuce will get you thuh win. One good pickll get you in 2 good picks you gone win. 10 will get you 20, 20 will get you 40.
(*Rest*)
Ima show you thuh cards: 2 red cards but only one spade. Dark winner in thuh center and thuh red losers on thuh sides. Pick uh red card you got a loser pick thuh other red card you got a loser pick thuh black card you got a winner. Watch me watch me watch me now.
(*Rest*)
Ok, 3-Card, you know which cards thuh deuce of spades?
Booth: Yeah.
Lincoln: You sure? Yeah? You sure you sure or you just think you sure? Oh you sure you sure huh? Was you watching Links lighting fast express? Was you watching Link cause he the best? So you sure, huh? Point it out. Now, place yr bet and Linkll turn over yr card.
Booth: What should I bet?
Lincoln: Dont bet nothing man, we just playing. Slap me 5 and point out thuh deuce.

> Booth slaps Lincoln 5, then points out a card which Lincoln flips over. It is in fact again the deuce of spades.

Booth: Yeah, baby! 3-Card got thuh moves! You didnt know lil bro had thuh stuff, huh? Think again. Link, think again.
Lincoln: You wanna learn or you wanna run yr mouth?
Booth: Thought you had fast hands. Wassup? What happened tuh "Links Lightning Fast Express"? Turned into uh local train looks like tuh me.
Lincoln: Thats yr whole motherfucking problem. Yr so busy running yr mouth you aint never gonna learn nothing! You think you something but you aint shit.
Booth: I aint shit, I am *The* Shit. Shit. Wheres thuh dark deuce? Right there! Yes, baby!

Lincoln: Ok, 3-Card. Cool. Lets switch. Take thuh cards and show me whatcha got. Go on. Dont touch thuh cards too heavy just—its a light touch. Like yr touching Graces skin. Or, whatever, man, just a light touch. Like uh whisper.

Booth: Like uh whisper.

> Booth moves the cards around,
> in an awkward imitation of his brother.

Lincoln: Good.

Booth: Yeah. All right. Look into my eyes.

> Booths speech is loud and his movements are jerky.
> He is doing worse than when he threw
> the cards at the top of the play.

Booth: Watch-me-close-watch-me-close-now: who-see-thuh-dark-card-who-see-thuh- dark-card? I-see-thuh-dark-card. Here-it-is. Thuh-dark-card-is-thuh-winner. Pick-thuh-dark-card-and-you-pick-uh-winner. Pick-uh-red-card-and-you-pick-uh-loser. Theres-thuh-loser-yeah-theres-thuh-red-card, theres-thuh-other-loser-and-theres-thuh-black-card, thuh-winner. Watch-me-close-watch-me-close-now: 3-Card-throws-thuh-cards-lightning-fast. 3-Card-thats-me-and-Ima-last. Watch-me-throw-cause-here-I-go. See thuh black card? Yeah? Who see I see you see thuh black card?

Lincoln: Hahahahhahahahahahahah!

> Lincoln doubles over laughing.
> Booth puts on his coat and pockets his gun.

Booth What?

Lincoln: Nothing, man, nothing.

Booth *What?!*

Lincoln: Yr just, yr just a little wild with it. You talk like that on thuh street cards or no cards and theyll lock you up, man. Shit. Reminds me of that time when you hung with us and we let you try being thuh Stick cause you wanted to so bad. Thuh hustle was so simple. Remember? I told you that when I put my hand in my left pocket you was to get thuh Mark tuh pick thuh card on that side. You got to thinking something like Links left means my left some dyslexic shit and turned thuh wrong card. There was 800 bucks on the line and you fucked it up.

(*Rest*)

But it was cool, little bro, cause we made the money back. It worked out cool.
(*Rest*)
So, yeah, I said a light touch, little bro. Throw thuh cards light. Like uh whisper.
Booth: Like Graces skin.
Lincoln: Like Graces skin.
Booth: What time is it?

> Lincoln holds up his watch. Booth takes a look.

Booth: Bitch. *Bitch!* She said she was gonna show up around 8. 8-a-fucking-clock.
Lincoln: Maybe she meant 8 *a.m.*
Booth: Yeah. She gonna come all up in my place talking bout how she *love* me. How she cant stop *thinking* bout me. Nother mans shit up in her nother mans thing in her nother mans dick on her breath.
Lincoln: Maybe something happened to her.
Booth: Something happened to her all right. She trying to make a chump outa me. I aint her chump. I aint nobodys chump.
Lincoln: Sit. I'll go to the payphone on the corner. I'll—
Booth: Thuh world puts its foot in yr face and you dont move. You tell thuh world tuh keep on stepping. But Im my own man, Link. I aint you.

> Booth goes out, slamming the door behind him.

Lincoln: You got that right.

> After a moment Lincoln picks up the cards.
> He moves them around fast, faster, faster.

SCENE SIX

> Thursday night.
> The room looks empty, as if neither brother is home.
> Lincoln comes in.
> Hes fairly drunk. He strides in,
> leaving the door slightly ajar.

Lincoln: Taaadaaaa!

(*Rest*)
(*Rest*)
Taadaa, motherfucker. Taadaa!
(*Rest*)
Booth—uh, 3-Card—you here? Nope. Good. Just as well.
Ha Ha *Ha Ha Ha*!

> He pulls an enormous wad of money
> from his pocket. He counts it, slowly and luxuriously,
> arranging and smoothing the bills
> and sounding the amounts under his breath.
> He neatly rolls up the money, secures it with a rubber band
> and puts it back in his pocket. He relaxes in his chair.
> Then he takes the money out again, counting it
> all over again, but this time quickly,
> with the touch of an expert hustler.

Lincoln: You didnt go back, Link, you got back, you got it back you got yr shit back in thuh saddle, man, you got back in business. Walking in Luckys and you seen how they was looking at you? Lucky starts pouring for you when you walk in. And the women. You see how they was looking at you? Bought drinks for everybody. Bought drinks for Lucky. Bought drinks for Luckys damn dog. Shit. And thuh women be hanging on me and purring. And I be feeling that old call of thuh wild calling. I got more phone numbers in my pockets between thuh time I walked out that door and thuh time I walked back in than I got in my whole life. Cause my shit is *back*. And back better than It was when it left too. Shoot. Who thuh man? Link. Thats right. Purrrrring all up on me and letting me touch them and promise them shit. 3 of them sweethearts in thuh restroom on my dick all at once and I was *there* my shit was there. And Cookie just went out of my mind which is cool which is very cool. 3 of them. Fighting over it. Shit. Cause they knew I'd been throwing thuh cards. Theyd seen me on thuh corner with thuh old crew or if they aint seed me with they own eyes theyd heard word. Links thuh stink! Theyd heard word and they seed uh sad face on some poor sucker or a tear in thuh eye of some stupid fucking tourist and they figured it was me whod just took thuh suckers last dime, it was me who had all thuh suckers loot. They knew. They knew.

> Booth appears in the room. He was standing
> behind the screen, unseen all this time.
> He goes to the door, soundlessly, just stands there.

Lincoln: And they was all in Luckys. Shit. And they was waiting for me to come in from my last throw. Cant take too many fools in one day, its bad luck, Link, so they was all waiting in there for me to come in thuh door and let thuh liquor start flowing and thuh music start going and let thuh boys who dont have thuh balls to get nothing but a regular job and uh weekly paycheck, let them crowd around and get in somehow on thuh excitement, and make way for thuh ladies, so they can run they hands on my clothes and feel thuh magic and imagine thuh man, with plenty to go around, living and breathing underneath.

(*Rest*)

They all thought I was down and out! They all thought I was some NoCount HasBeen LostCause motherfucker. But I got my shit back. Thats right. They stepped on me and kept right on stepping. Not no more. Who thuh man?! Goddamnit, who thuh—

> Booth closes the door.

Lincoln
Booth
(*Rest*)
Lincoln: Another evening to remember, huh?
Booth: (*Rest*)
Uh—yeah, man, yeah. Thats right, thats right.
Lincoln: Had me a memorable evening myself.
Booth: I got news.
(*Rest*)
What you been up to?
Lincoln: Yr news first.
Booth: Its good.
Lincoln: Yeah?
Booth: Yeah.
Lincoln: Go head then.
Booth: (*Rest*)
Grace got down on her knees. Down on her knees, man. Asked *me* tuh marry *her*.
Lincoln: Shit.
Booth: Amazing Grace!
Lincoln: Lucky you, man.
Booth: And guess where she was, I mean, while I was here waiting for her. She was over at her house watching tv. I'd told her come over Thursday and I got it all wrong and

was thinking I said Wednesday and here I was sitting waiting my ass off and all she was doing was over at her house just watching tv.

Lincoln: Howboutthat.

Booth: She wants to get married right away. Shes tired of waiting. Feels her clock ticking and shit. Wants to have my baby. But dont look so glum man, we gonna have a boy and we gonna name it after you.

Lincoln: Thats great, man. Thats really great.

Booth

Lincoln

Booth: Whats yr news?

Lincoln: (*Rest*)

Nothing.

Booth: Mines good news, huh?

Lincoln: Yeah. Real good news, bro.

Booth: Bad news is—well, shes real set on us living together. And she always did like this place.

(*Rest*)

Yr gonna have to leave. Sorry.

Lincoln: No sweat.

Booth: This was only a temporary situation anyhow.

Lincoln: No sweat man. You got a new life opening up for you, no sweat. Graces moving in today? I can leave right now.

Booth: I dont mean to put you out.

Lincoln: No sweat. I'll just pack up.

> Lincoln rummages around finding a suitcase
> and begins to pack his things.

Booth: Just like that, huh? "No sweat"?! Yesterday you lost yr damn job. You dont got no cash. You dont got no friends, no nothing, but you clearing out just like that and its "no sweat"?!

Lincoln: Youve been real generous and you and Grace need me gone and its time I found my own place.

Booth: No sweat.

Lincoln: No sweat.

(*Rest*)

K. I'll spill it. I got another job, so getting my own place aint gonna be so bad.

Booth: You got a new job! Doing what?

Lincoln: Security guard.
Booth: (*Rest*)
Security guard Howaboutthat.

> Lincoln continues packing the few things he has.
> He picks up a whiskey bottle.

Booth: Go head, take thuh med-sin, bro. You gonna need it more than me. I got, you know, I got my love to keep me warm and shit.

Lincoln: You gonna have to get some kind of work, or are you gonna let Grace support you?
Booth: I got plans.
Lincoln: She might want you now but she wont want you for long if you dont get some kind of job. Shes a smart chick. And she cares about you. But she aint gonna let you treat her like some pack mule while shes out working her ass off and yr laying up in here scheming and dreaming to cover up thuh fact that you dont got no skills.
Booth: Grace is very cool with who I am and where Im at, thank you.
Lincoln: It was just some advice. But, hey, yr doing great just like yr doing.
Lincoln
Booth
Lincoln
Booth
Booth: When Pops left he didnt take nothing with him. I always thought that was fucked-up.
Lincoln: He was a drunk. Everything he did was always half regular and half fucked-up.
Booth: Whyd he leave his clothes though? Even drunks gotta wear clothes.
Lincoln: Whyd he leave his clothes whyd he leave us? He was uh drunk, bro. He— whatever, right? I mean, you aint gonna figure it out by thinking about it. Just call it one of thuh great unsolved mysteries of existence.
Booth: Moms had a man on thuh side.
Lincoln: Yeah? Pops had side shit going on too. More than one.
He would take me with him when he went to visit them. Yeah.
(*Rest*)
Sometimes he'd let me meet the ladies. They was all very nice. Very polite. Most of them real pretty. Sometimes he'd let me watch. Most of thuh time I was just outside

on thuh porch or in thuh lobby or in thuh car waiting for him but sometimes he'd let me watch.

Booth: What was it like?

Lincoln: Nothing. It wasnt like nothing. He made it seem like it was this big deal this great thing he was letting me witness but it wasnt like nothing.

(*Rest*)

One of his ladies liked me, so I would do her after he'd done her. On thuh sly though. He'd be laying there, spent and sleeping and snoring and her and me would be sneaking it.

Booth: Shit.

Lincoln: It was alright.

Booth

Lincoln

> Lincoln takes his crumpled Abe Lincoln getup
> from the closet. Isnt sure what to do with it.

Booth: Im gonna miss you coming home in that getup. I dont even got a picture of you in it for the album.

Lincoln: (*Rest*)

Hell, I'll put it on. Get thuh camera get thuh camera.

Booth Yeah?

Lincoln: What thuh fuck, right?

Booth: Yeah, what thuh fuck.

> Booth scrambles around the apartment
> and finds the camera.
> Lincoln quickly puts on the getup,
> including 2 thin smears of white pancake makeup,
> more like war paint than whiteface.

Lincoln: They didnt fire me cause I wasnt no good. They fired me cause they was cutting back. Me getting dismissed didnt have no reflection on my performance. And I was a damn good Honest Abe considering.

Booth: Yeah. You look great man, really great. Fix yr hat. Get in thuh light. Smile.

Lincoln: Lincoln didnt never smile.

Booth: Sure he smiled.

Lincoln: No he didnt, man, you seen thuh pictures of him. In all his pictures he was real serious.

Booth: You got a new job, yr having a good day, right?

Lincoln Yeah.

Booth: So smile.

Lincoln: Snapshots gonna look pretty stupid with me—

Booth takes a picture.

Booth: Thisll look great in thuh album.

Lincoln: Lets take one together, you and me.

Booth: No thanks. Save the film for the wedding.

Lincoln: This wasnt a bad job. I just outgrew it. I could put in a word for you down there, maybe when business picks up again theyd hire you.

Booth: No thanks. That shit aint for me. I aint into pretending Im someone else all day.

Lincoln: I was just sitting there in thuh getup. I wasnt pretending nothing.

Booth: What was going on in yr head?

Lincoln: I would make up songs and shit.

Booth: And think about women.

Lincoln: Sometimes.

Booth Cookie.

Lincoln: Sometimes.

Booth: And how she came over here one night looking for you.

Lincoln: I was at Luckys.

Booth: She didnt know that.

Lincoln: I was drinking.

Booth: All she knew was you couldnt get it up. You couldnt get it up with her so in her head you was tired of her and had gone out to screw somebody new and this time maybe werent never coming back.

(*Rest*)

She had me pour her a drink or 2. I didnt want to. She wanted to get back at you by having some fun of her own and when I told her to go out and have it, she said she wanted to have her fun right here. With me.

(*Rest*)

[And then, just like that, she changed her mind.

(*Rest*)

But she'd hooked me. That bad part of me that I fight down everyday. You beat yrs down and it stays there dead but mine keeps coming up for another round. And she hooked the bad part of me. And the bad part of me opened my mouth and started promising her things. Promising her things I knew she wanted and you couldnt give her. And the bad part of me took her clothing off and carried her into thuh bed and had her, Link, yr Cookie. It wasnt just thuh bad part of me it was all of me, man,] I had her. Yr damn wife. Right in that bed.

Lincoln: I used to think about her all thuh time but I dont think about her no more.

Booth: I told her if she dumped you I'd marry her but I changed my mind.

Lincoln: I dont think about her no more.

Booth: You dont go back.

Lincoln: Nope.

Booth: Cause you cant. No matter what you do you cant get back to being who you was. Best you can do is just pretend to be yr old self.

Lincoln: Yr outa yr mind.

Booth: Least Im still me!

Lincoln: Least I work. You never did like to work. You better come up with some kinda way to bring home the bacon or Gracell drop you like a hot rock.

Booth: I got plans!

Lincoln: Yeah, you gonna throw thuh cards, right?

Booth: Thats right!

Lincoln: You a double left-handed motherfucker who dont stand a chance in all get out out there throwing no cards.

Booth: You scared.

Lincoln: Im gone.

Lincoln goes to leave.

Booth: Fuck that!

Lincoln: Yr standing in my way.

Booth: You scared I got yr shit.

Lincoln: The only part of my shit you got is the part of my shit you think you got and that aint shit.

Booth: Did I pick right them last times? Yes. Oh, I got yr shit.

Lincoln: Set up the cards.

Booth: Thought you was gone.

Lincoln: Set it up.

Booth: I got yr shit and Ima go out there and be thuh man and you aint gonna be nothin.

Lincoln: Set it up!

Booth hurriedly sets up the milk crates and cardboard top.

Lincoln throws the cards.

Lincoln: Lean in close and watch me now: who see thuh black card who see thuh black card I see thuh black card black cards thuh winner pick thuh black card thats thuh winner pick thuh red card thats thuh loser pick thuh other red card thats thuh other loser pick thuh black card you pick thuh winner. Who see thuh black card who see thuh black card? You pick thuh red card you pick a loser you pick that red card you pick a loser you pick thuh black card thuh deuce of spades you pick a winner who sees thuh deuce of spades thuh one who sees it never fades watch me now as I throw thuh cards. Red losers black winner follow thuh deuce of spades chase thuh black deuce. Dark deuce will get you thuh win. 10 will get you 20, 20 will get you 40. One good pickll get you in 2 good picks and you gone win.
(*Rest*)
Ok, man, wheres thuh black deuce?

Booth points to a card. Lincoln flips it over.
It is the deuce of spades.

Booth: Who thuh man?!

Lincoln turns over the other 2 cards,
looking at them confusedly.

Lincoln: Hhhhh.
Booth: Who thuh man, Link?! Huh? Who thuh man, Link?!?!
Lincoln: You thuh man, man.
Booth: I got yr shit down.
Lincoln Right.
Booth: "Right"? All you saying is "right"?
(*Rest*)
You was out on the street throwing. Just today. Werent you?
You wasnt gonna tell me.
Lincoln: Tell you what?
Booth: That you was out throwing,
Lincoln: I was gonna tell you, sure. Cant go and leave my little bro out thuh loop, can I? Didnt say nothing cause I thought you heard. Did all right today but Im still rusty, I guess. But hey—yr getting good.
Booth: But I'll get out there on thuh street and still fuck up, wont I?

Lincoln: You seem pretty good, bro.

Booth: You gotta do it for real, man.

Lincoln: I am doing it for real. And yr getting good.

Booth: I dunno. It didnt feel real. Kinda felt—well it didnt feel real.

Lincoln: We're missing the essential elements. The crowd, the street, thuh traffic sounds, all that.

Booth: We missing something else too, thuh thing thatll really make it real.

Lincoln: Whassat, bro?

Booth: Thuh cash. Its just bullshit without thuh money. Put some money down on thuh table then itd be real, then youd do it for real, then I'd win it for real.

(*Rest*)

And dont be looking all glum like that. I know you got money. A whole pocketful. Put it down.

Lincoln

Booth

Booth: You scared of losing it to thuh man, chump? Put it down, less you think thuh kid who got two left hands is gonna give you uh left hook. Put it down, bro, put it down.

> Lincoln takes the roll of bills from his pocket and places it on the table.

Booth: How much you got there?

Lincoln: 500 bucks.

Booth: Cool.

(*Rest*)

Ready?

Lincoln: Does it feel real?

Booth: Yeah. Clean slate. Take it from the top. "One good pickll get you in 2 good picks and you gone win."

(*Rest*)

Go head.

Lincoln: Watch me now:

Booth: Woah, man, woah.

(*Rest*)

You think Ima chump.

Lincoln: No I dont.

Booth: You aint going full out.

Lincoln: I was just getting started.

Booth: But when you got good and started you wasnt gonna go full out. You wasnt gonna go all out. You was gonna do thuh pussy shit, not thuh real shit.

Lincoln: I put my money down. Money makes it real.

Booth: But not if I dont put no money down tuh match it.

Lincoln: You dont got no money.

Booth: I got money!

Lincoln: You aint worked in years. You dont got shit.

Booth: I got money.

Lincoln: Whatcha been doing, skimming off my weekly paycheck and squirreling it away?

Booth: I got money.

(*Rest*)

> They stand there sizing eachother up. Booth breaks away, going over to his hiding place from which he gets an old nylon stocking with money in the toe, a knot holding the money secure.

Lincoln

Booth

Booth: You know she was putting her stuff in plastic bags? She was just putting her stuff in plastic bags not putting but shoving. She was shoving her stuff in plastic bags and I was standing in thuh doorway watching her and she was so busy shoving thuh shit she didnt see me. "I aint made of money," thats what he always saying. The guy she had on the side. I would catch them together sometimes. Thuh first time I cut school I got tired of hanging out so I goes home—figured I could tell Mom I was sick and cover my ass. Come in thuh house real slow cause Im sick and moving slow and quiet. He had her bent over. They both had all they clothes on like they was about to do something like go out dancing cause they was dressed to thuh 9s but at thuh last minute his pants had fallen down and her dress had flown up and theyd ended up doing something else.

(*Rest*)

They didnt see me come in, they didnt see me watching them, they didnt see me going out. That was uh Thursday. Something told me tuh cut school thuh next Thursday and sure enough—. He was her Thursday man. Every Thursday. Yeah. And Thursday nights she was always all cleaned up and fresh and smelling nice. Serving up dinner. And Pops would grab her cause she was all bright and she would look at me, like she didnt know that I knew but she was asking me not to tell nohow. She was asking me to—oh who knows.

(*Rest*)

She was talking with him one day, her sideman, her Thursday dude, her backdoor man, she needed some money for something, thered been some kind of problem some kind of mistake had been made some kind of mistake that needed cleaning up and she was asking Mr. Thursday for some money to take care of it. "I aint made of money," he says. He was putting his foot down. And then there she was 2 months later not showing yet, maybe she'd got rid of it maybe she hadnt maybe she'd stuffed it along with all her other things in them plastic bags while he waited outside in thuh car with thuh motor running. She musta known I was gonna walk in on her this time cause she had my payoff— my *inheritance*—she had it all ready for me. 500 dollars in a nylon stocking. Huh.

> He places the stuffed nylon stocking
> on the table across from
> Lincolns money roll.

Booth: Now its real.

Lincoln: Dont put that down.

Booth: Throw thuh cards.

Lincoln: I dont want to play.

Booth: Throw thuh fucking cards, man!!

Lincoln

(*Rest*)

2 red cards but only one black. Pick thuh black you pick thuh winner. All thuh cards are face down you point out thuh cards and then you move them around. Now watch me now, now watch me real close. Put thuh winning deuce down in the center put thuh loser reds on either side then you just move thuh cards around. Move them slow or move them fast, Links thuh king he gonna last.

(*Rest*)

Wheres thuh deuce of spades?

> Booth chooses a card and chooses correctly.

Booth: HA!

Lincoln: One good pickll get you in 2 good picks and you gone win.

Booth: I know man I know.

Lincoln: Im just doing thuh talk.

Booth: Throw thuh fucking cards!

Lincoln throws the cards.

Lincoln: Lean in close and watch me now: who see thuh black card who see thuh black card I see thuh black card black cards thuh winner pick thuh black card thats thuh winner pick thuh red card thats thuh loser pick thuh other red card that's thuh other loser pick thuh black card you pick thuh winner. Watch me as I throw thuh cards. Here we go.
(*Rest*)
Ima show you thuh cards: 2 red cards but only one spade. Dark winner in thuh center and thuh red losers on thuh sides. Pick uh red card you got a loser pick thuh other red card you got a loser pick thuh black card you got a winner. Watch me watch me watch me now.
(*Rest*)
Who see thuh black card who see thuh black card? You pick thuh red card you pick a loser you pick that red card you pick a loser you pick thuh black card thuh deuce of spades you pick a winner who sees thuh deuce of spades thuh one who sees it never fades watch me now as I throw thuh cards. Red losers black winner follow thuh deuce of spades chase thuh black deuce. Dark deuce will get you thuh win.
(*Rest*)
Ok, 3-Card, you know which cards thuh deuce of spades? This is for real now, man. You pick wrong Im in yr wad and I keep mines.
Booth: I pick right I got yr shit.
Lincoln: Yeah.
Booth: Plus I beat you for real.
Lincoln: Yeah. (*Rest*)
You think we're really brothers?
Booth: Huh?
Lincoln: I know we *brothers,* but is we really brothers, you know, blood brothers or not, you and me, whatduhyathink?
Booth: I think we're brothers.
Booth
Lincoln
Booth
Lincoln
Booth
Lincoln

Lincoln: Go head man, wheres thuh deuce?

> In a flash Booth points out a card.

Lincoln: You sure?
Booth: Im sure!
Lincoln: Yeah? Dont touch thuh cards, now.
Booth: Im sure.

> The 2 brothers lock eyes. Lincoln turns over the card that
> Booth selected and Booth, in a desperate break
> of concentration, glances down to see
> that he has chosen the wrong card.

Lincoln: Deuce of hearts, bro. Im sorry. Thuh deuce of spades was this one.
(*Rest*)
I guess all this is mines.

> He slides the money toward himself.

Lincoln: You were almost right. Better luck next time.
(*Rest*)
Aint yr fault if yr eyes aint fast. And you cant help it if you got 2 left hands, right? Throwing cards aint thuh whole world. You got other shit going for you. You got Grace.
Booth: Right.
Lincoln: Whassamatter?
Booth: Mm.
Lincoln: Whatsup?
Booth: Nothing.
Lincoln: (*Rest*)
It takes a certain kind of understanding to be able to play this game.
(*Rest*)
I still got thuh moves, dont I?
Booth: Yeah you still got thuh moves.

> Lincoln cant help himself. He chuckles.

Lincoln: I aint laughing at you, bro, Im just laughing. Shit there is so much to this game. This game is—there is just so much to it.

> Lincoln, still chuckling, flops down
> in the easy chair. He takes up the nylon stocking
> and fiddles with the knot.

Lincoln: Woah, she sure did tie this up tight, didnt she?

Booth: Yeah. I aint opened it since she gived it to me.

Lincoln: Yr kidding. 500 and you aint never opened it? Shit. Sure is tied tight. She said heres 500 bucks and you didnt undo thuh knot to get a look at the cash? You aint needed to take a peek in all these years? Shit. I woulda opened it right away. Just a little peek.

Booth: I been saving it.

(*Rest*)

Oh, dont open it, man.

Lincoln: How come?

Booth: You won it man, you dont gotta go opening it.

Lincoln: We gotta see whats in it.

Booth: We *know* whats in it. Dont open it.

Lincoln: You are a chump, bro. There could be millions in here! There could be nothing! I'll open it.

Booth Don't.

Lincoln

Booth

(*Rest*)

Lincoln: Shit this knot aint coming out. I could cut it, but that would spoil the whole effect, wouldnt it? Shit. Sorry. I aint laughing at you Im just laughing. Theres so much about those cards. You think you can learn them just by watching and just by playing but there is more to them cards than that. And—. Tell me something, Mr. 3-Card, she handed you this stocking and she said there was money in it and then she split and you say you didnt open it. Howd you know she was for real?

Booth: She was for real.

Lincoln: How you know? She coulda been jiving you, bra. Jiving you that there really *was* money in this thing. Jiving you big time. Its like thuh cards. And ooooh you certainly was persistent. But you was in such a hurry to learn thuh last move that you didnt bother learning thuh first one. That was yr mistake. Cause its thuh first move that separates thuh Player from thuh Played. And thuh first move is to know that there aint no winning. It may look like you got a chance but the only time you pick right is when thuh man lets you. And when its thuh real deal, when its thuh real fucking deal, bro, and thuh moneys on thuh line, thats when thuh man wont want you picking right. He will want you picking wrong so he will make you pick wrong. Wrong wrong wrong. Ooooh, you thought you was finally happening, didnt you? You thought yr ship had come in or some shit, huh? Thought you was uh Player. But I played you, bro.

Booth: Fuck you. Fuck you FUCK YOU *FUCK YOU*!!

Lincoln: Whatever, man. Damn this knot is tough. Ima cut it.

> Lincoln reaches in his boot, pulling out a knife.
> He chuckles all the while.

Lincoln: Im not laughing at you, bro, Im just laughing.

> Booth chuckles with him.
> Lincoln holds the knife high, ready to cut the stocking.

Lincoln: Turn yr head. You may not wanna look.

> Booth turns away slightly. They both continue laughing.
> Lincoln brings the knife down to cut the stocking.

Booth: I popped her.

Lincoln Huh?

Booth: Grace. I popped her. Grace.

(*Rest*)

Who thuh fuck she think she is doing me like she done? Telling me I dont got nothing going on. I showed her what I got going on. Popped her good. Twice. 3 times. Whatever.

(*Rest*)

She aint dead.

(*Rest*)

She werent wearing my ring I gave her. Said it was too small. Fuck that. Said it hurt her. Fuck that. Said she was into bigger things. *Fuck* that. Shes alive not to worry, she aint going out that easy, shes alive shes shes—.

Lincoln: Dead. Shes—

Booth: Dead.

Lincoln: Ima give you back yr stocking, man. Here, bro—

Booth: Only so long I can stand that little brother shit. Can only take it so long. Im telling you—

Lincoln: Take it back, man—

Booth: That little bro shit had to go—

Lincoln: Cool—

Booth: Like Booth went—

Lincoln: Here, 3-Card—

Booth: That Booth shit is over, 3-Cards thuh man now—

Lincoln: Ima give you yr stocking back, 3-Card—

Booth: Who thuh man now, huh? Who thuh man now?! Think you can fuck with me, motherfucker think again motherfucker think again! Think you can take me like Im just some chump some two lefthanded pussy dickbreath chump who you can take and then go laugh at. Aint laughing at me you was just laughing bunch uh bullshit and you know it.

Lincoln: Here. Take it.

Booth: I aint gonna be needing it. Go on. You won it you open it.

Lincoln: No thanks.

Booth: Open it open it open it open it. *OPEN IT!!!*

(*Rest*)

Open it up, bro.

Lincoln

Booth

> Lincoln brings the knife down to cut the stocking.
> In a flash, Booth grabs Lincoln from behind.
> He pulls his gun and thrusts it into
> the left side of Lincolns neck.
> They stop there poised.

Lincoln: Dont.

> Booth shoots Lincoln.
> Lincoln slumps forward, falling out of his chair and
> onto the floor. He lies there dead.
> Booth paces back and forth, like a panther
> in a cage, holding his gun.

Booth: Think you can take my shit? My shit. That shit was mines. I kept it. Saved it. All this while. Through thick and through thin. Through fucking thick and through fucking thin, motherfucker. And you just gonna come up in here and mock my shit and call me two lefthanded talking bout how she coulda been jiving me then go steal from me? My *inheritance.* You stole my *inheritance,* man. That aint right. That aint right and you know it. You had yr own. And you blew it. You *blew it,* motherfucker! I saved mines and you blew yrs. Thinking you all that and blew yr shit. And I *saved* mines.

(*Rest*)

You aint gonna be needing yr fucking money-roll no more, dead motherfucker, so I will pocket it thank you.

(*Rest*)

Watch me close watch me close now: Ima go out there and make a name for myself that dont have nothing to do with you. And 3-Cards gonna be in everybodys head and in everybodys mouth like Link was.

(*Rest*)

Ima take back my inheritance too. It was mines anyhow. Even when you stole it from me it was still mines cause she gave it to me. She didnt give it to you. And I been saving it all this while.

> He bends to pick up the money-filled stocking.
> Then he just crumples. As he sits beside Lincolns body,
> the money-stocking falls away.
> Booth holds Lincolns body,
> hugging him close. He sobs.

Booth: *AAAAAAAAAAAAAAAAAAAAH!*

End of Play

Fire in the Basement
(1974)

By Pavel Kohout (1928 –)

Introduction

Czech author and playwright Pavel Kohout is less well-known than his compatriot, Vaclav Havel, but the two share a history of repression and censorship. Since both were political dissidents in Soviet-controlled Czechoslovakia, they were banned from producing their plays in the theater (a circumstance which led Kohout to form a company that produced plays secretly—in people's living rooms). While Havel was imprisoned in the late 1970s, Kohout was merely exiled from Czechoslovakia, and took up residence in Austria. The reputation and success of both playwrights is based on productions of their plays in Western Europe and the United States, since their work could not be performed in their home country prior to the Velvet Revolution of 1989.

Kohout wrote *Fire in the Basement* (a play which could be—and might originally have been—performed in a basement) sometime between 1970 and 1973, and the play had its professional premiere in Germany in 1974. This one-act satire of bureaucracy (subtitled "*Fiery Farce*") begins as a screwball comedy incorporating nudity and slapstick. Ultimately, however, the play's tone becomes one of menace as we learn that the two main characters of the play, a newlywed couple, are not the victims of a mere prank but instead of an indoctrination and conscription.

Engl and Jartchi begin the play in the midst of their honeymoon, which they are celebrating at home. Their sexual play, involving fruit and animal noises, is hilarious but also suggestive of a state of natural innocence and freedom. The play begins with the couple in their own world, without clothing, without conventions, without even names that might circumscribe their roles.

Their romp is interrupted by a group of four firemen—or perhaps actors pretending to be firemen—who violently enter the apartment under the pretense of extinguishing a fire in the kitchen. The complication here is that the couple was not aware of any fire, and the firemen, led by Vodicka, must convince them that a fire was indeed ablaze. This takes some doing, since the firemen must overcome their own over-the-top theatricality in order to impress the seriousness of the situation upon Engl and Jartchi. The firemen smash through doors that aren't even locked and rely on ridiculous props, including a jock strap and the mysterious "Valkyrie" device.

Engl and Jartchi eventually accept that their kitchen has burned up, and their savings with it; here, the firemen's plot becomes darker and more convoluted, resulting in strife for the newlyweds. Vodicka convinces the couple to sign an insurance policy and falsifying the date so that it will appear that the policy took effect before the fire took place. In his attempt to convince the couple that the firemen dabble in the insurance industry, Vodicka quips, "One can't live by fires alone." The policy promises such a large payout that Engl and Jartchi will be able to afford a new standard of living, and the firemen themselves will take a generous cut from the fraudulent claim. Here, Engl's interest in the truth conflicts with his role as Jartchi's husband. Engl's concern about falsifying the insurance report prompts Jartchi to remind him, "I told you I'd only marry you if you stopped acting like an idiot. And you promised you would."

When the conflict becomes familial rather than farcical, we see Kohout's social critique at work. Just as the "firemen" engage in a bureaucratic con game not out of inherent evil but because they have to make a living (and we never discover whether they are actually firemen, insurance assessors, or merely thieves), Engl enables and perpetuates the fraud not out of greed but because it is simply easier to go along with a falsehood than to sacrifice one's family for a principled stand. When Engl finally agrees to become a "fireman" himself, his assimilation is complete. However, even though "society" has made a successful intrusion into Engl and Jartchi's former paradise, it has made them no guarantees—they are not certain of their safety or well-being, and they are not even confident that they know the truth. It is no surprise, on account of this, that the Czech authorities were uncomfortable with public showings of this work.

Dark. A sudden scream, which gradually dies away. Quiet. A light cuts across the foot board of a large double bed. A pair of naked legs, obviously female, are hanging over it. Far off in the distance the whine of a fire truck siren.

HIS VOICE: Grrr!
HER VOICE: Miow!
HIS VOICE: Grrr, grrr!
HER VOICE: Miiiiiow!
HIS VOICE: Grr, grr, grrr!
HER VOICE: *(Moaning.)* Miiowiiooowwwwooo!

(The legs jerk up, give in, gradually sink and disappear behind the bedboard. The fire truck siren is much closer. A young man shows up behind the bedboard. Exhausted he leans his chest against the board and stretches out his hand. Light illuminates the whole set: a tiny basement room, a door on each side, in the back a window onto the street or courtyard, which lets in a little daylight. The room is very sparsely furnished; the walls are decorated with posters, and aside from the bed the only piece of furniture is a table. On it a glass and some empty soda and beer bottles as well as a pile of banana and orange peels. A bridal gown and a wedding suit are hanging on a clothes stand behind the bed. The young man rummages around in the banana peels until he finds a whole banana. He begins to peel it.)

HER VOICE: Mrrrrra!

(The young man stares at a fixed point; he is completely concerned with something behind the bedboard. But he continues to peel his banana.)

ENGL: Quaquaqua …
HER VOICE: Mrrra, mrrraaa!
ENGL: Quaquaquac …
HER VOICE: Mmmrrrraaaaaa!
ENGL: Yauyauyauyauhooooo!

(He yells and disappears behind the bedboard. The siren wails again, this time very close by. The bed seems to be dancing to the craziest sounds, which come from it. This time two pairs of naked legs, remarkably intertwined, appear for a moment behind the bedboard just as the doorbell rings sharply. The legs freeze. The bell rings again. The legs plummet. His head and her head take their place above the

bedboard. Both young people are about twenty. In contrast to the young man, who seems to be a small innocuous guy, she seems like a pretty big, tough girl; she has the banana in her mouth. The bell keeps ringing, though not continuously.)

ENGL: Who's that?

JARTCHI: *(Throws the rest of the banana on the table.)* It must be your dopey friends.

ENGL: Ah come on. Where did you get that idea? Why them?

JARTCHI: You said they'd probably try something or other.

ENGL: All I said was that we should have invited them.

JARTCHI: Especially the chorus girls, right?

(Pounding on the door.)

JARTCHI: Nice friends you've got there!

ENGL: How do you know who's there?

JARTCHI: You don't know? So go open up. You can invite them right into bed.

ENGL: Why should I invite them into bed?

JARTCHI: You did say, we should have invited them, didn't you?

ENGL: Yeah, but I didn't say anything about bed.

JARTCHI: But why not? I'm sure they'd enjoy a return visit to such a familiar spot.

ENGL: Okay, okay, I'll open up, and then you can see for yourself about these fabled girls from the theatre, who I never had anything to do with.

JARTCHI: So it is them. It didn't take them long to find you, did it?

ENGL: How am I supposed to know if it's them!

JARTCHI: I thought you said you were going to open up.

ENGL: I only said that because you said … Jartchi, how can you be jealous already?

JARTCHI: Me? Jealous? Are you kidding? *(Disappears behind the bedboard.)*

ENGL: *(Listening.)* They're gone … Jartchi. Why would I want anybody else when I've got you?! You know? Grrrrr … ! Well? Grrrrrr … ! What about it?

JARTCHI: Grouuuuu!

(She drags him behind the bedboard. Her head and shoulders appear, this time from behind. Again meaningless noises, and the bed begins to shake. At this moment a metal pole sinks down through the basement window, and a fireman in full regalia comes sliding down. A powerful searchlight is attached to his helmet.)

JARTCHI: *(Terrified.)* Help!

(At the same time she pulls the covers out from under Engl, so abruptly that he flies on the floor. She throws the covers over her head and disappears behind the bedboard. Engl tries to cover up as quickly as possible and also hides behind the bedboard. The fireman runs around him to the door, and rattles the doorknob.)

VODICKA: Keep it calm! Don't panic! *(Bends over the lock and yells in the direction of the basement window.)* Hurnik!
HURNIK: I'm listening.

(Every time a fireman in the room speaks with one outside, he flips on the microphone, which is attached to the strap of his helmet at his throat. The voice is projected through a loudspeaker built into his helmet.)

HURNIK: *(Above.)* Yeah!
VODICKA: The door splitter!
HURNIK: Roger. Will do!
VODICKA: *(Turning to Engl.)* Is there a child in there?
ENGL: *(Speechless, shakes his head.)*
VODICKA: Brothers or sisters?
ENGL: *(Shakes his head.)*
VODICKA: Any old folks?
ENGL: *(Shakes his head.)*

(A gigantic fireman comes sliding down the pole. He is carrying a very large and very savage-looking axe.)

VODICKA: Hurry up, Hurnik!
HURNIK: Will do! *(Runs to the door.)*
VODICKA: Relatives or friends?
ENGL: *(Shakes his head.)*
VODICKA: Subletters? Anybody else? Let's go, man!
ENGL: *(Finally manages to blurt out something.)* No …

(While Hurnik fumbles around with the lock, another fireman comes sliding down the pole. His regalia is slightly less impressive than Vodicka's, and he is the only one who isn't wearing gloves. Instead he is holding between his teeth a roll of documents tied together with a string.)

VODICKA: *(Immediately starts reporting to him.)* Imperiled persons—two!
TVRZNIK: Roger. Notice taken. Janik!
JANIK: *(From above.)* I'm listening.
TVRZNIK: To UPOR! Imperiled persons—two!
JANIK: Roger. Will be reported.

(Hurnik smashes the axe into the door.)

ENGL: What are you doing?
VODICKA: Don't worry! We got here just in time.
TVRZNIK: *(Pushes aside the pile of banana and orange peels on the table, unrolls his documents and straightens them out. They consist of a series of forms attached to a clipboard.)* Do you have a dog in there?
ENGL: What? No.
TVRZNIK: A cat?

(Hurnik begins a rhythmical smashing of the door.)

ENGL: Wait a minute! *(Jumps up, but ducks back behind the bedboard in the nick of time.)*
TVRZNIK: A cat?
ENGL: The key is in the lock!
VODICKA: Well, why didn't you say so in the first place? *(Unlocks the door, we see a staircase, which leads from the basement to the upstairs.)* There's no fire here! *(Locks it again, and followed by Hurnik, races to the other door.)*
TVRZNIK: A cat??
ENGL: What?
TVRZNIK: Do you have a cat in there??
ENGL: No, for God's sake!
VODICKA: *(Examining the lock.)* Janik!
JANIK: *(From above.)* I'm listening.
VODICKA: Lock explosives!
JANIK: Right away!
TVRZNIK: Canary?
ENGL: No.
TVRZNIK: Goldfish?
ENGL: No. Listen here, what the hell is …

(A ladder is dropped down through the basement window. As Hurnik climbs up it, a young fireman with another savage-looking axe comes sliding down the pole. He and Hurnik have simple uniforms with a differing number of wires and helmets with searchlights.)

VODICKA: Let's go, Janik!
JANIK: All set.
TVRZNIK: Other animals?

(Janik smashes the second door with his axe.)

ENGL: But that one's not even locked!
VODICKA: Well, why didn't you say so right off? *(Opens the door a hair, slams it immediately, and blows on his fingers, although he is wearing gloves.)* Oh boy!
TVRZNIK: Other animals?
VODICKA: Hurnik!
HURNIK: *(From above.)* I'm listening.
VODICKA: The asbestos stuff!
HURNIK: Will do!
ENGL: *(Finally getting control of himself.)* Jesus Christ, Jartchi! There's a fire in here! *(Shakes her behind the bedboard.)* Please help me out with her!
TVRZNIK: First things first. Other animals?
ENGL: No we're alone … Jartchi!
VODICKA: *(Holds a thermometer up to the door, yells at the window.)* Hurnik!
HURNIK: I'm listening.
VODICKA: Put on the Fahrenheit defense system! With boots!
HURNIK: Will do.
TVRZNIK: *(Has replaced the old form with a new one.)* Do you have any originals in here?
ENGL: What kind of …
TVRZNIK: a) paintings b) sculptures c) others?
ENGL: No, no we don't …
TVRZNIK: Objets d'art?
ENGL: No … Jartchi. I beg you to …

(Janik climbs up the ladder as Hurnik slides down the pole. He is wearing an asbestos suit over his head and body, an eyeshield and asbestos boots. Various objects are dangling from his armor—things like asbestos pouches, etc.)

TVRZNIK: Antiques?

ENGL: No.

TVRZNIK: Persian rugs or gobelins.

ENGL: Where would we get them? Can you hear me, Jartchi?

VODICKA: Do you use gas in there?

ENGL: Yes, I mean, no, not gas, we have …

TVRZNIK: Manuscripts or inventions?

ENGL: No.

VODICKA: Kerosene oven?

ENGL: No, but …

TVRZNIK: Family jewels?

ENGL: No.

VODICKA: Propane-butane?

ENGL: No, I mean, yes! We have a propane-butane!

VODICKA: *(Whistling in surprise.)* Stove?

ENGL: And an oven …

VODICKA: Janik!

JANIK: *(From above.)* I'm listening.

VODICKA: Jock strap.

JANIK: Will do.

TVRZNIK: Gold or silver?

ENGL: No, well—silverware.

TVRZNIK: Where?

ENGL: In the kitchen cabinet.

VODICKA: *(Below the basement window. Takes the jock strap and puts it on Hurnik.)* Yell, Hurnik!

HURNIK: *(Nods.)*

TVRZNIK: Value?

ENGL: Jartchi inherited it … Jartchi!

VODICKA: Bombs?

ENGL: What do you mean bombs?

VODICKA: The propane-butane! Gas bottles!

ENGL: Yes, Two! Jesus Christ …

VODICKA: *(Bellowing.)* Janik!

JANIK: *(From above.)* I'm listening.

VODICKA: The armor shield too.

JANIK: *(Whistles in disbelief.)* Right away.

TVRZNIK: Savings books?

ENGL: The bombs could go up any minute, couldn't they?

TVRZNIK: Savings books?

ENGL: *(Shaking the bedcovers.)* Jartchi, stop the baloney! We've got to get out of here.!—She's out like a light …

VODICKA: Listen, be glad. Somebody will turn her back on soon enough. Is it too tight, Hurnik?

HURNIK: *(Shakes his head.)*

(Janik comes sliding down the pole and gives Hurnik something, which looks like a medieval shield.)

VODICKA: Ready, Hurnik?

HURNIK: *(Gives the thumbs-up sign.)*

TVRZNIK: Are there any savings books in there?

ENGL: No, there aren't.

VODICKA: Janik, the timing device! *(Janik takes a large alarm clock with a horn from his belt and hangs it on a hook next to the door.)* Timing device ready for action.

ENGL: Can't you at least help me to carry her out!

TVRZNIK: First things first. Other valuable items?

VODICKA: Set it at thirty.

JANIK: Set at thirty.

VODICKA: Hurnik, if the butane goes off, get out fast!

HURNIK: *(Nods.)*

TVRZNIK: Other valuable items?

ENGL: No, no …

VODICKA: Ready! three,—two—

JARTCHI: *(Bolts up behind the bedboard, and pokes her head out from under the bedcovers.)* What do you mean, no? All the money we have is in there!

VODICKA: *(Stops counting.)*

TVRZNIK: How much?

JARTCHI: More than five thousand! *(To Engl.)* I can't even afford to faint around here! You won't take care of anything!

TVRZNIK: Where?

JARTCHI: In the clothes closet! There's a kind of handbag with a chain on it. Please, try and get it!

VODICKA: Did you year that, Hurnik. Try to fight your way through to the handbag!

HURNIK: *(Nods and gives the thumbs-up sign.)*

VODICKA: Ready! Three-two-one-now!

(Janik presses the alarm, the horn sounds. Vodicka opens the door slightly, and with Janik's help, pushes Hurnik in, and slams the door behind him. Janik climbs back up the ladder.)

JARTCHI: I told you to put the money in the bank! Didn't I say that?
ENGL: Yeah sure, but how the hell was I supposed to know that …
JARTCHI: What are you, a man or a mouse? What if it all goes up in smoke?
TVRZNIK: *(Placing another form on the clipboard.)* Name?
ENGL: What? Oh … Engl.
TVRZNIK: Full name.
ENGL: Engl Jaroslav.
TVRZNIK: Papers!
ENGL: Papers … *(Searches around on his naked body.)*
TVRZNIK: Do you have your papers?
ENGL: Of course. Just a second.

(Covers up with a pillow, gets out of bed and backs himself up to the clothes stand. With his free hand he rummages through the pockets of his wedding jacket.)

JARTCHI: He lets five thousand crowns just burn up!
ENGL: But—
JARTCHI: Will you please just shut up!—What is it that caught fire?
JANIK: *(From above.)* Janik here, sir.
VODICKA: I'm listening.
JANIK: UPOR wants to know if we'll need the roof winch?
VODICKA: They can keep it for the time being.
JANIK: Roger.
VODICKA: Also all the floor winches and stuff.
JANIK: Roger.
VODICKA: The basement winch will be enough, if it's working.
JANIK: In working order, sir.
VODICKA: Bon. In a few minutes I will give the positional announcement.
JANIK: Roger. Will be reported.
ENGL: I must have left it on the kitchen cabinet.
JARTCHI: You're just impossible!
TVRZNIK: This is getting serious.

JARTCHI: He lets his papers just burn up!

TVRZNIK: Who's going to vouch for your identity?

ENGL: She will, of course! Jartchi … !

TVRZNIK: Hold it. I'll ask the questions around here.

(*The horn blows. Vodicka opens the door slightly. Hurnik, accompanied by a cloud of black smoke, stumbles out. Vodicka immediately slams the door behind him.*)

VODICKA: How does it look?

HURNIK: (*Gives the thumbs-down sign and begins to mumble incomprehensively.*)

VODICKA: (*Puts his ear to the Plexiglas shield, and listens attentively.*) Gotcha.

JARTCHI: Did he get the handbag?

TVRZNIK: First things first. (To *Engl.*) Start counting.

ENGL: What?

TVRZNIK: Start counting out loud, so you don't hear her. I want to check you over.

VODICKA: (*To Hurnik.*) Gotcha.

HURNIK: (*Mumbles on.*)

ENGL: Here, it's on my business card!

TVRZNIK: In so far as it's yours.

ENGL: Why shouldn't it be mine?

TVRZNIK: You're acting as if the fire were somewhere else. Keep counting.

ENGL: My God … (*Starts counting.*)

TVRZNIK: Louder!

ENGL: (*Counts more loudly.*)

VODICKA: Gotcha. Will be reported. Quiet here!

TVRZNIK: Quiet!!

ENGL: (*Stops counting.*)

JARTCHI: Did he find the handbag?

VODICKA: Janik!

JANIK: (*From above.*) I'm listening.

VODICKA: Communication for UPOR: Position report number one. Epicenter kitchen, steps six to seven, progressive tendency, visibility zero = zero, cause as yet undetermined, measures taken to localize. Commander Vodicka.

JANIK: Roger. Will be reported.

ENGL: What did that all mean?

VODICKA: That things are getting hot around here. Janik!

JANIK: I'm listening.

VODICKA: Hydrants and hoses. At least three rolls.

HURNIK: Will do.

(Three sets of hoses come unrolling through the window. Vodicka disentangles them and gives Hurnik the nozzles.)

JARTCHI: *(Leaps up. The bedsheet covers her like a toga.)* I hope you're not planning on shooting that thing around in here!

ENGL: They've got to put it out, Jartchi.

JARTCHI: *(Ignoring him.)* Listen, Commander, it's already so damp in here, we'll never get it dry. Isn't there any other way of putting it out?

VODICKA: Bon. *(Calls up.)* Come back, Hurnik! Take the Valkyrie!

JANIK: Will do.

(Slides down the pole wearing on his back an apparatus that looks like a flamethrower.)

VODICKA: Swiss invention. We don't like to use it much. Refills use up too much foreign currency. It smothers the flame, and finally you just sweep up the fire.

JARTCHI: You're a real pal. We'll repay you somehow.

VODICKA: I'm sure you will. We sure are pulling out all the stops for you!

JARTCHI: *(To Engl.)* Do you hear that? And you would have let them flood us out.

TVRZNIK: Keep counting!

ENGL: *(Starts counting again.)*

TVRZNIK: *(To Jartchi.)* What's your name?

JARTCHI: Jaroslava Englova.

TVRZNIK: *(To Engl.)* That'll do.

ENGL: *(Stops counting.)*

TVRZNIK: *(Pointing to Jartchi.)* What's her name?

ENGL: Jaroslava Schoberova.

JARTCHI: How could you forget that we're married?

ENGL: Englova! Sorry, in all this ... I'm just ...

JARTCHI: You really are hopeless.

ENGL: We just got married.

TVRZNIK: Do you have a marriage certificate?

ENGL: Of course ... *(Searches through his jacket pocket again.)*

VODICKA: *(With Janik's help he has fastened the apparatus on Hurnik's back and now hands him the nozzle.)* Janik, adjustments!

JANIK: *(Turns a nozzle on the tank.)* Adjustments concluded.

VODICKA: Ready, Hurnik?

HURNIK: (*Gives the thumbs-up sign.*)

VODICKA: Timing device at one hundred twenty.

JANIK: (*Sets the alarm.*) One hundred and twenty it is.

JARTCHI: Please the handbag. It has a kind of chain on it.

VODICKA: Did you hear that, Hurnik? Try to fight your way through to the handbag.

HURNIK: (*Nods and gives the thumbs-up sign.*)

VODICKA: Three, two, one, now!

(*Janik presses the alarm. The horn sounds. Vodicka opens the door slightly. Smoke pours out. Janik and Vodicka shove Hurnik in and slam the door behind him. Janik climbs back up.*)

ENGL: (*Suddenly remembering.*) You've got it in the handbag!

TVRZNK: This is getting serious.

JARTCHI: Didn't I tell you to keep it yourself? Didn't I say that, huh?

ENGL: How was I supposed to know …

TVRZNIK: Sir!

VODICKA: I'm listening.

TVRZNIK: These people cannot produce any identification.

JARTCHI: He just lets the marriage certificate burn up!

VODICKA: Oh, oh, that looks bad.

JARTCHI: I can swear that he's really my husband.

TVRZNIK: In so far as you're his wife.

ENGL: But she is my wife.

TVRZNIK: In so far as you're her husband.

ENGL: But why should we want to lie to you?

VODICKA: No offense, Mister—okay what do I care—Engl. Have you ever heard of something called arson?

JARTCHI: Come on Commander. We wouldn't set fire to our own apartment!

TVRZNIK: In so far as it's your apartment!

ENGL: But of course it's our apartment!

TVRZNIK: Do you at least have the lease?

ENGL: Of course … Jartchi where's the lease?

JARTCHI: You had it!

ENGL: Then I gave it to you.

JARTCHI: To me?

ENGL: In your—in your handbag.

JARTCHI: Christ Almighty. Is there anything you didn't put in the handbag to burn up? He just …

TVRZNIK: First things first. Who's the apartment manager here?

ENGL & JARTCHI: *(To each other.)* Who's the apartment manager here?

TVRZNIK: Do you know any of the neighbors?

ENGL: We just moved in three days ago.

TVRZNIK: You must have run into somebody in three days.

ENGL: We haven't been out.

TVRZNIK: You were sick?

ENGL: No, we …

JARTCHI: *(To Vodicka.)* You must know by now what caught fire in there!

VODICKA: *(Listening at the door. Calls up.)* Janik!

JANIK: I'm listening.

VODICKA: Call UPOR. Tell them to send an ambulance fast in case the butane goes up.

JANIK: Will do. Will be reported.

ENGL: Shouldn't we get out of here?

TVRZNIK: Why haven't you been out in the last three days?

JARTCHI: *(Completely returned to normal.)* Is that so important right now? Why don't you help them put it out?

ENGL: Jartchi … !

VODICKA: My colleague Tvrznik is the fire damage inspector. He has nothing to do with the fires as such, just with their causes and consequences.

ENGL: Please, we didn't mean anything, it's just that it's all so …

VODICKA: Okay okay, we understand. It's not every day you have a fire.

JARTCHI: I'd like to know how the fire could break out in the kitchen! *(The sheet has slipped down over one of her shoulders.)*

TVRZNIK: Why don't you put some clothes on?

JARTCHI: Now just a second … Jarda!

TVRZNIK: You're her husband?

ENGL: That's right.

TVRZNIK: And you don't care if, and with strangers around, too …

VODICKA: My colleague Tvrznik just got married too. So you've got to be shown some understanding yourself.

ENGL: Please, put something on!

JARTCHI: What, may I ask? All my stuff is in the other room.

TVRZNIK: *(Pointing to the clothes stand.)* And who might this belong to?

JARTCHI: But that's my wedding dress!

VODICKA: If I were you, I'd put it on. Then at least you'll have something for the new start in case the butane goes up.

ENGL: Please, hurry up. (*Begins to get dressed himself.*)

JARTCHI: (*Getting unsteady; forces herself to the clothes stand, still wrapped up in the sheet.*) A great idea to put the clothes in the kitchen!

ENGL: But that was your …

JARTCHI: For Christ's sake, can't you stop talking. Why don't you tell me what could have caught fire in the kitchen!

JANIK: (*From above.*) Janik here, sir.

VODICKA: I'm listening.

JANIK: UPOR wants to know if we need lifesaving nets.

VODICKA: They can keep them.

JANIK: Roger.

VODICKA: And they can keep the chutes, too.

JANIK: Roger.

VODICKA: But we need all the outflow blockers and the sewer pipe rammer!

JANIK: Roger. Will be reported.

(*In the meantime Engl and Jartchi, squatting behind the bed, have put on their wedding clothes, which under the circumstances look pretty pathetic.*)

JARTCHI: Pull up my zipper at least!

ENGL: (*Doing it.*) Listen, shouldn't we get out of here?

TVRZNIK: Why didn't you go out for three days?

JARTCHI: Is that so difficult to figure out when we were married the day before yesterday.

TVRZNIK: In so far as you are married.

JARTCHI: Did you notice the clothes we're wearing?

TVRZNIK: In so far as they belong to you.

ENGL & JARTCHI: What?

TVRZNIK: In so far as the real groom and the real bride are not also … (*Points to the kitchen.*)

ENGL: But that's … that's really … Commander!

VODICKA: Mister—Okay, let's say—Engl, fire is the best detective because it often turns up at the right place at the right time. Once we had a case where a guy had knocked off his aunt, and just as he was pouring gas all over her, there's Hurnik hanging in his window in order to tell him that the house was on fire underneath him.

(While Engl and Jartchi are speechless, the horn sounds twice. Vodicka opens the door a crack. Hurnik staggers out, accompanied by a cloud of black smoke. Vodicka slams the door behind him and supports Hurnik.)

VODICKA: How does it look?

HURNIK: *(Gives the thumbs-down sign and mumbles.)*

VODICKA: *(Puts his ear to the Plexiglas and listens.)* Gotcha.

JARTCHI: Did he *get* the handbag?

TVRZNIK: First things first. Miss—okay let's say Mrs. Englova, in so far as you are Mrs. Englova—, you must know what's behind this door.

JARTCHI: The kitchen, of course.

VODICKA: Is that right, Hurnik?

HURNIK: *(Nods.)*

TVRZNIK: What's in the kitchen?

JARTCH: Clothes cabinet, kitchen cabinet, refrigerator, and … the oven.

VODICKA: Hurnik?

HURNIK: *(Nods.)*

TVRZNIK: What's in the oven?

JARTCHI: Nothing.

TVRZNIK: And in the refrigerator?

JARTCHI: Vodka, beer and a roast duck.

VODICKA: This?

(Hurnik lifts his hand. In it he is holding a charcoal object which might have been a bird at some point.)

JARTCHI: Christ Almighty … is that what it's like in there … I thought you claimed you would just sweep it up … !

VQDICKA: Where was this duck, Hurnik?

HURNIK: *(Mumbles.)*

VODICKA: Understood. Will be reported. Janik!

JANIK: *(From above.)* I'm listening.

VODICKA: To UPOR: Position report number two. Cause of fire: Oven with duck not turned off.

JANIK: Roger. Will be reported.

JARTCHI: *(Yelling.)* No! No! That's not …

VODICKA: Wait a second, Janik! Hold that report!

JANIK: Roger. I'm waiting.

JARTCHI: I'm absolutely sure that I turned off … that the duck…

(Hurnik again holds up the charcoal skeleton, and Jartchi breaks down in despair. Engl on the other hand takes the opportunity to show himself to be master of the house.)

ENGL: I told you to take the duck out. Did I tell you that or didn't I?

JARTCHI: *(Breaks into tears.)*

ENGL: And then she asks how the fire started!!

VODICKA: Oh don't blame the little woman too much, Mr. Engl. Things like this happen to people with more experience, too, you know. Once we had a case where a lady forgot to turn off the oven. She erred, she confessed and promised it'll never happen again. Right, young lady?

JARTCHI: *(Cries even more.)*

TVRZNIK: *(In the meantime he has filled out a sheet and hands it to Engl on the clipboard.)* Bottom left.

ENGL: Yes … *(Takes the pen from him and wants to sign.)*

TVRZNIK: Don't you want to read it through?

ENGL: No, what's the point … ?

VODICKA: Read it out loud, Tvrznik. You see how excited the two of them are.

TVRZNIK: Roger. *(Reads.)* "The fire was caused by reckless neglect of the female renter of the apartment in failing to switch off duck in oven."—Right?

ENGL: But that's pretty . . . Couldn't you somehow …

VODICKA: Somehow what?

ENGL: Somehow tone it down. For Jartchi's sake …

VODICKA: I like that, Mr. Engl. I like it when a family sticks together. Tvrznik, cut out "in oven." It's not necessary.

TVRZNIK: Roger. *(Crosses something out.)*

VODICKA: How does it read now?

TVRZNIK: (Reads.) "The fire was caused by reckless neglect of the female renter of the apartment in failing to switch off duck."

VODICKA: Okay. Satisfied, Mr. Engl?

ENGL: Yeah, sure, but … Does Jartchi have to be … I mean so directly …

VODICKA: I really like you for that, Mr. Engl. I wouldn't leave my wife in the lurch either. Tvrznik, cross out "female renter of apartment." We don't have to know that.

TVRZNIK: Roger. *(Crosses something out.)*

VODICKA: How does it read now?

TVRZNIK: *(Reads.)* "The fire was caused by reckless neglect in failing to switch off duck."

VODICKA: Well, see. Everything's okay now, right?

ENGL: Yeah, sure … only …

VODICKA: Come on, out with it! Only what?

ENGL: Only if it wasn't so clearly stated that … that somebody was negligent.

VODICKA: I see. You know, Mr. Engl, our motto is: live and let live. We don't want to be harder on you than the fire was. If it will make you happy—Tvrznik, cross out "reckless neglect in failing to switch off."

TVRZNIK: Roger. *(Crosses something out.)*

VODICKA: And how does it read now?

TVRZNIK: *(Reads.)* "The fire was caused by duck."

VODICKA: Good. Let them try and figure that out!

ENGL: That's really nice of you.

TVRZNIK: *(Again hands him the paper with the clipboard.)* Bottom left, Mr … You are really Mr. Engl?

ENGL: *(Intently.)* I swear it! I wouldn't lie to you when you've been so decent to us! *(Signs.)*

TVRZNIK: I believe you. *(Handing the paper to Jartchi.)* Bottom left, Mrs … you are Mrs. Englova, aren't you?

JARTCHI: *(Nods while crying.)*

TVRZNIK: I believe you.

(Jartchi signs. Vodicka tries the light switch on the wall. A light goes on and illuminates the whole mess.)

VODICKA: You've got lights! Why didn't you say so right away?

(Janik slides down the pole and helps Hurnik to take off his asbestos suit. Then the two of them begin to roll up the hoses.)

ENGL: Could you please tell us how the clothes cabinet looks?

VODICKA: Hurnik?

HURNIK: I'm listening.

VODICKA: The clothes cabinet?

HURNIK: Kindling wood.

ENGL: And the kitchen cabinet?

HURNIK: Ashes.

JARTCHI: *(Holding back tears.)* And my handbag?

(Hurnik gives Vodicka a piece of blackened chain, which he hands on to Jartchi. She starts crying again.)

 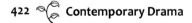

VODICKA: Don't cry, little lady ... the insurance company will pay off for those few crowns and the other junk without a second look.

JARTCHI: *(Sobbing, to Engl.)* I told you to take care of the ...

VODICKA: *(Whistling in amazement.)* What? You're not ... ohohoh!

(Hurnik and Janik are alternatively sliding down the pole and climbing up the ladder. Gradually they clear the room of all the paraphernalia which they had previously brought in.)

ENGL: *(Again deflated.)* We had nothing worth ...

JARTCHI: And for two years we saved up for this nothing! *(Starts crying again.)*

VODICKA: Tvrznik!

TVRZNIK: I'm listening.

VODICKA: Could we ah ...

TVRZNIK: You're the boss, sir.

VODICKA: I think so. They're nice young people. We should try and help them out.

TVRZNIK: *(Bows, takes another form from his file, fastens it to the clipboard and hands it to Engl.)* Bottom right.

ENGL: *(Not believing his eyes.)* But that's a ... Jartchi, it's an insurance policy!

JARTCHI: *(Stops crying, takes the form.)* Let me see that!

VODICKA: My colleague Tvrznik also moonlights for the insurance company as an assessor. It's only reasonable. One can't live by fires alone.

ENGL: But you can't do that—after the fact ...

VODICKA: Who said anything about after the fact? Only the date is given, not the hour. You could have taken out the policy just before the fire broke out! Once we had a case where lightning struck during the actual signing.

JARTCHI: And they recognized the validity?

VODICKA: And how. My colleague Tvrznik enjoys complete confidence. And we testified as well.

ENGL: Only ... this didn't happen before the fire ...

VODICKA: Okay, if that's the way you want it, Mr. Engl. *(To Jartchi.)* Is he really your husband?

JARTCHI: Jarda, if you don't accept this offer ...

VODICKA: Cool off—be glad that Mr. Engl has principles, young lady. Of course nobody would notice anything, but the more expensive the principles, the more you can enjoy them.

(Tvrznik starts to put the form away, but Jartchi stops his hand, takes the form from him and hands it to Engl.)

JARTCHI: I told you I'd only marry you if you stopped acting like an idiot. And you promised you would. Did you promise or not?

TVRZNIK: Bottom right.

ENGL: *(Signs.)*

JARTCHI: Me too?

VODICKA: The head of the family is sufficient—and I assume that that is Mr. Engl. The main thing is that you don't forget to pay the first premium, which is due today, and comes to …

TVRZNIK: Three hundred and twelve crowns.

ENGL: And where are we supposed to get that?

JARTCHI: I told you to put the money in the bank. I told you …

VODICKA: But listen kids. You're already burned out. What's the sense of fighting about it? Somebody will lend you the few crowns.

ENGL: If you hadn't chased away all my friends …

VODICKA: Wait a minute, wait a minute! Where there's smoke there doesn't have to be fire!

JARTCHI: Don't worry. I'll get the money somewhere, even if I have to start walking the streets. I'm just sorry the fire didn't reach this room. At least we could have bought a bed that hadn't been used!

VODICKA: Young lady, you know, I like you. That's why I want to tell you the following: You've been here for only three days, and nobody has even visited you. So we're the only ones who know what actually burned up.

JARTCHI: What do you mean?

VODICKA: Tvrznik …

TVRZNIK: I'm listening.

VODICKA: Could we …

TVRZNIK: You're the boss, sir.

VODICKA: Well, I just want the best for these two, because they're so nice and decent. It's actually surprising that you two don't own anything other than a refrigerator, a kitchen cabinet, a clothes cabinet and an oven with duck. We saw a bunch of other things here.

ENGL: What kind of things.

VODICKA: For example—Tvrznik!

TVRZNIK: *(Placing another form on the clipboard and reading aloud.)* An Empire trumeau.

ENGL: What's that?

TVRZNIK: *(Reads.)* A small antique table with mirror. Value about 8000 crowns.

VODICKA: It was over there next to the door, right? Hurnik!

HURNIK: I'm listening. *(Opens a pouch.)*

VODICKA: What's left of it?

HURNIK: The fittings. *(Takes out a piece of blackened metal.)*

VODICKA: *(Looking at it.)* That's really too bad. Go on!

TVRZNIK: *(Reads.)* The Portrait of a Lady by the academy painter Chily. Approximate value 10,000 crowns.

VODICKA: Grandma, I suppose. Hurnik!

HURNIK: *(Hands him a scorched piece of wood.)* A piece of the frame.

VODICKA: *(Looks at it.)* It's enough to make you cry, no?

TVRZNIK: *(Reads.)* One three quarter length fur coat, chinchilla, purchase price 6021 crowns.

HURNIK: Here are the buttons.

VODICKA: And so forth, etc. You'll read through it later, right?

HURNIK: *(Shakes out a pile of burned objects on the table.)* Here's the rest of it.

TVRZNIK: (Reads.) The total damage comes to 57,344 point 20 crowns. *(Hands the list and the pen to Engl.)* Upper left.

JARTCHI: *(As if in a dream.)* Fifty-seven thousand …

VODICKA: Well, do you want it?

ENGL: But it's …

VODICKA: What?

ENGL: But it's just …

VODICKA: Well, what's the matter, Mr. Engl? Did you want to say: fraud? You did, didn't you? And you'd be surprised: of course it's fraud! But the insurance itself is a hundred times as big a fraud. My colleague Tvrznik could tell you how many people stuff it like a piggy bank for as long as they live and never get even a single fire out of it. One pensioner has figured out that with all that insurance money, he could have … what was it he could have done?

TVRZNIK: Made a trip around the world.

VODICKA: And?

TVRZNIK: He went crazy.

VODICKA: You see, thanks to our efforts there are so few real fires that getting insurance is like throwing your money down the drain. We work ourselves to the bone and they pocket the premiums. So you shouldn't be surprised if we try and double-cross them once in a while. Of course, if you're not interested …

(Tvrznik starts to put the form away, and Hurnik shoves the burned stuff back in his pouch. Jartchi lays her hand on the paper.)

JARTCHI: Wait a minute. *(To Engl.)* Go count for a while! *(To Vodicka.)* Just so we understand each other, Commander, can we do anything for you in return?

VODICKA: Why, of course you can, young lady. We should all get a piece of the pie.

JARTCHI: And how big might the slices be?

VODICKA: Ah, that's a good woman for you. You've made a fine choice, Mr. Engl.—Just like we were home, right? Everyone gets the same size slice. There are four of us and two of you. So—one third for you. That makes …

TVRZNIK: 19,114 point 73 crowns.

JARTCHI: That doesn't seem fair to me.

VODICKA: What? Why not?

JARTCHI: You delivered the goods, but we cooked it up right here.

VODICKA: Very good. I like that. You should really get half.

TVRZNIK: 28,672 point 10 crowns.

JARTCHI: *(Shakes her head.)*

VODICKA: Still too little? How come?

JARTCHI: Everyday can be a holiday for you, but for us it comes only once a lifetime.

VODICKA: Isn't she adorable? You don't know how lucky you are, Mr. Engl, that I'm no longer as combustible as I once was. Okay. Keep two thirds. That makes …

TVRZNIK: 38,229 point 46 crowns.

VODICKA: No, no, no, that will have to do. I've got expenses, and then my boys here might go off and take a better offer, probably right from the insurance people. Right, Hurnik?

HURNIK: Right, sir.

VODICKA: Okay, agreed?

JARTCHI: And the five thousand?

VODICKA: What five thousand?

JARTCHI: The ones that burned. You can't slice that up.

VODICKA: You win. Tvrznik. Add that to it.

TVRZNIK: 43,229 point 46 crowns.

JARTCHI: Did you hear that, Jarda? Think about it: we'd have to save for eight years to get that much together.

ENGL: *(Stubbornly.)* Four … !

TVRZNIK: *(Ceremoniously hands the form to Vodicka.)* Commander, the registry of the damages.

JARTCHI: But we'd be eating pork and beans for four years, too.

ENGL: *(Stubbornly.)* I like them.

VODICKA: Let's see … *(Goes through the list.)* Trumeau, Chily, chinchilla … *(Reads incomprehensibly.)*

JARTCHI: Jarda, don't be an idiot! Almost everybody does it!

ENGL: Well, I'm sorry, but maybe I'm not just everybody …

VODICKA: He agrees. *(Signs.)* Hurnik! Janik!

HURNIK: *(Below.)* I'm listening.

JANIK: *(Above.)* I'm listening.

VODICKA: Sign here!

(Janik slides down, both step simultaneously to the table.)

BOTH: Right. *(They sign.)*

JARTCHI: So you're not everybody! And just who do you think you are? Onassis?

ENGL: You married me. So you must know …

JARTCHI: I don't care if you're just a chauffeur, but when you break your word … you swore you would do anything for me. Did you say that or not?

ENGL: But not fraud …

JARTCHI: Then you should have said that. You should have said: sweetheart, I'll do anything for you, except commit fraud. But you didn't say that. You were even ready to kill somebody.

ENGL: Me?

JARTCHI: Didn't you say you'd kill Kubr if he didn't stop calling me?

ENGL: *(Spreading his hands helplessly.)* But that's the kind of thing you just *say* …

JARTCHI: You just *say* everything!

VODICKA: Come on, kids, what's the matter? In that case just forget it. The money involved isn't worth it if it ruins your honeymoon.

JARTCHI: We're not talking about the money, we're talking about the principle of it.

VODICKA: I'd be careful if I were in your place. Once we had a case where a school burned down because the principal on principle wouldn't let us in with street shoes on.

JARTCHI: Is it valid if I sign it by myself?

ENGL: Jartchi!

VODICKA: Your signatures are only a formality anyhow. Fire victims aren't taken seriously. They're always asking for the moon. What counts is the signature of the official authorities—and that's us.

JARTCHI: May I? *(Tvrznik hands her pen and paper.)*

TVRZNIK: Upper left.

ENGL: If you do that …

JARTCHI: *(Belligerent, but somewhat uncertain.)* What then??

ENGL: Then I don't want to know anything about it.

JARTCHI: *(Turns away in disdain and signs.)*

TVRZNIK: *(Takes the form from her and hands it to Vodicka.)* The forms, Commander.

VODICKA: *(Tears out the carbon copy, and bowing, gives it to Jartchi, while Tvrznik replaces the original with another form.)* If you please, young lady … *(But when the carbon copy is at the tip of her fingers, he grabs it back and gives her the other paper with his other hand.)* Pardon me, this here too …

JARTCHI: What's this?

VODICKA: Confirmation that you have received a private loan from the four of us in the amount of 14,114 point 74 crowns. To be paid back immediately upon receipt of 57,344 point 20 crowns from the insurance company. The rest—43,229 point 46 crowns belongs to you. In order, young lady?

JARTCHI: *(Studies the paper.)* Yes, I think so …

TVRZNIK: In the middle.

JARTCHI: *(Signs, exchanges the paper for the other ones, which she stares at as if it were a valuable prize.)* We should drink to that, shouldn't we? If it weren't for the fire, I could offer you something … *(She looks and notices for the first time that almost all the fire-fighting equipment has disappeared.)* Is the fire already out?

VODIGKA: But, young lady, that's what the fire department is for! You know what we say: "Does your fire need some aid?

JANIK & HURNIK: Call on Vodicka's Brigade!"

VODICKA: My colleague Tvrznik wrote that himself.

TVRZNIK: *(Bows.)*

JARTCHI: I'm so happy! *(Kisses Vodicka on the cheek.)*

VODICKA: You certainly are fiery, young lady. You should have married a fireman.

JARTCHI: The least you can do is thank them, Jarda!

ENGL: *(Stubborn.)* I didn't set any fire.

JARTCHI: What's that supposed to mean? You should thank them and me as well. Otherwise you'd be getting pretty desperate for cigarettes and beer after eight years. *(Notices that Janik and Hurnik are gnawing at the banana peels, and Vodicka is sucking out the last drop from the glass.)* My God, you must be hungry and thirsty … maybe something survived in the refrigerator!

(She runs to the kitchen. Hurnik gets in her way. At first it looks like a clumsy accident, but then Janik cuts her off, too.)

VODICKA: Leave that to my boys, young lady. They're equipped for it. After you use the Valkyrie, it hangs in the air of an hour. Your dress would look like a Swiss cheese. Janik!

JANIK: I'm listening.

VODICKA: Go get some … didn't somebody say something about vodka?

JARTCHI: Tell him to take anything he can get his hands on.

JANIK: *(Unlocks the kitchen door and reaches for the door knob.)*

VODICKA: Janik!

JANIK: I'm listening.

VODICKA: *(Reprimanding.)* At least take the armor shield!

JANIK: Roger. Will do.

(Hurnik lets him and his armor shield in. A thin waft of smoke comes out. In the meantime Engl has sat down on the bed. Overjoyed Jartchi kneels at his feet and attempts a reconciliation.)

JARTCHI: Jarda! *(Gives him a kiss.)* Are you really mad?

ENGL: Oh no …

JARTCHI: Don't get angry. Be happy! With forty-three thousand we can turn this dump into a palace and … You know what else? We'll be able to afford a … (*Whispers in his ear.)* What do you think?

VODICKA: See? Fire is a stern master but an obedient servant. I hope you'll take us for a ride too some day.

JARTCHI: I didn't mean a car …

VODICKA: No, well what then?

(Janik comes out of the kitchen. He's carrying bottles on his shield as if it were a tray. Hurnik locks the door behind him.)

VODICKA: Well, Janik?

JANIK: Contents of the refrigerator not damaged, Commander. Vodka, beer and … *(as he puts the shield on the table he turns it around. Behind the bottles is a pan)* a duck. *(Engl and Jartchi stare at the duck as if they had seen a ghost.)*

VODICKA: Congratulations! I can see you're not overburdened with chairs. It's about time you got burned out. Hurnik!

HURNIK: I'm listening.
VODICKA: Turn the bed sideways!
HURNIK: Will do.
VODICKA: You'll have to excuse us, Mr. Engl …

(Engl gets up mechanically, Hurnik leans against the bed and turns it sideways, until it stands next to the table like a long bench.)

VODICKA: Let's go boys. Sit down.

(All the firemen sit down next to each other on the bed. Janik and Hurnik on the ends, Tvrznik and Vodicka in the middle. Vodicka takes the duck, rips it to pieces, and passes it around.)

VODICKA: All work makes Jack a dull boy. It's lucky that a refrigerator like that is a *de facto* fireproof safe. Once we had a case—I hope it's all right, young lady, for us to eat with our fingers like we do at home—where all the personnel and the customers at a meat outlet had saved themselves in a big freezer like this, a total of—
TVRZNIK: Three men and eighteen women.
VODICKA: And not a single one of them had gotten so much as a blister. It was just too bad for them that we didn't find them until a month later. But who could have expected them to be in there, huh? A delicious duck! *(To Engl.)* Don't you want some?
ENGL: *(Beaten down.)* Okay …
VODICKA: Well then sit down with us!

(Engl starts to obey, but Jartchi holds him back and finally says something.)

JARTCHI: Hold it!
VODICKA: And just take what you want, young lady. Do you want a piece of the tail?
JARTCHI: I want to look in the kitchen.

(The firemen continue eating and drinking good-naturedly. But Engl is very nervous.)

ENGL: What do you want to see in there?
VODICKA: Come on, young lady, don't spoil the meal. First it's got to die out completely in any case.
JARTCHI: I'll put on the asbestos!

VODICKA: That wouldn't do you any good. No, no, young lady. It's a man's job.

JARTCHI: *(To Engl.)* Then you go look!

ENGL: Me? Why?

JARTCHI: You're a man, aren't you. I want you to go and look.

ENGL: But I …

VODICKA: Tvrznik!

TVRZNIK: I'm listening.

VODICKA: Couldn't we—

TVRZNIK: Whatever you say, Commander.

VODICKA: I'm very much for it. Mr. Engl is a grown-up, he's rational, and he has principles, he loves his wife—Why shouldn't he take a look in? I think we'll make an exception and look the other way.

ENGL: Not for my sake …

VODICKA: Just to satisfy the little lady, Mr. Engl. She is your wife, isn't she?

ENGL: Yes, but—

VODICKA: Well then. Why not take a look in if it will make her happy? That would make you happy, young lady, wouldn't it?

JARTCHI: *(Becomes uncertain.)* Yes …

ENGL: I don't want to!

VODICKA: But, but what is that supposed to mean, Mr. Engl? We have to hold the little lady back by force, and you're afraid to go in at all? That's a great prospectus for your marriage.

ENGL: I'm not afraid.

VODICKA: Well, congratulations. Janik!

JANIK: I'm listening.

VODICKA: Give him the asbestos stuff and the boots. And Hurnik!

HURNIK: I'm listening.

VODICKA: Go with him, and take care of him.

JANIK & HURNIK: Will do.

VODICKA: *(While Engl is being dressed.)* Don't stay in there too long, Hurnik. Just long enough for Mr. Engl to look around.

HURNIK: Roger.

VODICKA: As for you, Mr. Engl, chin up! Thanks to your little wife you'll look back on this calamity as if it was Christmas. Ready, Mr. Engl?

HURNIK: *(Indicating to Engl that he should put his thumbs up.)*

ENGL: *(Already wearing the equipment, hesitatingly puts his thumbs up.)*

VODICKA: Okay, then—Off you go!

(He opens the door, and with Janik's help, pushes Engl in. Hurnik follows with the axe. Vodicka slams the door and blows away some smoke with his hand. Jartchi makes a motion in the direction of the kitchen.)

JARTCHI: Jarda!

VODICKA: *(Steps in her way.)* Don't worry, young lady. Hurnik will make sure that he doesn't roast.

JARTCHI: Let me by!

VODICKA: *(Scolding.)* Not like that, young lady. I don't like you at all like this. We come to you as friends and you treat us like strangers.

(The door opens and Engl comes out, accompanied by Hurnik: Janik locks it behind them.)

VODICKA: Now see. Nothing happened to us. We're back already. Janik, Hurnik, quick, get that stuff off him before he collapses on us!

BOTH: Will do. *(Takes off his helmet, chest protector, and boots.)*

ENGL: *(Smoothes out his hair, is very upset.)*

JARTCHI: Well??

VODICKA: A real mess, eh, Mr. Engl?

JARTCHI: How does it look?

VODICKA: Not a nice sight, eh?

JARTCHI: Say something, Jarda!

ENGL: It's like this, Jartchi …

JARTCHI: Like what??

ENGL: The clothes cabinet is …

VODICKA: … Kindling.

ENGL: *(Nods.)*

JARTCHI: And the kitchen cabinet?

ENGL: Ashes. Everything is …

VODICKA: Well, what do you say, Mr. Engl? Were you lucky or not?

ENGL: Yeah. *(Sinks heavily onto the bed.)*

(All the firemen sit down again. Engl sits between Vodicka and Tvrznik. They have great difficulty all fitting on the bed. The firemen fish out their portions from the pan and continue eating.)

VODICKA: Well, you see? Don't think about it anymore. Have a bite to eat instead. I saved a wing for you. (*Hands him a portion.*) Just so you can fly away in case the little lady tries to beat you up.

(*All the firemen laugh. Engl begins to gnaw mechanically; Jartchi is the only one still standing. She is thinking things through.*)

VODICKA: Sit down with us, young lady. At least you'll get warm. Come on, boys. Shove over!

JARTCHI: Wait a minute.

VODICKA: Now what?

JARTCHI: If the duck got all burned up, what's this thing here? (*Vodicka and the other firemen stop chewing.*)

VODICKA: (*Harshly.*) Well, Mr. Engl, can you clear this up for us?

ENGL: I …

VODICKA: Just among us women folk: isn't it likely that there were two ducks?

JARTCHI: Two?

VODICKA: Didn't you just happen to roast the second one yourself as a little surprise for the little lady? Huh?

ENGL: Yes …

JARTCHI: When for heaven's sake? I would have known that!

VODICKA: Didn't it just happen to be in the middle *of* the night?

ENGL: That's right …

JARTCHI: … But why didn't you say anything to me about it?

VODICKA: Well? Why didn't you inform the little lady, Mr. Engl?

ENGL: I forgot …

VODICKA: Come on, come on. At your age? You better watch out, young lady—Once we had a case where some clown like this forgot to save his mother-in-law, his wife and his two kids from a fire. (*All the firemen laugh loudly and continue chewing.*)

JARTCHI: I was sure I had turned off the oven and put the duck in the refrigerator … But that means …

VODICKA: (*His mouth full.*) You're getting warmer, young lady.

JARTCHI: That means—that you're the one who didn't turn off the oven!

VODICKA: Now it's getting really hot, eh Mr. Engl?

ENGL: Prabably …

JARTCHI: And you were going to just sit there and let me take the blame?

VODICKA: That's not true either, I'm on Mr. Engl's side here. Don't you remember how stoutly he defended you when we made up the official report? He has no cause to have a guilty conscience. And furthermore if you want to be fair: now the one who really earned this …

TVRZNIK: 43,289 point 46 crowns.

VODICKA: … is him. Right?

JARTCHI: That was just sheer luck!—And now tell me why you're roasting a duck in the middle of the night when there's already one in the fridge?

ENGL: I …

VODICKA: Didn't you happen to want to have some friends over in private, Mr. Engl?

JARTCHI: *(Understanding.)* Jarda! You were … *(As if spellbound she looks at each of the firemen in turn.)* Wait a second!

(She starts moving and the others notice too late that she's headed for the kitchen. All but Engl jump up, their hands and mouths full of duck, but Jartchi reaches the door with a jump, turns the key and opens it. The scene freezes for a second. Then Jartchi goes into the kitchen. Engl closes his eyes. Pause. Jartchi comes back out, carrying in her hand a metal canister, which is still sending out a bit of smoke: a smoke bomb. She starts laughing. She laughs so hard that she has to lean on the door. Vodicka joins in laughing. Then the other firemen. The room echoes with laughter.)

JARTCHI: *(Finally catching her breath.)* Well, you really put me on! You know you really put the fear of God in me for a while.

VODICKA: Oh no, really?

JARTCHI: I even cry at the movies, when I know they're just acting. How was I supposed to guess here in my own place that you guys get all this *(pointing to their uniforms)* from the theatre?

VODICKA: Yeah sure!

JARTCHI: Jarda was always saying: If you don't let me keep on acting in the theatre group, they'll pay you back. But as soon as somebody yells "Fire," everybody goes crazy!

VODICKA: Yeah sure!

JARTCHI: You know I think I'll let him go back to it. He's a better actor than I thought.

VODICKA: So you see …

JARTCHI: Sit down, don't stand around. Please just make yourselves at home.

(The firemen sit down and begin eating again. They drink freely from the bottles.)

JARTCHI: But there's one thing I won't forgive you for. I could already smell the money. That's right, love, you'll feel sorry about the beautiful fire, too, when you're eating pork and beans for the third straight year! *(The firemen roar with laughter.)* Forty-three thousand … You really pushed it to the limit! *(To EngL)* Wouldn't you like to introduce me to your friends?

ENGL: *(Softly.)* I've never seen them before in my life.

(The firemen stop chewing. Once again the scene freezes.)

JARTCHI: Come on, enough's enough. Or I might get really scared!

ENGL: They're not from the theatre group …

(Hurnik and Janik stand up. Jartchi, terrified, moves back, but Hurnik just goes to the door to the stairway, and Janik to the basement window. They take up positions there as if they were standing guard. Vodicka and Tvrznik wipe off their hands.)

JARTCHI: *(Anxiously.)* Who are you?

VODICKA: Don't be so nervous, young lady. We're the firemen!

JARTCHI: And … what do you want here?

VODICKA: What do we want? We've just been doing our duty.

JARTCHI: But there wasn't any fire here!

VODICKA: What! No? Come on, young lady! Women certainly tend to be forgetful, don't they, Mr. Engl?

JARTCHI: Let him alone. He's just as normal as I am!

VODICKA: Well, I'll grant you that, young lady!

JARTCHI: Who do you want to convince that there was a fire here??

VODICKA: Why should we want to convince anyone of anything? You're both normal people, and we've got your signed statements. That'll do.

TVRZNIK: *(Opens his file, and reads.)* The fire was caused by us. Jaroslav Engl, Jaroslava Englova.

JARTCHI: What a lie!

ENGL: *(Particularly harassed, since he is still squeezed in between Vodicka and Tvrznik.)* Jartchi …

JARTCHI: But what we signed said: "The fire was caused by duck!"

VODICKA: But young lady, you can't have something that stupid in an official statement! Look for yourself, Mr. Engl.

TVRZNIK: *(Shows him the statement.)*

JARTCHI: What you quoted wasn't what we signed!

VODICKA: Let's not quibble about words, young lady. The fact is that you signed this statement about a fire. Or didn't you?

JARTCHI: But that's not worth anything! That's fraud!

ENGL: Just a second, Jartchi ... Gentlemen, would you mind telling us what you actually—

JARTCHI: Will you please be quiet! You've already let them make an ass of you! How can you be so thick? Can't you see that they're trying to blackmail us!

VODICKA: We blackmail you? That's really too much, young lady.

JARTCHI: But you won't get away with it. That promissory note isn't valid, either.

VODICKA: Which one?

JARTCHI: The one for fourteen thousand.

VODICKA: Fourteen thousand? Oh you mean the one for—

TVRZNIK: 14,114 point 74 crowns.

JARTCHI: Yeah, that one.

VODICKA: And why do you think it's not valid?

JARTCHI: Because nothing burned down here, not to kindling and not to ashes. Absolutely nothing. Not even the duck!

VODICKA: Really? What about the—

TVRZNIK: (*Takes out another form and reads.*) Empire trumeau.

JARTCHI: I don't even know what that is!

TVRZNIK: Portrait of a Lady by the academic painter Chily.

JARTCHI: We never had anything like that on our walls!

TVRZNIK: One three quarter length fur coat, chinchilla.

JARTCHI: How could we afford that?

VODICKA: Well, in that case why did you sign this statement which claims that everything was there this morning? I hope it wasn't in order to collect ...

TVRZNIK: 57,344 point 20 crowns.

VODICKA: ... from the insurance company?

JARTCHI: That was your idea!

VODICKA: Better be careful, young lady, don't do anything too drastic. That is after all a serious charge. How do you propose to go about substantiating it?

JARTCHI: Jarda ...

VODICKA: This document containing your signatures states that the items were here. If they were not here, that certainly would be fraud—on your part, of course. A case of fraud, which according to—

TVRZNIK: Paragraph 132, section 1, letters a through c.

VODICKA: —is punishable with ...

TVRZNIK: Imprisonment for no less than two years nor more than five.

VODICKA: Which I really would not like to believe, young lady. *(Brightening up.)* But—if the things really were here, that's proof enough that there really was a fire. Right? *(Quiet. Tvrznik carefully ties his file back up,)*

JARTCHI: For God's sake, Jarda. Say something!

ENGL: What am I supposed to say?

JARTCHI: Christ Almighty! What kind of man are you? Call somebody or just throw them out. If we tell them what really happened, nobody could blame us.

ENGL: Maybe we'd better come to some kind of agreement, Jartchi.

VODICKA: I like that, Mr.Engl. There's nothing you couldn't learn how to swallow. Right?

JARTCHI: Do you know what I think you are? *(Goes behind the back of the bed.)* A great big zero. And do you know what I'm going to do now? *(With a leap she is at the bed, rips the file out of Tvrznik's hands, runs under the basement window, through which Janik has just climbed, and starts to yell.)* Help! Help!

ENGL: *(Jumps up.)* Jartchi, for God's sake!

(Vodicka and Tvrznik remain calmly seated. Then we hear Janik's voice over the loudspeaker.)

JANIK: Sir, UPOR is calling.

JARTCHI: *(Stops yelling.)*

VODICKA: Go ahead.

JANIK: UPOR wants to know if we still need the ambulance.

VODICKA: No, they can keep it.

JANIK: Roger.

JARTCHI: Heeeelp!

VODICKA: But tell them to send the hearse. We probably won't be able to force our way through to the people in time. I can hear them screaming.

JANIK: Roger. Will do.

(Jartchi has stopped screaming and, terrified, is looking at Vodicka.)

VODICKA: Hurnik!

HURNIK: I'm listening.

VODICKA: The Valkyrie.

HURNIK: Will do.

(Janik comes sliding down the pole again and helps Hurnik put the familiar apparatus on his back.)

VODICKA: Were you in the military, Mr. Engl?

ENGL: Yes.

VODICKA: Rank?

ENGL: Private first class.

VODICKA: So, now that the excitement has died down, you will surely be able to tell us what the Valkyrie *defacto* is.

ENGL: A flame-thrower.

VODICKA: Very good, private. *(To Tvrznik.)* Take his name down, Tvrznik.—I'll make sure you'll be a Corporal any day now. I assume you know what a flame-thrower is used for?

ENGL: *(Shakes his head.)*

VODICKA: Sometimes we have cases where the people are gradually suffocating, and we can't get to them. Or they panic and are threatening the others. During a really big fire, Private, martial law goes into effect, and what is best for the majority is by definition the most humane course of action. Since the little lady claims that there hasn't been any fire here … Hurnik!

HURNIK: Will do.

(Steps into the middle of the room and aims the nozzle at Jartchi. Vodicka and Tvrznik have finally stood up and move as far as possible behind the bed, as does Janik.)

VODICKA: You better come back here, Private. There's an average of two deaths per basement holocaust, but we grieve for every single life.

ENGL: *(Pulls himself together, jumps up, and yells.)* Wait!

VODICKA: Yes? I'm waiting, Private.

ENGL: *(Goes to Jartchi, who is frozen with fear, and takes the documents from her.)* Will you spare us if I give this back to you?

VODICKA: Why not?

ENGL: What's our guarantee?

VODICKA: The best one you could hope for. After all you owe us …

TVRZNIK: 14,114 point 73 crowns.

VODICKA: Of course, that's only after you receive your—

TVRZNIK: 57,344 point 20 crowns.

VODICKA: We're fair people to deal with, Private. And naturally we don't intend to harm ourselves either.

ENGL: Why are you doing it?
VODICKA: *(Stretching out his hand.)* The papers!

> *(Engl goes and gives them to him. Vodicka hands them to Tvrznik. Hurnik lowers the nozzle. Janik takes the apparatus from him.)*

VODICKA: I'll tell you why, Corporal. Everybody's got to live, right? We firemen live off fires. The more fires, the more firemen, the better the positions, higher salaries, improved equipment. But—the more firemen and the more effective the equipment, the fewer the fires … You understand?
ENGL: *(Nods numbly.)*
VODICKA: So what choice do we have left to us if the only thing we know how to do is put out fires. When your business is putting out fires, you may find that you have to start up a holocaust or two now and then. Right, boys?
HURNIK & JANIK: Will do. *(They start carrying things up the ladder again.)*
VODICKA: But we take care of the others too—, as long as they don't spoil the fun. The young lady got it straight, even if she got her wires crossed later on. But we'll consider that over and done with, right, young lady? We have a successful mission and you have a dowry.
JARTCHI: *(Goes to the bed, sits down exhausted and leans her head on the bedboard.)*
VODICKA: Bon. The main thing is you stood by her when it counted. But that's why people get married. So there's only one detail left: when there's a fire, and we are not quite sure how it started, and afterwards the victims seem to be upset, the rule is that we leave a fire-guard behind at the burned location. Not necessarily forever, but for as long as is needed to make sure that everything is nice and quiet again. Hurnik and Janik are the most logical candidates. Pick out which one you like the best.

> *(Hurnik and Janik come sliding down the pole with a folding cot and other equipment. They stand at attention next to each other. Jartchi's shoulders begin to quiver.)*

VODIGKA: Little lady, you don't have to worry. The guard will stay in the kitchen and be quiet as a mouse. That has the advantage that if you roast a duck again … oh, let's forget it.
ENGL: Commander, Sir.
VODICKA: I'm listening, Corporal.
ENGL: Maybe you could come up with another suggestion?

VODICKA: *(Turns to the firemen.)* Did you hear that? Bravo, Corporal. I think I'll promote you to Platoon Leader!

TVRZNIK: *(Opens the papers and notes it down.)*

VODICKA: As a Platoon Leader, you see, you could stay here by yourself.

ENGL: I'm—

VODICKA: A Platoon Leader of the fire department can fulfill the function of fire guard without assistance.

ENGL: But I'm not …

VODICKA: Everybody—Attention!

(Janik and Hurnik stand at attention. Tvrznik opens the file and hands it to Vodicka. Instinctively Engl also snaps to attention.)

VODICKA: Corporal Engl Jaroslav, I herewith promote you to the position of Platoon Leader of the fire department. At ease! *(Gives the file back to Tvrznik.)*

TVRZNIK: *(Hands Engl the file and a pen.)* Anywhere.

VODICKA: We're making an exception, mainly to calm down the young lady. By the way she'll have to stand guard herself, of course, when you're at work. From now on you'll receive an additional salary of 2000 crowns every month.

JARTCHI: *(Stops crying and dazed, lifts her head.)*

VODICKA: Well, Mr. Engl?

ENGL: *(Without saying a word, he signs.)*

VODICKA: My congratulations, Platoon Leader. *(Shakes his hand, embraces him and kisses him.)*

(After that Janik, Hurnik, and Tvrznik shake his hand. Then Janik takes the folding cot back out.)

VODICKA: With this signature you have formally recognized your obligations. And now as for your rights …

TVRZNIK: *(Hands him various vouchers from his file.)* Voucher for the helmet … For the uniform … For the equipment … As well as a cash advance of 312 crowns. *(Pays him in bills and coins.)*

VODICKA: Well, look at that! That happens to be just enough for the insurance premium.

JANIK: *(From above.)* Commander, UPOR is calling.

VODICKA: I'm listening.

JANIK: UPOR wants to know why we've been here so long.

VODICKA: Why? Is there a fire somewhere?

JANIK: No.

VODICKA: Report to UPOR. Action successfully concluded. Departure shortly. Receiver remains on.

JANIK: Roger. Will be reported.

VODICKA: We will proceed according to plan.

JANIK: Roger. Will not be reported. (*Outside a motor starts turning over. It starts up.*)

VODICKA: Everyone—Forward march!

FIREMEN: Roger. Will do.

TVRZNIK: (*Ties up the papers, takes them between his teeth and climbs up.*)

VODICKA: Platoon Leader Engl!

ENGL: (*Standing at attention.*) I'm listening.

VODICKA: You take over the fire watch.

ENGL: Will do.

VODICKA: Best of luck in your new job and marriage.

ENGL: Roger.

(*Vodicka climbs out. Hurnik, who is carrying the flame thrower on his back again, aims the nozzle at Engl and Jartchi, makes a hissing noise, and then makes believe he is setting the whole room on fire like a kid playing soldier. Then he too climbs out. Right after that the ladder and pole are pulled up. The truck starts away. The fire siren sounds and moves away quickly. Engl has been standing at attention until this point. Now he rushes desperately to the stairway door. It is locked, and the key has disappeared. He runs to the basement window and tries to jump up and pull himself up in vain.*)

ENGL: (*Screams.*) Jartchi! Come and help!

(*Desperately he tries to shove the clothes stand through the window, and see if he can climb out like that. That also doesn't work. Jartchi doesn't move. He drops everything and runs to her.*)

ENGL: Do you hear? We've got to go to the police right away!

JARTCHI: (*Lost in thought, she just shakes her head.*)

ENGL: You were right. They'll understand that we had no choice. They were capable of anything … So hurry up!

JARTCHI: (*Without saying a word, she takes off her wedding dress.*)

ENGL: What are you doing?

JARTCHI: *(Wearing only panties and bra, she takes a bucket, a broom, and some rags from the corner.)*

ENGL: What are you doing now?

JARTCHI: Cleaning up.

ENGL: What … ? For God's sake!

JARTCHI: What do you mean … ! The clothes cabinet is kindling … the kitchen cabinet is ashes …

ENGL: Jartchi, have you gone crazy?

JARTCHI: *(Begins to clean up.)* On the contrary.

ENGL: What do you mean, on the contrary? Stop it. *(Tries to grab the broom.)* I'm telling you, we've got to go to the police!

JARTCHI: *(Defending herself)* Let me go!

ENGL: Jartchi …

JARTCHI: *(Pulls away from him, sharply.)* Did you get three hundred and twelve crowns from them?

ENGL: Yes, but—

JARTCHI: So what do you want the police for? Hurry up and pay the insurance premium, so that you get today's date on it!

ENGL: But we're not going to accept this money!

JARTCHI: Forty three thousand? And why not? Can you tell me that?

ENGL: So that we'll be completely in their power?

JARTCHI: You idiot! You idiot! You should get down on your knees and thank me. They had us so completely in their power that if it weren't for their fear they would calmly have burned down the whole damned place, everything, us included, just to chalk up Brownie points with the authorities. Come on! We got off easy!

ENGL: Now you probably expect me to stand guard?

JARTCHI: And why not? They probably won't bother you if you're one of them.

ENGL: Jartchi, be reasonable! Think what you're asking me to do! Come on …

JARTCHI: Why don't you try and be reasonable. You're not a little baby. You have a wife, you want to have a family … Well, do something for them. What good are the police, if the firemen come back?

(The fire truck signal is heard in the distance. Terrified Jartchi immediately leaps into the bed and covers herself with the sheet. The siren dies away. Engl stands next to the bed, unsure of what to do next. Then he kneels down in front of her.)

ENGL: Jartchi … I love you … I don't want you to have to be afraid … Are you listening? … I'll do whatever you think is right. Do you hear me? I'll pay the insurance. I'll put our money in the bank, and then everything will be like before.

JARTCHI: (*Under the covers.*) Then get going! Hurry up!

(*Engl stands up, goes quickly into the kitchen. Pause. Then he laughs shrilly. He comes to the doorway and laughs like a crazy man. In one hand he's holding an empty silverware chest, in the other an open handbag with a chain.*)

JARTCHI: (*Can't stand it any longer and looks out from under the covers.*) What's the matter with you?

ENGL: The money—the silverware—everything gone! They were … just thieves!

(*Stunned she stands up in the bed, then he grabs her and whirls her madly around the room, until she is caught up in the feeling of relief, and joins in enthusiastically in the romp. Then they both fall on the bed, and the laughter changes into sudden passion.*)

JARTCHI: (*Hisses like a tigress.*)

ENGL: (*Hisses like a lion.*)

JARTCHI: (*Hisses more strongly and rips off his jacket.*)

ENGL: (*Hisses even more strongly, rips off her bra and stops short.*) And what if they're not really thieves?

JARTCHI: (*Uneasy again.*) What if it's just as a bonus that they …

BOTH: (*Unison.*) —steal?

END

Breinigsville, PA USA
08 September 2010
245001BV00003B/1/P